Oil Companies and Governments

OIL COMPANIES AND GOVERNMENTS

*An Account of the
International Oil Industry
in its Political Environment*

J. E. HARTSHORN

FABER AND FABER

24 Russell Square

London

First published in mcmlxii
by Faber and Faber Limited
24 Russell Square, London, W.C.1
Second impression mcmlxii
Second (Revised) edition mcmlxvii
Printed in Great Britain
by Ebenezer Baylis and Son Limited
The Trinity Press, Worcester, and London

(Published in the United States under the title
'Politics and World Oil Economics' by
Frederick A. Praeger, Inc.)

To
WANDA
and
DAVID

Contents

CONTENTS

Part Two (cont.)

Maps

Tables

Foreword

THIS book looks at the kaleidoscopic international circumstances of an industry in course of change: it is of necessity impressionistic and selective. For ease of reading, I have avoided footnotes within the text; but some notes regarding published sources, a short bibliography, a few maps and charts, and some pages of salient statistics about oil are appended.

For current detail I have depended heavily upon the industry's outstanding trade journals—*Petroleum Intelligence Weekly* and *Platt's Oilgram* internationally; the *Petroleum Press Service* and *Petroleum Times* in Britain; the *Oil and Gas Journal*, *World Petroleum* and the late *Petroleum Week* in the United States; *Pétrole Informations* in France; the *Middle East Economic Survey*, *Arab Oil* (Tripoli) and *Review of Arab Petroleum and Economics* (Baghdad). I have used figures of petroleum both in the terminology of 'tons a year' that is often used in Europe, and that of 'barrels a day' that is used almost invariably in America and the Middle East. In the simple rule of thumb of the trade, a barrel of oil a day roughly equals 50 tons of oil a year.

My personal acknowledgments are legion. Any understanding of the oil industry in the pages that follow has been gained from the extraordinarily patient explanation of friends in the companies, the governments, and among the consultants and commentators who serve the industry: I am indebted to them for hospitality, time and argument. But the book is not sponsored by any company, government, or other interest: and its conclusions are entirely my own. Any understanding of business behaviour in general that I have been able to bring to this business was gained almost entirely in the service and the companionship of *The Economist* newspaper.

The mistakes may be legion too. Only those are wholly mine.

Note on the Second Edition
This revision of the original text was completed during 1966; in

FOREWORD

general, the examples cited have been brought up to date to the end of
1965. The revision, however, has gone somewhat beyond mere up-
dating. At a number of points, I have modified and attempted to clarify
my views. In particular, the analysis of oil pricing has been wholly
rewritten; and I have revised my views of the way that oil concession
formulae might evolve to take account of the way that the Organization
of the Petroleum Exporting Countries has of late been able to hasten
their evolution.

When I wrote this book in 1962 I was an economic journalist looking
at this industry wholly from outside; incidentally, for the first time.
Shortly before I completed this revision, at the end of 1965, I left
journalism for energy consultancy, and a somewhat closer, professional
relationship with a number of oil companies and governments. But that
is a profession at which I am still a tyro. This book cannot pretend to
any expertise: it remains the view of an outside, and I hope detached,
observer.

J.E.H. 1966

Part One

CHAPTER I

By Way of Introduction

On 19th and 20th January, 1966, all the 24 companies holding oil concessions in Libya agreed to convert the financial terms of these concessions into line with an amendment to the Libyan Petroleum Law made by royal decree two months before, on 20th November, 1965. This amendment provided for Libyan income tax to be charged on their oil 'profits' as if all the oil had been sold at its 'posted' or published price, less an agreed discount—regardless of the actual prices at which the oil had been sold, which had recently, in many cases, had been very much lower. This discount was in line with offers that had first been made to the Libyan government late in 1963, by six of its concessionnaires; and which during 1965 had been agreed with certain other Middle East governments by ten of the companies with concessions in Libya. Only five of these ten, at the time, were actually producing oil in Libya—though together they accounted for the bulk of the country's production.

None of the other 14 concessionnaires in Libya had been parties, directly, to those agreements. These others included two of the three companies jointly controlling the country's second most prolific oil concession, output from which had been rising particularly fast. But these three companies had achieved such rapid growth only by selling their crude oil at market prices far below the prices posted for it—and had been able to do so only because they had so far paid tax on whatever prices they got for the oil. So this change in the basis on which they reckoned their tax—from the prices actually received to much higher, fictitious prices (which nobody would have been prepared to pay in the open market)—greatly increased these companies' liabilities to pay the government revenue on this oil. For certain companies, it more than doubled the amounts they had so far paid the Libyan government on each barrel of oil they exported (even though these payments, initially low because of heavy exploration write-offs, would in 1965 anyway have risen somewhat).

The concessions that these companies held at the time did formally provide for tax payments to be related to the posted prices of oil; but the companies were allowed to deduct as a 'marketing expense' the discounts that they could satisfy the Libyan government they had had to grant their customers to meet competition. (Just what size of discount could have been justified strictly to meet competition, admittedly, was already a bone of contention between these companies and the government—which was far from satisfied.) Their concession agreements— which they had already agreed to amend once before, to fit an earlier Libyan amendment to its petroleum law, in 1961—also contained guarantees that no later amendment or repeal of the law following 1961 could alter their contractual rights on their concessions without their consent. Why, then, did these companies consent to accept this new 1965 amendment? They did so, ultimately, after the Libyan government obtained the approval of its parliament to take whatever action it considered necessary to compel them to accept. And the Prime Minister declared that he was prepared to stop exports by any company that would not consent: that is to say, force it out of business in Libya.

There were other sanctions and incentives to back the government's pressure—exerted finally on only six recalcitrant companies, the rest having agreed already to alter their concession terms. Libya was considering bids for some further oil concessions that it had to offer, and existing concessionaires were prominent among the many companies interested. The government said that new concessions would not be granted to any companies that did not accept its new formula related to posted prices on all the concessions they held or might be granted. Moreover, to all concessionnaries agreeing to change over it offered a 'quit-claim', confirming without further argument their income tax returns for previous years, over some of which it had threatened to argue very hard indeed. And finally, other oil-producing countries' governments that are members of OPEC, the Organization of the Petroleum Exporting Countries, let it be known that they had passed a resolution saying they would not grant any new concessions in their countries, either, to Libyan concessionnaires that held out against the new Libyan amendment.

Nobody outside these six companies can know how much these other sanctions—which were legitimate enough—weighed with them. But the sequence of events is clear. It was not until the Government, with its parliament's consent, made the definite threat to stop exports—that is, to act unilaterally in breach of its written contracts—that these last recalcitrant companies gave in.

This was not the first time that the 'host government' of an oil-producing country had threatened to break the contracts in its oil concession agreements. Some had in fact done so, and 'nationalized their oil' in one way or another. But the circumstances in Libya were rather special, and may have future repercussions for all oil concessionnaires everywhere. They deserve examination. For this was the first time that any host government had ever threatened to break the contracts of some private oil companies to impose conditions that were part of an agreement with other private oil companies.

Most of the companies that had agreed the discount off posted prices for tax purposes with the governments of certain Middle East countries were the 'international majors', the biggest companies in the world oil trade. They had done so as part of a wider settlement with these governments, all members of OPEC, after negotiations that had dragged on for two and a half years. What the OPEC governments had been seeking was the 'expensing' of royalties, i.e. the payment of oil royalties separately, as a charge against income for tax, instead of 'crediting' these fixed royalty payments for oil against the income tax reckoned without counting them. The effect of this 'expensing', on an income tax at say 50 per cent, meant a considerable increase in government payments. These companies, in the other oil-producing countries with whose governments they had made this settlement, were already paying tax reckoned on the basis of posted price—in spite of the fact that any oil sold at arm's length from those countries could only fetch much lower prices. To mitigate somewhat the full financial burden of the new expensing system, these companies had stipulated, and the governments had agreed, that a certain specified scale of discounts should be allowed for tax purposes off the posted prices that they accepted as a royalty basis.

This settlement had been offered to all the OPEC governments concerned in virtually the same terms. Libya had been one of the governments to whom the offer had been made, and it had agreed in principle at the end of 1964. But in practice a settlement including an agreed discount off posted prices for tax purposes had at that time no clear meaning in Libya. For in Libya, under its existing law, concessionnaires had been paying taxes on the selling prices actually realized, and arguing later to justify the discounts they had granted. The government might

19

perhaps have considered changing the law to provide for the expensing of royalties, and have pursued the question of the 'OPEC discounts' in the tax arguments about discounts in general that it was already engaged in with some of the companies. Or it might possibly have reached some agreement with all its concessionnaires to 'phase' their discounts gradually into line with those agreed with other OPEC member governments. But how could it apply the OPEC formula generally agreed, with graduated (and moderate) discounts off posted prices for tax purposes, to companies that were already granting far larger discounts, and claiming that these larger discounts were justifiable as a proper basis for tax under existing Libyan law?

Libya might have sought to make the best of this awkward situation by applying the agreed discount only to companies with whose tax returns it was already satisfied, because they had been exporting at higher prices; and going on arguing with the companies granting the really big discounts. But in fact this course of discriminating between companies was not open to it. For the companies that had offered this general settlement to the OPEC governments had understandably stipulated, as part of it, a 'most favoured company clause'. This was a stipulation that no company agreeing to this settlement should be obliged to pay any *additional* revenue per barrel as a result if, under the terms of any other concession extant in the country, applied to their own circumstances, it would have stood to pay less. In no case was this clause to be interpreted actually to reduce a company's payments per barrel *below* what it had been paying before the OPEC settlement; but it did offer the signatory companies protection against discriminatory lenience by governments prepared to offer other concessionnaires easier terms. In most of the other OPEC countries involved few other companies were producing on really comparable concession terms, and in general the terms set for new concessions were tending to become stiffer, not easier. But in Libya there were far more concessions than in any of these other countries. And while financial practice differed considerably between companies, their formal concession terms were in principle much the same, under the same petroleum law.

In practice, only Standard Oil of New Jersey and Amerada Petroleum, out of the companies that had voluntarily accepted the change to the new basis in Libya, were at the time large-scale producers in Libya, though some others among them were just coming into significant production or had already, like Royal Dutch Shell, arranged to buy large amounts of Libyan output. And Standard Oil of New Jersey, the world's largest oil company, colloquially known in the industry as 'Jersey' or 'Esso', appeared to have been invoicing the great majority of its Libyan exports—from its producing company there to other affiliates of the Jersey group—at considerably higher prices than those at which the heaviest discounters were selling. Initially, Jersey appeared to have invoiced its crude exports from Libya at no more than a small 'marketing expense' discount off posted prices; and even by 1964, the Libyan government later stated, the company had been paying it over 90 cents a barrel in royalties and tax. In the increasingly competitive conditions in markets for Eastern hemisphere crudes in general, this might well have changed even if the law had remained the same. By 1965, it is quite possible that Esso Libya too might have claimed larger discounts than before. But for 1965, in the event, with the change to royalty expensing and the OPEC discount, the relevant price became $2.03 (against the posted prices of $2.21 and $2.23); and Jersey stood to pay the government about a dollar a barrel.

Most of the remainder of Libyan output up to that time had come from the Oasis group, owned by Amerada and two other American companies, Continental Oil and Marathon Oil. Amerada, which was in process of concluding a long-term deal for the sale of a half-share in its third of the concession to Shell, one of the companies involved in the original offer to Libya, agreed to change to the new law. Marathon had taken no part in any discussions with the other OPEC countries, and objected to having to accept terms following upon an agreement to which it had not been a party. Continental, as the owner of a very small share in the Iranian Consortium,[1] had signed the supplementary agreement with Iran amending the terms to royalty expensing with OPEC discounts, including the 'most favoured company' clause. But it did not accept the new terms set out in the amended Libyan petroleum law as following logically from an agreement it had signed with another country where the whole tax basis was already quite a different one.

All these three Oasis partners were large, experienced American oil companies, but relative newcomers to the oil markets of the Eastern hemisphere, without international marketing networks of their own. So in order to obtain markets for their Libyan crude oil, they had had to sell a large proportion of it to independent refiners in the open market. And this had meant accepting very low prices indeed. In the early years of the sixties, as Oasis output had built up, the crude had been sold at prices varying between about $1.40 and $1.60 a barrel. This made for a rapid growth in Oasis output, faster even than Jersey had built up its own output from its original Zelten field. But with a tax rate of 50 per cent, with royalties originally offset against this tax and taxable income reckoned on actual selling prices, it also meant that the Libyan government was asked to bear the cost of half the discounts below the posted price that these companies allowed, in contrast to the higher and more stable revenues per barrel it had been obtaining from Jersey's sales. The actual government revenue per barrel from Oasis sales, in those initial years of production, was held down by the large deductions allowed against taxable income to write off exploration and capital expenditures before production had started. So in many cases total government revenue per barrel would not have been much more than the level of the bare royalty, 12½ per cent of the posted price, or 27 cents.

By 1965, presumably, the main effect of these heavy write-offs would have passed; moreover, with rising output, costs per barrel for Oasis would have been coming down, increasing its margin of taxable profit from any given level of prices. So the levels of revenue per barrel received by the government from the different groups were probably already moving somewhat closer. But even so, the government reckoned that in 1965, if it had accepted the heavy discounts Oasis was allowing, it would still not have been getting more than about 55 to 60 cents a barrel from this group's exports. These exports were becoming a bigger proportion of the country's total exports; other concessionaires would not necessarily have been ready or indeed able to export at steadily higher prices than Oasis; the average price declared for tax purposes had already, the Bank of Libya later reported, come down from $2.19 in 1961 to $1.77 in 1965, for all companies. So it was clear to the Libyan government that it was unlikely to be able to get any additional payments from the companies that had made the original offer, and might nationally suffer a loss in income—*unless*, in line with the 'most favoured company' clause, it could manage to bring the companies that had been selling at big discounts into line. The country had ambitious development programmes, and needed extra income badly. Even so, aware that the heavily discounted sales had been partly responsible for continuing its very rapid growth in export tonnage, it hesitated for some months before deciding to put the pressure on these companies.

It is much easier to see why the different parties in this situation should have become aggrieved and insisted on what they considered their rights than to sort out any objective right or wrong. To the government, its rights were clear and simple. As part of OPEC, it had by bargaining achieved the promise of an increase in revenue per barrel from its largest producing concessionnaire, and from several other companies as well. The companies objecting to the change in its petroleum law were among the concessionnaires selling at the heaviest discounts. These concessionnaires, selling at such heavily discounted prices, seemed to the government to be taking advantage of the fact that Libya had granted them much more generous terms as regards marketing expenses than they could obtain in almost any other significant producing country. Their heavily discounted sales, moreover, were helping to bring down the general level of prices in the international oil market—which could affect all Libyan oil revenue directly.

To Continental, Marathon and other concessionnaires who felt the November amendment to Libya's oil law was an abrogation of terms they had been granted and guaranteed, their rights seemed equally clear. Libya, admittedly, had begun by granting extremely generous concession terms to attract exploring companies. Once oil had been found, it had gone back on those original terms, significantly stiffening certain conditions. But at that time it had done so by the legitimate method of offering further concessions only to companies that accepted changed terms on all their old ones as well. And considering the evidence they had by then of the likely profitability of Libyan oil, all the companies had chosen to change over. The post-1961 Libyan concession terms still remained relatively generous compared with those in the main Middle East concessions. But it was partly because of that remaining generosity that Libyan output had been able to grow, in the early sixties, at a spectacular pace. European markets, when these newcomers began trying to sell crude there, were very largely supplied by the international major companies. The newcomers argued that they would have been unable to sell Libyan oil there if they had had to bear a tax burden per barrel comparable to the 90 cents or so that up to 1964 Esso, more strongly established already, could afford; and certainly it could have brought their return down towards the kind of level one might expect from manufacturing, rather than from production achieved after all the risks of international oil. And after all, they would argue, whatever level of revenue per barrel Esso Libya had been paying the Libyan government had arisen from the fact that it chose to transfer crude to other Jersey affiliates at higher prices than they themselves could get from independent buyers. They assumed that in terms of its total commercial circumstances and tax situation across the world, this suited the Jersey group; that was its business. But this seemed to these companies no reason why the Libyan government should threaten *force majeure* to compel them to accept radically stiffer concession terms than those they believed it had guaranteed in 1961.

To any international major company producing in Libya, again, the rights of the matter must have looked quite different. Newcomers such as the Oasis partner companies, in its view, had been spoiling the international market for oil since the late fifties by selling at knockdown prices. Such prices did not provide an adequate return on capital to established companies, which owned not only producing ventures but also large and costly distribution organizations in the market—and which, on the majority of their crude oil sales internationally, had to pay tax on the basis of posted prices, whether they transferred the oil at posted price or not. In the final market for refined products, where the oil was sold to the consumer, no company, for long, could get more than the competition would allow. Even if a major international company invoiced its oil out of Libya at posted price, it would still not be able to get significantly more for the products refined from this than its Libyan competitors, providing they were selling in the same final markets. Somewhere in between, within its integrated company structure, it would have to accept effectively the same discount. Now the international major companies, the 'responsible' competitors in the industry, had agreed to fresh increases in the revenue per barrel that they paid host governments. There was no reason why their 'less responsible' competitors, producing oil under similar conditions and laws, should escape this extra burden; or if they could escape it, there was no reason why the international major companies should carry it alone. The 'most favoured company' clause, to such companies, seemed a merely prudent stipulation. It was Libya's responsibility to decide whether, and if so how, it applied the clause. When the government asked these companies to accept the amended law voluntarily, they did so because the law merely applied a formula they had already offered in the OPEC settlement. It has been said, however, that one or more of the major companies did protest to the Libyan government as new steps towards compulsory action appeared to be under serious consideration by the government, and before it sought parliamentary approval for such steps. And when the government decided nevertheless to force the recalcitrants into acceptance, all the international majors protested against the final threat of unilateral action; they had not yet formally signed their acceptance of the new petroleum law, and might still have withdrawn. In fact, perhaps because of this, the government never promulgated the measures for which it had gained parliamentary support. It never needed to. The same night, the companies holding out gave in.

(Both the Libyan government and the independent companies that had held out longest, it may be said, publicized their views on this issue at considerable length.[2] None of the major companies that accepted gave their views publicly. So the views I have set out above—not the facts— are a matter largely of surmise. Only Esso, among the majors, had very significant production in Libya at the time. Most of the others had concessions there; some were coming into production. Most of them, from early on, agreed to convert their concessions to the basis of the new Libyan law—though one of the international majors, the Gulf Oil Corporation, was among the 'recalcitrants' that held out until the last. On the other hand, there were independents, including the Oasis partner Amerada, among the nearly 20 companies that had agreed to amend their concessions in Libya before the final threat.)

Whatever the rights of the matter, the recalcitrant companies finally gave in. Some of them, it is said, appealed to Washington for diplomatic support against the threat to stop exports unless they accepted new terms. Whether the American government gave this, we do not know. One of its officials, three months later, said that the Libyan independents 'would need some tax relief' from the Libyan government to carry on their 1966 and 1967 exploration programmes; but that view came long after the event. If any representations were made at the time, they did not dissuade the Libyan government from making its threat; and soon after that the argument with the companies was over.

From this moment on, it was only a matter of time until the next 'host government' of a major oil-producing country might decide to amend its concession terms unilaterally, by the same threat of direct action in breach of contract. The doctrine that radicals in such countries have often urged, 'Legislate, don't negotiate', had been given a new and considerable boost.

Within a few months officials in Kuwait, another OPEC member country where original acceptance of the royalty expensing settlement had been followed by frustrating problems with tenant oil companies, were also threatening to legislate unilaterally. It was never clear what new law they had in mind, directed against whom; and in practice it seemed almost certain that Kuwait could reach and ratify an acceptable agreement with British Petroleum and Gulf, the two major companies concerned, without any unilateral moves whatever. But threats were certainly coming back into fashion. The Government of Iran, during 1966, put pressure on the Consortium of oil companies responsible for nearly all Iranian oil production to increase output far more sharply than they had planned. The chairman of its national oil company, the prime minister, and indeed the Shah of Iran himself all hinted ominously at the measures Iran might have to take to protect its national interest if its demands were not met. Hints or none-too-cloaked threats, these were effective; before the end of the year the Consortium had agreed to raise its own output faster, to provide the national company with attractively-priced crude that it could sell to Eastern Europe, and to relinquish part of its operating territory several years in advance of the timetable set in its agreement.

Libya's successful action in January, 1966, in the perspective of time, will come to seem less of a precedent for change than it appeared there and then, and more of a crystallization of change that was already quickening. There is no reason to assume that the Government of Syria needed any Libyan example to help it decide to 'nationalize' 300 miles of pipeline carrying Iraq oil through its territory at the end of 1966, over a dispute about the level of transit charges. Nor did the Government of Iraq—whose oil income was liable to be cut in half by its Arab socialist neighbour's move—need any precedents from anywhere in continuing to put pressure on the Iraq Petroleum group of companies. Its own 'Law 80' of 1961 was a piece of unilateral legislation that had seized all but a tiny percentage of these companies' concession area; and succeeding governments had declined to ratify a new agreement worked out between Iraq government negotiators and the companies in mid-1965. The Iraq government may well have been uneasy about the implications of Syria's demands to increase transit charges on Kirkuk oil piped to the Eastern Mediterranean. But its immediate reaction, predictably, was to increase its own pressure on its tenant companies, seeking short-term financial assistance and longer-term 'improvements' in the new agreement they had initialled eighteen months before.

At the consuming end of the business (and this book is written by an oil consumer) there had been perhaps a couple of events worth noting too. In Britain, the country most advanced in nuclear power generating investment, tenders had been let for nuclear stations to come into commission in 1970–71 offering costs nearly as low as in the latest American stations—costs which would offer power much more cheaply than from European coal, and close to the cost at which it could at the time be generated from fuel oil in Europe. And with natural gas from the enormous reserves of Slochteren in the Netherlands at length beginning to be used on a growing scale in Holland, and exports planned to Belgium, Germany and France, large-scale discoveries of natural gas had also been made during 1965 and 1966 under the British Continental Shelf of the North Sea.

These, at the time this book was being revised, were elements in the forefront of change. At the time that it was originally written, in 1962, it seemed to me that this period of accelerated change had begun just on two years before, about the time that OPEC was set up in autumn 1960: it still does. In the introduction to the first edition of this book I wrote of the Baghdad meeting at which this organization was set up as 'one that may turn out to have been of seminal importance in the current history of the international oil industry'. All I should wish to amend now in hindsight would be the words, 'may turn out to be'. It did turn out to be.

That was a meeting of governments: the governments of five countries that, at the time, were supplying some 80 per cent of all the oil that moves in world trade. After four days' discussions, it was announced that the governments of Iraq, Iran, Kuwait, Saudi Arabia and Venezuela had decided to form the Organization of the Petroleum Exporting Countries, 'for regular consultation amongst its members with a view to co-ordinating and unifying the policies of the members.'

The kind of co-ordinated policy that these governments have in mind was indicated by the first resolution they had passed at their meeting, which is worth quoting in full. They agreed:

'That members can no longer remain indifferent to the attitude heretofore adopted by the Oil Companies in effecting price modifications;

'That members shall demand that Oil Companies maintain their prices steady and free from all unnecessary fluctuation; that members shall endeavour, by all means available to them, to restore present prices to the levels prevailing before the reductions; that they shall ensure that if any new circumstances arise which in the estimation of the Oil Companies necessitate price modifications, the said companies shall enter into consultation with the member or members affected in order to fully explain the circumstances;

'That members shall study and formulate a system to ensure the stabilization of prices by, among other means, the regulation of production, with due regard to the interests of the producing and the consuming nations, and to the necessity of securing a steady income to the producing countries, an efficient, economic and regular supply of this source of energy to consuming nations, and a fair return on their capital to those investing in the petroleum industry;

'That if as a result of the application of any unanimous decision of this Conference any sanctions are employed, directly or indirectly, by any interested Company against one or more of the Member Countries, no other Member shall accept any offer of a beneficial treatment, whether in the form of an increase in exports or any improvement in prices, which may be made to it by any such Company or Companies with the intention of discouraging the application of the unanimous decision reached by the Conference.'

Oil from beneath these countries of OPEC is produced and exported almost entirely by private companies, not by these governments. Its original resolutions, and those since, have been of deep interest to the companies. And their purport, to the big companies that produce oil in the OPEC countries, has often seemed at once ironic and menacing.

For there was little that the member governments of OPEC demanded that oil companies should do that the big companies were not, in broad terms, anxious to do; yet that little, potentially, could have disrupted the whole way that they are accustomed to do business. No government was more anxious than every large established company to keep prices steady and get them back to higher levels. A steady income to the producing countries, and economic and regular supplies to consuming nations, are both things that any sensible oil company is anxious to maintain in the smooth conduct of its business; and the declared purpose of its business is to obtain the fair return on capital of which the OPEC resolution spoke. Since autumn, 1960, the managements of established oil companies have indeed continued to sigh wistfully for these things.

The demand for prior consultations with the governments of these countries before they changed their prices, however, challenges one of the central prerogatives of any businessman, and the idea of governments regulating production challenges another. These particular companies are not given in general to exactly frenzied price competition; they are more often credited with or criticized for an extreme desire to hold prices stable than with any wish to change them too often. But power to set prices and to control 'offtake' from the various areas where they produce oil remains crucial to the management of their business.

Admittedly, prices and offtake have become, by the terms of their tax arrangements in these oil-producing countries, crucial to the revenues of the OPEC countries as well. And oil revenues represent by far the largest element in the national budgets—indeed, in the national incomes —of these countries.

The Organization of the Petroleum Exporting Countries did not come out of the blue, any more than other claims of governments upon this industry had done. It came as a direct reaction, as the wording of its first resolution made plain, to one of the rather infrequent changes in price in this industry—a reduction, just about a month before, in the posted price of crude oil in the Persian Gulf. The attitudes that were finally expressed in the formation of OPEC had begun to form many years before. But it took cuts in posted prices in August, 1960—which seem likely to have been the last that these companies would ever make in posted prices, in their then form—to crystallize them.

Without those price cuts, the Organization of the Petroleum Exporting Countries would almost certainly have not come into being—at that time. To the outside observer, it seems certain that it would have come sooner or later. Five weeks after OPEC was formed, there was a public demonstration of the underlying reason why.

In October, 1960, Shaikh Abdullah Tariki, who was at the time a director appointed by the government of Saudi Arabia to the Arabian American Oil Company, presented a paper to the Second Arab Petroleum Congress in Beirut entitled 'The Pricing of Middle East Crude Oil and Refined Products'. In it he accused the eight major international companies who in various groupings own Aramco and the other main operating companies which actually produce the oil in the Middle East of swindling their 'partners', the host governments, out of $2,737,145,066, or just on a thousand million pounds.

Shaikh Abdullah's thesis was based on a complex argument about crude oil prices which it would be beside the point to summarize here; it is considered briefly in a fuller discussion of pricing in this industry (which appears in Chapter IX). It was not, I think he would even then have been prepared to agree, more than an attempt from outside to rationalize the pricing behaviour of the oil companies, as shown by the prices they posted for Middle East oil between August, 1953, and August, 1960; and I am not sure whether he would stand by all the details of this analysis now. But over-tortuous or not, the reasoning served to lead Shaikh Abdullah to a conclusion about which in essence if not in detail he clearly felt no doubt. This was that ever since the institution of the fifty-fifty profit-sharing system, in continuing bad faith, the eight major oil companies that control oil operations had 'posted' lower prices for Middle East crude than they were in practice able to realize, so that the half-share in profits on those posted prices accruing to the host governments in the Middle East had been artificially depressed over a period of years. Few Arabs of note had up to then been more closely exposed to the workings of the Western oil companies; and this is what this one thought of them. Shaikh Abdullah was one of the founders of OPEC; much of its work has expressed a similar suspicion and determination to analyse this industry independently, on behalf of the host countries.

Since that first meeting in Baghdad in 1960 OPEC has come a long way—broadly, though not directly—towards its original aims. It never managed to get those 1960 cuts in posted prices reversed, and indeed finally accepted them for tax purposes as part of the royalty expensing settlement of early 1965. But that settlement did indirectly bring some of its Middle East members benefits, retrospective to the beginning of 1964, about equal in cash per barrel to what they had lost in revenues as a result of the 1960 cuts.

It has not formally gained any acceptance from the companies, either, of its right to consultation before they alter posted prices in future. But in fact, since 1960, they never have altered posted prices there again. Moreover, under the royalties settlement, the OPEC governments concerned did gain acceptance of their right to be heard before the companies make any further changes in the 'OPEC discounts' for 1967 and after—and a guarantee that the discount will not be increased further. This guarantee does not formally extend to the posted prices to which the discounts apply. But the guarantee would have no meaning if in practice it did not cover the posted price benchmark for tax as well. Up to the time that this book was revised, the point had not been tested in practice. But OPEC could at least plausibly argue that its member governments had been given a bigger say in the prices that affect tax. And it is certainly arguable that in their turn the oil companies operating in OPEC countries have surrendered some part of their commercial prerogative as regards prices.

As regards the control of the volume of 'offtake', or exports from these countries, the companies have not openly surrendered any of their prerogative; but this too is under challenge. OPEC's own initial attempt at 'programming' production had not been ambitious, and even this had run into difficulties. Certain of the companies in member countries that had purported to place limits on the percentage increases in their exports had appealed to arbitration under their concession agreements. Few of the governments involved seemed ready to be limited by the percentage increases they had been allocated and the main challenge to the companies' control of offtake came from governments who wanted their production increased, not limited. But for a variety of reasons—including, notably, the unilateral action of Libya, an OPEC member, to raise its taxes—it seemed possible that 1967-68 would see some increase in oil prices. OPEC might take heart from this. It was not yet in a position to take much credit. Nevertheless, its impact on the oil business in five years had already been profound, and far-reaching. Give it another five years, and the relationship between producing governments and oil companies could be changed beyond recognition.

At the other end of the business, collective organization of consumer governments has progressed less spectacularly since the beginning of the sixties. But these governments, too, have not been idle. Given a world market in which prices have been generally soft, such consumer governments might seem to be comfortably placed. Not all, however, are equally comfortable; moreover, some of them are solicitous for the home comforts of higher-cost fuel industries. In the early sixties, hence, we have often had the spectacle of consumer governments, in countries such as Germany, India, or Australia, putting pressure on integrated companies to reduce the prices, and the foreign exchange outgoings, on the crude supplied to refining affiliate there; or querying the losses or very low profits earned by these affiliates, which comes to the same thing. At the same time—and sometimes in the same countries—governments have been putting duties on cheap imported oil in order to help their own higher-cost coal, or sometimes local oil, sell in the home markets.

Occasionally, pressure to handle cheaper oil has led to disputes as bitter as any at the producing end of the business. Having had their refineries and marketing businesses in Cuba nationalized in summer 1960, and used ever since to handle Soviet oil, the same major companies had in 1962 and 1963 undergone rather similar action in Ceylon, and in later years had also encountered government favour for Soviet oil in Pakistan and India. From Venezuela to Brunei, countries where oil was produced have demanded higher incomes from oil operations: from Japan to Tanganyika, countries that consume oil have pressed for yet lower prices as a condition of supplying their markets. The United

States government shows little sign of thorough reconsideration of its own statutory import restrictions; the European Economic Community, with Britain once again tip-toeing towards the edge of it, remains worried about the 'security of supply' of its 'cheap energy'.

This is an outside reporter's book about the oil industry and its international circumstances, not an expert's. Its evidence is therefore at best secondhand, based on asking questions, over a period now of about five years and more thousands of miles of travel than I like to remember, of people inside this industry, or in a position to influence it, about what they are doing and why. Among the reasons that finally impelled me to get it down on paper were the events of 1960–62 in this industry and the background to them. Many of the changes in the oil industry between 1960 and 1966 began in the Middle East; but this is not a book about the Middle East, with which my acquaintance is even more glancing and external than with the oil industry. The background to these events lies wider; and this book is an attempt to set out analytically some of the circumstances in which the international oil industry now has to live with governments all round the world, and not merely in the underdeveloped countries where much of the world's oil happens to be produced.

These international circumstances, I believe, are already constricting, and for some time at least will increasingly constrict, the independence with which oil companies operate abroad, for reasons which at any rate seem legitimate to the many governments concerned, and some of which would probably seem legitimate to any unprejudiced person. Good arguments can be advanced for many of the measures that governments have taken and are taking which deliberately or incidentally limit some area of this industry's operations; at any rate, when these measures are considered singly. Together, however, they may soon reach a point where the huge job of international logistics carried out in the world oil business, as it is at present organized, will become very hard to continue efficiently. That present pattern of organization is neither perfectly efficient, nor necessarily the only one under which the international supply of a commodity becoming steadily more essential to the world could be carried on successfully. The pattern is indeed continuing, somewhat painfully, to evolve. But it is the only one we have, and its results continue to be vital to all of us. So major changes of any kind that any government is tempted to press upon the oil business have to be judged primarily in terms of how such changes—in concatenation with the other changes that other governments may be pressing at the same time—would affect the efficiency of world oil supply.

The oil business as it now exists is a curious international phenomenon, one of the few economic phenomena that have ever achieved such importance on such a stage. There is a powerful internal logic within its interlocked operations—though its structure, so far, has been organic and developing rather than simply rational, and embodies large elements of accident and luck. It cannot avoid rather more involvement in politics than most ordinary businesses: but politically as well as commercially, it would probably argue that its operating success depends upon sticking to 'strictly business' principles as much as it can. The logic of its business behaviour, however, comes of necessity into contact and at times into conflict with a phenomenon that in our century has manifested even greater power, nationalism in developed as well as in underdeveloped countries. This phenomenon is very easy to recognize and label when somebody else is displaying it—particularly for Westerners, when the somebody is in Asia or Africa. When we display it ourselves, whoever and wherever we are, we tend to identify it as 'the national interest—another thing altogether'. That is part of the universal strength of nationalism. And that is what makes the lot of any independently international organization such as the international oil industry, which exists mainly to move a resource vital to most nations across national frontiers, a vulnerable one.

The host countries where the oilfields are present themselves obviously as areas where nationalism impinges on this industry: but I believe one can both misjudge their actions and miss the main point by assuming they are in this sense exceptional. The oil industry of the United States is tightly regulated by state agencies and of late largely insulated from the world market by government restrictions—which may have done as much to reveal the world surplus that broke oil prices in 1960 as the behaviour of the state-controlled Russian industry did. The British government was the first one ever to take over a controlling share in the ownership of any major oil company: the French state owns large holdings in most French oil companies, and controls the business behaviour of all oil companies in France, whoever owns them, more tightly than almost any other country in the non-Communist world. Nationalism and governmental influence on the oil industry are not confined to any one country or group of countries.

In assessing the possible spread and effects of that influence, it is

c 33

convenient to begin by considering what is being influenced. The first part of this book is designed, therefore, to give as simple a sketch as possible of the business behaviour of the international oil industry as this is at present organized. It outlines the extent to which the world depends on oil; the geography of petroleum and the long, complex chain of exploration, production, transport and marketing which that necessitates: and as clearly as an outsider can comprehend and describe them the economics of its financing, its pricing, and its company structure. Having considered the special characteristics of competitive and uncompetitive behaviour in this industry, the second part of the book goes on to describe how its operational flexibility, in almost all countries where the industry operates, is nowadays circumscribed, for good reasons or bad, in the entirely legitimate name of the national interest. Whether the industry likes it or not, it is inevitable that the governments of consumer countries in which oil has now risen to dominate the fuel market should take an interest in the economic circumstance of its provenance. And the countries from which it is produced and exported have, generally speaking, few other economic circumstances for their governments to be interested in.

This is a descriptive book with some attempt at analysis, for the person generally interested in oil rather than the expert in any particular aspect of it. I have offered some comments on the way, but not I hope irritating hasty solutions to other people's problems—which are not necessarily susceptible of any neat, lasting, or inevitably happy solutions. These are problems in which nobody who is at all concerned with oil—and who, nowadays, is not in some sense?—need apologize for trying to understand further. The oil industry spends more money, effort and intelligent people on explaining certain aspects of its world-wide operations to the public of every country than any other I know. Yet somehow it also often contrives to give an impression of remoteness, perhaps through its sheer size and its international depth, from any one outside its periphery. Oilmen on occasion are apt, too, to treat its inner workings as something of a craft mystery, beyond the ken of mere mortals outside. But more and more people—and more and more governments—have come to feel that the oil business is too important to be left to oilmen. That is what this book is about.

CHAPTER II

Oil as a General Fuel

B y any measure we can apply, the world is now becoming rapidly more dependent on oil and natural gas, the petroleum fuels. During the sixties, for the first time in history, man has begun to obtain more heat and mechanical energy from petroleum than from any other fuel. By 1965, petroleum was providing more of the world's supplies of commercial energy than all other fuels put together. For something approaching a century, in these senses, coal had been the world's dominant fuel; but now the balance has tipped over.

These are broad statements; but it is only broadly that any statement about the quantities of energy consumed right across the world can pretend to be true, and historically the perspectives are even more blurred. For large parts of the world no figures exist, reliable or unreliable; and where any figures do exist, they vary enormously in scope and quality.[1] Fortunately for this kind of figuring, most of the areas for which statistics are entirely lacking are places where people use little fuel or at least buy practically none, relying mainly on wood and farm wastes. Statisticians generally find it convenient to exclude these fuels from their figuring as 'non-commercial'. They are still burned in huge quantities: as recently as 1875, for example, three-quarters of the fuel consumed in the United States is reckoned to have been wood, and today some guesses would still put the contribution of such fuels to total energy consumption in the world at more than a tenth.

But under the heading of 'commercial energy', then, the statisticians rank only the fuels supplied for sale in response to a defined market demand—coal and other solid fuels such as lignite; petroleum, liquid and in the form of gas; hydro-electricity; and nuclear electricity, though production of this new 'primary fuel' is still too miniscule to show at all on any graph of world supplies. During 1965, the world appears to have burned, either as raw fuel or in secondary forms, the equivalent of close on 5,400 million tons of coal. Of this total, coal and lignite

35

together accounted for some 2,250 million tons, or 42 per cent; hydro-electricity[2] for the equivalent of 120 million tons, or about 2 per cent; production of nuclear electricity was still tiny. The remaining 56 per cent came from oil products equivalent to about 2,100 million tons of coal and natural gas equivalent to just over 900 million tons. In 1960, solid fuels had 50 per cent against petroleum's 46 per cent; but since then coal has abdicated its kingdom. For consumption of coal, right across the world, is now growing only very slowly, while consumption of oil and natural gas, taken together, is still growing at perhaps 6–8 per cent a year. The consumption of hydro-electricity is still growing as fast as that of oil, though not nearly as fast as consumption of natural gas; but it remains a very tiny percentage of total fuel consumption in the world today. Moreover, hydro-electricity is one fuel of which 'reserves' can be pretty well identified, and for which the best sites are steadily being developed one by one. Its percentage share seems unlikely to get larger.

Over the past thirty years, moreover, oil and natural gas have accounted for about two-thirds of all the increase in the world's consumption of fuel. They have not been the only dynamic elements in the rapid growth of the use of commercial energy during that period. The exponential curve of electricity consumption, which has continued over many years with hardly even a ripple to acknowledge the occurrence of slump or war, shows an even more dramatic rise. But electricity is a 'secondary fuel', one of the convenient ways that man has devised to make use of energy, not a source of energy in itself; it has to be made from some 'primary fuel' such as coal, oil, falling water or fissile uranium. The surge in consumption of the two petroleum primary fuels has probably also resulted partly from the fact that these are convenient to use. The specialized secondary fuels that you can refine from crude oil are convenient for many purposes and practically indispensable for some; and natural gas is a primary fuel that starts out with all the convenience that coal can only achieve rather expensively through the processes of traditional gas manufacture. But our growing dependence on petroleum has not come wholly from the fact that consumers prefer convenience. In the first decade after the Second World War, in particular, oil and natural gas supplied the lion's share of the extra energy the world required simply because it was easy to develop additional supplies of them rapidly. That was emphatically not true of coal. Vast new sources of petroleum were steadily developed, and the pipelines, tankers and refineries were brought into being to deliver them to the consumer, at a time when a comparable investment of capital in some of the world's coal industries was having practically no visible effect at all on a depressingly inflexible level of output. Sheer availability, when the coal that people would ordinarily have used was not there, opened many markets to oil and to natural gas.

So far, we have been generalizing about the availability and competitive performance of the different fuels in a largely imaginary 'world market' for fuels that are bought and sold. In reality, such a market hardly ·exists; all these world figures are a blurred aggregate of the patterns of many different markets for fuel, and of bewildering diversity. Some of these fuels, though not all, move between the separate markets in world trade: but even with the vast international movement of oil, world trade only deals with perhaps 15–20 per cent of all the fuel burned in the world at present. And there is probably one division we need to make to gain any useful impressions from all this 'global' figuring about fuel. That is the division between the countries controlled by Communism and the rest of the world. So far as fuel consumption is concerned, this division is only incidentally political, nor does any Iron Curtain prevent the movement of fuels in trade. During the last five to ten years, the fact that oil in particular can and does move from the Communist areas of the world to the non-Communist—though hardly at all the other way—has been of growing significance in the world oil business. This division between capitalist and Communist countries is one between two largely independent markets, organized in quite different ways; and significantly, it is also a division between two quite different patterns of energy consumption.

For outside the Communist sphere, in what it is conventional and convenient to call 'the free world', petroleum is well in the lead. What is happening to the whole world in the sixties had already happened, tipping the balance by the middle of the fifties. But the switch towards oil and natural gas has gone much further in the free world than in the Communist countries. This seems to have occurred partly because those countries succeeded rather better in redeveloping their coal industries after World War II than some countries in the West, and went on expanding production until much more recently. But it is also partly because the Communist governments decided to switch their plans towards a growing dependence on oil and natural gas only some years after the same switch had begun, partly planned and partly unplanned, in Western Europe.

In the free world, by 1965, oil on its own had already overtaken coal as the largest single source of energy. Counting in natural gas, the petroleum fuels accounted for about 65 per cent of total energy consumption: coal was down to about 32 per cent. On the other side of the political divide, under Communism, petroleum fuels, by 1965, still probably accounted for only just over 30 per cent of the total energy consumption; solid fuels, supplying nearly 70 per cent, were still overwhelmingly the main source of energy there.

The Communist world at the beginning of the sixties, that is to say, used energy in roughly the same proportions as the rest of the world say thirty years before. The changeover to oil, and its consequences, are already fully upon us in the West; for the Communist countries, it still lies perhaps a couple of plans ahead. Another difference, which may become more important in future years, is that the main areas of consumption in the Communist sphere are under the same government as the main sources of their oil. In the West, most are not.

During most of the history of the petroleum industry—which is little over a century old—its rate of expansion has been set by a dominating demand for one or another of the specialized fuels that can be refined from it. In its earlier years, large amounts of crude oil were burned raw without refining, but very little is burned today. Not only fuels can be refined from crude oil; indeed, the one thing refined from it for which our mechanized civilization might be hardest put to find a substitute today is not a fuel at all, but lubricating oil. But it has been the specialized fuels that have supplied most of oil's historical momentum (along with most of its profits) over the last 40 years.

When crude oil first began to be refined in Europe and later in the United States during the last century, people were mainly after kerosene (alias 'paraffin oil') to burn in lamps and stoves, and this actually remained the most important single product of the oil industry until well into the twentieth century. Gasoline (alias 'petrol' in Britain) was originally just a nuisance, a light by-product of refining that would vaporize and explode too easily to be safe in oil lamps and stoves. But before the turn of the century these very properties were making it suitable as a specialized fuel for the internal combustion engine; and by the end of the First World War gasoline was becoming the most important product of the petroleum industry, as the internal combustion engine established itself as the most important technical and economic innovation of the early twentieth century. And there is no effective substitute for gasoline in this specialized role, except another petroleum product, diesel oil. Demand for gasoline swelled enormously with the spread of motor transport, followed by other applications of the internal combustion engine, across the world; the petroleum industry could profitably allow all other products to fall in behind this one. During most of the first two decades of this century, the volumes of the black oils sold—that is, of gas, diesel and fuel oils—exceeded sales of kerosene or gasoline. In the thirties, sales of the two groups of products ran roughly level. During and since the 1939–45 war the black oils went ahead again in volume. Nowadays their consumption exceeds that of gasoline by more than 50 per cent. But they have never enjoyed any comparable invulnerability to competition. They are sold in competition with other general fuels on the market, as the by-products of processes operated primarily to give high yields of gasoline or other products. And the rates of growth in their output are largely set by demand for these more profitable products.

If the rapid growth of oil consumption during the first half of this century has been associated with the most widely-ramified technical innovation of that period, the internal combustion engine, it has also borrowed momentum from the fact that the industry developed first and farthest in the United States. One cannot perhaps clearly distinguish the two: the automobile and the United States, as phenomena contributing to world economic growth, overlapped during the first half of this century so far as to be in some ways inseparable. During the first half of this century, the United States was not only the largest and richest country in the world, but also among the most rapidly growing of the industrial countries. During most of the hundred years that span the real history of the petroleum industry, this one country has been the largest single consumer (and producer) of commercial energy. North America still consumes about 40 per cent of the world's oil, and three-quarters of all the natural gas. The oil industry of the United States was the first to be developed on any significant scale; it remains the largest in any country, and American companies own a larger share of oil production and marketing overseas than any others. The sheer size of the American economy and its possession of oil and gas reserves have been tremendous elements in the rise of world consumption of petroleum.

During the last thirty years, petroleum consumption has been growing rapidly, as standards of living have risen, in the other developed countries that are poorer than the United States, but much richer than the rest of the world. The consumption of petroleum—as indeed of most of the other commercial fuels, and of most industrial materials and manufactures—is still extraordinarily concentrated within a relatively small part of the world's inhabited surface and population. About 58 per cent of all commercial fuel used in the world, in 1965, was burned in North America and Western Europe; another 25–30 per cent, probably, inside Russia and the other European Communist countries. The poorest 70–75 per cent of the world's population used less than a fifth of the commercial energy sold in it. In the non-industrial parts of the earth, where consumption per head of fuel as of most other commodities comes down in the statistics to forbiddingly small quantities, warmth is provided by burning wood and even dung; tractive energy by the horse, the ox and the human. There is a familiar correlation between the amount of fuel used per head in each of the world's economies and the comparative standard of living there. And until very recently, at least, the statistics tended to show also that these standards are rising faster in the developed countries than in most of the underdeveloped. The rich are getting richer; and relatively, many of the poor are getting poorer.

Businessmen concerned with oil seldom like to consider it as a simple commodity, or raw material. But, in the economic sense, recently, oil and the countries that produce it have fared like other commodities and primary producers. The terms of trade have been moving against them: that is to say, the amount of manufactured goods that they can exchange with their customers for a given amount of the primary material they produce has been falling and for a time may go on down. To anyone living in a country exporting manufactured goods and importing primary materials, this remains hugely, fortuitously convenient. But it has also become one of the most disturbing tendencies in the world economy today.

Standards of living in all countries are now being raised by the fact that liquid petroleum is perhaps the first really easily transportable fuel that the world has yet developed. Oil is essentially a fuel on the move (indeed, this was vital to the formation of the oilfields from which we tap it). Flowing along a pipe or pumped, it is immeasurably easier and cheaper than coal to load into and out of every kind of container, without degradation of its quality. Being of a higher calorific value, it is anyway better able to bear the cost of transport than coal ever has been, or than electricity or gas made from coal are yet, over long distances. The economics of transporting gaseous petroleum are favourable too, though a good deal less so than with oil. And this inherent ease of transporting oil has fitted rather neatly into the historical circumstances in which it was developed. The petroleum industry could never have grown as it has without coal, as a base for the development of iron and steel and of the engineering industries that use them. But the oil, once developed, could be transported readily for use in the economies where industrialization had begun on a foundation of coal. Coal needs to be used as near the source as possible, if it is to be cheap, and a market tends to be developed wherever it happens to be. Oil does not.

It is increasingly as a general fuel rather than as a specialized one that petroleum has come to dominate world energy consumption in the sixties. Gasoline, the specialized fuel to which this industry owes the biggest part of its expansion, became and has remained the industry's major product in economic terms. But sales of gasoline have never been as much as half of the total volume of oil products consumed throughout the world; and of late, consumption of certain other products refined from crude, to say nothing of natural gas, has been growing much more rapidly.

In the United States, which is still by far the world's largest market for petroleum, the total quantity of the black oils consumed—gas and diesel oils, distillate and residual fuel oils, and crude burned raw—passed that of kerosene by 1910, and was not exceeded in volume by gasoline until about 1930. Today gasoline represents about 40 per cent of oil consumption in the United States, while the black oils account for only about 35 per cent. But these are no longer the only forms of petroleum competing in the general market for fuel there; natural gas has captured a sizeable share of total fuel consumption, and its sales are still growing much more rapidly than those of the fuel oils.

In the next largest market for petroleum, Western Europe, natural gas did not appear on the market in significant quantities until recently. Throughout the fifties this market was consuming more and more oil as a general fuel—its consumption was growing much more rapidly than the American. The petroleum that was used as a general fuel on the European market consisted almost entirely of the black oils refined from crude. So far as oil alone is concerned, therefore, European demand for the heavier oil products, in the fifties, rose faster than for gasolines. In broad terms, across the world, one can say that consumption of natural gas and of the black oils is much larger and has lately been growing faster in most of the world than sales of any specialized oil product.

Its steadily widening involvement in the general fuel market during the fifties began to present the oil industry with some new problems, economic and political. From the late fifties onwards, these problems were sharpened. At the same time certain economic problems with which the industry had become grimly familiar in the past returned to plague it.

Of these, the central problem was the return of a world surplus of oil—or rather of reserves available for rapid development at costs well below the prices ruling in the market. As late as 1955, in economic terms, and as late as 1957, in political terms that were still blurred by the consequences of shared folly at Suez, forecasters inside and outside this industry were dominated by the mental climate of anxiety over fuel shortage that had prevailed since the end of the Second World War. In the fuel markets of most European countries, judgment was blurred at that time by the apparent continued impossibility of getting enough of the general fuel upon which we were accustomed to depend, coal, in spite of the investment that had been poured into attempts to raise the output. So far as the oil industry itself was concerned, potent business decisions had been made and vast sums had been staked upon the assumption that the oil business in the United States might prefer to buy its oil in the cheapest market and hence to rely to an increasing degree upon importing foreign oil more cheaply than it could produce oil at home; made, incidentally, by some of the most astute businessmen concerned with oil both inside and outside the United States.

Fortunes—including those of whole nations—depended upon those decisions; and they began to appear wrong, in some cases, within months of being made. The United States decided not to rely on increased imports of oil, and has not so far been obviously the worse for it. Coal output outside the United States and the Communist sphere remained almost as hard to increase; but the ranks of the customers who had been forced to switch to oil were soon swelled by others who positively liked the idea, and within a couple of years coal changed from being hard to get to being hard to sell. The host governments of oil producing countries who had been made partners in the bonanza of cheap oil flowing from under their deserts, and given half of the richest 'economic rent' of all time, were suddenly asked to share lower unit profits in leaner years. World demand for fuel was still increasing, and petroleum was still the abundant residual supplier of all the extra fuel the world wanted. But there was more of it ready for development, profitably, at current prices than the world was prepared to buy for the moment; and more was becoming available every day.

Today's continuing surplus of oil, offering the world a potential abundance of cheap energy, has to be considered against a certainty of continued growth in energy demand. Forecasting of energy demand, over the last decade or so, has undergone considerable refinement in technique. But it has to be applied to a range of markets quite unlike in pattern and in rates of economic growth; moreover, the nature of the data upon which forecasts have to be based may still be so unreliable as to offset refinements in figuring. Also, it is often impossible to appreciate in advance the eventual 'net' significance of major technological shifts in consumption or supply.

At the beginning of this century, forecasters had to try to assess the consequences of electricity, a fuel that was clearly fantastically easy and efficient to use, though in terms of thermal efficiency inherently wasteful to produce. On balance, what effect would it have on the growth of fuel consumption? In fact, it accelerated the consumption of energy—and the general rate of growth—in the industrialized economies where it was first applied. But at the same time, from the nineteen-twenties onward, its efficiency in use, and its substitution for other fuels, brought about a significant growth in general productivity, and a reduction in the amount of extra energy and other resources needed for any given amount of general economic growth. It does not seem likely, revising this book in 1965, that the eventual arrival of competitive and cheapening nuclear energy will have as profound a net effect upon productivity and growth in mature or developing economies as electricity has already had on the mature ones. But it would be stupid to pretend to any certainty.

Today, forecasts of world energy demand over the next 10–25 years[3] postulate rates of growth from $2\frac{1}{2}$ to 4 per cent compound per annum. In 25 years' time, that range implies that total effective demand for commercial energy may be from 85 to 167 per cent more than it is today. Hydro-electricity is unlikely to contribute much of that massive increase. Coal production will certainly grow more slowly than total energy demand for a generation or so, though it is arguable that by the end of the century the ruling price of energy, owing to rising costs in other fuels, might rise enough to justify some more rapid growth in coal exploitation, and perhaps some recovery in its share of world energy supply. Within five years, nuclear energy will probably set an upper limit to the price at which it will be possible to sell fossil fuels, and will contribute most of the increase in electricity generated in areas where these fuels are expensive. But its contribution to the growing total of world energy will probably still, by the end of the century, be a limited one. The bulk of the increase in energy requirements, over the next generation, can only come from one basic source—petroleum, liquid and gaseous. And the circumstances of its provenance will be a vital national interest in every country in the world.

CHAPTER III

Geography: Sources and Markets

'Oil is where you find it' is perhaps the most frequently quoted truism in this industry: but rather often during oil's commercial history, that has not been where you want it. Sheer geography would have been an inhibiting factor in the oil industry, sharply limiting the areas over which its markets could economically spread and imposing checks on its rate of development, if oil had not, providentially, turned out to be inherently easy to transport. As it is, the pattern of its geography has gradually made this industry, during this century at any rate, more genuinely international than almost any other has ever been. There are still, certainly, two great areas of relative self-sufficiency for oil, in North America and the Soviet Union. But no other fuel—including so far, natural gas—has ever been consumed in such vast quantities so far away from where it is produced.

The physical geography of petroleum, as its name indicates, derives from geology, which might be called the petrified history of the earth. The fuel's own historical origins remain a matter of some argument among geologists (and are the first of the many fascinating technical aspects of oil into which this book is not competent to follow the expert). Most of them appear now to agree that it was formed, over many millions of years, from organic materials of one kind or another accumulated at the bottom of oceans or inland seas, or washed inland during periods of inundation, and gradually covered by mud or lime deposited on top; there is less agreement about just how. Through the action of temperature or pressure, of particular processes of decomposition, or perhaps simply of time, these organic sources became converted into the characteristic mixture of hydrocarbon compounds that constitute petroleum—varying from nearly solid asphalt, through the liquid form, to gaseous forms such as methane. Being formed as a fluid, petroleum could move through any underground strata that were porous and permeable. Being lighter than the salt water also found in the pore spaces of the strata surrounding it, it tended to make its way gradually upwards. So where it is now discovered may not necessarily be where it began to be formed. That propensity to migrate has considerably complicated the geologists' ideas of just how petroleum could have originated; however, it is also mainly what has made petroleum available to man. For the characteristic underground pool of oil-permeated rock that forms an oilfield seems generally to have come into being when oil, moving upward or laterally through porous layers of rock, had its general progress towards the surface stopped by some impervious layer or 'caprock'. These deposits are found in particular where folding and wrinkling of the earth's crust has formed 'anticlines', dome-shaped formations under which the upward-migrating oil was sealed and gradually collected. There are many other formations and 'traps' of rock strata in which oilfields have been located, but almost all seem to satisfy certain prerequisites: porous strata such as sand or limestone in which the oil can collect, and impervious rock or clay above and around parts of such strata that can hold the petroleum sealed in. And those geological prerequisites, as it happens, seem more often than not to exist under parts of the earth's surface where so far industrial civilization has not been developed sufficiently to use the products of petroleum in really large quantities.

Any fuel or mineral extracted from the earth, to the extent that it can be used raw or processed simply, obviously creates as much of a local market as it can. But from almost the beginning of the large-scale commercial exploitation of petroleum—which to all practical purposes one can date from the opening up in Pennsylvania of the Appalachian fields, from 1859 onwards—most of the oil began to be moved quite a long way to market. Some of the biggest sales of kerosene for lighting and heating, as the American market developed, were in rural areas and behind the frontier as it moved westward. In the more developed markets of the Eastern cities, coal, and later gas and electricity, could offer kerosene much more competition. During the first thirty years of oil's history in the United States, the industry was nearly always exporting a third of its total output of refined products, and sometimes selling as much as two-thirds to foreign markets. On the earth's surface as well as under it, oil has proved a migratory fuel.

For lighting and to a lesser extent for general heating, kerosene was only one fuel among others, and one best able to compete in rural or underdeveloped areas; hence 'oil for the lamps of China'. Gasoline, on the other hand, was a fuel almost without a rival, and essentially a fuel of advancing industrialization and rising standards of living. And the first great surge of automotive consumption happened in the United States where the crude oil was produced. But even there the markets that developed earliest and fastest were rather remote from where the oil came out of the ground.

By the time that the gasoline era of this industry was beginning, the great centres of oil production had shifted from Pennsylvania, New York, West Virginia and Ohio to Texas, California and Oklahoma. In these areas, remote from coal, the black oils could develop local markets as a general fuel for railroads, heating and industrial steam-raising. But automobiles were bought all over the continent, and particularly in the larger centres of population in the East, and the oil had to be taken there. In the same way, in Europe, Russian and Rumanian oil was originally developed for small-scale local use, but demand for it rose faster in the cities and later in the richer and more developed economies of Western Europe. North America remained up to the early sixties the greatest single source of oil produced and market for it. But the very size and rate of expansion of its market caused early anxiety about exhaustion of reserves—anxieties that have been regularly disproved, but have recurred, during the whole history of the petroleum industry. It sent the nation's oilmen overseas to look for fresh supplies; and all the biggest reserves of oil discovered since about 1935 have been outside the United States.[1]

At the turn of the century the only oil industries developed on any significant scale were in the United States and Russia; there was some production in Burma as indeed there had been for centuries, and the exploration for oil was beginning in Persia. In the first twenty-five years of this century oil consumption grew at a rapidly rising rate in the United States, much faster than extra reserves were discovered there; but there were important discoveries in Mexico, Venezuela, and Persia. Fears of exhaustion of American reserves spurred the search at home; in the late twenties and early thirties huge new fields were opened up in East Texas, California and Oklahoma. But these fears also encouraged American oilmen and American diplomats to seek a firm footing in the developing Middle East (as against the British, who were already largely established there economically and politically, developing oil in Persia and later in Iraq). Moreover, there came a sharp decline in demand as slump spread throughout the world; the new American fields were produced at high rates that simply pushed prices and returns on investments down to ruinous levels until the governments of the main oil-producing states began to regulate the level of output. Between 1935 and 1945 the growth of oil output and additions to reserves in the United States, already very heavily drilled, tended to slacken: five years of that decade were years of war and materials shortage, admittedly. But for the world as a whole, reserves 'proved' by exploration rose much more than production of oil did. In the Middle East, in particular, the thirties were a period of major oil discoveries, in Bahrein, Kuwait and Saudi Arabia, as well as in Iran and Iraq. Since the war, significant new oilfields have been discovered in Venezuela and the Middle East; moreover, the estimates of oil reserves in already developed fields have gone up steadily. Canada came in at the end of the forties as a new producer, and by the end of the fifties a sustained effort of exploration had developed large-scale production in certain parts of Africa, primarily the Sahara, Libya, and Nigeria. Of late, the biggest new discoveries, once again, have been in the Middle East.

The significance of the truism quoted at the opening of this chapter is that in spite of all the preliminary scientific surveys one can make of likely areas, oil can defy the geological signs and still not be where the indications suggest. On existing theories, one can rule out large areas of the world's surface where oil almost certainly isn't. Without drilling, however, one cannot say definitely where it is, even in promising areas; and without further drilling once an oilfield is discovered one cannot estimate how much oil it may be possible to get out of it. As a result the number of new fields discovered must be to some extent a function of the amount of effort and money that companies have been prepared to put into all the costly techniques of explorations, especially into drilling.

The amount of oil that one actually discovers for a given amount of drilling varies enormously, not only between areas already heavily explored and exploited such as the United States and newer areas such as the Middle East, but also between different areas developed more recently. In all, up to end-1964, only about 550 wells had been drilled in Kuwait since exploration began there, 'proving' reserves estimated (conservatively) at 70,000 million barrels of oil. In Algeria, from 1952 to 1964, nearly three times as many wells had been drilled, but only some 6,000 million barrels of oil have been located. It is said that it took only 17 'wildcat' wells to find the first 13 major oil reservoirs in Saudi Arabia, Kuwait, Qatar, and the Basrah area; yet 130 wells were drilled in Canada before the discovery of its first significant field, Leduc.

In any given programme of exploration, the dominating factor is the uncertainty and randomness of reward for this effort.

The reserve-production ratio, which is an important yardstick for oil-fields, countries, and for companies in this industry, takes into account also the current output of any given area; and unless more oil is located as fast as output rises, this ratio will necessarily tend to decline as the years go by. And there are other factors, not wholly economic, that are still, even with far more oil on tap today than the world needs, encouraging a very high rate of exploration. One can count on some continuing improvement in the techniques of searching for oil: but the area of the main sedimentary regions of the earth's surface still unsurveyed, from dry land at least, is steadily decreasing. The industry has only just begun on oil exploration in the 'continental shelves' of the oceans: there are intriguing possibilities too, in the 'seaway' beyond the limits of the shelf. Drilling in already intensively explored areas has steadily to go deeper: in the United States, ever fewer 'barrels of oil proved per thousand feet' drilled are being added from exploratory wells as the years go by.

For the world as a whole, the total of 'proved oil reserves', over the industry's whole history, has at most times kept pace with the growth of consumption. But following the huge discoveries in the Middle East during the thirties the reserve production ratio rose to embarrassing levels. In 1939, total proved reserves were put at 32,000 million barrels, representing 16 years' production at the previous year's rate; by 1950, they had nearly trebled, representing 24 years' output at a much higher rate; and by about the middle of the sixties 'published proved reserves' were more than three times as high again, at 357,300 million barrels or just under 48,000 million tons, about 31 years' production at 1965 rates. The geographical distribution of the world's proved reserves had also altered radically. In 1939, half of the total was located in the United States—as against about 60 per cent both of world output and of world consumption. By the end of 1965, the United States, still producing more than 25 per cent and consuming 36 per cent of the world's oil products, possessed only about 11 per cent of proved reserves. More than 61 per cent of reserves were in the Middle East nations. Countries in this area were just about passing the United States as a producer—although they were themselves consuming no more than two per cent of the world's oil. Another rapidly rising share of world proved reserves has been in the Communist bloc, where proved reserves of oil are approaching those of the United States.

D
49

What one means by 'proved' reserves, in the most rigorous conventional definition, is a measure of the quantities of oil that have been located by drilling and are estimated to be recoverable by the production systems in operation at the time, plus undrilled resources so close to the drilled areas that there is every probability that they will produce when drilled. Even that definition, framed by the American Petroleum Institute, involves a large amount of estimation and leaves a good deal of room for optimism or pessimism.[2] It is important to remember, moreover, that the number of years' production in the reserves that any country or oil company has proved and published is related within limits to the amount of effort it has chosen, or found profitable, to put into drilling. Provisions in the tax systems of certain countries make a high rate of exploration and development of new wells advantageous financially as well as in maintaining a company's technical position. The United States is one of the most expensive places in the world to find an additional barrel of oil for one's reserves; at the beginning of the sixties its reserves represented about 12 years' production (there are some indications that the Russians like to work on a roughly similar number of years' inventory).[3] To keep that ratio around 12–13 years, certainly, was involving the American oil industry in a prodigious and steadily growing drilling effort—some 45,000 wells a year, exploration and development. Perhaps 10,000 of these were exploratory 'wildcat' wells, of which no more than one in nine finds oil and no more than one in forty-five finds a million barrel field, which is what one needs to make it worth commercial production. The rest of the wells drilled are development wells, of which three in four reach oil; these 'prove up' existing oilfields but don't really locate fresh oil.

In other parts of the world it is very doubtful whether 'proved reserves' prove as much as in the United States. Wells are often farther apart than would allow the proving of 'connected fields' on the API definition. Not all companies or even producing countries want to advertise just how much oil they know they have. One or two countries, perhaps, are close-mouthed because they wish they had more; but some of those in the Middle East find it more convenient to be conservative about their inventory of buried wealth. Total 'proved reserves' for that area, in 1965, were published as 215,000 million barrels: yet Mr. Wallace Pratt, one of the industry's leading geologists, had reckoned as early as 1955–56 that the Middle East had 240,000 million barrels of 'conservative and proved reserves'. Companies operating in Kuwait and Saudi Arabia, for example, publish proved reserves totalling about 70,000 and

60,000 million barrels respectively: many oilmen in the Middle East are prepared to guess that the companies in Saudi Arabia at least have pretty strong evidence of the existence of reserves two to four times that size. Moreover, when the present consortium began operations in Iran in 1954, it published figures of proved reserves a good deal higher than had ever been reported by Anglo-Iranian: yet there had been no drilling in the meantime. Companies striking it rich in new areas, such as Standard Oil of New Jersey, towards the end of the fifties, in Libya, are cautious about indicating reserve figures: and their rivals in the oil business are even more cautious about taking any figures at face value. Figures of proved reserves, collected according to as rigorous and stable a definition as one can hope to get observed, are meaningful in indicating the extent of primary development of the general 'resource base' of the industry and the 'stock' of oil that could be tapped at fairly short notice. But one should not ignore the fact that the primary data represent no more than companies want to tell their competitors. Even published data, however, show Middle East reserves at well over 75 years' production at current rates. That is far more oil than any company would find it 'efficient' to have on tap for ready development.

Estimates of 'ultimate reserves', on the other hand, have generally been made for the industry as a whole. And these figures, from the outside, sometimes seem to represent so little that has any tangible meaning that the industry does not care in the least what it tells its competitors (though it would as soon dismay them as not). Definitions of the term vary, but it is usually taken to imply an estimate of the total petroleum recoverable, both from current proved reserves and from reserves that will be discovered in future, in terms of current production techniques (usually assuming an unchanged level of recovery techniques). This last convention was challenged a few years ago, quite logically within the terms of such speculation, by two American economists in a study which suggested the alternative concept of the 'resource base.[4] This is an estimate of the total quantity of oil *in situ*, to which one may if necessary then apply recovery percentages based on the techniques that one hopes may have been invented by the time that the oil in question comes to be taken out. The trouble is that what you arrive at is not susceptible of any form of periodical checking with what is actually discovered in the meantime; which opens the question whether such estimates have any practical meaning at all.

One of the few purposes served by estimates of ultimate reserves is to reassure people who fear the world may soon run out of oil, as people may who simply apply current rates of growth in consumption till, say, the end of the century and compare how much oil we may by then cumulatively have taken out of the earth against the figures of 'proved reserves'. Another purpose, it is difficult not to suspect, may be simply to bedevil forecasters in other fuel industries. Some planners in other industries, such as coal, base their own ideas of the amount of capacity they ought to keep in being on the argument that the oil industry's own forecasts of growth in consumption imply quite sharply rising costs for petroleum by about the end of the century. Whether or not such estimation is ever wise, it is almost predictably upset, within a year or so, by some far more optimistic estimate of the 'ultimate reserves' of oil likely to be available by another (or even the same) famous oil geologist: the latest figures suggest that some 2,000,000 million barrels may be recoverable by primary techniques, and another 1,500,000 million barrels by 'secondary recovery' techniques. But the constant upward revision also seems to represent in part simply the geologists' state of mind—which is characteristically sanguine, and on experience so far has good reason to be.

It is probably safer to settle for another of the oil industry's generalizations—'There is still a good deal more oil left in the earth than has ever been taken out.' Even in terms of 'published proved reserves', that is still true, as a statistical statement; and estimates of the world's proved reserves, as we have seen, have of late been growing rapidly. It is not true of the United States now, counting production to date against proved reserves, even allowing for increases. Given current orders of cost and a finite reservoir of this exhausting resource, many oilmen there believe that the peak rate of American output may be passed during the next ten years. And North America is the only major area of the world that has ever supported a really high rate of petroleum consumption out of its own resources. (Russia in the early sixties used no more oil per head than Samoa.) The only other centres of really high consumption, primarily Western Europe, Japan, and parts of the British Commonwealth, have never had very significant proved oil reserves of their own at all: about half of one per cent of the world's oil reserves. In 1965, Western Europe produced in fact nearly one and a half per cent of the world output; but this amounted to only about one-eighteenth of the amount of oil that it consumed.

This pattern of oil geography, therefore, makes a very large part of the world's consumption of oil dependent on long-distance seaborne trade between the main exporting countries that produce most of it but use hardly any, and a group of consuming countries which use large and growing amounts but produce practically none. Until the mid-twenties most of the oil moving around the world came from Mexico and the United States. For the next generation Venezuela was the dominant supplier. Since about 1950, the Middle East has been in the lead. The United States began to import oil between the wars, but did not become a steady net importer until about 1948. Up to now, though its imports cover only about a fifth of its consumption, they are far the largest of any country in the world. As a region, however, Western Europe has long been the destination for the biggest imports; in 1965, it brought in about 7¾ million barrels a day, well over twice as much as North America. Gradual shifts between the sources from which oil is carried to the main importing countries, allied with the switch of certain countries from exporting to importing, have transformed the pattern of the world's oil trade, at the same time that its total volume has been growing rapidly like everything else in oil. But they have only sharpened the distinction between have and have-not, consume-not and consume, which is responsible for that trade.

Are any developments in sight in the world's oil industry that may greatly alter this interlocking pattern—and basic interdependence—of consumer and producer nations? In what it is fashionable to call 'the foreseeable future'—say over the next 25 years—one can obviously expect the countries from which oil is exported, some of them already rich though not industrialized countries, to develop standards of living that consume much more energy; and the energy they consume is unlikely to be anything but petroleum. The United States, as a policy, has reduced the rate of growth of its net imports; and if it remains prepared to accept the somewhat higher—though not necessarily rising—cost of energy produced at home, it may not make such demands on the main exporting countries as it expected some years ago. New major oil-producing areas, such as North Africa, are already rising in importance, particularly where they are located nearer the big importing areas than the present Middle East and Caribbean suppliers. The present industrialized importing areas—in particular, Western Europe—are beginning to be explored for oil more intensively than ever before. They cannot necessarily be written off in terms of production; North-west Europe has found large reserves of natural gas, and has even larger hopes.

Nevertheless, if one assumes peace and even moderate rates of economic growth, it is difficult to expect anything but a continued rise in imports of energy into Western Europe. Less developed economies are likely to be growing faster; so will their consumption of oil; and a number of them have been able to reach self-sufficiency in oil—at a low consumption level. But the absolute lead in living standards of the highly industrialized societies, and their lead in population over all but a few of the others such as India and China, are likely to mean that their total consumption remains a very large proportion of the world total. There seems little chance, moreover, of any massive shift in the geographical balance of world industrialization during say the next twenty-five years. The economies newly becoming industrialized are far less dependent on coal than those developed earlier, and certain materials of construction now rising in importance, such as aluminium and the plastics, may reduce a developing economy's dependence even on steel. Natural gas, again, might possibly turn out to be more of a 'resource-locating' fuel than oil has ever been. It certainly seems likely that certain bulk chemical commodities will be made from natural gas at source, and moved by tanker around the world in large volumes, from now on. But one specialized job that oil and gas have not until recently been able to do, the smelting of iron, has served coal well. Moreover, the institutional 'weight' in the world market of the economies built on coal retains a considerable magnetism for capital—and for educated manpower.

If the import requirements of the developed Western economies are then certain to remain a huge and possibly growing proportion of the world oil trade over the next generation or so, where they may be met from is perhaps something that it is less wise to prophesy, even in purely economic terms. Did many experts guess in 1929 how the centre of gravity of world petroleum would shift, over the next thirty years, to the Middle East? Yet when one considers the enormous reserves of oil now available in that region, and the likelihood of further discoveries there, given any really intensive drilling—even apart from the relatively low cost of oil there, of which we have said nothing so far—it is hard to believe that any other area can replace it over the next generation. Diversity in sources of supply is something that customers might seek for economic reasons alone, even if there were no political reasons pressing them into doing so. It is also something that companies which develop and purvey oil throughout the world may logically also go on seeking, even in times of surplus. But we ought probably to assume that the industrialized areas of the world are likely, on balance, to become even less self-sufficient in fuel; and that a very high proportion of the fuel they import will still have to come from the major exporting regions of today, give or take one or two significant areas.

This separation of oil resources from oil markets, over the industry's history, has brought immense benefits to many otherwise under-developed parts of the world, as well as to the developed powers that supplied the knowhow and capital, and the companies that have done the job. Oil is a kind of fuel for which there is still no practical way of providing autarchic substitutes. It has been the source of possibly the greatest single wave of overseas investment in history, and of a fantastic acceleration of economic advancement in some areas. It has been developed, so far, by companies domiciled originally in developed countries—and in particular by a handful of very big ones, inter-national in scope, mobile in operations and dealing on terms approach-ing equality with the governments not only of exporting but of con-suming countries. These oil companies fulfil, primarily, an economic role—though it quite often does not seem to the governments concerned to remain simply economic, and perhaps could never have been expected to remain so. For both the economics of oil development and the institutions that have evolved to carry it out are rather unusual.

CHAPTER IV

Operating Economics: I. Crude Oil

Nobody outside the oil industry can hope to gain more than the sketchiest idea of its technology; indeed, few people inside would claim they know it all. Along with the chemical industry, it was among the first of the 'science-based' industries; today, from one end of its long chain of operations to the other, it is still involved in steady refinement of the complex techniques that it employs, so that they are constantly becoming more complex. Here, the technology is outlined merely to describe some peculiarities of the operating economics of the industry. Oil production is an extractive industry, exhausting deposits discovered underground by exploration of which the results are hardly predictable. It supplies the raw material extracted, via the largest single bulk transport operation in the world, to a complex manufacturing industry. This refines crude oil into a wide range of products, in proportions that can be varied deliberately only to a limited degree. Many of the techniques used in exploration, transport, refining, and the marketing of certain major oil products are entirely specialized to oil. And frequently—in the free world outside the United States one can say characteristically—all these activities from exploration to wholesale distribution are controlled by the same integrated group. It is a pretty safe generalization to say that this industry has a characteristic pattern of high fixed costs and low running costs; but the conclusions commonly drawn from that can be misleading. To put economic meaning on the bones of these generalizations, we need to consider the cost pattern of each of the main stages in the industry's operations.

The production of oil can logically be linked with exploration for it (in the past; unfortunately, there is no automatic link between present exploration and future production). For convenience rather than in logic, this chapter also includes a sketch of the specialized forms of long distance transport used to move oil. Tankers and pipelines, obviously, are used to move products as well as crude oil. But crude accounts for a growing proportion—now some three-quarters—of the oil moved in international trade.

PRODUCTION AND EXPLORATION

At the end of 1964, about 700,000 oil wells were in operation through the world; with 28 million barrels a day, or 1,400 million tons a year, of total output, that gave an average yield of less than 40 barrels a day, or 2,000 tons a year, for each well. But that average is utterly misleading. About 600,000 of those wells were in the United States, producing in all about 7·8 million barrels a day, which is a sizeable proportion of the world's output, but an average of no more than 13 barrels a day, or 650 tons a year, from each well. In the Middle East, on the other hand, only about 1,800 wells were in operation throughout the oil-producing territories, for an output of 7·7 million barrels a day, producing an average of 4,300 barrels a day (215,000 tons a year) each. In Iran and Iraq, with only about 140 and 130 wells respectively in operation, the averages were 14,000 and 10,000 barrels a day from each well. Between these extremes of dribble and flood came the 11,000 wells in Venezuela, each producing about 300 barrels a day; those in Indonesia, with an average of about 200 barrels a day; and the 41,000 or so wells of the U.S.S.R., producing about 100 barrels a day each.[1] And within each of these countries, there are further variations between the old and the new, the richer and the less productive oilfields. In the United States, in particular, the number of wells is inflated by governmental regulation that keeps uncompetitive wells producing—and makes the average production impossible to compare realistically with countries where oilmen close down uneconomic wells.

This fantastically wide variation between rates of output from the wells that this industry considers it worth while keeping in operation results from various factors. These include the different volumes and conditions in which the oil lies in the earth in different places, the depths from which it is being taken out, the working age of any given well, and the number of them that have been drilled to tap the same oil reservoir. When the pressure in the oil reservoir that one is tapping is high, it will gush to the surface at a very high rate; and so will crudes in which there is a very high proportion of dissolved gas, even if they are found at great depths. Over the working 'life cycle' of every oil well, a 'production decline curve' establishes itself, with the gradual loss of pressure as oil and gas are taken out. There is normally an initial period on 'natural drive' with the oil flowing to the surface of its own accord.

Then comes one form or another of 'artificial lift' which lengthens the wells' working life. Both these phases are classed as 'primary recovery'. Finally the well declines to operation as 'a stripper', exhausting its last few barrels a day, unless the operator has in the meantime decided to invest in more elaborate forms of 'secondary recovery'. The techniques used are generally those of 'fluid injection' with gas or water. When applied early in a well's producing life, this is known as 'pressure maintenance'. But when it is applied only when the well's natural pressure is becoming exhausted, as 're-pressuring' and 'water flooding' along with more complex techniques, it ranks as 'secondary recovery'.

The period that any well runs on 'natural drive'—obviously its time of lowest costs—will vary according to underground conditions and possibly also according to the number of wells that have been drilled into its reservoir of oil. Over-drilling, which has occurred in some parts of the United States and elsewhere at certain periods, can waste the underground pressure in a reservoir and indeed reduce the proportion of the oil in it that one can hope to get out without resort to costly methods of secondary recovery. Most of the wells in the Middle East are still on natural drive, and conditions in the reservoirs there are such as to keep them flowing without assistance from the surface for many years; but pressure maintenance is already being applied. In the United States, on the other hand, nearly 90 per cent of all producing wells, in 1960, were 'on the pump'; that is to say, that the oil was being raised with the help of various kinds of pump or by other techniques such as 'gas lift', which involves injecting gas under pressure into the column of oil contained in the well, to reduce the weight of it and enable underground pressure to keep it flowing to the surface.

Between the end of the Second World War and the middle of the sixties, the total of proved oil reserves in the world rose by about 290 billion barrels, or 40,000 million tons. During the same period, from the end of 1945 to the end of 1965, the oil industries of the world produced about 130 billion barrels or nearly 17,500 million tons of oil for consumers. The amount of new oil proven in reserves, therefore, was of the order of 420 billion barrels. This was the result of a prodigious effort of exploration, plus development of known oilfields. An enormously costly one, too—though the cost was inflated because of the concentration on keeping up American reserves. Together, exploration and production in the free world alone have been reckoned during the decade 1953–62 to have cost some $60 billion (about £20,000 million). These figures, published in 1964 by the oil committee of OECD, show that $42 billion was invested in production and exploration in U.S.A., with a gross addition to reserves in the ten years of 29 billion barrels (nearly 4,000 million tons). In the Middle East, with production/exploration investment of only $2 billion, additions to reserves amounted to 144 billion barrels (19,400 million tons).

This postwar surge of exploration for oil was partly to match a rapid expansion in demand and to provide for the development of a greatly expanded capacity to match the growth of future demand. Oil, like other extractive industries, has constantly to provide against the depletion of the resources it is working. In terms of the actual physical depletion of reservoirs, this factor is really significant perhaps only in the areas where production has been established on a large scale for a long time. In the United States, for example, every producer seeks to find another barrel for each barrel of oil he takes out (and he may have to spend practically all the profit he gets out of the one in finding the other).

Outside America concessions are limited in time; and in a number of Middle East countries the reserves already discovered, allowing for the inevitable 'rating up' of estimates as the years go by, are huge in relation to any predictable growth in output. So the incentive to add to reserves is smaller—for the concessionnaire. Governments of these areas, however, may think differently. Nowadays a concessionnaire is often obliged to carry through a minimum programme of drilling and to bring any fields located into production within a given period, or relinquish his rights to explore. And to abandon or drastically to reduce exploration in an area where one may have invested many millions is a heavy decision to make because at any one time the market for finished petroleum products may happen to be weak. It is seldom, after all, that any significant supplies of oil come on to the market from a new oilfield in less than about three years from the time the find is made, and in that time the state of demand can have altered quite radically. Outside the Soviet sphere, again, we are not concerned in this industry with managements who imagine they can do what is best for whole industries. The people who have to decide are concerned with the present and future of individual companies. Moreover, they may always be pushed into exploring any given area by the feeling that if they do not somebody else will take the gamble—and perhaps the winnings, which may eventually be huge. The next oil you find may be lower in cost, or nearer to market: if someone else finds it, it will undersell some of yours.

In the process of finding oil and developing production, very large amounts of money have first to be gambled on what may be no more than an experienced geologist's hunch. Even if this gamble pays off, a good deal more money will have to be invested, not only in determining the extent of the field and installing the production facilities. Often, particularly in the underdeveloped areas where most drilling goes on, much capital has to be invested in providing transport facilities to move the oil and living accommodation, with some standards of amenity, for the people who will be responsible for getting it out of the ground. A large proportion of the money spent on exploration, particularly the early stages of it, tends to be wasted—except for the negative indications that even dry holes give the next explorer.

The chances of finding oil when one drills a 'wildcat' well in exploration are often quoted at one in nine. In practice, this figure comes from the United States, where the statistics are more reliable than anywhere else but the circumstances encourage drilling in less promising conditions than would be commercially wise almost anywhere else. Once again, such averages are misleading. There are areas of the world where the chances of finding oil are extremely good, and the chances that if you do it will be cheap to produce and bring to ocean-going transport are very high. The Japanese Arabian Oil Company, which began drilling off the shore of the Saudi Arabia-Kuwait Neutral Zone in 1959, not far from the existing Safaniya field of Saudi Arabia, discovered commercial oil with the first well that it sank. Yet during the same twelve months a number of major companies had decided to pull out of Papua, where some years and millions had been spent in pursuing what seemed a good chance of finding oil; and Shell and B.P. were finally able to achieve an output of 10,000 barrels a day from two fields in Nigeria, in finding which they had spent about £30 million over a period of nearly twenty-one years. And even in as promising a Middle East area as the Kuwait offshore concession, for which Shell bid so high in 1960, no oil had been discovered up to the time that this book was revised in 1965.

An oil company does not begin to put down the heavy stakes in the gamble of exploration until it begins drilling; any refinement in preliminary techniques that will reduce the risk of 'dry holes', therefore, is eagerly sought. The ordinary sequence of searching for oil begins with a preliminary reconnaissance by the geologists, which may take anything up to a year for a large area on which little data exists. If this is favourable, it will be followed by surface geological mapping and air photography. Geophysical survey of likely areas, by techniques that measure fractional differences in the earth's gravitational or magnetic fields, or by seismic methods akin to echo-sounding, follows. But all these stages can at best assess the probability that oil may be found in certain places. Nowadays, petroleum can only be found with the drill—and indeed it may be necessary to drill 'stratigraphic' test wells to investigate the nature of the rock strata before taking the decision whether or not to go ahead in drilling actual test wells for oil. The preliminaries will probably cost hundreds of thousands of pounds, when you count in the cost of accommodating and administering the expeditions involved, and may run into millions. A drilling programme is fairly certain to cost millions.

It was estimated in the middle fifties that 60 per cent of the oil contained in proved reserves in the major oil-producing areas of the free world lay between 1,000 feet and 5,000 feet below the surface, and another 30 per cent between 5,000 and 8,000 feet down. It is still possible to happen on new and highly productive fields within these depths; but exploration teams are tending to have to drill more and more of their wells between say 3,000 and 10,000 feet, and many go much deeper. The deepest hole ever drilled into the earth's crust (until American and Russian geophysicists began seeing who could dig down farthest purely in the interests of national prestige) was by an oil company in West Texas. It went to some 25,000 feet, before the company decided to stop. Almost inevitably, it was a dry hole (though production has now been achieved from wells below 21,000 feet). The rigs involved in drilling are large and fairly elaborate pieces of equipment. Though they are constantly being rendered more mobile, in remote areas they need backing up with supply services and all the people concerned need accommodation and provisions, so that the exercise is inherently costly, at times running into hundreds of pounds per foot drilled. To say that rotary drilling consists of rotating a toothed bit in the earth on the end of a string of pipes, while pumping through it a specially-compounded mud that carries to the surface the debris—and the evidence—is broadly true but hopelessly inadequate to describe what goes on. Over the years drillers have perfected ways of dealing with the myriad difficulties that can arise in carrying on a boring operation in which the bit may be two or three miles out of sight below your feet, but test drilling will probably never become a routine operation. Nor can it ever be anything but a financial risk.

The places that the oil industry picks to explore are those that seem to its managements the likeliest places to find the lowest cost additional reserves—considering nearness to markets as well as geology. Each management is thus reacting rationally to a selection of variously 'prospective' areas, ranging downwards in likelihood and upwards in cost. Its choice may be mistaken, but that will be demonstrated only in hindsight. However, the occurrence of oil deposits, geographically, is random; so is their size distribution where oil is found. So it is hard to make any guess about the amount of oil reserves likely to be discovered for any given amount of exploration. A programme of exploration may produce nothing at all—or enormous deposits such as some of those in the Middle East, which when they were discovered in the thirties and forties were outside all previous experience in the industry anywhere. This can cause an unpredictable bunching of additions to reserves, and sharp fluctuations over short periods in the 'stock' of proved oil reserves available for development cheaply and at short notice.

Even to locate oil is not nearly enough. You have to estimate the 'pay thickness' and then the extent of the oil reservoir. Then you have to decide whether the investment so far and the probable life of the reservoir at a rate of extraction that will justify putting in transport facilities—almost certainly a tanker terminal, and frequently a long pipeline to feed it—make the further investment of bringing the find into production worth while. Once the decision is made, an oil company has to invest more years and millions before the first oil from this new underground source flows into world trade. Getting the oil to the surface, in the initial stages, may be no problem, since it often lifts itself up to be stoppered and led off from the characteristic 'Christmas tree' of valves and gauges. But the correct spacing of wells to take off the required volumes of oil, the assessment and utilization of pressure conditions in the underground reservoir, and the installation of surface equipment to separate gas in solution and to treat any of its other special properties, are technically demanding and costly. Pipes to take the oil away, tank farms to hold some limited amount in store (though one seldom wants to store much crude anywhere but in the best place, under the earth), and ocean terminals to load it into tankers (assuming that the oil is discovered remote from refineries and markets) require further investment. Complete townships, such as Ahmadi in Kuwait and Dhahran in Saudi Arabia, may have to be developed to house the technical staff and management involved, in what may well be in its own right a very big business indeed.

In economic terms, this business of oil exploration, development, and production is fairly capital-intensive; and the time-table of the investment involved has a peculiar effect upon the production costs of oil. In many cases the running costs of producing oil are very low indeed; they are almost always low in relation to the burden of capital charges that the product has to bear. As a result, oil production from any one reservoir has sharp economies of scale up to the limits of well capacity; and for a time at least, once the producing pattern of wells is established, its average costs decline as more and more oil is taken out without any additional investment. Oil is thus in a different cost situation from those of the other extractive industries, which include one of its main competitors, coal. Oilmen generally bridle if you say to them that oil mines itself. And when you consider the vast effort and expense, in many cases fruitless, that has to be put in before a barrel of oil is produced from a new well, they have every reason. But after those resources are committed, successfully, for a while the oil comes up on its own.

At some point in the working life of any given well the normal pattern of diminishing returns that must eventually apply to any industry extracting a wasting asset does certainly begin to assert itself. So long as the well is flowing freely—mining itself?—its average costs diminish; when it is shifted over to its next stage of artificial lift, such as straight pumping or the injection of gas to help it to the surface, its costs rise sharply by one further 'step'. But this upward step again is mainly a fixed addition to the capital investment embodied in the well; the running costs are increased, but do not become very high and remain the same for a considerable time. So for another longish period in the well's working life its average costs are again probably diminishing. Eventually, perhaps, it reaches a point where the flow, even assisted, becomes such a trickle that without exceptional and yet more costly techniques of secondary recovery, the owner may turn off the tap. The well, or on a rather wider scale the field, is gone; so is the investment. The owner has undoubtedly been looking for reserves to replace those he is taking out; indeed, the point at which he finally decides to take the expiring well out of production will often be decided by the relative cheapness of new production he has found elsewhere.

Professor M. A. Adelman has recently reminded the industry[2] that this is not the same thing as saying that oil production, uniquely among extractive industries, enjoys 'increasing returns', or decreasing marginal costs. That would be so if at each moment in time, given that its demand were one barrel higher, the industry could produce the further barrel at less than its average cost for all the rest. For a given well, reservoir, or indeed oil producing area working at less than its installed capacity, that may be true, as it might be in individual plants or regions for any other industry. But nothing inherent in oil economics makes it necessarily true for the whole industry. Whatever the demand upon the industry at any one time, its commercial aim is to supply that amount from the least-cost combination of sources. To the extent that it is fulfilling that commercial aim properly, to supply one barrel more at that time would involve it in tapping the next lowest-cost cost source for that additional barrel. Economically, therefore, there is nothing peculiar about oil. When allowed to act with commercial logic, it operates in circumstances of increasing marginal cost, and diminishing returns.

Political constraints, however, may prevent the industry acting logically. Restrictions on oil imports into the United States, for example, mean that at present any given demand for oil there is supplied by calling into production the next lowest cost oil available inside U.S. frontiers. That next barrel of oil would not even necessarily be the cheapest additional oil that could be produced there, owing to regulations that share demand between high and low cost wells 'rateably'. And along with many of the barrels of U.S. oil already being produced, that next barrel would certainly be much more expensive than oil which in a free world market for the commodity could be imported from abroad. In many other market areas of the world where local oil production exists, similar constraints operate: additional demand is in practice met by using higher cost oil than would be available abroad. In the world today, a great deal of high cost oil is being produced and sold. The next barrel of United States demand could certainly be supplied at lower than average cost—if it were allowed to be brought in from the Middle East or Libya. These are facts not to be wished away by calling them distortions of the free market: they are main contributory factors to this industry's largest problems. Nevertheless, they are political facts; and to assume that they reflect some inherent peculiarities of the industry's economics may simply blur one's understanding of them.

Oil's pattern of low operating costs and very large economies of scale makes competition with it intensely difficult for coal, an industry extracting solids from the earth by cutting them out of the seams underground and lifting them. Mechanically or with hand labour—and there is no doubt that most of the coal industries of the world have stayed more dependent on hand labour, and over a longer period, than they should have done—this job is one in which running costs are high and often increasing over time, if only because each next ton one wins is farther away from the surface or the shaft bottom. Where it

comes into direct competition with coal, oil's peculiar pattern of
tion cost—a pattern that tends to be repeated in later stages of it.
gress to market—gives it considerable inherent advantages. But
same pattern of cost can have considerable embarrassments for the o.
industry itself in internal competition. Large amounts of new capital
may be attracted into oil, particularly in the most productive areas, by
the very high returns that entrepreneurs can on occasion earn there.
But the return that can be earned on oil production depends on getting
the oil to market—and without full use of his capacity to do so, the
new producer may find it necessary to unload his oil at prices that offer
very low returns indeed.

TRANSPORT

Once at the top of the well, oil is ready to flow where the producer
wishes. Its very nature as a liquid is the essence of the ease and cheapness with which it can be transported, in comparison with other fuels
and indeed with most other commodities that move in world trade—just
as it is essential to the consumption of oil and is the property around
which the technology of its processing has been developed. This liquid
has to be contained to be handled at all, and generally in a specialized
container: once the volume is large enough, it is convenient to combine
the container and the means of transport. In the pipeline the product
moves, not the container. The ocean tanker, on the other hand, gains
economies of scale from the principle that the containing 'skin' of any
receptacle rises as the square of its dimensions, whereas the volume
enclosed rises as the cube of them.

On any one day in the middle sixties, there might have been about
35 million tons of crude oil and products moving in perhaps 39 million
deadweight tons of tankers around the world, and a like tonnage of
tankers in ballast on their way back to be filled up again. There are
not many return hauls in the crude oil trade, and vessels are generally
employed over any given period on crude or on products, but not
both. In the movement of petroleum products, some of which may
be in surplus in one refinery area and some in others, the shipping
departments of the oil companies can make rather more use of 'tri-
angular' routeing of their ships, but this too is limited. World-wide
movement of oil, at the beginning of the sixties, was carried out by
a world tanker fleet that totalled, at the beginning of 1965, nearly 82
million deadweight tons, representing about one-third of all merchant

shipping in the world. This total was nearly five times as big as in 1939, and over 40 times as much as in 1914: over the last generation, in particular, tanker tonnage has been by far the most rapidly growing element in world shipping. And it has been increasing much faster in carrying capacity than in tonnage, because average speeds have steadily risen too, and the new, faster tankers are the larger ones. Before the war, companies were building tankers mostly of say 12,000 tons dead-weight and operating speeds of say 11–12 knots. The T–2 standard tanker, turned out in vast numbers by American shipyards during the war, was of 16,800 tons with an operating speed of 14–16 knots. Since the war standard sizes have risen rapidly. Early in the fifties a vessel of 32,500 tons d.w. ranked as a 'super tanker'. Today most new tankers are of 50,000–80,000 tons d.w., with some giants of 200,000 d.w. in or coming into service. Operating speeds have risen to 17–18 knots.

One cannot give any comparable figure of the total capacity of pipe-lines throughout the world: the capacity of a pipeline depends on the number of pumping stations, as well as on the diameter, and stations can be added as required. The total length of pipelines in being in 1965 has been put at 1,030,000 miles (apart from the Communist countries, where large developments are in train): of this total some 770,000 miles carried natural gas, and 270,000 miles carried oil. The majority of this was crude oil, the biggest mileage of lines carrying crude from inland oilfields to refineries or tanker terminals. The use of pipelines for the movement of refined products, hitherto economic only in the United States, has now spread to Europe, where another current development is the building of crude pipelines from ports to refineries far inland. There has been talk of building undersea pipelines for both oil and gas from North Africa across the Mediterranean to Europe, or even from the Middle East to Europe; but so far there is only one major crude pipeline in the world that operates in direct competition with ocean tankers. This is TAPline, the 754-mile line completed in 1950 from Sidon in the Lebanon to Qaisumah in Saudi Arabia, where it joins a 314-mile pipe-line to the Abqaiq oilfields in Arabia. TAPline can deliver 470,000 barrels of crude a day (23 million tons a year) to the Eastern Mediter-ranean; when working to full capacity, it will at any time contain about 5 million barrels of oil. In operation, it has somewhat reduced the growth of seaborne movement of oil, by reducing the number of tankers that have to go from the West right round to the Persian Gulf. A similar effect has been experienced from the use of the trunk pipelines from Northern Iraq to the Eastern Mediterranean, though these lines, from far inland, can hardly be called directly competitive with tankers. Certain large trunk lines were built from Texas to the north-east coast of the United States during the war for the movement of crude, but the distances involved then offered insufficient advantage over coastwise tanker shipment, and these lines are now used to move natural gas. Big trunk lines from the Russian oilfields to Central Europe have now come into operation; these are playing a real part in the world oil trade and moving oil that might have come, at least from the Black Sea onwards, by tanker. But up to now TAPline has been the only major line to play a big part in the free world's international trade in crude oil, and practically all the oil that it delivers to Sidon is loaded into tankers for further movement. In the movement of crude oil, so far, pipelines and tankers have been much more complementary than competitive.

In Western Europe, however, pipelines have recently begun to play a larger part, by moving crude oil from the southern coast of Europe to refineries built inland. Oil from the Persian Gulf that moves to the Eastern Mediterranean by TAPline instead of tanker can now go from Marseilles to Stuttgart or Strasbourg by pipeline instead, possibly, of sailing round the North Sea to be transhipped into smaller tankers to sail up the Rhine; a long distance has thus been lopped off each end of the tanker haul to North-West Europe. That is one new development that is tending to moderate the growth of the total ton-miles travelled by tankers in the seaborne movement of oil. Another is the rapid development of production much nearer Europe, in Algeria and in Libya. A third—which is only partly economic, and belongs properly to our later discussion of nationalism—is that in the early sixties the movement of oil from the Middle East to the United States did not grow to the degree that was foreseen in the fifties.

The greater part of the oil movement around the world flows towards the shores of the North Atlantic; but in comparison with pre-war years, a far larger amount now comes from the Eastern hemisphere, and the bulk of this from the Middle East. By the early sixties, indeed, the movement of crude oil from the Western hemisphere to consuming countries in Europe and points East was simply a balancing factor; because the most rapid rise in European demand was for fuel oil, and Venezuelan crudes offer relatively high yields of fuel oil. Considerable quantities of products, however, were still being exported from Venezuela to Europe to keep balance between demand and European refinery capacity.

During the early postwar years, with this big shift in the network of oil movement, the average distance that a ton of oil moved to market steadily rose: it was about 3,600 miles, 12 days' steaming for a 14-knot tanker, by 1955, some 13 per cent farther than the average for 1938. During the fifties, looking forward ten years or more as it is necessary to do in planning all the facilities that a capital-intensive industry such as oil needs in a period of fast and steady growth, forecasters in the major companies reckoned that the average distance would continue to lengthen. The interruption of oil supplies during the Suez crisis emphasized that in future large quantities of oil might have to be shipped from the Persian Gulf round the Cape, instead of through an international waterway under nationalist and potentially hostile control. This strengthened the forecasters' conclusions; they may indeed have put an extra margin for security into their calculations about the tanker tonnage required. By the beginnings of the sixties, some of the factors we have mentioned above—supplies nearer Europe, pipelines within Europe, and restrictions on American imports—were beginning to weaken the basis of that reasoning.[3] But the tankers—some 35 million tons ordered between 1954 and 1957—were coming down the slipways by then; the money was spent.

It was a vast amount of money; the 30 million tons on shipyard orderbooks around the world at the peak in 1956–58 represented, at then prices, perhaps £2,750,000,000 (though in many cases this new building was postponed, and in some the prices per ton were adjusted downwards as quotations fell in the ensuing shipbuilding slump). Means of transporting oil always take sizeable investment—one among the many in this industry. There is one saving, however, of which the company investing in tankers can take advantage: remarkable economies of scale. It takes less labour, steel, and shipyard design to build a tanker to carry 100,000 tons of crude oil than it does to build two to carry 50,000 tons each; and less than twice as much shaft horse-power to drive it through the water at a given speed, and hence less bunker fuel. The crew needed on the larger tanker is little larger than on one of the smaller ones, and up to a point insurance costs per ton of cargo fall as size increases. 'Up to a point' applies to all these economies; there could come a point where the construction costs and certain running costs 'fault' upward sharply, before economies of scale again begin to apply at the higher level. But by 1965, some companies were ordering 250,000–300,000 tonners.

The main thing that limited the extent to which tanker owners were prepared to seek economies by building bigger, during the building boom just after the Suez incident, was the question where the vessels could sail and could profitably be employed. If the Suez Canal had remained closed, and the same amount of oil had had to be moved to the West from the Persian Gulf, the industry would have needed more capacity to move it round the Cape. This might have been had most cheaply by building very big tankers; or more pipeline capacity from the Gulf to the Eastern Mediterranean; or some combination of both. The most economical tanker capacity to build for the longer run, indeed, might have been vessels of say 100,000 tons d.w. or more. But these would not have had the alternative of going through the canal if it were open, because they would draw too much water to transit the waterway even after all existing plans to deepen it were carried out, and even if they were only part-loaded and riding high in the water. The canal did not stay closed. Shifts in the rate of growth of American demand for Middle East oil, and in the sources of supply for Europe, gave a chance of moderating the flow of crude oil to the West if the companies had to do so. The companies also pressed forward their plans to increase the capacity of the existing pipelines to the Mediterranean, though the cutting of the line from Kirkuk to Tripoli, during the Suez affair, did not exactly predispose them to lay down more capital immovably on the ground in the shape of new lines; and by the time the new pumping capacity on existing lines from Iraq was completed the companies were in bitter dispute with its government. The limited depth of anchorage within reach of the main consuming centres of the world, and the need to keep as costly a single item of capital as a tanker of this size fully and regularly employed, mean that an investment in super-tankers has to be supported by heavy investment in terminals to take them. Companies did, certainly, begin to construct a number of large terminals, in Europe as well as the United States, to and from which super-tankers could operate. Moreover, supplies from the Middle East to Japan, and also to the United States, favoured use of the 100,000 tonner and upwards.

The big ocean-going tanker is still certainly the cheapest way of moving oil—provided that it is not so big that its savings in cost are offset by losing the flexibility of operations that tankers ordinarily enjoy. It is a highly mobile unit of 'fixed capital'; by contrast, the pipeline is fixed in the physical as well as in the accounting sense. The pipeline is a highly efficient form of continuous one-way transport of fluids; but it is itself immovable. Its costs are almost entirely fixed costs, and the unit cost of moving oil therefore falls fairly steadily up to the limits of its capacity. This capacity depends largely on the diameter of the pipe and the pressure gradient from one end to the other: you can move the same amount of oil in a given time by a large-diameter pipe with a small pressure drop, or a smaller diameter with a larger pressure drop, and the choice may depend on the cost of pumping stations, to move the oil along the pipe. One can move 800,000 barrels of oil a day (40 million tons a year) along a 36-inch pipeline, the largest diameter so far in general use.

Unit costs of fluid movement along a pipeline, unlike those in most other forms of transport, do not depend mainly on distance. The main cost is the pipe, and another mile of route takes another mile of pipe and a corresponding fraction more power. Administrative costs tend to fall as the length of a line extends: but these are relatively insignificant anyway. But the unit costs that a pipeline actually achieves, as against those it can potentially offer, depend upon the extent to which it is used. Its costs rise significantly when it is used below full capacity, and in the short term it has a rigidly defined total capacity without the possibilities of overload in times of emergency possible for most other forms of transport—and for most of the other expensive capital plant that the oil industry uses.

It is usual to begin operating a pipeline with the minimum pumping power—a single pumping station theoretically, would do for a line some hundreds of miles long, provided it traversed flat country—and later build up its capacity towards the theoretical limit by installing more stations. The optimum for large-diameter lines has been put at one pumping station per 60 to 150 miles; obviously costs of pumping are higher where a station has to be installed in remote country without any basic services at all, but the stations can use the fuel that is being moved in the line, and are increasingly being remotely controlled. Since TAPline was installed in 1950, its capacity has been increased almost 60 per cent by increasing the permissible pressure and putting in extra pumping units; the extra investment required amounted to no more than 12 per cent of the $200 million that it originally cost to lay the line. But in some recent years TAPline has been moving oil at below its full rated capacity. A commercial reason for this was that its costs were unable to compete with those of large efficient tankers in a very depressed freight market. Politically, too, the claims of more than one government upon the revenues of the line may have inhibited full utilization.

Many comparisons have been published from time to time of the cost of moving oil in various forms of transport; it is not easy to keep these realistic when costs of one form of transport vary primarily with the utilization of capacity and those of most others mainly with distance. Moreover, the cost of tanker operations is one thing: freight rates at any particular time may be another. Over equal distances, no crude pipeline has ever yet been able to compete even with the average tankers of today, let alone the super-tanker on an efficiently organized run. Product pipelines are perhaps cheaper than road or railway movement over equal distances for quantities of anything over a million tons a year; and cheaper than major river transport for about the same quantities. And it has to be remembered that the pipeline can usually go a far shorter way from A to B than any other form of transport and can operate regardless of weather conditions. Costs for tankers and most other forms of transport fall with distance, because one only has to load and unload once however long the journey: those of the pipeline do not. For the movement of crude, pipelines are an essential complement to tankers, but seldom compete except where much shorter distances can be achieved. For products, though problems arise for viscous fluids such as heavy fuel oil, which may need preheating and heavy insulation of a pipe (or the mixing of fuel oil, like some solid fuels, with water), they are coming in logically as inland centres of consumption develop. For natural gas, as will be seen later, they form so far the main practicable means of transport, though tankers for liquefied gas can now compete for long-distance transport. The operating economics of petroleum transport, as we have seen, vary considerably in detail. But both of the main specialized forms require very large capital investment, and need operating to high capacity in order to achieve their inherent economies of scale.

71

CHAPTER V

Operating Economics: II. Refined Products

Oil, which is now becoming the world's most widely used fuel, is very seldom burned raw. All crude oil is a mixture of a long series of hydro-carbon compounds, but the nature of the mixture varies considerably between crudes from different oilfields and types of sedimentary strata. Here we are concerned with the chemistry of petroleum only in terms of the range of products that can be processed from these crudes; broadly, they can be ranked in three main families, paraffinic, asphaltic, and mixed base crudes. Paraffin based crudes, when refined, will give a high yield of gasoline and a fairly high yield of kerosene, a residue from which lubricating oils can be made, and solid paraffin waxes as a by-product. Asphaltic based crudes give a low yield of the lighter products, and a large yield of the black oils, with a semi-solid residue that is marketed as bitumen. Mixed base crudes come in between the other two. The first crude oils commercially refined, from the Pennsylvania fields in the eighteen-sixties, were paraffinic crudes rich in light products (which suited the early demand for lamp oil, though the gasoline yield was a nuisance). Venezuelan, Mexican and Californian crudes are asphaltic with a particularly high yield of fuel oil. Most of the crudes produced in the Middle East and in the main basins of the United States are of mixed base, with yields of products between the two extremes; those of North Africa, so far, have a high yield of light products.

The main range of liquid petroleum products, again, can be ranked in terms of end-use. There are a range of light products, primarily the gasolines, but including diesel oil, from which energy is best obtained by explosive combustion; these are mainly used in road and air transport. Then come a range of diverse general fuels, from kerosene to heavy fuel oil, from which one obtains energy mainly by simple burning—though kerosene is used in aircraft jet engines. Certain gases, in particular butane and propane, are separated as by-products of refining processes: these have long had a role as fuels for special purposes, and are now, like natural gas, entering the general fuel market, though in far smaller quantities. And outside the fuel field, there comes the vast family of lubricants, general and specialized; waxes and bitumens for a variety of uses; and the range of hydro-carbon compounds used as raw materials in chemical industry, which represent a small proportion of the volume of oil products used throughout the world but have been growing in importance and value to the industry faster of late than any other single group of oil products.

The translation of liquid petroleum from its original complicated mixture into a range of still complex but better-sorted-out products ready for use is effected by a specialized technology of petroleum engineering. This begins by distillation, boiling off the different 'fractions' of the crude oil; so that in refining terms, one talks of the variable yield of products one can get from any given crude in terms of the proportion of its volume that boils off within different bands of the temperature range. Distillation is the main process of separation available to the refiner; but some compounds can also be separated out by solvent extraction, in which a particular solvent may be added to a mixture of hydro-carbon compounds to dissolve and thus separate out those compounds that are soluble in it and leave those that are not. But these 'straight run' processes, which separate the products naturally available in the crude, do not give the refiner the various products in the proportions that he may have a market for them.

A wide range of conversion processes have therefore been developed in order to convert those of which he gets more than he can sell into those of which he cannot get enough to satisfy the market. This family of processes, which began with thermal cracking, the treatment of surplus separated products under high temperature and pressure, has been steadily elaborated through various forms of catalytic conversion and polymerization. Up to the sixties, the elaboration of the refinery technique had been in the direction of obtaining more light products, in particular high-grade gasolines, from a barrel of crude oil. Since the late fifties, with demand for fuel oil rising faster than for motor spirit, there has been a theoretical case for processes to produce more fuel oil out of the barrel, which would be technically possible providing a market could also be found for large amounts of products such as liquid petroleum gases. But in practice this shift in demand has been met by building more of the new refineries as the simpler types, such as 'topping units' which merely 'skim off' the light products and leave the straight-run residue of black oils. The third main family of processes in refining is concerned with the purification of the products produced, one particular impurity with which refiners are concerned being sulphur. But many other impurities have to be cleaned out of oil products before they are sold to the customer; the general degree of purity across the whole range of products is far higher than could have been achieved thirty years ago.

That over-simplified classification of the main types of process that go on in oil refining can give no idea of the wide variety of techniques employed and the complicated way in which these are linked together. But the fact of their linkage is not without importance in petroleum economics. The continued development of oil refining has brought into being over the last forty years or so a new 'steady-state' technology of chemical processes. In a modern refinery there is a sequence of processes going on unceasingly while the mobile feedstock flows from one on to the next, continuously undergoing chemical and physical change. In continuous flow processes such as these the operating conditions in any one vessel or item of plant remain the same all the time; the liquids and gases undergo the change as they move spatially through the successive items of plant. This assemblage of processing units in each of which conditions are unchanging, but between which balance has continuously to be maintained, do not so much lend themselves to automatic control as require it. In the balancing of certain modern refinery units, it is no longer a question of how many men a given bank of instruments and automatic controllers has replaced. Men could not do the job at all as it is now set up, because it would be impossible for a group of them to co-ordinate their own manipulation of pressure, temperature, flow and the other variables quickly and precisely enough.

Any form of technology where labour simply cannot do much of the operating is by definition capital-intensive. An oil refinery is one of the most capital-intensive among a group of industries in which capitalization is generally high, the 'primary conversion' industries that process basic industrial fuels and materials from their raw state. In mid-1965 there were refineries in the world with a total capacity of close on 32 million barrels a day, or 1,600 million tons a year, representing a capital investment approaching $25,000 million. Like tankers and pipelines, refineries can take advantage of economies of scale in their construction and operating costs. There is a minimum scale of throughput below which it is hardly economic to build one—say 15,000 barrels a day or 750,000 tons a year—though the further economies to be gained become smaller as one moves up the scale.

Limits to refinery size may be set by the managerial capacity required to head such a plant and make all the decisions that have to be made (though the computer is coming in here to lighten the executive load of actual operations). Limits are in practice rather more likely to be set by external factors—the size and stability of the market that can economically be served from the refinery, which at giant size will have heavy additional costs to bear from operating at times below capacity. Few giant refineries have been built in the West since Abadan reached its present scale, though some new plants in the Communist bloc are of the same order. Many refiners would argue that with a throughput of say 60,000 barrels a day or 3 million tons a year, one has attained all the economies of scale that are worth while without bringing in extra complications.

As an exceptionally highly-capitalized item of process plant, with high overheads and comparatively low running costs, the refinery has the same characteristic pattern we have seen in exploration and transport of oil—diminishing average costs for each extra barrel up to the limits of its capacity. But the nature of its processing—the separation and conversion of the crude oil into a wide range of different products—introduces another special complexity into its operating economics. Almost all its costs are joint costs, in economic jargon—i.e., one cannot have any of the final products without the whole cost, and incidentally without each other. (As noted above, the refiner has a battery of techniques that enable him to get a larger proportion of any one product; but he can never wholly eliminate the rest of the range.)

This situation of joint costs is a familiar concept in economics (the classic example is another fuel industry, the joint manufacture of gas and coke). With only two products coming from a process, one can postulate a formula for allocating these costs, not in terms of any technical valuation (e.g. the calorific value of the two fuels in heat units), but of the demand for them. One charges all the costs on to the one which is in most demand and which therefore sets the scale of operations; sells the other for whatever it will fetch in the market; and credits its proceeds against the cost of the whole operation to determine the price at which one can sell one's primary product. That is broadly the rule of thumb used in the pricing of gas, coke and the other by-products of traditional carbonization plant. Either gas (in a gasworks) or coke (in coking plant) may be the major product of the process. But one can never properly speak of the average 'cost' of gas or coke (apart from the cost of ancillary operations peculiar to either one). And in the same way, in oil refining, it is hardly meaningful to speak of 'the cost of gasoline' or 'the cost of fuel oil'.

Refining a barrel of oil has a perfectly measurable cost, and the refiner has to get this cost back plus a return on his investment; but none of the products he sells from that barrel has any fully identifiable average cost at all. The oil industry has never managed to get this point over to the public, or to its competitors, very effectively. Coalminers, for example, feel that some swindle is going on when fuel oil, competing with their product, is sold for less than the price that the crude oil from which it is refined cost the refinery. This may well happen when the refiner can get most of his return out of selling other products, such as gasoline, more remuneratively. (And since some consumers, if put to it, could burn crude, the price of fuel oil cannot exceed that of crude.) But there is no trick in it; the price at which it pays the refiner to sell any given product will depend upon the range of prices at which he can sell the rest. Pricing in the oil industry is dealt with in a later chapter. Suffice it to say here that the relative prices of products, which together make up the return on the refinery investment, will depend largely upon the relative strength of demand for each and the degree of competition in its market, including the cost of entry into each market. Some products are always liable to be sold at low 'by-product' prices to give even a small addition to the refiners' total return on the barrel of crude. Equally, if refinery capacity has to be expanded primarily to meet demand for one product that is growing faster than for the rest, the whole 'marginal cost' of increasing output can be attributed to this particular product. Argument about when a product ceases to be a by-product and should be expected to contribute more of the total return is perfectly legitimate. Argument about the average cost of individual refined products is not—except in relation to specialized facilities put in to purify or treat particular products.

The volume of saleable products from an oil refinery is today, though it has not always been, almost as large as the volume of the raw material. This volume of products, moreover, costs rather more to store and to transport than crude does, because it has to be segregated in separate tankage and moved in separate containers, generally smaller and less efficient than the means of transport that crude uses. A refinery need not necessarily be located as close to the source of its raw material, therefore, as for example, an iron and steelworks (into which about six tons of ore, fuel, and scrap have to be transported for every ton of finished steel that goes out). The economies of scale that we have mentioned in refining would in a sense act as location factors favouring refining near the source of crude, simply because nowhere else could one justify refining on a giant scale that may be beyond the capacity of most single markets to absorb. Refining close to the source, again, should theoretically give the greatest flexibility in supplying products to terminals as close to the ultimate market as one can get them. But other factors enter in.

Originally, refineries were located as a matter of course fairly close to the source of crude, or at least within the producing country. The United States early this century was in any case not only the greatest producer and exporter of oil but also the greatest market. Moreover, when kerosene was the only important product, transporting crude would have meant moving a large tonnage of waste; only about 30–40 per cent of the volume of the crude could be sold. But the growth in sales of black oils and of gasoline changed that. Between the wars certain refineries were built in market areas rather than where the oil was produced: a certain volume of crude began to move in seaborne trade, which until then had consisted almost entirely of products. Some refineries in consuming countries were built for autarchic reasons: others because it was argued that the continuance of crude supplies could be relied on more than that of supplies of refined products. But in general crude was refined as close as could be to where it was produced.

After the war various special factors combined to shift the balance towards refining near the market areas. Successively, the European countries' markets for petroleum products developed to the size and variety that justified a refinery with some minimum economic throughput—say 15,000–20,000 barrels a day. There was a need for rapid expansion of refining capacity after the slowing down of the industry's investment during the wartime years, and there were a number of small specialized refining units in market areas, mainly in Europe, that could be expanded relatively quickly into full-scale refineries. But the influences shifting refining towards market areas were by no means simply economic, or at any rate had little to do with oil economics proper. Europe, a growing market, was short of dollars in that immediate postwar period, and sought to establish 'import-saving' to ease its balance of payments. A variety of currency deals were worked out to facilitate oil imports. But the establishment or expansion of an oil refining industry often, in most European countries, with Marshall Aid, seemed certain to reduce these costs. Later anxieties after the nationalization of Iranian oil and the growth of nationalist pressure in other host countries may have added reasons of security. And oil companies seeking to secure markets, in developed or underdeveloped areas, found not infrequently that the price of entry was building a local refinery, whether or not the market really justified it immediately.

Continued rapid growth of consumption in Western Europe has gradually accumulated the economic justification for the large number of refineries that were constructed around the coasts of Europe in the post-war years for partly non-economic reasons. Moreover, the growth of markets far inland in Europe has gone far enough to begin to justify the location of refineries inland too, fed by the crude pipelines mentioned in the last chapter. Such refineries are generally built in anticipation of the development of markets for them to serve: one can always bank on some market response to sheer abundant availability. But it is possible that the development is occurring more slowly than the groups investing in pipelines had hoped. These pipelines and refineries have been projected during a period of intense competition for the European market.

Another justification for locating those postwar refineries in Western Europe has been the rapid development of petroleum chemical production in areas where it was virtually unknown, and in which certain of the world's most advanced chemical industries relying entirely on coal had lacked the world's most convenient raw material for the synthesis of many organic chemicals. Petrochemicals today form the fastest-growing elements in the world's chemical industry. The ethylene and butylene gases that were at one time 'tail gas' residues of the refining process are now in considerable demand as feedstocks for synthesis; so now is naphtha, or low-grade gasoline. The kind of technology involved in forming many of the products that can be made from them, such as detergents and synthetic rubber, is akin to refinery engineering and can be neatly fitted on to the end of it.

Advanced petrochemical production, in its present stage of rapid innovation, seems an activity that it might be hard to develop far from large scale markets with high standards of living, fed by highly developed engineering industries on the spot. Innovation in new materials needs to be allied with the development of products one can make out of them. Projects for simpler 'bulk' petroleum chemical development to use gas from the oilfields of the Middle East, however, have been put forward in recent years; fertilizer plants are now being put up in Iran, Kuwait and Saudi Arabia, following the example of a successful venture based on the natural gas of Trinidad.

MARKETING

The whole object of this industry's elaborate organization is to get petroleum to where the consumer wants it, in the form and the quantities that he is prepared to buy. The distribution and selling of refined products is always a vital element in the industry's operations. At times—and the last decade has been one of those times—access to markets may be the most important asset that any company in the oil business can command. Quite a significant investment, in this final stage of a capital-intensive industry, is always required to gain entry to a market. Once in, a company will have to spend a good deal more money to secure and defend its market position.

In physical terms, marketing is the organization of onward movement, plus the necessary stocks, between the refinery and the consumer; and here many of the same elements enter as are concerned in the transport of crude from well to refinery. Most of the products, being liquids, can physically be moved by any of the means employed in crude transport; but the extent to which marketers can take advantage of the economies of scale inherent in these means depends upon the size and rate of growth of the markets he is serving. An oil marketer is selling and has to move many products, not one, and the nature of his wares, service, and customers varies—even if at any one time one product is likely to dominate his turnover and his profits. He has to move fairly large volumes of products from refineries to storage depots convenient to his various market areas, and often uses coastwise, river, or canal tankers for this medium-scale movement—though rail may offer competitive costs when full trainloads, rather than single truckloads, can be made the unit of movement.

In few countries has the market become large and concentrated enough until very recently to justify the movement of products by pipeline: the United States, as always, proving the exception. Fuel oil, the product for which demand in Western Europe has been growing fastest since the early fifties, is too viscous a liquid to move conveniently by pipeline: it can be done, but it requires heavy insulation of the pipeline, pre-heating of the oil, or the mixture of the oil with water to reduce viscosity. It is only recently that any major centres of consumption in

Europe have developed beyond the fairly high level of consumption for which it may be economic to build a products pipeline. And geography does not always necessitate it; the London area, for example, is one of the largest centres of consumption of all oil products in Europe, but it is concentrated around one of the continent's largest ports. The first significant development of products pipelines for commercial purposes in Britain, at the end of the fifties, was for certain single points of consumption taking very large amounts of a given product. Gasworks and chemical plant, buying tail gases or chemical feedstock in very large and stable quantities, ensured steady operation of the line at high capacity. Airports are another kind of consumption point that typically require very large supplies of one or two products, high-octane gasolines and the paraffin or 'wide-cut petrol' fuels used as turbine fuels.

Transport fuels, since the development of the internal combustion engine, have become the dominant products of the oil industry, and have supplied much of the return on the range of products it markets. A large proportion of these motor fuels are sold to commercial consumers, in large quantities and by competitive tender, but the dealer gasoline market selling to the motorist forms the most important single element in this business. Motor spirit has to be available in storage, today in perhaps three grades, at a large number of selling points dispersed widely around the main areas of vehicle population and along the main flows of motor traffic (which can alter quite frequently over say ten years). There are about 180,000 filling stations in the United States, and 39,000 in Britain. The motoring customer is highly mobile; and though the oil industry spends a great deal on advertising in an attempt to differentiate companies' own motor spirit, 'brand loyalty' tends to fade when the petrol gauge gets near empty or one has to turn across an oncoming traffic stream in order to get Brand A against Brand B. Price competition in gasoline is discussed later. In general the industry reckons that this gains an individual company little after costing all the companies who engage in it a lot. Nevertheless, price wars break out sporadically in the United States and in the last five to ten years have developed in European markets.

The companies want contracts with stations on the major traffic routes, on which the main volume of occasional sales are made; but to an even larger extent, in most countries the companies seek to sign up those at local points of high density in the automobile population. The companies' usual method of securing a filling station for their brands is to negotiate exclusive dealing contracts for a period of years. During this time, in return for some capital assistance and probably a slightly better margin on his sales, the dealer agrees to sell no other gasoline (and possibly to favour the company's brands of lubricating oils as well). The 'free house' still exists among filling stations, as it does among British public houses. But it is unlikely to get as favourable margins on the petrol it sells as the large garage whose custom offers the companies' tankers much more storage for each grade of gasoline. The more gasoline that can be delivered at one time, the more distribution costs can be reduced. Intense competition to secure the best sites between major companies has at times, in most countries, encouraged an excessive proliferation of filling stations. This is moderated nowadays by the regulation and zoning which the multiplication of small stations at every cross-roads has provoked; though this town planning, by its very nature, may create local monopoly positions which dealers are not slow to exploit. But the volume of motor spirit sales tends to be much more concentrated, even in this dealer market, than the wide spread of filling stations might suggest.

Lubricating oils for automotive transport are sold partly through the same filling station network; but they are also sold widely throughout industry. This is one of the parts of the market in which the specialist blender and marketer tends to buy his base oils from the refiner and to compound and brand his own specialized product. In the general fuel market, particularly where long-term contracts or large single consignments can be gained, the oil companies tend to trade direct. As small-scale domestic central heating business spreads in Western Europe, there is a tendency for the wholesaler, sometimes selling other fuels as well, to include oil in his range of wares. Certain products sold primarily to the domestic user, such as kerosene for free-standing home heaters, are sold through ordinary retail shops, generally encouraged by the companies to offer delivery. But in the sales of fuel oil, for example, to commercial, institutional and industrial customers, the marketing company tends to supply—and compete—direct.

The pattern of marketing petroleum products is a changing one. The physical organization of distribution tends to change as total oil consumption grows—as it has never yet ceased growing in any country—and as fresh products develop from the sphere of specialized fuels into a wider market. In Europe, at the beginning of the sixties, the liquid petroleum gases, propane and butane from refineries were just graduating from the tiny and specialized markets of heating country cottages and lighting for caravans and cabin boats into significant use as highly convenient and relatively mobile fuels for industrial heating, taking advantage of their relatively high calorific value for a given amount of tankage space in storage tanks. Nor are these the only forms of petroleum gas competing with fuel oil in the European market during the sixties.

CHAPTER VI

Operating Economics: III. Natural Gas

Natural gas is one of the forms in which petroleum is found under the earth, and much of the world's output is produced along with oil from the same wells: yet it is not too easy to fit into an economic rationale of the oil industry. It is generally a joint product of the exploration stage of the oil business and sometimes of the production stage, just as most saleable oil products are joint products of the later refining stage. But unlike oil, it is sold almost without processing, as a raw fuel, and it has competed from its early beginnings in the general fuel market, without special advantages in any specialized use. It can be transported long distances overland, though not nearly as cheaply as oil, but it has only just begun to be moved across the sea. It has entered international trade, therefore, mainly across certain land frontiers—notably in pipelines from Canada to the United States. But even with that limitation natural gas has developed more rapidly than any other primary fuel since the last war. By 1965, it supplied about a third of all the fuel consumed in the world's richest market, the United States, and in the previous year its consumption in the rest of the free world was probably seven times as much as it had been in 1950—though still only 2–3 per cent of the total energy used.

Wherever you find worthwhile deposits of oil there is gas too: but the converse does not hold good. Gas exists in an oil reservoir sometimes as 'cap gas' compressed between the top level of the crude oil and the sealing 'caprock' above it; but also, nearly always, dissolved in the crude oil. At a given temperature and pressure, oil will dissolve a given volume of gas. If it contains more, this will tend to come out of solution into a gas cap: if it has less, the gas does not help much in bringing the oil to the surface. When gas is stripped out of the oil at the surface it may be put down the well again for 'repressuring' (providing this is not 'unsaturated' oil that would simply dissolve it) or for 'gas lift' to keep the oil coming. Gas, however, may exist in reservoirs on its own. Its

83

main constituent is methane, a rich hydro-carbon gaseous at any but very low temperatures, but it usually contains some 'natural gas liquids'.

Exploration for petroleum is virtually indivisible: when you drill a wildcat well you are looking for 'oil and/or gas', and glad to find either. Until recently, moreover, the discovery of gas was considered largely as a by-product of drilling for oil. Gas alone was hardly worth the high cost and risk of wildcatting, though once located, even alone, it could justify development provided it was within practicable reach of a market. In the United States—and now also in Western Europe—drilling for gas alone is now becoming a more reasonable commercial proposition. Where encouraging geological indications occur in the midst of industrialized areas that could offer ready markets, they may justify quite a systematic drilling programme. Between 1956 and 1961, for example, the British gas industry spent £5 million on exploring for natural gas in several promising areas of Britain; it found some caverns in which gas could be stored, but almost no gas. However, since 1964, several European countries have begun exploration programmes, mainly hoping for gas, under the seabed of the North Sea. By 1965, some very large discoveries had been made.

But over a large part of the world petroleum exploration is a gamble on the discovery of oil, in which finds of gas alone provide no pay-off whatever. And in many others, exploration and much of the development of any given field is counted as a joint preliminary cost against the oil and gas that may be produced together, presuming that the gas finds a separate market and is not used merely as an agent to assist extraction of the oil. Traditionally, in this joint accounting one would charge the costs against oil as the main product and throw in as a credit whatever one managed to get for the gas; this is now becoming an inadequate formula. The costs of development drilling, in some cases, can be divided more accurately between gas and oil; and those of production, in most cases, can be partly distinguished once the oil and gas pass the separating equipment at the top of the well. One American consultant reckons typical well costs as say 30 per cent for exploration, 40 per cent for development and 30 per cent for actual production, but reckons that at best only half the development and production costs —i.e., one-third of the whole—could be identified as between oil and gas.

Gas can only reach the final consumer along a pipe (a point that is recognized in the nationalization statutes of certain state-owned gas industries, which are given a monopoly of 'piped public supply', not of gas manufacture or production). Its first large-scale development, in the Appalachian fields of the United States in the eighteen-eighties, awaited the advent of the iron pipeline—one that served Pittsburgh from Murrysville, Pennsylvania, was perhaps the first of real importance. The first high-pressure pipeline, serving Chicago from the very large gas fields discovered in Ohio and Indiana, came before the turn of the century. But it was not really until after the thirties that the long-distance welded pipeline came into its own—and transformed natural gas, across the vast overland expanse of the United States, from a localized to a nationally available fuel. During the war the United States government financed the construction of two large oil pipelines, the 'Big Inch' (a 24-inch line running 1,250 miles) and the 'Little Big Inch' (a 20-inch line running 1,475 miles) from Texas to the Atlantic Coast states, to economize in the use of tankers. After the war these lines were taken over by the natural gas industry; successful experience with them was followed by the laying of a network of large-diameter lines across the continent. By the middle fifties almost all of the states in the Union, except one or two in its north-eastern and north-western corners, had a supply of natural gas; and plans were in existence to pipe gas to some of these from Canada. Across the border in Canada, even in spite of administrative delays over the laying of pipelines, consumption rose about sixfold during the fifties, to make it the free world's second largest consumer and producer of utilized gas. (Consumption in the U.S.S.R., with its far larger area and population, was much larger than in Canada, but less than 15 per cent of the United States consumption.)

When you move gas along a pipeline under high pressure, you move fewer heat units for a given diameter of pipe than in pumping oil along the same line. All the same economic peculiarities of any pipeline apply—the high investment in an immovably fixed asset, the need for very high utilization of capacity to achieve economical transport, the transport costs varying only very little with distance. But the gas line needs to move 170 cubic metres of natural gas (at atmospheric pressure) to equal one barrel of oil; and the eventual cost of transporting energy may work out at twice to three times as much as for oil. On the other hand, gas is in some applications an even more convenient general fuel than the oil products with which it competes; and industrial demand, which makes up a half to two-thirds of the sales in the U.S., is very responsive to the low prices charged for 'off-peak' supplies. Gas is clean, and the consumer requires no storage, though the distributor needs a high-cost network of distribution mains, often utilized below capacity. Its first competitive impact in the United States was on an inconvenient solid fuel, coal, and on the gas made, by techniques becoming obsolescent, from that coal. Only later did it make inroads in the United States upon fuel oil's share of the general fuel market. It was made available around the United States at prices which were particularly low for industrial consumers who could take large quantities outside the periods of peak consumption, or 'interruptible' supplies, and its sales multiplied enormously. And the business yielded a return to the distributors, the pipeline companies and the gas producers that may have been low in unit terms but grew impressively in aggregate.

None of this was of any consolation to oil producers who could not help raising huge quantities of gas to the surface, but had no markets within reach of a pipeline where they could sell it. In Venezuela and the Middle East the gas produced with oil was originally flared off to waste as the cheapest way of getting rid of it. More recently, it became of use in many Venezuelan fields for maintaining the flow of oil wells where underground pressure was falling; and large volumes are also pumped back underground in the Middle East, though in most fields there pressures seem adequate to keep the oil flowing on natural drive for many years. The amounts being flared in both of these oil-exporting areas, it was estimated in 1960, had been reduced to about 100 million cubic metres a day, the equivalent of 600,000 barrels of oil a day. But even this was a frustrating reminder of the industry's inability to make use of a rich fuel that it could not help producing, and of rich gasfields that had been discovered in these areas only to be shut in. Projects for pipelines running miles from the Middle East to Europe were studied: the political complications of crossing a dozen or more borders, apart from the economics, put these out of court. But there are political complications too, with 'host governments', when concessionnaires do not utilize or sell the oil.

And during the middle fifties there came a chance—and for Western Europe an added incentive—to move natural gas across the sea to market. Methane can be liquefied at a temperature of minus 161 degrees Centigrade, which is around half-way down towards absolute zero. The technique of liquefaction offers no particular problems; but though the use of liquefied methane had been discussed several times before the war, technical problems concerned with the storage and transport of a liquid refrigerated to such a degree had deterred experiment.

In 1950, however, through the initiative of a Midwest stockyard and cold storage company that felt it was paying too much for its locally-produced fuel, experiments were begun again with refrigerated barges designed to move natural gas liquefied near its source up the Mississippi to Chicago. The liquefaction plant was built; barges were insulated in a new way to carry the liquid methane. But the river authorities and insurance companies raised difficulties about this new and seemingly dangerous form of transport up the Mississippi; and in the meantime the Chicago stockyards managed to get a better price out of their local fuel suppliers. The project might have foundered at that point, which had little to do with the technique or the economics of the actual transport of liquid methane. But its proponents managed to get in touch with a customer of a much larger magnitude, to which liquid methane, providing it could be had economically, offered powerful attractions—the British gas industry. This nationalized industry is the largest manufacturer of coal gas 'for its own sake' in the world: the United States and Germany make a greater volume of gas, but make most of it primarily as a by-product of carbonization industries of which the main product is metallurgical coke. The British industry was experiencing severe competition from oil and electricity; in a growing market for fuels of convenience in Britain, it was failing to hold its own.

The British gas industry had already turned to making gas out of oil to relieve some of its problems; but to import gas direct, perhaps much cheaper than it could make gas from new equipment, seemed an opportunity not to be missed. The Gas Council put up capital, jointly with the companies that had originated the idea for the conversion of a small tanker to carry liquefied methane (later the Shell group took an interest in the transport company too). The *Methane Pioneer* carried through a series of experimental voyages carrying frozen natural gas from the Texas Gulf to the banks of the Thames, where it was stored in refrigerated gasholders and later mixed with lower-grade gas manufactured from oil to produce town gas of standard British calorific value.

For commercial operations, originally the natural gas was to have come from Venezuela, where supplies were offered cheaply on a long-term contract. But when the project began to be discussed more seriously in Britain at the beginning of the sixties, the source that its sponsors had in mind had changed, not surprisingly. Their attention had shifted —as had most of Western Europe's—to the Sahara.

Development of the Saharan gasfields during the late fifties was providing the nations of Western Europe with a powerful added incentive to devise some way of moving gas across the sea. Within Europe, the economy of Northern Italy had gained a powerful impetus from development of natural gas in the Po Valley; France was fitting gas from its Lacq deposits into its pattern of fuel consumption; and France again, as a leader in the European Common Market, was anxious to get both liquid and gaseous petroleum from its 'franc zone' widely accepted within its partners' economies. Elaborate studies were made for undersea pipelines, following various alternative routes across the Mediterranean, to Spain or Italy, from which the gas could be piped north to north-western and central Europe. But a pipeline already existed from the Hassi R'Mel gasfields to the Algerian coast; and a long contract was soon made between the French nationalized companies exploiting this natural gas, a company formed by Shell, Continental Oil, and Union Stockyards of Chicago to develop ocean transport of methane in refrigerated tankers, and the British Gas Council. Since it was made Algeria has become independent, and its politics, though more peaceful, remain none too stable. But export of its gas, liquid in special tankers, has begun on a large scale, and in 1965 Libya too began to make contracts for large exports of liquefied natural gas. Nigeria and Venezuela, too, are potential sources; and Alaska may soon supply Japan.

In regions where natural gas has been the first large-scale source of gas available, it is consumed virtually raw, after separation of liquids and in some cases after removal of troublesome impurities. This is undoubtedly the ideal way to use it; it is a rich gas and cheaper per unit of heat to transport along pipelines (though similarly liable to losses through leakage) than town gas mixtures of lower calorific value. But when it is introduced, initially perhaps in relatively small quantities, into an existing supply of gas of lower heat value, it presents a dilemma. The equipment with which a consumer burns gas is not flexible enough to accommodate gases of such different qualities. To switch over all the burners in a house carcassed for town gas of European quality to methane gas, in the renewal of burners, might cost some £15–30 per consumer. And even if the gas supplier is prepared to accept this high capital cost, it may not necessarily be able to guarantee any such consumer the whole of his supplies in the form of natural gas for quite a long time. In such circumstances, when introducing natural gas initially as a supplement to existing gas supplies, the authorities may opt to sell it only to large-scale consumers who can afford to convert their equipment; but even this involves separate supply mains.

Discovery of further really large deposits of natural gas in the industrial areas of north-west Europe—such as the huge discoveries made in Holland or those now found by explorers in the North Sea—

III. NATURAL GAS

may possibly slow the pace of development of either tanker or pipeline transport for Saharan gas. But these would simply be alternative ways of supplying natural gas in these areas. It seems fairly certain, given the current state of the technology of moving natural gas and current attitudes towards the economies of doing so, that natural gas from one source or another will make deeper inroads into this rich market. If this happens, one possible and significant result may be to reduce the divergence of the pattern of demand for oil products in Western Europe from that of the United States, a divergence that was so marked a feature of these two oil markets in the fifties.

The main reason why the United States still refines a much larger proportion of gasoline from its crude oil and a considerably smaller proportion of fuel oil is not that its demand for motor spirit in road transport is still expanding much faster than its demand for energy in other sectors of the economy, or that American coal is able to stand up to oil competition so much better than coal elsewhere. The reason is that natural gas has accounted for much of petroleum's advance in the general fuel market of the United States. If one adds together the growth of consumption of fuel oil plus natural gas in both areas, the combined shares are more in line than their consumptions of fuel alone. To the extent that supplies of natural gas become available in very large quantities in Western Europe, one might expect the pattern of oil product demand in this region to shift back more towards that of the United States. But it would be unwise to exaggerate the speed of any such swing back towards common refining patterns. There remain considerable uncertainties about the trans-oceanic transport, at any rate, of natural gas; and while some of these are political, others are economic.

To say that demand for petroleum, both liquid and gaseous, over the medium run at least, will be increasingly for consumption as a convenient general fuel implies that demand for the petroleum products which serve specialized uses will not rise as fast as total demand for petroleum. These specialized products command a premium for their peculiar value in particular applications—which in some cases amounts to irreplaceability. If demand for these products rises less rapidly than demand for oil products that have to meet competition in the general fuel market, one would expect combined revenue from a given mixture of petroleum products used, and the total products refined from say a barrel of crude oil, to fall.

This point is often acknowledged when people discuss the effect on refining margins of more rapid growth in demand for fuel oils than for gasolines. At first sight, the introduction of natural gas into the general fuel market beside fuel oil might seem to assist matters, by allowing the refiner to adjust his balance of products towards a more traditional pattern. But when one realizes that this is simply achieved by bringing the rate of growth of demand for fuel oil down more into line with that for gasoline, it is clear that the net effect must reduce the rate of growth for all oil products. And in terms of return on capital, the natural gas that one sells instead may rank as a poor relation even of the fuel oil. If one considers gas and oil as products of a single industry—and they are, at the least, nearly always joint products of petroleum exploration—then the traditional pattern of prices of this industry may seem a mixed blessing.

This is a problem that has not yet been resolved in the world's greatest market both for oil and for gas, the United States. Gas, originally, was sold there for whatever it would fetch in whatever markets it could reach. Its wellhead price therefore reflected a highly competitive price for general fuels in the distant market less the cost of transporting the gas by pipeline. Originally, this meant extremely low prices at the wellhead; but the producer was glad to take whatever he could get. This was a perfectly reasonable policy to adopt in fostering a market for a new product that commanded no particular area of monopoly value except rather more convenience than some of the competition. But external influences operated to freeze this approach to the market into a permanent stance.

Long-distance pipelines gave natural gas distribution throughout the nation; they also made it a product moving in inter-state commerce, subject to rate regulation of its transport charges. And the products with which American natural gas naturally competed were produced by public utilities. Gas, too, began to be regulated as a public utility, in the states where it was finally sold, early in its history, and since 1954 its wellhead prices too have become subject to general supervision by the Federal Power Commission. None of the traditional criteria used in the regulation of public utility prices—ascertained costs, the capital employed as a 'rate base', or a stable rate of return on capital—can easily be applied to the wellhead price of gas. This is a fuel some of the costs of which are joint costs, in which some elements of the 'capital' invested are customarily written off in the same year as they are spent, and in which the rate of return expected customarily reflects a habit of self-financing plus a rather high degree of risk in one's initial investment. One can forgive the administrative authorities concerned for some uncertainty in seeking for reasonable criteria in regulating prices; but also question whether regulation of gas *producers'* prices makes much sense anyway.[1]

The petroleum industry in the United States, therefore, is its own best competitor. In the market, its prices for alternative fuels have to be broadly competitive; and though wellhead prices have been rising in recent years, the higher cost of transporting gas to market generally has meant that in terms of heat content, at the wellhead, the price one can get for gas is substantially lower than that of crude oil. So every time that gas displaces oil in consumption, or even captures a market from coal that fuel oil might without it have gained, the eventual total revenue of the petroleum industry may go down.

This does not necessarily imply that investment in the natural gas business, in its current expanding circumstances, is unattractive. In American wildcatting, the discovery ratio of gas is significantly higher than that of drilling for oil, and the reserves-production ratio for gas is higher than that for oil. Replacing the cubic metre of gas one has just sold with another cubic metre of reserves, that is to say, does not cost as much as finding the next barrel of oil to replace the one that you have just sold. Moreover, though it is subject to regulation of prices, gas is not subject to as much control over the volume of production as oil production is in most of the United States. Producing more gas, even with a low return, may well suit the particular circumstances of particular companies. One should never, in a free economy, assume that 'the industry' is a single thing with a single set of interests and responses. In spite of much overlapping in operations and ownership, the gas producer and the oil producer in the United States do not speak with quite the same voice, and the short-term decisions of one cannot always be expected to take account of the longer-term interests of the other.

What this rather complex interaction of gas and oil upon one another in the United States may imply for the development of natural gas consumption in the rest of the world, and now in international trade, is that the balance of advantage in such developments may not be as simple as it seems at first sight. When gas that has been moved long distances expensively is sold cheaply enough to supplant one of the joint products of crude oil that itself was a joint product with the gas, and which could have been moved more cheaply to the same market, is the original allocation of costs blurring the producer's commercial judgment? When there is a surplus of crude oil, traditionally the main product of petroleum exploration and production, should the other product still be sold at give-away prices that will enable it to be transported to new markets and to seize business that fuel oil, which might offer a slightly better return, may already have been in the way to capturing?

One developed economy confronted almost overnight with the opportunity of becoming a large-scale natural gas producer, Holland, has chosen a quite different way of marketing it from this traditional American way. In marketing gas from deposits in Northern Holland which are now known to be clearly the largest in Europe, the Dutch government, Shell and Esso have decided to sell it at home and for export, to start with, as a 'premium fuel'—i.e. at prices suited to a rather cheap manufactured gas, but not in cut-price competition with the cheapest coal and fuel oil. This may mean a relatively slow and controlled growth of the natural gas market, though higher unit returns on the gas sold. It will not displace fuel oil and coal in the general industrial fuel market or in power generation or chemical manufacture as widely and rapidly as it might otherwise have done.

One may criticize this policy for not giving Holland the cheapest possible energy immediately, or for taking too much care of established fuels, both home-produced and imported. On the other hand, the Dutch government is treating this gas bonanza as a rich windfall, but one that in the history of the country may be counted as short-lived. It thinks the developers should get the best possible return out of this windfall without dislocating its basic, less rapidly-changing, energy supply pattern. For gas development in an already industrialized country—without the same need as remote sources have to quote rockbottom prices in order to gain the gas any market at all—this method of exploitation has some logic. For the petroleum industry as a whole, considering reserves of natural gas that are universally much smaller and shorter-lived in relation to consumption than oil, it might seem a logical method too. But how much chance oil and gas suppliers in other countries have of switching to this system—and indeed whether Holland can maintain it—is another matter.

Much depends, obviously, on how much business there remains in any given market that either fuel might capture from coal in its raw form or from its secondary fuels, manufactured gas and electricity. And much also depends, as always in this industry, upon the business situation of the particular petroleum producers concerned. But the outside observer of this industry is sometimes tempted to feel that the peculiar history of the natural gas business in the United States, and the sheer lack of it to sell, until recently, in most other producing countries, have absolved the petroleum industry from ever fully thinking through the economics of developing natural gas in a competitive market for energy.[2]

Commercial development of natural gas in Europe, also, seems to be repeating a similar pattern of State regulation—or participation, since the forms of enterprise involved have differed from the start. In Italy, ENI, a special State corporation, was given the monopoly of natural gas development in the Po Valley, and built up on profits from this a formidable position in the oil market of the country as well; its production has now levelled off, but it is becoming, again, the country's main importer of liquefied gas (from Libya). In France, the Lacq field was developed by the nationalized *Gaz de France*, and this corporation, too, will be the single national buyer of Dutch gas for French consumption. In the development of the enormous Slochteren gasfield in the Groningen province of the Netherlands, NAM, the Shell-Esso joint subsidiary that discovered the gas, was obliged to accept the Dutch government and the Dutch nationalized *Staatsmijnen* as partners in development and in wholesaling the gas within Holland. And discoverers of gas under the North Sea, on Britain's Continental Shelf, are obliged to offer a 'first refusal' of it to the nationalized Gas Council, with its internal sales monopoly.

In exporting the gas from Holland to its European neighbours, NAM Gas Export is on its own without Dutch partners, and in sales to Belgium and to Western Germany it has been able to secure a shareholding in the bulk transmission pipeline companies which sell the gas wholesale to local gas undertakings and also, where practicable, to bulk industrial customers. But in both of these customer countries NAM has been obliged to accept a degree of State regulation of prices, and in Belgium also State participation. It has not been able to secure a shareholding in the bulk transmission of any gas it may sell to France, and now seems unlikely to be able to make a bargain with the British nationalized Gas Council for supplies by undersea pipeline across the North Sea. Other companies exploring for gas and oil in Holland—where under the traditional *Code Napoleon* exploration licences have been granted readily but no explorer can begin to bargain about the terms of his concession until he has found the 'mineral' concerned—may also be obliged to accept State shareholdings in any development of successful discoveries.

Now that natural gas has been found in large quantities under the

Continental Shelf of the North Sea—explorers are naturally thinking in terms of 'more Slochterens'—then the conditions of development and disposal will again be crucial for the oil companies concerned. (In 1964 and 1965, in the British section of the Shelf alone, a variety of groups committed themselves to invest something over £100 million in exploration over the ensuing six years.) In Britain and probably in some of the other states sharing the Shelf, the successful discoverer is confronted by a nationalized 'monopsonist' buyer of gas, hoping to offer only a price fairly tightly drawn to give a very moderate return on his risky venture. In disputes over what might be a 'reasonable price', the discoverer would generally be faced with some form of governmental arbitration. In unregulated competition with other general fuels, such North Sea gas, presuming its costs were low, as they would be if any find approached 'Slochteren scale', would probably be able to secure a sizeable economic rent. Though offshore exploration and the laying of undersea pipelines is costly, the enormous locational advantage of such gas, against Algerian gas or Middle East oil that has to travel several thousand miles to market, would afford this economic rent if it were offered at prices set slightly to undercut competitive fuels. The question would be how that economic rent would be shared, in practice. Between explorer, government, and gas wholesaler, and in what proportions? Or might the consumer share too, by really sizeable cuts in his going price for energy? This basic question, and the various forms of price structure that may be chosen to introduce large quantities of natural gas into developed markets that have had little of it before are becoming large, if hopeful questions for the countries bordering on the North Sea, and particularly Britain, towards the end of 1965. For companies engaged in the search for petroleum under the North Sea, however, these questions are not unmixedly hopeful, in terms of their own private commercial interest. There was no doubt that most of them would have been a good deal more pleased to find oil there. They know how to market that—on their own.

CHAPTER VII

Investment and Returns

Reckoned in terms of what was originally spent to bring it into being, the free world's petroleum industry, at the end of 1964, may have had a gross book value of about $136 billion; written down, the 'net investment' involved in it must have been of the order of $74 billion, or well over £25,000 million. A comprehensive analysis of the industry's capital investment made by the Chase Manhattan Bank of New York suggested that at the end of 1964, the industry's gross investment in the United States was $71,100 million against a 'free foreign' total of $64,525 million.[1] American oil thus represented about 55 per cent of the whole, though ever since 1955 oil investment outside the United States has grown faster than inside it, and since 1958, the amounts invested annually outside America have been larger than those inside.

A word, first, about what 'investment' means in oil. Very large amounts of money have to be spent to find and develop oil reserves: these do not always produce 'fixed assets' for the industry, nor in accounting terms are they always treated as are the sums invested in productive facilities for other industries. When an oil company surveys a fresh section of a concession area in which it already has production and income, it may be able to 'expense' the whole cost of its preliminary search, such as geophysical work, against taxable income in that year, as one of its current costs: it usually does the same with the current cost of drilling operations. If the well it sinks discovers oil and this is developed into production, it takes the actual cost of the tangible assets involved—casing in the hole, Christmas tree of valves at the top, gas separation equipment, pipe for gathering, storage tanks, and the like— on to its books as an investment, capitalizing them and writing them down over an agreed period of depreciation like any other fixed assets. The whole cost of drilling development wells in areas after

95

oil is discovered, also may have to be capitalized and written down, not partly 'expensed'. Practice and tax rules differ between countries and companies.

If the well does not find oil, and is abandoned as a 'dry hole', the whole cost of it can usually be expensed as a current cost against the company's other income in the producing country. But if the company has no other income in that country, there is nothing to write it off against. In an integrated group the tax authorities in its parent country will often allow the resultant loss to be charged against current income from other areas, but that depends upon the institutional structure of the group. If the company finds oil after a period of unsuccessful exploration, the cost of its exploration up to the point of success can be written off for tax purposes against the income that eventually arises. The same may be done for rents paid during the period of exploration before oil is found—'dead rents'—and on occasion for bonuses and premiums paid to get a concession, though less often. The precise rules settling which items in oil operations can be written off as expenses in the same year, which written off by instalments, and which capitalized with amortization according to a depreciation formula, vary as between countries, companies and concessions. American tax rules are fairly generous here, and have often been taken as a model overseas, but in recent years countries granting new concessions have become tougher about what they concede in these parts of the 'fine print' of the concessions.

These preliminary costs certainly represent money that has to be spent to find oil, or to go on developing reserves. Are they capital investment? It is a nice conceptual point. Is an array of dry holes abandoned all over the world—and for every successful exploratory well, there will be a number of dry holes—part of the 'fixed assets' of the oil industry? Are the 'intangible' costs of geophysical survey and drilling, written off against current income in the year they were incurred, part of the 'book value' of the industry? In accounting terms, few companies would show them as such in the books. Yet if you look for oil anywhere, these form a large part of the initial stake you will have to put up; and if you do not find oil and have no other income against which to offset them, they are lost even more irretrievably than any clear 'capital' assets in any unproductive investment. You can adopt any convention that you (or the tax authorities you are currently dealing with) choose: what is important to realize is that the convention will be arbitrary, and that the net cost to you of searching for and developing oil may depend to a considerable extent upon it. This becomes a significant factor when one considers rates of return on investment in this industry, particularly in production: what 'investment' is one talking about? The conventions adopted in the totals we are now considering, those compiled by the Chase Manhattan Bank, exclude the costs of geophysical search and the rentals paid for leases or concessions from the figures for 'capital investment'; but they do include any bonuses paid to obtain concessions and the whole cost of drilling.

Technologically, as well as geographically, a 'map' of this global valuation emphasizes the spread of the industry's commitments. About 42 per cent of the net value of assets in 1964 was in production facilities (including exploration and development); about 18 per cent in pipelines and tankers; 21 per cent of refining and petrochemical plant; 17 per cent in marketing facilities. But the United States alone accounted for two-thirds of the total assets in the production stage, a far larger proportion than its share of assets in any other stage of the industry. Outside the United States, the distribution of assets was oriented considerably less towards the countries that produce and export oil than the total breakdown by 'departmental' figures might suggest. The big investment in refining and marketing oil in Western Europe makes this area the second largest geographical concentration of fixed investment in oil in the world: and an even larger technological concentration was the world's ocean-going tanker fleet, with a net book value of $7,965 million in 1964. (In terms of the net value of fixed assets, there was estimated in 1964 to be more oil investment in Canada than in the Middle East or Venezuela at that time.) These book values put no valuation on the oil in the ground, which indeed the oil industry outside the United States normally does not own, but works under leases or concessions.

Gross or net 'investment values', at any one time, lump together an assortment of expenditures made at times when the price levels will have varied considerably: it is as well to supplement them with figures of new expenditure by the industry over recent periods. Between 1953 and 1962, an OECD oil committee reported in 1964,[2] the oil industry spent $106,000 million on developing its capacity. In the United States, oil investment over this period represented about a sixth of total fixed capital formation by business. In the 'free foreign' world as a whole the proportion was probably nearer a third, though in Western Europe, the biggest consuming area relying on imports, such investment in oil as had to be made within its borders probably represented no more than 5 per cent of fixed capital formation by all business there. About 70 per cent of what these figures showed as capital expenditure in the oil industry of the United States during these years went into exploration, development, and production, about 13 per cent into refineries and petrochemicals, about 6 per cent into transport and about 8 per cent into marketing facilities. But in the 'free foreign' world outside the proportions ·were very different: less than 40 per cent into exploration and production, about a quarter into transport, and another quarter into refining and petrochemicals, and about 16 per cent into marketing.

Oil is thus, as the outline of its technology and commercial arrangements in previous chapters has suggested, a highly-capitalized industry though not an evenly-capitalized one in all areas of the world. It may not be much more heavily-capitalized, to be sure, than some of the other energy industries, and particularly those that supply energy processed into highly convenient forms. Comparisons of capital requirements in all these industries are highly debatable, whatever yardstick one chooses. But some recent estimates suggest that outside the United States, at any rate, the investment required to expand oil production by a ton a year is no more than is required to increase coal capacity by an equivalent amount (say $1\frac{1}{2}$ tons a year, as the oil has a higher calorific value). The oil is almost never used raw, while large tonnages of coal still are; transport, processing and marketing may add twice as much again to the investment required to bring oil products to the consumer. But if the coal has to be processed into fuels of a convenience to compete with petroleum products, substantial further investment has to be put into power stations or gas-making equipment. Coke ovens, for example, are as capital intensive items of plant as oil refineries; hydro-electricity and, so far, nuclear power stations are indeed even more capital-intensive than oil, gas or thermal electricity.

Petroleum, however, has for some decades achieved a faster rate of expansion than any other fuel industry except electricity; and it has an element of specialized long-distance transport built into its capital requirements that is unknown in most other energy industries. Its processing plant and specialized storage and distribution facilities cannot be dispensed with. And it is mainly a privately-owned industry, whereas other highly-capitalized energy industries tend to be public utilities, regulated and often owned by local or national governments. These are often guaranteed some degree at least of monopoly: they are not expected to earn much more than a low and stabilized rate of return; and

98

some in practice fail to earn even that and at the same time to maintain the value of their assets intact. Among privately-owned industries that are expected to earn a commercial rate of return, oil is by any measure one of the most highly-capitalized as well as one of the most rapidly growing. Moreover, its initial investment is often peculiarly risky.

During the fifties various rules of thumb were worked out about 'capital requirements per annual ton of additional capacity' for use in long-term forecasting in the oil industry. In 1964, the Oil Committee of OECD reported that during the fifties the oil industry had invested about $321 per annual metric ton added to producing capacity in the United States and about $118 per annual ton added in the rest of the free world. This figure is measured against producing capacity added, but it covers investment in all stages of the industry. Inside the United States, fiscal and regulatory incentives to drill for oil are peculiarly high, and therefore the investment per ton put into exploration and development there tends to be exceptionally high (though the technical efficiency of drilling is high there, and the cost per foot drilled lower than elsewhere). Those figures may have been inflated by over-investment during the fifties; at any rate, more recent estimates come out lower. Mr. A. S. Ashton, treasurer of Jersey's British affiliate, estimated early in 1965[3] that capital requirements per annual ton, for the whole free world industry, might now be about £35 (say $100): £15 for production, and about £6–£7 each for transport, refining and marketing. He said that in the United States, production alone required an investment of about £35 per annual ton; in the Middle East and North Africa this would be only about £4–£6. In Western Europe refining and marketing might need investment of about £11 per annual ton; in the underdeveloped countries, lacking basic facilities, about twice as much investment per annual ton would be needed.

Such figures are averages that mask a wide range of values for different circumstances. One has only to recall the millions spent in Nigeria before payable oil was proved and the Japanese success with their first well off the Saudi-Kuwait Neutral Zone; the contrast between rates of production per well in the United States and in the Middle East; the sharp difference in cost between a refinery incorporating all the techniques such as catalytic cracking and 'platforming' to increase its yield of light products, and of a topping unit that merely strips out the heavy products and may simply re-cycle the surplus light fractions back down the well. Average capital requirements for tankers and pipelines during any period depend on the rate of growth of demand in

different areas, near and far; those for refineries on the pattern of production developing during the period, and on technical change.

In the long run, the capital that will have to go into finding and
developing any wasting natural resource may be expected to rise; but
with oil that can be a very long run. Drilling technology, in particular,
seems to be developing fast enough to offset much of the greater physical
effort involved in going steadily deeper. In some countries finding oil
is probably becoming on the average a steadily more expensive gamble:
but there are probably many bonanzas to be happened upon still, and
there is also a lot more cheap oil already located than anybody has ever
yet cared to develop to its full capacity. Nor is capital intensity in
transport and refining as certain to rise as seemed likely ten to fifteen
years ago. Larger tankers cost less per ton to build, and larger diameter
pipelines take less steel per ton of oil moved. A switch from the one to
the other, as in the new pattern of supplies to some parts of Europe,
means substitution by a slightly more capital-intensive form of transport;
but the saving in distance involved tends to offset this. In refining,
because demand for products that require less specialized treatment,
and for natural gas, is rising faster in many markets than demand for
the specialized fuels, the industry has of late been building less complicated and expensive refineries in many areas, requiring less investment
for a given increase in petroleum consumption. But one must expect
continued pressure for purification of the less specialized products;
treatment to reduce the sulphur in fuel and diesel oils, for example,
may soon be a legal requirement in many countries. And factors that
are not wholly economic may cause more separate refineries, and smaller
ones, to be built than economics alone would dictate.

Two elements in the capital investment of this industry that lie
slightly off the track beaten from well head to petrol pump deserve
special note. Technical research and development in this industry are
somewhat analogous to exploration for oil, in that they represent
expenditure on seeking fresh opportunities for successful investment.
It has been said that they offer a roughly similar chance of success; and
the expenditure involved, like the exploration, can usually be expensed
as current income, rather than treated as investment and written off by
amortization. The oil industry ranks as a fairly heavy spender on research and development among those industries that pay for their own,
though it does not compare with the heaviest spenders of all such as
aircraft and electronics, industries that can usually get the government
to finance most of their technical endeavours on defence grounds. This

is an element of 'pre-investment' in oil that seems likely to go on rising, particularly even during a régime of cost-cutting. Any industry with so diverse an array of expensive techniques must offer a myriad of opportunities for improvements, from the increasingly complex equipment being developed for undersea exploration and well completion to the computer that works out all the possible programmes of operation for a refinery and 'optimizes' its production of a given range of joint products. And there is always commercial pressure to diversify the range of products further. The oil industry cannot guarantee a steady flow of the best ideas by employing an army of trained men to consider technical problems. But it can ensure that the possible innovators learn what its problems really are, and increase the likelihood that good ideas from outside the industry (which have offered many of its basic improvements in technique) are picked up and assessed without delay.

Petroleum chemicals, the most rapidly developing part of the world's chemical industries, have been developed from research into refining technique and into the properties of petroleum hydro-carbons. It was at the end of the fifties the most rapidly growing area of petroleum industry investment. In tonnage, it is still small: in 1964 in Britain, for example, it accounted for only just over 3 million tons, or 5 per cent of total refinery throughputs. (For the Shell group in 1959–60 it was said to represent about 9 per cent of turnover, 5 per cent of profits, and 25–30 per cent of expenditure on research.) Petroleum chemicals are usually extensions of refining technology, with a similarly capital-intensive array of plant. Oil companies have varying policies as to the extent that they process and re-process these chemical intermediates towards the finished product and some have been dissuaded by bitter price-cutting in chemicals too. But in general they have tended to move farther into this growing branch of chemicals over a period when profits have been less easily come by in their basic business of producing fuels.

Some forecasts of capital requirements produced for this industry in the middle fifties, before the fact of surplus became plain, will probably have been as exaggerated as much other fuel forecasting was then; but the rate of capital expenditure in the oil industry in the sixties and seventies is still liable to be prodigious. The OECD oil committee estimates referred to above were made as the basis of forecasts of capital requirements in the future. This oil committee has calculated that between 1963 and 1972 the industry would probably have to invest about $158 billion (much more than the gross value of all its assets today) in order to provide the facilities necessary to meet demand for oil in the free world, which certainly continues to rise steadily. Mr. Ashton offered forecasts too, and though his specific figures of investment per ton of capacity were much lower, his estimates were from a higher base year, 1965, and for a longer period, 15 years. His estimate of the total capital investment required from 1965 to 1980: £95,000 million ($266 billion).

If one thinks in terms of a notional 'world oil industry', quite a large part of the 'investment required' in such an estimate, during the sixties, might not in an absolute sense be 'required' at all. Everybody postulates a continued growth in world demand for petroleum. Refinery capacity was not, at the beginning of the sixties, in practice, much larger than total demand: so one must postulate an investment in new refineries roughly in line with market development. Distribution and retail selling capacity is more difficult to assess. Some part of the new gasoline marketing capacity has to be geared to the shifts in traffic flows, and in particular to the building of new motor roads, rather than to the rise in total demand for gasoline: but elsewhere larger throughputs at existing stations could in theory mean rather better utilization of the capital equipment there and of the distribution organization that supplies them. How far the distribution of other petroleum products may require new capital investment—for example, in terminals and storage—is not easy to judge. But the development of products pipelines in Europe certainly will, and if the disproportionate growth of demand for the black oils and for liquid petroleum gases goes on, distribution facilities for them will have to be expanded to match. If natural gas takes over some of this growth, investment may have to be greater, because gas distribution is more capital-intensive. But gas marketing will not necessarily be a matter for the oil industry. Nor will petrochemicals. Investment in these may be commercially worthwhile: if so, it can attract the capital. Perhaps from oil companies; but it is hardly a 'capital requirement' of oil supply.

In exploration and development, moreover, it is difficult to estimate what amount of capital investment would absolutely be 'required' to meet the continuing increase in world demand for crude oil: certainly less than the oil industry is planning to spend. If oil were free to move around the world simply in accordance with the arithmetic of how much was required at given places at a given cost, there might not need to be much more net investment at all, for some time, in oil *production* in the United States. The same reasoning, in the circumstances of the early sixties when this book was being written, also applied to Venezuela

—where indeed, of late, exploration has slowed down, with much capacity shut in and few major fields being significantly developed. Over the years, additions to reserves occur from the reassessment of existing fields, as well as the discovery of new ones. It could well be that comparatively little real exploration would be needed over the next 10–15 years to support the growth in demand that is forecast; merely the development and 'proving up' of reserves already located. A number of major fields in the Middle East could alone probably sustain the current rate of increase in world demand for quite a period of years, given continued investment in development, pressure maintenance, and loading facilities, without enough depletion of their reserves to worry the 'world oil business'—if such a business, single-minded and monopolistic, were to exist.

It does not: so the forecasts of capital expenditure made in the late fifties may not turn out to have been as wrong as theoretically they might be argued to be. The minimum capital that might unavoidably need to be invested in physical facilities to supply the amounts of oil that the world will need in the next decade or so is an interesting subject for speculation. What will be invested while doing so is another thing. 'Capital requirements' as the OECD Oil Committee hardheadedly reckons them are its best guess at what the institutions in the oil industry, as actually organized, will choose to invest in doing so. Their national circumstances will affect this: those are political factors dealt with later in this book. So will their institutional circumstances. This is an industry organized in different units, which are differently placed in terms of commercial advantage; and the men running many of those units cannot think in terms of one decade only, but are concerned with the long-run advantage of their organizations. A high rate of exploration for new reserves of oil has continued during a period when existing output is still far below the capacity that could readily be developed and total reserves are immense. This has been partly because some of the companies with the best marketing positions have not commanded sufficient reserves of low-cost crude. But it also arises from geography. New reserves, such as those of Libya, have been discovered much closer to market than oil already developed or 'proved'. And even companies with very low-cost oil elsewhere cannot refrain from searching in any promising locality nearer to markets, such as the North Sea. For gas or oil found there is a potent competitor for Middle East reserves however cheap they are, simply because of its transport advantage.

However much capital the oil industry of the free world requires

or decides to invest in the sixties, it is likely to generate a large proportion of the finance from within. This has always been *par excel-
lence* an industry of self-financing, accumulating from earnings most
of what it invests. Between 1955 and 1964, for example, one representative selection of major companies—mainly American, plus Shell
and BP—is reckoned to have provided 95 per cent of all the capital that
it put into fixed investment and working capital from internal resources.
(About 65 per cent came from depreciation provisions; roughly 60 per
cent of the industry's investment in any year, tends nowadays to be
for replacement.) This means, essentially, getting the wherewithal to
expand from one's customers, through price, rather than by asking one's
shareholders or other investors to invest it in oil: shifting the decision,
that is to say, from the plane of the individual investor to that of the
collective management. The proportion of self-financing in oil has since
the war been considerably higher than in most other industries in the
United States or Britain, even though the industry's rate of expansion
has been much greater too. The industry is inclined to say that this was
inevitable because it would have been quite impossible to raise such
sums from the capital markets of the world. It is certain that in the
postwar era, while those capital markets were restoring themselves
painfully, this would have been so. At the same time, the reverse of the
medal has to be considered: such amounts of money did not become
free for investment partly because the oil companies did not pay out to
their shareholders as much as they could have done. The argument is
circular, and partly affected by the general business climate of the
period. Capital appreciation was more palatable to many shareholders
than income on which they were heavily taxed, and most industries
tended to adopt cautious dividend policies—though not many, con
sidering what was being earned, policies as cautious as the oil industry.
In this industry as in others, managers feel it unlikely that the shareholder, or the investor at large, will re-invest all of his dividends, or can
decide as sensibly as they where capital ought to be ploughed in to sow
future benefits. They think it safer not to give him the option.

During the last five years, there have been some changes in this
attitude within the management of the privately-owned oil industry.
Various of the major international companies, for example, have had
more recourse to the capital market for new finance. Some pressure has
developed, of late, for these international companies to rely partly on
local capital—pressure not only from governments on the spot, but from
the American and British governments, both of which have been suffer-

ing persistent difficulties on their balances of payments and are anxious to moderate net capital outflows. But most investment decisions in this industry are still taken largely in terms of the cash flow generated in its international operations, of the investment opportunities it sees open within its own spheres or others into which its experience may make 'diversification' worth while, and—in many cases but not all—of its long-run prospects in the oil business. A company that is 'long' on marketing facilities, such as Shell, is prepared to invest heavily in seeking new crude, however long on crude others may be. One without sufficient facilities to dispose of its supplies in the markets open to its oil, like Gulf in Europe in the early sixties, will invest more heavily than others need to in gaining entry to new markets.

What rate of return does the oil industry expect and obtain on the vast capital that it employs? There are many statistical series relating to oil company earnings; but it is not too easy to arrive at meaningful comparisons with other industries. One run of figures calculated a few years ago by the First National City Bank of New York for a group of international oil companies runs over a very long period.[5] It shows a net return on the 'net worth' of these companies of about 10–11 per cent in the late twenties, falling drastically in the thirties (though only in 1931, on the average across the industry, showing a loss). Returns were stabilized at about 7–9 per cent in the war years (partly by wartime taxation): but the average jumped up to 15 per cent or more for the early postwar years. Since 1951, the bank's figures show the average return running down slowly, from nearly 17 per cent in 1951 to about 10 per cent in 1958 and 1959, and rising gradually to reach 11·4 per cent by 1963. (In the study cited above, Mr. Ashton calculated that the international industry would need a return of 11 per cent to go on self-financing say 90 per cent of its future investment requirements.)

The same bank, since 1961, has produced calculations relating to the profits of the major international companies that operate outside the United States, attempting to separate out the part of their profits attributable to operations in the Eastern hemisphere and moreover to divide this as between production and 'downstream' operations. (Few companies have ever published any geographical breakdown of profits; and most of them would hesitate to divide profits between stages of the integrated business.)

Such a separation must at best be rather rough and ready. Very large quantities of oil are still traded between the Western and Eastern hemispheres, and the profits shown on refining and marketing in either hemisphere may relate partly to the processing or sale of oil from the other. Many of the tankers that move crude from or around the Eastern hemisphere, once again, are owned by companies that have their head-quarters and show their profits in the Western hemisphere (more often in Panama, Honduras, or Bermuda, the havens of 'fleets of convenience', than in the United States where the final owners may be).

The bank, in its calculations, extracted, from published reports of the seven major international companies, what it was satisfied were the net profits of these companies in the Eastern hemisphere. It then took the revenue paid to each host government in the exporting countries in any given year, and reckoned that according to the 50–50 formula the total oil company profit from production in these territories should have been exactly the same. Subtract these calculated 'production profits' from estimates of Eastern hemisphere profits on all operations, and the difference should show the return on non-producing 'downstream operations'. The answers this exercise produced were that while in 1954 'non-producing profits' amounted to about 27 per cent of the profits shown on production, by 1957 they had dropped to almost nil, and that from then onwards until 1964 these subtraction sums produced very substantial minus answers. The companies' total net return on Eastern hemisphere operations, that is to say, fell some $250–500 million short each year of the amounts paid to producer governments. The bank took these minuses, with some qualifications, as representing 'downstream losses'—i.e. losses on the transport, refining, and marketing operations in this hemisphere, in which some 70–80 per cent of the industry's net assets in the area are employed.[6]

These calculations certainly showed that producing governments were doing better out of Eastern hemisphere oil than the major oil companies were. What they proved about downstream losses for the whole hemisphere is more debatable. By the early sixties, any assumption that the governments' 'take' must represent 50 per cent of profits made by selling crude at full posted prices had become merely formal. All companies were selling to third parties at heavy discounts; some at least were giving their downstream affiliates discounts too. The hemispheric estimates, again, could be affected by the varying patterns of company structure. Total Eastern hemisphere profits would exclude some profits earned in non-consolidated joing subsidiaries retaining profits and paying no dividends; and would also be net of some losses incurred in unsuccessful exploration by affiliates that had not yet achieved any trading income. Annual statistics of foreign investment published by the United States Department of Commerce have shown, since the late fifties, a steady decline in net profits in most consuming countries in this hemisphere; but up to 1964 the aggregate was still positive, around $100 million profit for *all* American companies operating there.

In its own latest study, the First National City Bank reckoned that at the end of 1958, the net fixed investment of these companies in the Eastern hemisphere was of the order of $6,359 million, and that by the end of 1962 this had grown to $9,375 million. Some earlier estimates of net fixed assets in petroleum facilities in this hemisphere (by its colleague, the Chase Manhattan Bank of New York), had valued them at $5,525 million for 1955 and $12,475 million for 1960, for all companies. (The 1960 figure is not easy to reconcile with the First National City Bank's estimate of less than $8,000 million for the seven international majors, but these apparently precise figures have inevitably a wide enough margin of error.) For 1955 a very rough allocation of the Chase Manhattan total might have credited the seven major companies, which with the French CFP then controlled practically all Eastern hemisphere oil production outside the Soviet orbit, with say $4,000 million of net fixed assets. The 'Eastern hemisphere profits' of the seven major companies, according to the First National City Bank, amounted to some $950 million for 1955 and $1,102 million for 1960. This would imply a net return on integrated operations in the Eastern hemisphere of the order of 20–25 per cent in the mid-fifties; but falling to about 15 per cent by 1958 and to 13 per cent in 1960 and 1962.

By the same token, if practically all this net profit was shown on the production of oil, with practically none on 'non-producing activities', then the percentage return on production would be very much higher. The Chase Manhattan Bank's estimates of capital employed in this industry suggest that of the total net investment in oil facilities in the Eastern hemisphere only between a quarter and a third consisted of production facilities, or were invested in producing countries. So the assumption that all the industry's profits in this hemisphere were earned in production—which is an assumption which can, as we have seen, be drawn from the companies' prized formula of 50–50 'profit-sharing'— would imply that in the mid-fifties the major international companies operating in the Eastern hemisphere were earning net profits of the order of 60–90 per cent on the net capital employed in production there, after paying like sums to the host governments that shared these profits equally. These rates too would have been cut by nearly half by the early sixties. But again, it can be noted that only about a third of oil production investment in the Eastern hemisphere is located in the Middle East which produces the vast majority of the oil and the profits. So the return on production there must be much higher than the average for the hemisphere.

Many estimates have been made in recent years of returns in investment in Middle East oil production, which has become politically a highly controversial figure. Of these, it is perhaps worth selecting two: one made for the host governments, and one made by the parent government of most of the international majors. A study prepared for OPEC by the American consultants. Arthur D. Little in 1962 estimated that the returns on investment by the main concessionnaires in Middle East member countries other than Kuwait during the period 1955–60 averaged approximately 66 per cent, compared with 20 per cent for Venezuela (30 per cent in 1956 and 1957, falling to 12½ per cent for 1959 and 1960).[7] A United States Department of Commerce survey of American investment abroad, in mid-1961, put the average book value of capital investment in the American petroleum business in the Middle East for 1960 at $1,195,000,000, the turnover of these businesses at $1,745,000,000, and their profits after tax at $610,000,000: for Venezuela the book value of investments was estimated at $2,071,000,000, the turnover at $1,902,000,000, and the profits at $595,000,000. This figuring suggested rates of return for American oil companies on the book value of their investment as about 50 per cent in the Middle East and 29 per cent in Venezuela. These figures were lower than A. D. Little's, but they will have included other oil companies' operations, some of them on exploration not yet producing any returns, and also returns on pipeline, refinery and marketing investment in Middle East countries that produce no oil. The Department of Commerce figures were not easy to link with those of the First National City Bank, which however was concerned purely with the largest international groups; nor with the figures of total asset values estimated by the Chase Manhattan Bank. But the answers they suggest are of the same order. These Department of Commerce figures are published regularly. For 1964 they suggested net profits of $893 million on Middle East oil assets valued at $1,238 million, or about 70 per cent; and a comparable figure of only about 21 per cent for Venezuela.

Both of these studies, it is worth noting, give pretty modest figures compared with the guesses anyone can hear in comparatively informed quarters on the spot. Few people in the Middle East oil business seem to doubt that the notional rates of return on the book values of assets of the operating companies there are at least as high as these governmental estimates. One small American company with interests in the Iran Consortium—where all presumably fare alike—once published figures suggesting a net return approaching 100 per cent on its net assets after depreciation: Aramco has at times shown profits of the order of 70 per cent. Informed guesses at the rate of net profits achieved in Iraq (by trading companies rather than the IPC group itself) put this in between Aramco and Iran; and some oilmen in other companies will argue that net profits on the comparatively modest investment in Kuwait, by the various companies who gain a direct or indirect share of these, must be higher than in any of the other oil-producing territories of the Middle East. Profit figures for Libya, the latest graduate to the 'big league' of OPEC oil producing membership, appear to have been higher in terms of cents per barrel, at least for pioneering companies such as Esso, than in the Middle East. But most other companies producing there were up to 1965 selling at very heavy discounts, and earning much less profit. Moreover, a large proportion of the investment and exploration expenses put into Libya have still to bear fruit in production and profits. So the return on investment is as yet probably still low. Not until Libyan oil growth has settled down towards the OPEC average will it become meaningful to hazard comparisons.

Is this 'where' the profits on oil are really 'earned'? It is certainly where the major companies show these profits to the many governments to which they pay taxes. Can it be rationalized in economic terms? It might, certainly, be possible to argue that once an entrepreneur has located cheap oil he could acquire the capital required for some if not all the later stages in the oil business—tankers, pipelines, refining, at any rate—for no more than the long-term cost of borrowing, which for a major oil company could be very low indeed. Certainly many people would agree that the largest elements of risk in this business are concentrated at the earliest stage of exploration. On such an analysis you might argue that the later stages of an integrated operation 'need' no more than some riskless 'public utility' return on the capital employed, after depreciation but before tax; and that the capital would be forthcoming on these terms to anybody, and more particularly to any big company, that had found cheap new oil. You cannot argue rationally that capital in these later stages needs no return at all, or can be run at a loss, which is what some of the integrated companies have found themselves doing in recent years on this kind of accounting. Moreover, in practice the capital requirements of these later stages are in aggregate very high; whether or not these stages of the business incur much risk, they do pose the newcomer a very high 'cost of entry'. Probably 70–80 per cent of the fixed capital employed in this business, outside the United States, appears to be in stages later than production. A company that was earning say 13 per cent on its total integrated operation, as in the early sixties most of the majors probably were in the Eastern hemisphere, could on this argument allocate a considerable proportion of its net profits to the early stages. If it accepted a return that covered no more than the net cost of borrowing, which might be of the order of 2–3 per cent, allowing for the charging of interest against tax, on say 75 per cent of its capital employed, this would leave net profits of about 45 per cent for the capital employed on its smaller but much riskier investment in exploration and production. Alternatively, if one were to allow a return of say 10 per cent for 'downstream' investments, then production in the Eastern hemisphere would have yielded the companies operating there a return of about 22 per cent on the average, with higher rates in the more productive areas such as the Middle East.[8]

In practice, according to the figures of the First National City Bank, the major international companies have in recent years been accepting even lower rates of return than this net cost of borrowing on the large amounts of capital employed in their affiliates in some consuming countries; and at times, in some areas, may have shown even larger returns on their productive activities than the figures above. It is possible to rationalize these differences, too, according to the argument that suggests the profits should be where the risks are. For the even higher rates of return on countries such as Kuwait are in places where the risky gamble of exploration has paid off most handsomely. For each of these several exploration enterprises may have had to be abandoned in other countries. The average return on exploration that an entrepreneur might require to put his capital into oil exploration and development would be lower than this; but the entrepreneur takes higher returns than average out of his bonanzas to go on exploring in other places. At any one time the oil industry, or an integrated company, is exploring for oil in a number of countries. In some this is paying off already; in others it has not yet; in some it never will. You can quibble about the actual rate of exploration that the industry needs to engage in at any one time; but even to keep pace with the normal growth of oil consumption during a period of surplus some substantial rate would probably be required. And in practice the industry tends to finance all of this from profits made in the most successful areas.

This question of the 'proper' rate of return on risk capital in the oil business is crucial in the relations between oil companies and governments. It is one in which the governments both of countries where the major companies produce oil and those where they process and sell it take a growing interest. But in economic terms much of the argument about 'where' the profits are made in the oil business can only be regarded as notional. A case for argument that the bulk of the profits 'needs' to be made on production has been set out above. But it would be as easy to produce an argument that at least 65–75 per cent of the profits ought to be made on stages following production. Would allocation of profit according to the investment involved at each stage be any less logical than the allocation of it according to the degree of risk involved, which is anyway not easy to 'quantify' in any real sense?

In reality this is a profit on an integrated operation—the whole expenditure on exploration, development, production, transport, refining and marketing is required to give crude oil in the ground any value at all. Most of the oil is not sold until after it has been refined into products and distributed to final markets; it moves to that point under the same ownership. And where the major companies do sell large quantities of crude, they do so at prices differing from the posted prices that can be used in exercises such as the above to show 'where' profits are made in the oil business. To say that there is a large profit on the production of crude oil and none on say, refining in Europe—as has purported to be the case in recent years—is a matter largely of accounting practice, rather than of the actual occurrence of profit at different stages of the business.

This is not to argue, as some critics of this industry would, that the integrated company is at all times wholly free to choose where it shall take its profits. The profits shown at different stages at any given time will represent the result of decisions taken at different times in the past, many of which an integrated company cannot easily reverse. Moreover, the integrated company is subject at certain stages of its business to differing degrees of competition on price. It will ordinarily be under some pressure to set its transfer prices from one 'department' to another, and hence the profits it can allocate to any stage, broadly in accordance with competitive rates in the general market for that stage of the business—if significant competition exists there. Up to the mid-fifties, in some stages, there was little competition, and the major companies were free to set transfer prices as they chose. Since then, competition has returned, and they have lost most of this freedom. Moreover, governments at various points in any company's spread have a growing concern with the foreign exchange transfers—and taxes—that its chosen pattern brings about.

Whatever other critics of the companies would argue, the consumer may be inclined to feel that in the past the companies decided to take a high and disproportionate share of their profits at the stage of production, or at any rate to 'post' prices at this stage that offered the host governments a large revenue from tax which it was convenient to call a half-share in the profits. This formula has been of tremendous advantage to the oil-producing countries in the past, in terms of revenue, and by no means inconvenient for the companies which could set off taxes there against tax liabilities on foreign income elsewhere. But it is now causing them considerable difficulty. The Middle East governments' understandable opposition to any reduction in the posted price, because this would automatically reduce the 'profit-sharing' revenue they receive, has now developed into pressure to push discounted market prices up to these artificial levels—while consumer governments' pressure is largely in the opposite direction.

An international oil company concerns itself primarily, however, with its rate of net return on capital as a whole, not with the rate of return that may be attributed to any particular part of it. There is such flexible and continuing movement of resources between parts of the world in this industry, for companies that have a really wide spread of business, as largely to blur the geographical analysis of oil profits.

Two interlocking factors that affect capital investment in this industry have had considerable significance in the structure of organization that it has in fact assumed. The first, as we have seen in the discussion of operating economics in oil, is that at most stages in its operations there are significant technical economies to be gained by operating on a large scale, and that with continued growth of the total market these can be achieved in more and more markets. A second factor, allied with the first, is that in most parts of this industry the cost of entry for a newcomer is very high. To secure concessions over the very large areas that until recently been characteristic of oil exploration in most countries except the United States, for example, or equally to establish oneself to sell petroleum products in any of the developed markets of the world, very large initial investments are generally required. These factors militate against entry into this industry, today, on anything but a very large scale, unless one can gain some political privilege in entry; and perhaps even then. This large entrance fee to the industry constitutes a stake that a company may find it advisable or imperative to protect by gaining control of other stages in operations—integrating backwards and forwards. The integrated company is in part a product of the characteristic high cost of entry into oil operations. And the dominance of integrated companies in the international industry tends, in its turn, to perpetuate and even to raise the cost of entry for newcomers.

CHAPTER VIII

Bigness in the Oil Business

I n glancing at the operating economics of the petroleum industry in the last few chapters, we have seen various factors that make it convenient to have big units of ownership. Many of its operations are highly-capitalized, and in some there are considerable economies of scale. Moreover, the large areas over which rights to explore for oil have become available, in many parts of the world outside the United States, have raised the cost of entry into this one stage of the industry where one might expect to find adventurous individual businessmen—though one sometimes still does. These elements make for big units of ownership at particular stages of the industry's operations—that is, for 'horizontal integration'. They may also, indirectly, make for 'vertical integration', or the ownership of more than one stage of oil operations. In practice, oil companies frequently own or directly control almost all the operations that are applied to petroleum, from exploration right down to selling the processed products. There is still great diversity in the company structure of this industry; many small units or largish non-integrated units survive and flourish. But integration does dominate at most levels in the structure; and whether or not one regards it as an inevitability in the development of such an industry, it certainly has played a logical part in the way this industry has developed in practice.

First, the facts. Here, as in other ways, there are marked differences between oil in the United States and in the rest of the free world, even though many of the same companies are involved in both, and American companies own the largest single share of the privately-owned oil industry outside their borders. In particular, the share of vertically-integrated oil companies, and of the seven great 'international majors', is much greater outside the United States. Here the oil industry developed later than inside America, and the shape that it adopted, historically, was in some ways a reaction to the structure and strength of American oil companies at the time.

In the oil industry of the United States bigness is too common for even any giant to dominate ownership of the industry. Only occasionally has the degree of concentration in the industry been measured in detail.[1] In 1959, the four biggest companies in American oil refining accounted for about a quarter of total deliveries, which was rather less than the average 'concentration ratio' for American manufacturing industry (and had fallen from a third in 1954); the share of the top 15 companies in oil, however, was three-quarters, much more than the average for other manufacturing industries. These top 15 producing companies, in 1959, produced probably 44 per cent of the crude produced in the United States. In 1955, the top 20 companies accounted for 85–90 per cent of the crude moved through pipelines; and about the same proportion of refinery throughput was in the hands of a similar number. The top 20 marketers were responsible for about 80 per cent of all sales of gasoline, though for only about 55 per cent of service station sales.[2] There were two fields of operations in which ownership by large companies was fairly insignificant: small companies or specialists drilled three-quarters of all new oil wells, and very few service stations nowadays are actually owned by big companies. But a large proportion of the drilling was done by specialists under various risk-sharing arrangements with the largest companies. And practically all the service stations through which these companies sold gasoline, though no longer owned by the refining and marketing companies, were tied by exclusive contracts or leases to them.

Those estimates, properly, are measures of concentration—that is, of the share controlled by the largest units in particular stages of the industry—not of the share controlled by vertically integrated companies. But in practice, there appears to be not much difference. Among the top twenty companies in American crude oil production, refining, gasoline sales, and the top twenty in terms of total asset value, in 1958, there were only twenty-four different names. In 1950, there were 50 fully integrated companies in American oil. These accounted for just on 60 per cent of crude production in the United States and for 99·6 per cent of crude produced by American companies abroad; for about 90 per cent of American refinery capacity and a fractionally higher percentage of actual refinery runs; for 60 per cent of bulk sales of products and 58 per cent of gasoline sales at service stations.[2] By 1964 there were 68 integrated and semi-integrated companies (buying crude from 9,000 producers), plus 61 other companies in marketing. These marketers worked with 20,000 jobbers, 14,000 distributors, and nearly

200,000 service stations.[3] Bigness, in the world's largest oil industry, is therefore cheek by jowl with smallness amounting at some stages almost to fragmentation of ownership (kept in existence at the production level largely by official policies guaranteeing the small man a living). And integration co-exists with large numbers of non-integrated companies at each stage, in many cases highly prosperous ones. The Texas millionaires, for example, are generally independent explorers, producers, and dealers in oil leases: selling to the majors, but not within them. But for the most part big business and integration coincide.

Records of the performance of a group of about 30 of the largest oil companies operating in the United States have been maintained for years by the Chase Manhattan Bank.[4] In 1950, this group was responsible for 85 per cent of American refinery throughput and for 52 per cent of the country's crude oil production. By 1964, the refining percentage had grown a little, to 88 per cent; the percentage of crude oil output had grown significantly, to 65 per cent. In 1964, their refineries processed 55 per cent more crude than they produced in the United States and they took three-quarters of the crude produced by independents. (The wells these integrated refiners owned were working below full capacity. In theory, they could have satisfied more of their crude oil needs from their own wells, almost certainly more cheaply. But output regulation in the United States requires most wells to be produced to the same degree of capacity working—and thus obliges integrated refiners to buy some crude that they have enough capacity to produce themselves.)

In 1950, this same group of companies was responsible for 68 per cent of refining operations for the whole non-Communist world. By 1964, this proportion had come down to 57 per cent. The group's share of refining in the non-Communist world outside the United States had some down somewhat; but the main reason for the decline was that operations in this 'free foreign' area, where the group's proportionate share was smaller than in the United States, had been growing much faster than in the United States. In 1964 these companies were responsible for 38 per cent of 'free foreign' refining; and for about 55 per cent of 'free foreign' production. However, this grasp on the industry outside the United States was concentrated among only a few of them—the American-owned 'international majors', plus a number of American 'big independents'.

For in the free world outside the United States, oil ownership is much more concentrated into the hands of a few companies, whose operations are in general more fully integrated (not being subject to production control, as yet at any rate) than those of the Chase Manhattan Bank's selected group. And outside the United States, their dominance arose and has continued to be based upon the command of crude production, not primarily of refining operations. A 1956 estimate showed that 99 per cent of crude production outside the United States and the Soviet orbit was in the hands of fully integrated companies; 90 per cent of refining; and about the same proportion of marketing. The international integrated companies owned a notably smaller share of the world's tankers—some 34 per cent in 1956—but of the nearly 60 per cent owned by independent tanker operators, they had on charter a large part, so that perhaps three-quarters of the operating tanker fleet sailed on their account. Ownership of service stations by major companies has not developed as much outside the United States as it did there during some periods of the industry's history; but a similar network of leases and contracts ties the owners of most service stations to their suppliers of gasoline.

Essentially, this oil industry outside the United States is still largely dominated by seven of these fully-integrated majors—Standard Oil of New Jersey, Royal-Dutch/Shell, British Petroleum Company, Gulf Oil Corporation, the Texas Company, Standard Oil of California, and Socony Mobil Oil Company (to rank them in order of crude production). The French *Compagnie Française des Pétroles* ranks as an eighth of these majors, less in terms of sheer size than because it shares their joint operating companies in parts of the Middle East.

Since the mid-fifties, the operations of these companies in the international market—i.e. the non-Communist world outside the United States—has not grown quite as fast as total oil business there; so their proportionate share has shrunk a little. In 1964, the eight together accounted for some 80 per cent of crude production outside the United States and the Communist sphere, and perhaps 70 per cent of refinery throughput and of total oil product sales in this area. During the last decade, some sizeable newcomers have begun operating in the world oil trade, without as yet commanding any very large share of it. Some hundreds of American companies have re-entered international operations, or entered them for the first time since the Second World War; the most important of these are themselves fully integrated companies too. Certain nationalized or semi-nationalized companies, previously in the industry only as refiners or marketers, have been extending their operations backwards and outside their own borders into exploration and now into production of crude oil. In the refining and marketing stages, there remains a significant sprinkling of independent refiners around Western Europe (though many operate largely on contract to the international majors, becoming almost part of their integrated operations) and many independent marketers of particular products.

If one measures the degree of integration of an oil company primarily by the extent to which its crude production 'upstream' balances in volume with the throughput of its 'downstream' refining operations, the companies operating internationally differ considerably in degree. Of the eight international majors, only Texaco over the years has been steadily in broad balance, counting in its international operations. (Some people would argue that this is why it has more often than not earned the highest rate of return on its total operations.) Royal Dutch/Shell and Socony Mobil have been large-scale net buyers of crude, producing much less than they refined. In the last few years, however, both have been achieving somewhat greater self-sufficiency in crude, and tending to rely less upon the very large bulk purchase contracts they have with other majors—notably, Shell with Gulf and Socony with BP for crude supplies from Kuwait. Standard Oil of New Jersey, during most of the postwar period, has also been a net buyer of crude; but by 1964, with its large fresh production in Libya, it was much nearer balance between crude production and refining than the other two. The other four international majors all produce significantly more crude than they refine or market as products. Gulf, in 1964, produced 70 per cent more crude than it refined; CFP and BP around 50 per cent more; Standard Oil of California 10–15 per cent more.

	Refinery Throughput '000 b/d crude	Net Crude Production as % of Refinery Throughput	Sales of Products
S.O. New Jersey	3,632	88	107
RD/Shell*	3,364	66	100*
Texaco	1,674	99	105
B.P.	1,430	151	92
Socony Mobil	1,282	71	109
S.O. California	1,123	110	111
Gulf	1,084	174	100
CFP	434	147	101

(* includes sales of crude)

The balance between refinery throughput of crude and total sales of products seems to be a good deal less significant than that between crude production and refinery throughput. It will depend a good deal upon any company's geographical spread of production and the areas where it is expanding sales most. Refinery capacity and yields are seldom precisely fitted to the market demand in the areas they serve; a good deal of cross-sales between companies and areas is inevitable in any industry extended as widely and growing so fast. Certain of the largest groups, Jersey, Shell, and Socony, sell considerably more products than they refine. These are net buyers of crude. (But Standard Oil of California, because of its pattern of operations, manages to be at once a net seller of crude and a large-scale net buyer of refined products.)

Bigness and integration developed differently in oil inside and outside the United States because of geography, history and the different social and legal systems concerned. In its beginnings in the United States this industry had to be fitted into a settled pattern of land ownership that was perfectly well suited to the mining of coal and other solid minerals. The owner of the land on the surface was held to own whatever might be found under it; he was prepared to lease exploration and development rights in his subsoil for petroleum as for other minerals. This pattern of ownership, however, did not suit a mineral that might not stay where it happened to be found. If somebody drilling on your neighbour's land penetrated through to an extensive oil reservoir, he could begin emptying it out of the porous strata beneath your property as well as beneath your neighbour's. The law that applied here was the 'rule of capture'—that regardless of where the oil may have been *in situ* it belonged to the owner of the land where it was actually brought to the surface.

In wildcatting for oil, this rule of capture was an incentive to proliferate small units, not to create big ones. Nor did the simple techniques of early refining demand organization in large units, though they did require rather more capital and commercial acumen than drilling did. But the incentive not to let one's oil be sucked away by another driller, or alternatively to join in wherever someone had struck it rich, led to wasteful over-drilling, followed in some cases by the collapse of output in what had seemed tremendously rich fields. Refining capacity, similarly, was expanded as each rich new field was discovered and then hastened into over-production. Fears of scarcity of oil were regularly followed by the fact of surplus and severe price competition, particularly for refined products. Since cutting the price did not increase demand much, these price wars left most refiners with much the same share of the market as before, only poorer. With small-scale refining capacity duplicated to a point where in the eighteen-seventies it could have handled three times as much oil as was produced, the need for rationalization was obvious. The general desire for stability offered Rockefeller the chance to begin combination in refining. The strategic role of the transport that carried oil to market, first exploited by the railroads competing to secure large-scale oil traffic, offered him the chance to oust his competitors, and to secure virtual control of the market for crude. Development of the pipeline, where his large-scale organization could not only secure transport rebates but actually own the means of transport, sealed his control over the movements of oil from well to refinery.

Control of the transport of crude to the refinery, by owning part of the means of transport and contracting with the owners of the rest, was Standard Oil's first step backwards into vertical integration from the refining stage. Integration forward into the marketing of kerosene, once again seeking economies of larger scale through bulk delivery and local storage, was a logical sequel, securing Standard's grip on the market for what was then the key product of oil refining. The original combine did not buy its way into the ownership of actual crude production to anything like the extent that it bought up transportation and refining, and developed marketing; at no time did it own more than a third of American crude production. Its control was adequately exerted by transporting and processing the crude oil. The behaviour of this dominant combine, however, left room for other major entrepreneurs to enter crude production, the one point of entry then open to large-scale new independents, and to grow with the discovery of rich new oilfields. 'To avoid becoming in effect a part of Standard Oil Company's production department,' as W. L. Mellon once said of the beginnings of the Gulf Oil Corporation, it became essential for such companies to integrate forward into pipelines, refining and marketing.

Bigness as well as vertical integration thus proceeded largely from economic factors in this industry. When the first was checked by social attitudes embodied in American law, the other continued. The thirty-three separate corporations into which the Standard Oil group was dissolved by an anti-trust judgment in 1911 were not all balanced as oil businesses. Moreover, the dissolution came at a time when the rapid emergence of gasoline as the industry's new main product was beginning to overturn established patterns in the industry. Most of the former Standard affiliates tended to integrate backwards or forwards to complete their own vertical structures. At the same time other vertical combines in the business grew with the rapid development both of the new gasoline market and of rich sources of crude.

The largest of the American major companies, along with two or at the most three groups based in Europe, also dominate the privately-owned oil industry outside the United States. The structure of the international industry bears the stamp of the men who created it, at a time when the American oil industry was already in being and crystallizing in its ownership structure. But it also reflects the economic consequences of oil geography—and the social and legal attitudes towards business development both in the countries from which these creators came and in those where they developed the oil.

In the oil producing areas outside the United States the pattern of land ownership has led directly, not indirectly, to bigness. The only European petroleum industry that was of comparable size to the American by the turn of the century, that of Russia, was locked within the economic limitations of a feudal state; it never experienced the stimulus of America's automotive revolution, and the First World War removed it from private ownership (though not, for very long, from the world oil trade). No other European power found enough oil within its borders for its needs. European enterprise had to enter the oil business by way of oil exploration in countries where often no settled pattern of land tenure existed and where legal rights in the subsoil were not firmly vested in any surface landlord. Explorers for oil in these colonial and semi-colonial areas had to deal with rulers whose ownership of territory and subsoil was absolute (or was promptly presumed to be). The early concessions granted comprehensive rights to exploration and development over very large areas, and in some cases over whole countries. In the Middle East, the reservoirs developed have been huge, and it has certainly made for technical efficiency that they should have been developed under single managements. Moreover, the high costs of exploration and development in these under-developed countries required very large, speculative stakes, which only big companies could afford, initially, to risk there.

European attitudes towards oil abroad, on the part both of entrepreneurs and of governments, moreover reflected their lack of oil at home. The Royal Dutch/Shell grouping, which came together to compete with Standard Oil for kerosene and later gasoline markets outside the United States, was always concerned with finding the crude as well as moving it to market. It could not rely, as could Rockefeller, upon gaining control of the means of transport in the certainty that enough crude (or even more than enough) would be forthcoming. Its sources of oil were across the seas from its markets: this put the emphasis upon the development of the tanker, which originated in the European companies operating internationally as logically as the overland pipeline originated in the American. European pioneers in the oil business did not have to worry as much as American about social or political attitudes to the growth of their enterprises. European governments were less concerned with the ideology of small business and much more concerned with laying hands on the oil.

Governmental reactions to the combine of Shell and Royal Dutch before the First World War, therefore, were not to try to divide it up but to get into the oil business themselves. This, as well as securing oil for the Royal Navy, was a reason for the British government's investment in Anglo-Persian (later Anglo-Iranian, and today British Petroleum). German enterprise, private or governmental, was shut out of world oil by defeat in that First World War; the French government secured its share of right to oil development in Iraq and gave private enterprise, within the *Compagnie Française des Pétroles*, a share in exploiting this. After the Second World War France increased its own state and private participation in oil through the development of Algerian oil and gas; Italy, developing local gas through a state enterprise, began to market and refine oil and then sought with this state company to integrate backwards into oil production abroad; Japan encouraged some capitalists from outside oil to explore successfully in the Persian Gulf. All of these were consumer countries putting capital into the development of oil sources; logically, they were seeking integration, and with national backing some of them attained bigness.

Wherever the oil industry has grown to prominence you find bigness and vertical integration; the one, indeed, makes the other advisable. Operating units enjoy marked economies of scale, and have comparatively low running costs; either low or unstable rates of operation, therefore would raise their total operating costs. At the level of production, where each well for a time seems to enjoy increasing rather than diminishing returns, the owner whose investment is already sunk is tempted to work to full capacity at almost any cost. Yet reductions in price for crude or products do not, in general, significantly widen demand from the final consumer, and price wars may serve only to reduce everyone's return on capital. So the incentive to secure a share of the market by integrating forward is strong. The incentive to 'integrate backward'—i.e. for companies strong in marketing and refining to secure crude production of their own—depends more, perhaps, on the circumstances of the time. Given a proration system that obliges all wells to be produced to the same rate of capacity, as in the United States, actual ownership of large reserves of low-cost oil may not be as advantageous as it would in freer producing circumstances. In the international market, more often than not in the history of this industry, oil has been in surplus and companies that are net buyers of crude should have had the upper hand in bargaining with those that are 'long on crude'. But given the rise to predominance of any area such as the Middle East, with exceptionally low costs of production, and certain groups particularly well-placed, the strong marketer's bargaining advantages may seem less attractive. He may be able to buy crude from these groups more cheaply than from anywhere else; but that may still leave them exceptionally high profits on the crude to enjoy (or share with their host government). Some of the international majors that have been net buyers of crude, such as Shell, have spent very heavily on seeking, or sometimes buying up, command over a higher proportion of their own cost crude. There is still such a large element of luck in exploration that continued heavy expenditure on searching for oil may still leave the largest of companies short of low-cost oil reserves in the places that it would like. On the other hand, even a large integrated company happening upon exceptionally rich oilfields as BP and Gulf did together in Kuwait may be hard put to find a market for its new and abundant potential supplies of crude: and not infrequently marriages or less regular liaisons between differently-placed groups have been arranged.

Bigness may make it easier to finance expansion—either by the market power to obtain margins that allow for self-financing, or in this industry's infrequent recourse to finance from outside. Size and solidity have their attractions for the investor outside: so may an integrated situation even when the market prospects are not buoyant. And the very large company in an industry growing at the rate that oil is has a built-in pressure to expand. Its expenditure on exploration, for example, will be related not merely to its forward estimates of demand, its present reserve-production ratio, and its views of the chances in possible new areas. There remains, even after so many years of search throughout the world, a strong element of pre-emptive bidding. If one company does not look for oil in even an unlikely place, the next one may find it there; geology is not an exact science. And oil found by somebody else closer to market may reduce the relative value even of large reserves of low-cost crude farther away. The largest international oil companies are concerned with maintaining their own positions in the world oil business. These are entities imbued with the intention of permanence; and they are in business to stay, and ideally to stay with as big a share as they have today, if not bigger. And wherever oil is found, they prefer it to be in strong hands—preferably their own.

When one looks at the historical development of this industry, inside or outside the United States, it is hard to feel that the economic advantages alone of bigness or vertical integration need have been overwhelming. In each stage of the American industry, some independents have survived and thrived; nor has the independent ever been for very long shut out of the international oil trade. It is sometimes said that bigness is essential to research on the scale that the petroleum industry needs it. But in the United States, at least, many 'small' oil companies are large enough to carry on research on a scale that European firms in other businesses would find impressive. Independents and plant engineering firms have made many of the vital and continuing advances in technology of the oil industry. The record of every major company, in spite of the impressive contributions to its technology reaped from the money and effort it will have harnessed to research and development internally, is still studded with innovations adopted from outside.

During the fifties, the major companies were tending to bring the independent operator back into various stages of the business, under their own wings. Much of the exploration done on behalf of the major companies was in fact carried out by small individual specialist companies. In transport, the majors have been content to charter a large part of the extra capacity required to meet growing demand from independent owners—who have, indeed, led the way in innovation in each successive size group up the super-tanker scale. In research, again, the big company often puts specific investigations in the hands of the plant engineer or the sponsored research institute. This readiness to let specialists do the actual job displays a sensible apprehension about possible diseconomies of scale in the sphere of management and of communication. During the early sixties, these tendencies may have changed a little. In these years, many oil companies have concentrated on cutting costs; in such economic campaigns, activity farmed out to specialists often tends to be cut back first. Drilling contractors, in particular, had a number of lean years. But less temporary influences may have been at work, too. Inside big companies, communication has been almost revolutionized along with data processing. It has become possible for central management to assimilate and sift a far larger mass of operating data than anyone imagined a decade ago. With families of linked computers and the facility of a central computer to have instant access to the memory and the current data fed into each of the others, the shift may be from the decentralization preached a few years ago, back towards centralization. Nevertheless, decentralization of operating management remains essential for enterprises spread as widely as these (though the amount of real decentralization sought and achieved in practice differs quite considerably between the major international groups). And they do not find it easy to measure their performance against what others achieve—let alone to achieve optimum performance.

One notable disadvantage of bigness in any business is that people, rightly or wrongly, distrust it. Ever since Rockefeller hired Ivy Lee, the large oil companies have recognized that their growth and accumulating power breeds suspicion, even apart from envy. This is not confined to countries with an ideological attachment to small, competitive business, such as the United States. In countries where the oil industry is present only as a foreign capitalist, bigness serves to strengthen the feeling that the country is being unfairly exploited. And even in European countries with less emotional attachment to the ideal of competition than the United States, public attitudes towards the great oil companies that work from headquarters within their borders are often somewhat mixed. Their very international sphere of operations is in a sense suspect. It can give the impression of being always able to remove any issue from the context in which it is raised, and of taking decisions for reasons that are never wholly explained. Quite a significant element in oil's overhead costs goes into public relations departments in these companies, which have the task of explaining the companies' behaviour. Whether or not this task is ever adequately discharged, it is certainly never completed. The policies change with the years; so do the kind of people one has to explain them to. And responsibility for explaining themselves lies more and more with managers at the top, not with the expert practitioners in communication whom they have assembled to present however much they are willing to tell.

Such disadvantages of bigness, however, do not stop newcomers seeking to achieve it, and certainly seeking to achieve vertical integration. From the host countries to the countries that lack oil, all recent new entrants to this industry on any substantial scale have sought to integrate forward or backward: Italy's ENI back to the oil well, Kuwait and Saudi Arabia, perhaps, forward to the foreign market. Vertical integration may not be the only 'organic' structure that the oil industry could have assumed, though some integrated companies would probably have been important in any practical structure that did emerge. But there has been as much logic as accident in the way that vertical integration has predominated in the structure of the world's oil business. This integrated structure largely determines the amount of competition in this business and the way it occurs; and it largely though not wholly determines the level of prices at which the industry has delivered, over its history, so vast a volume of the goods.

CHAPTER IX

Pricing: I. Appearance and Reality

In mid-1965, you could buy a gallon of regular-trade gasoline at any service station in the United States for about 30 cents, which included about 10 cents of state and federal taxes: the average retail price excluding tax, in that year, was 20·2 cents. Forty-five years before it would have cost a motorist about the same, with practically no tax at all: the price excluding tax was 29·74 cents a gallon. In Britain, regular grade petrol cost 4s. 10½d. an imperial gallon (which is a fifth over an American gallon) in mid-1965, including tax; in 1920, this spirit (which like the 1920 gasoline in the United States would have been a much lower-grade product) had cost about 4s. a gallon, including only 3d. tax. Those prices relate to the main petroleum product of the 'gasoline era', which hardly dates back beyond the First World War. As to the raw material, crude oil sold in the United States averaged about 94 cents a barrel (of 42 U.S. gallons) in 1880; $1·19 a barrel in 1900; $3·05 a barrel in 1965. (Here again, over the years, the qualities of the many crudes whose prices make up the average will have changed considerably.)

Comparisons over the forty years of the gasoline era are perhaps rather unduly favourable for the prices of crude oil and what has become the main product made from it; the base date was a year of pretty high prices. Oil prices had risen sharply immediately following the First World War reflecting an apparent shortage (they did the same, after some years of price controls, immediately following the second). Reckoned against general wholesale or retail price indices, indices for petroleum and its products have risen somewhat less since 1947 than those of the other things a dollar could buy, but in the inter-war period often rose much higher and never came down as far. Comparison with some other fuels is perhaps more meaningful. Bituminous coal in the United States cost $1·25 a ton in 1880; $1·04 a ton in 1900; $1·12 a ton in 1910; $3·75 a ton in 1920; $1·91 a ton in

1940; $4·50 a ton in 1960; and $4·38 a ton in 1964. In Britain, where coal came on to the defensive against oil much later than in the United States, its price has risen seven times since 1920—and has not yet stopped rising. Natural gas in the United States, in 1964, was sold at an average of about 15·6 cents a thousand cubic feet, not much more than forty years before; in 1965 prices set for new contracts were about 16·5 cents. But that was a controlled (and controversial) price; so were the prices that utilities charged for electricity, another fuel that could beat even oil for price stability.

The oil industry, therefore, can fairly describe its products as cheap fuels with a quite remarkable record of price stability over a long period during which almost all other prices have soared. It repeatedly does: but that is almost all it has to say about the matter. Even inside the American oil industry, which has the most elaborate price reporting and statistical series of any oil business in the world, it is not too easy to get rational discussion of the way in which these prices are in fact formed. In the United States, the spectre of anti-trust proceedings broods over any such discussion, and its shadow extends wherever in the world American companies operate. Even so, it is notable and unfortunate that up to now most international oil companies, in particular, have left almost all the serious discussion of price formation in the international oil business to their critics—usually contenting themselves with the claim that oil pricing is the result of 'competition', naïvely defined.

The 'literature' on this subject consists largely of discussions by outside investigatory bodies, such as the Federal Trade Commission of the United States or the Economic Commission for Europe; or by independent students of the oil industry, such as Messrs. Levy, Frankel, and Ovens, or by academic economists such as Professors Adelman, Cassady, de Chazeau and Kahn, and Leeman.[1] Published contributions to the discussion of prices from people actually within the industry have been infrequent and unfortunately rather often anodyne, though when anyone else discusses prices there have always been spokesmen of the companies to emphasize how distorted a picture you can get from outside. They have taken this line notably towards people discussing oil prices from within oil-producing countries, such as Shaikh Abdullah Tariki, Mr Ashraf Lutfi, and Mr Ramadan Kamel.[2] On occasion, certainly, comments from these host countries have been easy to fault on factual detail and figuring—though such weaknesses can co-exist with penetration in separating out their countries' interests in the matter. But the companies, in replying, sometimes give an impression that they are more concerned to show that other people have the wrong ideas about it than to help them to get the right ones. Inevitably, the host countries have chosen to build up their own independent expertise. Since 1960, this has been one of the services that OPEC has begun to provide for them. Its economics department, built up by Dr Francisco Parra, has made a number of distinguished contributions to the discussions of oil pricing in the world market.[3]

In their own few positive contributions to discussion of the subject, company spokesmen have usually been hampered by having to postulate that prices in this industry are formed by processes of unbridled competition. This seems to be partly because the anti-trust laws require the pretence that this is how modern American industry actually behaves; but also partly because big oil companies, English as well as American, seemed to feel that this copybook economics was about as complicated an explanation as they could expect anyone outside the industry to understand without stirring up further embarrassments for themselves later on. To the interested outsider, this explanation may seem no more realistic than the opposite assumption from which some of their critics begin—that oil prices are fixed by an all-powerful and largely sinister cartel. During the last few years certain international companies, notably Royal Dutch/Shell, have shown a change in this attitude, and they have begun to discuss their pricing in more sophisticated and realistic terms.[4] But the general company attitude has not changed yet.

Most of the facts on record about oil prices, as I have said, are American. In Western Europe, by contrast, no systematic price reporting yet exists for oil, and price statistics are hence quite inadequate. At one time, oil moved quite freely in international trade; it still moves in greater volumes than any other commodity. In theory, up to the mid-fifties, you might still argue that in the non-Communist world it was traded in a fairly unified market. So logically, you could expect the prices of crude oil and products to bear some relation to prices in the dominant market, the United States. The international market is no longer unified, though some vestiges of the relationship remain between certain American oil prices and others in some parts of the world. In theory, again, in such a single market, the basic elements affecting the price or series of prices at which oil changes hands on its way to the consumer will be the final demand for petroleum products and the cost of obtaining the crude oil from which they are made; and the relation between the two should perform the function of bringing demand and supply into balance. Over the last five to ten years, oil prices have been falling. But they remain, so far, well above the cost at which extra supplies can readily be developed and supplied. So they still seem far from bringing the world oil market into balance. Some of the distortions in oil prices both inside and outside the United States arise from government policies. But any 'price structure' remaining high above the cost at which further supplies could be developed, for whatever reason, remains vulnerable.

LANGUAGE—AND MEANING

Discussion of oil pricing in the United States, as elsewhere, is generally couched in a rather specialized language. It is useful to get clear what these terms are supposed to mean—and also, in practice, how meaningful the prices thus described really are nowadays, which is rather a different question. One is concerned, at various levels, with schedules of published or 'posted' prices, and with the prices actually paid, which generally differ. That is not unusual in many industries. But in oil the pattern is variegated enough to demand some definitions.

A 'posted price' for refined products or crude oil is a statement of the price at which a buyer or seller of oil is ready to do business with all comers prepared to sell or buy in the quantities specified. It is, in practice, a guarantee to do business on those terms with anyone, provided the oil is available. Prices for refined oil products are 'posted' by a number of refiners in most of the main producing and refining centres of the United States; and also by refiners elsewhere, at a number of the main export refining centres of the world, such as the Caribbean and Persian Gulf refineries. In most other big markets, refining and marketing companies publish schedules of prices for the main different products, often on a delivered basis, varying by 'zones' according to the distance involved from the refining centre or bulk import terminal. The prices at which business is actually transacted in these products may differ significantly from the 'posted' or scheduled prices. Customers will be able to secure rebates according to the volume or term and regularity of their purchases. They may also, at times when the market is soft but published prices have not been adjusted downwards, be able to secure rebates generally, because of this.

In the United States there are daily price-reporting services, such as

Platt's Oilgram Price Service, which keep both marketers and customers up to date with news of the prices at which they learn that oil products have been sold, or at least offered, in different areas. There are quotations from export refiners in certain key refining centres, for products in 'cargo lots' at the 'refinery gate'; and also 'tank-wagon prices', which are delivered prices at various marketing centres, including transport and handling costs as far as the local distributor; and a broad congruence can be traced between the two. No comparable price reporting exists in any of the other main developed markets for oil across the world—though in one or two cases there are attempts at price reporting by private or governmental agencies, usually longer in arrear than in the United States. Inside some of these other markets, rebates are also conceded on the majority of sales to customers buying in bulk; but the extent of the rebates granted is not so widely and quickly known—particularly to consumers. This permits a certain amount of price discrimination between different customers within the individual markets, related to their knowledge and bargaining power. Given the very rapid growth of oil sales in the past decade in Western Europe and Japan, at any time there will have been even in these developed economies a sizeable proportion of new customers unaccustomed to buying oil.

That was too good to last, for the sellers, and it has not lasted. But on a broader scale considerable discrimination has also been possible between different national markets, according to the extent of competition in each from newcomers ready to cut prices to bargain their way in. There persisted until the early sixties considerable differences in product price levels between nearby countries in Western Europe, for example. Underdeveloped countries in Africa, Asia, and to a lesser extent Latin America, a number of which bought all their oil up to the sixties as refined products, tended to be charged prices closer to those generally posted. They had less bargaining power on questions of foreign exchange, and were less attractive markets—though easier to penetrate, sometimes—for price-cutting newcomers. As and when these graduated to having refineries built, however, with the chance for the company involved of a head start in markets that could only grow, some of them managed to conduct their Dutch auctions sensibly, and to achieve better prices for the crude supply rights that generally went with the refinery contract.

Posted prices for crude oil, on the other hand, differ even in nature between the United States and the rest of the world, because of the contrasted patterns of the American and the international industry (and because of governmental controls over United States production). In the United States, posted prices for crude are buyers' prices, not sellers'. They are posted by refiners, who thus notify the prices that they are willing to pay for crude oil at the wellhead from producers connected to their pipeline gathering systems. And these prices set the figures at which oil is held to have changed hands at any given time, though the actual purchases may take place continuously, without any re-negotiation in respect of a price change, under long-term 'open division' contracts between refiner and producers. This advertising of crude prices by the buyer and not by the seller, in the United States, reflects the structure of the American oil industry, where most of even the largest integrated companies produce much less oil than they refine, and are accustomed to being obliged by the State proration systems to make up their requirements by buying from a wide variety of independent producers (because all 'prorated' wells have to be produced to the same proportion of 'allowable' capacity).

Outside the United States, where most of the world's production is in the hands of very large-scale producers, integrated to differing degrees, posted prices for crude are set by the seller, f.o.b. from export terminals. Up to the early fifties, and during the short supply crisis following the closure of the Suez Canal in 1956, these posted prices represented the price at which such producers were prepared to sell to all comers in tanker cargo lots. Since then, most actual sales of crude have occurred at discounts off these posted price levels, the discounts growing steadily larger up to 1965. Up to 1960, the posted prices were adjusted downwards to some degree; since 1960, they have hardly altered, and not at all in the Middle East.

In the international market, at the present time, all arms-length transactions in crude oil are made at prices differing from these posted prices. Current discounts are known to be sizeable, though they are often not easy to measure precisely, since the benefit to the purchaser may not be expressed in cents per barrel at all. Many forms of advantage may be offered apart from actually cutting the offer price: long-term loans at low rates of interest, artificially low freight rates in a delivered price, offers to re-purchase some of the products that the refiner may make in excess of requirements in his market at more favourable prices than he could get there; or 'profit-splitting' deals that gear the crude price in to some extent with the prices the refiner gets for products. Moreover, the price may bear little relation to posted prices because the crude sold has no general price: 'reconstructed' crude or mixtures of crude are increasingly nowadays tailored to the requirements of each customer's particular market for refined products.

Discounting occurs, we have seen above, off the prices posted internationally for products at export refining centres, too. But these posted prices for products, in practice, seldom seem to become quite as insulated from actual prices in the market as those of crude. For all refined products, finally, need to be sold. Most of the crude produced in the world is never sold at all.

Even in the United States, perhaps 60 per cent of the crude is produced by integrated marketers and simply transferred by refining departments or affiliates of the same group. This would not necessarily mean insulation from the market: nobody would suggest that a market in which 40 per cent of the business represents arm's length sales cannot throw up competitive prices. United States prices for crude, and hence for products, *are* insulated from the world market, and are thus unrealistically high. But that is a result of Government policy: import restrictions that shut out far cheaper oil, paralleled by State proration systems that restrict internal output to 'market demand' at prevailing prices. It might be argued that if these government polices were dismantled, the integrated marketers could gain a far higher share of production, simply by being allowed to produce their own wells closer to capacity; and that this would recreate monopolistic tendencies within the American oil industry itself, making prices less competitive. But there is no reason to argue that current prices do not realistically represent current conditions in the American oil market. It is the general level of the market that is unrealistic—by government choice.

Outside the United States, only 20–30 per cent of the crude porduced is ever sold at all. The rest is moved within integrated channels, from producing affiliate to international trading (and perhaps tanker) affiliate to refining affiliate. The oil is sold only after it has been processed into refined products. Within this vast integrated flow of crude, there are some arm's-length transactions but fairly private ones. There are various inter-company bulk sales of crude under long-term contracts, and a variety of short-term inter-company sales as well. Within the joint operating companies of the Middle East, there is some production of crude for shareholder companies in larger volumes than these may be entitled to under jointly-agreed 'offtake' arrangements, which may involve them in paying penalties to other shareholders: these 'overlift prices' are very real ones to the groups concerned, even though they are never published. And under the concessions in which companies have entered into partnership with national companies, now becoming the rule in the Middle East, another form of 'hidden price' has been introduced. If the national company cannot dispose of its own entitlement of crude in the market, it can require its private partner to buy from it part or all of this entitlement at some price related to cost and to the posted price—sometimes a 'halfway' price. The integrated companies no doubt see these as elements of internal accounting, hardly prices; and nobody else sees them at all. But they are the only arm's-length transactions ever applying to a majority of the crude that these companies produce.

This majority of crude that moves through integrated channels, certainly, used often to be invoiced to marketing affiliates of the integrated group at transfer prices based upon the prices posted for crude internationally, plus estimated long-term averages for freights. And posted prices were sometimes used too for the valuation of crude exchanges at different points in the world between different integrated groups. In many cases, nowadays, posted prices do not serve either of these purposes. Marketing affiliates are invoiced at prices differing from 'postings plus long-term freight averages'—though the practice seems to vary as between the different internationally integrated groups, largely perhaps because of different tax practice in their own parent countries. But in any case, these transfer prices were and are important mainly to the governments whose foreign exchange and company taxes are involved. To the integrated group, what matters commercially is the range of prices that it can get for products in each market where the oil is finally sold, and what it has to pay to supply them. It considers what it calls the 'tax-paid costs' of the range of crudes from which it might supply the refining affiliate. Academic critics such as Professor Adelman[5] have reasonably challenged the notion that royalties and taxes are a cost of production; but for the present the integrated group takes them as unavoidable payments, however defined. It knows the cost of moving these crudes to the consuming country in its own or chartered tankers. A given refining affiliate will choose one or a number of these crudes, with or without tailoring, to minimize its own refining and marketing costs—both in terms of minimizing its processing costs and in terms of supplying its pattern of market demand with the least avoidable waste of excess products of one kind and another, which the group will have to sell off somewhere even if the international supply affiliate takes them off this particular refining affiliate's hands.

As for the 20 per cent or so of crude produced in the international market that is sold as such, to genuinely independent refiners who buy their crude at arm's length, the prices they pay bear no necessary relation to posted prices. They are always liable to be lower; over the last seven or eight years in the international market, they have often been far lower. 'Independent refiners' is not a precise or permanent definition; such companies from time to time tie themselves up with long-term crude contracts with major integrated companies, or refine on contract, or conclude deals that involve co-operation in marketing of the products. Whether they tie themselves up in this way or not, these refiners seldom make contracts for shorter periods than a year. So at any time, there will not be a large number in the market, or many deals being made. Mr Gripaios of Shell[6] has reckoned that in any one year the amount of total international crude output being traded in the market in these arm's-length deals may be no more than 7 per cent—i.e. about a third of the total sales to these independent refiners. It is easy to conclude from this that the prices agreed in such bargains 'are quite unrepresentative of the market as a whole'. But if these prices represent a third of the crude actually entering into actual sales, there is no particular reason to consider them unrepresentative. For the 70–80 per cent of crude moving through integrated channels, and never sold as such, is hardly part of the crude market in any ordinary sense of the word.

What is true is that there are comparatively few deals going on at any time; the price reporting is scrappy; and as we have seen above, many side arrangements can be entered into that such prices as are published may not give too clear an indication of the real terms on which business is being done. This does not mean that the market is unrepresentative; it means that the reporting of it is imperfect. It is not what the European Communities would call 'transparent'; i.e. people doing business in it cannot be sure that they know exactly how the bargain they make compares with the bargains the next two other people have just made. That is not particularly unusual in modern business; and in fact, after five to ten years of hard bargaining in the arm's-length crude market, the market information buyers and sellers now command in it is probably not at all bad. In this market, as in any other, businessmen have to sort out the 'distress sales', bargains made by companies with crude to sell in smallish quantities at prices that they could not necessarily repeat. But apart from these exceptional bargains, there is nowadays a steady trade in crude available on a long-term basis at sizeable (and up to the mid-sixties growing) discounts. This has occurred quite inevitably during a period in which, to quote Mr Gripaios again, 'it has not been expedient to reduce . . . postings, since 1960 in line with the deterioration of market prices'.[6] Various attempts have been made in recent years to record a steady run of these steadily discounted prices—for example by the European Coal-Steel Authority—and to rationalize the build-up of costs, taxes and profits that they now rest on. But what matters first is to accept that these discounted prices are representative of the only real international market for crude oil.

What, then, do posted prices for crude in the international market signify? And what purpose do they serve? These questions are not difficult to answer as regards the present time, and certain oil-exporting areas of the world. But even today the answers are not adequate everywhere. And it is a good deal less easy to define what these posted prices were and did in the past, and just how their function came to change.

Since 1960, in the Middle East, the meaning and purpose of posted prices for crude has been obvious for all to see: they are benchmarks for calculating host country royalties and taxes on the crude exported. This was recognized formally under the 'OPEC settlements' of early 1965, which *inter alia* reduced the companies' taxable income by fixed percentage discounts (declining progressively over a three-year period) from these posted prices. The discounted tax prices thus separated from postings were for the first time in the Middle East openly identified as 'tax reference prices'; but they remained defined by their relation to posted prices.

Another function that for years posted prices happened incidentally to fulfil, and which tax reference prices may often do from now on, is to dictate the foreign exchange transfers involved in the movement of crude oil across frontiers, whether it changes hands commercially or not. Declared c.i.f. values for imports of crude (and products) were for a long time generally based on these posted f.o.b. prices, plus long-term averaged values for freights (since the tanker movement might well be under the control of the same integrated company). These transfer prices, however, have always been open to query both by foreign exchange authorities and by the tax authorities interested in the profits or losses imputed to refining and marketing operations in consumer countries. In recent years, with posted prices becoming admittedly tax benchmarks at the producing end, a number of governments have been challenging these transfer prices.[7] These governments have been primarily those of consumer countries which are not the headquarters of integrated companies; but from time to time in the United States there have been suggestions that these transfer prices might be queried, and also the validity of foreign income taxes related abroad to price benchmarks rather than to prices in actual bargains done. The actual transfer prices used by companies may in fact depart from either posted or tax reference prices at the producing end. But where governments are in the habit of querying integrated transfer prices, the companies' international pricing departments like to have some outside reference prices to justify their figures.

These are the main functions now served by posted prices in the Middle East, Libya, and now Venezuela (which together account for about 75–80 per cent of the crude in world trade). In Algeria, from 1965 onwards, there is a tax reference prices agreed between two governments, and not formally related to the posted price of crude. In Indonesia and Nigeria the host government taxes related, formally at least, to the prices actually realized, not to posted prices at all (and up to the middle of 1966, they were in Venezuela too). Most of the crude moved under arm's-length sales from these countries also moves at large discounts off posted prices; but there may be one or two small exporters from which some actual small sales may be made at or near posted price. So in a few scattered niches of the world market, even now, posted prices could still have some vestigial linkage with the actual market. This was the situation at the turn of 1966; but it changes over time. There is no doubt that following Libya's lucrative example, all other exporters will now seek to move their tax basis up to posted instead of realized prices. In that case, these posted prices will increasingly take on the function they already serve for the Middle East majority of world crude exports.

But do posted prices for crude in some of these other countries, then, serve no purpose at all? (Unless, perhaps, to irritate their host governments, who inevitably consider prices actually realized in terms of the discount they involve off the prices posted?) The easiest way to answer this question would be to put the current condition of posted prices into perspective as the current stage of decay of a once realistic price structure. Most analysts would answer in that way, I think: indeed, discussion of the history of crude oil prices in the world market is quite heavily documented by now. And I think some brief tracing of that history cannot be dispensed with. But first it is worth noting that though posted prices are not crucial for the supply planning decisions of the integrated companies, they probably still have *some* interest and convenience for the companies. Not so much the absolute level of the posting or the tax reference price now tagged on below it; but the *relation* between these prices for different crudes. For in the Middle East and Libya, the government revenue per barrel will depend upon these prices; and since the cost charged for tax purposes can be taken as a datum, integrated choices between different crudes will be affected to some extent by the relationship between these prices, even if their absolute levels are unreal in market terms and perhaps no longer useful even as transfer prices internally. We have had evidence of this interest when the companies have taken their few opportunities, since Middle East crude postings became effectively frozen in 1960, of adjusting the differentials between these prices.

The 'structure' of these posted prices, when they were set and so long as they could be altered freely, was adjusted by the pricing departments of the integrated companies concerned in accordance with their export area's geographical position in relation of the markets where different crudes could be expected to compete; and in terms of their quality. Freight differentials between the loading points in the Persian Gulf are not very considerable (though they can still cause considerable argument whenever some company sets a posted price—and hence the government 'take'—for a new crude from a new terminal). And the freight differentials between the Middle East and their major competitors such as the North African crudes could be taken account of at the times, since 1960, when these North African crudes first had prices posted. Quality, and the values attached to it, can differ more widely between crudes from any given region—and these values can change over time.

Gravity, sulphur, waxiness, and a host of other elements in quality can affect refining costs and product quality, in so far as this affects the consumer's final choice between products. The assessment of quality differentials in this business is of necessity inherently difficult. The patterns of demand, for example the value put on light products as against heavier ones, differ from market to market: and in each market will probably change over time. So may the importance attached by consumers to particular qualities in oil products, for example sulphur in the smoke produced when power stations burn fuel oil. One might value each crude according to the value relative to other crudes placed upon it by a refiner in its 'natural market'. But at any time a refiner also has a range of possible processes (and costs) that he might apply to each crude or a combination of them; these processes change over time; and so may the tanker freights and potential competition from other crudes that might be taken to define the 'natural market' for any given crude. Until the advent of the computer, at any rate, it would seem to the outsider that determining quality differentials must have involved large elements of arbitrariness; otherwise, the reasoning could have become unendingly circular. The traditional 'gravity differentials' of about one or two U.S. cents per degree A.P.I. appear to have reflected demand and refining conditions in the United States as far back as the thirties. Internationally posted prices, at one time, were related to demand in refineries on the Eastern seaboard of the United States; and the quality differentials between them probably reflect too, vestigially, a slightly modernized version of that American pattern.

In mid-1961, when the Jersey group posted the first export price for Libyan crude, it set a price low in relation to those in the Middle East, after allowing for the savings in freight costs. Its Libyan crude is a light crude, yielding a lot of gasoline and comparatively little fuel oil. According to the traditional differential that values crudes according to gasoline yield (which still, broadly, holds good in the United States) it would have commanded a higher value than heavier crudes yielding larger proportions of the black oils. In the European market that it serves alongside Middle East crude, however, the most rapid growth at the time was in demand for fuel oils and middle distillates, with gasoline demand lagging behind. The levels of discount in the Middle East already reflected this, with light crude being discounted by much larger amounts than heavy ones. Jersey's posting for the Libyan crude could be rationalized in terms of these discounted prices—or in terms of a much lower than traditional differential for crude gravity, and one much more in line with the demand pattern of the market it was sold in.[8]

Nearly four years later, when the major companies agreed to expense royalties providing that they were allowed a discount off posted prices for the purposes of taxes in certain OPEC member countries, the same principle came in again. The rate of 'OPEC discount' was set in relation to one particular crude of a given gravity, for the year 1964. For 1965 and again for 1966, this average discount for tax purposes, was reduced slightly, thus slightly increasing the government's average tax per barrel on the crudes concerned. But only the particular 'base' crude was given exactly this average reduction in discount. For all the other crudes concerned, correction factors were applied according to their A.P.I. gravity, in relation to the gravity of the crude taken as a base for the calculation. And these correction factors—affecting the government revenue involved and thus did matter to the integrated companies—

tended to reduce the advantage that the posted prices on which taxes were formerly set had given to light crudes against heavy ones. Somewhat tortuously, this did adjust the gravity differential, as it affected government revenues per barrel, rather more into line with the value that the crude market was currently attaching to light as against heavy crudes.[9]

This concern that posted prices, whatever their absolute level, should have some justifiable relation to one another in terms of quality (and of declining freight costs as tankers get steadily more super) is thus not illogical so long as postings ultimately affect government 'take' and what the integrated companies think of as 'tax paid cost'. Nevertheless, there is allied with the current logic some tradition (and perhaps some hope that these prices may eventually again bear a more realistic relation to the market). This is where a brief glance at the history may not come amiss.

HISTORY AND OIL PRICES

Originally, the prices posted in the international market—for products and later, as some trade developed in it, for crude—were set in what the companies posting them considered a realistic relationship to one another. Some of these prices, for example in Venezuela, were prices at which a sizeable volume of arm's-length trading was probably done (though it seems doubtful whether this trading had much influence on the prices posted, and in some of these bargains the actual prices differed from the postings). Other posted prices, notably some of those in the Middle East, seem from the beginning to have been posted primarily to set royalty and tax benchmarks. But there is not the slightest reason to doubt that these too were set as realistically as possible in relation to the others. Any integrated and decentralized company, trying to run its business efficiently, will always prefer to have the transfer prices that it uses between different departments and affiliates as self-consistent as possible, and as logically linked to the other prices that competitors may be using. So the 'posted price structure' of international oil was originally as closely linked to 'competitive market reality' as the pricing departments of the integrated companies could make it.

'Competitive market reality' was not too easy to identify in the international oil business in say the thirties. But the companies in hindsight, and outside students of the industry analysing prices since, have generally been able to explain or rationalize that price structure, as it developed in the early years, in terms of the quality and freight relation ships that different supplies available around the world bore to demand patterns and supply prices in the dominant market that could be taken to set the pattern. Up to the Second World War, this market was the United States. Even though proration was already being invoked to try to control production in line with 'market demand at prevailing prices there', competition was not absent from its market. Outside, the international market was less competitive: it was seeking, with varying success, also to control output, the development of new reserves, and prices. But the decision of the companies concerned to link such prices as they quoted or posted around the world with the United States as a 'basing point' was not unreasonable. Even given much more atomistic competition in the world market, the United States might well have been dominant in setting price levels (even, too, if proration had tended to keep up the price levels it set).

During the past thirty years that linkage, so far as published prices are concerned, was first attenuated and then finally abandoned. But the prices were never fully adjusted to demand patterns in what became the marginal markets of the international market—Western Europe and Japan—or to the costs of the emerging marginal supply area, the Middle East. The adjustment began and continued, albeit slowly, during the fifties. But posted prices were never adjusted downward as far as actual discounts generally available in the market: partly perhaps because the integrated companies dominating production internationally refused to accept these discounts as representative, but partly too because they were uneasy about adjusting government revenues per barrel too far downwards, too. After their price changes in 1960 provoked so much government indignation and the formation of OPEC, they ceased to adjust posted prices at all. The actual prices paid in arm's-length transactions continued on down; and latterly, even the transfer prices within integrated companies seem to have been moved down too. But commitment to these tax benchmark prices of one kind and another, plus an understandable reluctance to accept that discounts would become as large generally as they now have done, has delayed any formal recognition of the newer international price structure that is perhaps now gradually crystallizing out.

For many years American postings for crude oil and the prices for products reported from the 'spot' market at the United States Gulf represented not only the nearest thing to an atomistically 'free' market in the oil business anywhere, thin market though this was. This was also the market that set the price at which American products or crude oil became available to the rest of the world, and set a ceiling to the prices at which producers or refiners anywhere else could sell oil to the United States: the point of commercial contact between the world's largest oil producing area, and market, and the rest of the world oil business. Up to the late twenties the United States was, moreover, the main 'marginal supplier' of crude or products. As such, the prices ruling in it could logically be used to set a ceiling over the world price of crude oil and of products. It was not possible to sell oil to anybody anywhere in the world for more than the price at the United States Gulf plus the cost of moving it to the market concerned, which there were independent buyers and sellers ready to do. Texas had a large surplus of oil for export: whether or not it was the cheapest supplier of a single cargo at any one time, it tended until the thirties at least to be the cheapest dependable supplier from which buyers anywhere in the world could count on large and continuing supplies.

How long it would in practice have remained so is a matter of argument. From the late twenties to the mid-thirties the world oil market was in a state of surplus, with large amounts of existing capacity 'shut in' for lack of buyers, and prolific new fields such as East Texas and eastern Venezuela coming in to swell potential supplies. By the mid-thirties Venezuela was producing about 9 per cent of world oil output and exporting virtually the whole of this, supplying perhaps 40 per cent of the world export trade in oil, only slightly less than the United States. The major oil groups, at this time, were attempting to consolidate agreements to control most current production, to keep the development of new oil areas such as the Middle East 'orderly', and to limit price competition in many markets throughout the world, with varying degrees of success. The thirties in oil, indeed, had much in common with the sixties. And much of what the major companies tried, not altogether successfully, to achieve by agreement was not dissimilar to what some oil-producing 'host governments' would like to have happen today.

One thing these agreements did achieve, however, was generally to maintain 'Gulf plus' as the basis for the delivered price of oil almost everywhere in the world. No marketer, regardless of any agreements, could have got more for his oil than the c.i.f. price at which comparable oil could have been delivered from Texas. The question as the thirties wore on was whether in circumstances of unbridled competition buyers everywhere need have paid as much as 'Gulf plus'. At the beginning of the thirties, with oil running to waste in East Texas at ten cents a barrel, this was a very low price indeed, but by the late thirties it had become a fairly high one in relation to the cost of oil from, say, Venezuela or Rumania. The development of conservation in Texas and other parts of the United States, 'pro-rationing' output in most cases into line with 'market demand' as well as with efficient production of the oilfields concerned, soon tended if only incidentally to stabilize American oil prices at a pretty respectable level compared with the giveaway prices of a few years before. As the major international groups, in setting prices abroad according to the 'Gulf plus' principle, used freight rates reckoned according to long-term averages, rather than the often wildly fluctuating spot rates for single voyages, this element in world oil prices too became relatively stable. (Moreover, by the mid-thirties international tanker schemes were in operation which also tended to keep freight rates fairly steady.) The general world price level for oil, though here and there discounts or price-cutting could make it cheaper, was thus set by these companies on a logical, but also relatively high and stable basis. For most non-American markets, moreover, the potential suppliers from Texas or the Caribbean would have been some of the same international companies: these had no incentive to undercut themselves.

Moreover, the international groups had even less incentive than integrated companies operating in the United States to compete in ways that would push down the general level of prices in final markets. They were, clearly, in a situation of 'oligopoly'—that is, of competition between a few sellers, as distinct on the one hand from single-firm monopoly and on the other from the 'perfect competition' of many sellers in the market. Smaller independent operators existed; but at no stage of the integrated world oil trade were these as important as they were in the oil industry of the United States. Each major group, moreover, sold oil in many places; could press, but equally was vulnerable, on many fronts. Under conditions of oligopoly, action to alter price or rates of output by any one of them was certain to affect the general balance of the market for all the others. Each international group had to consider that if it cut the price of oil, its competitors would almost certainly match the cut and possibly cut further; so its initial decisions involved deciding how to react to the reactions that its move would be likely to provoke. This situation of oligopoly is frequently present in oil marketing. But for the international companies it existed on a wider than national scale. Price cutting to put pressure on a competitor in one market might bring pressure in return in some other part of the world where that competitor happened to be better placed.

Like marketers in the United States, the international groups were occasionally disposed to embark on price competition to enter some new market: but the thirties had seen a series of truces to some extremely painful price wars in international oil, which those remaining in the trade were not anxious to renew. They were not quite universally able to get landed prices for all products corresponding to the delivered price from the Gulf of Texas. But the prices of oil products from export refineries throughout the world, in general, did correspond, after allowing for the costs of transport, with the cost of supplies laid down from the United States Gulf; and later, as the main source of exports shifted to Venezuela, from the Caribbean. The companies supplied each market throughout the world from the source that gave them the best net return, considering local production and refining costs, the cost of transport and insurance to market areas, and their tax situations at all points. But consumers at any one place in the world paid the same wherever the oil came from. This 'single basing point system' of pricing meant that suppliers from elsewhere than the base area got different 'netbacks', or proceeds at source, according to where they sold the oil.

Up to the Second World War, it should be noted, world trade in oil was basically a trade in petroleum products. Comparatively little crude oil was shipped across oceans: it was generally accepted as more economical to process oil near its source in big refineries, and to ship the products, which were higher in value, had less waste in them and did not necessitate the later 'cross-hauling' of products that local refineries' markets might not be able to consume. The only really large-scale movement of crude by sea was originally not international but coastwise. This was from the producing areas bounding the U.S. Gulf to the great market-oriented refining centres in the north-east United States such as New Jersey.

During the thirties there was a shift in this Western hemisphere pattern of trade, through considerations of integrated return rather than of availability or of open price competition. Oil was in surplus and cheap in Texas: but output of crude and refined products was mounting in the Caribbean, with a much higher output per well and hence lower physical costs of production than in the United States. The Caribbean crude terminals and export refineries are somewhat nearer by sea to the north-east seaboard of the United States than those on the U.S. Gulf. (Eventually, too, the fact that coastwise shipping around the U.S.A. had to pay U.S. maritime labour rates became a considerable factor in comparative transport costs.) American companies with access to their own oil at cost in Venezuela, but which were for various reasons obliged to purchase a good deal of any supplies they used inside the United States at posted prices from other producers, began to use this alternative source of supply to serve markets to which Venezuelan oil involved lower transport costs and a better profit margin than they could get from the same delivered price by moving more Texan oil. These markets included Western Europe and Latin America, served almost entirely with refined products: but also the north-east United States, where Venezuelan crude began to be supplied to the main refining centres.

A $10\frac{1}{2}$ cent duty was imposed on crude imported into the United States in the early thirties: this did not limit the flow of oil from the Caribbean, but it did slightly reduce the price that the supplier could realize for his crude there. The netback value of Caribbean crude oil could be no higher than the price of comparable oil shipped from the U.S. Gulf to eastern seaboard refineries less the duty, and less the freight from the Caribbean to the same refineries. Effectively, when prices began to be posted at ports in the Caribbean, these differed from U.S. Gulf prices by virtually the amount of the American duty. Higher duties on products such as gasoline confined the trade in products from the Caribbean to the United States to fuel oil, which it did not pay American refiners to manufacture and for which some Venezuelan heavy crudes were particularly suitable.

While the United States was ready to absorb all the crude oil on offer at prices based on delivery from the Texas Gulf, there was no reason for any international marketer to accept less than a corresponding 'netback' price anywhere in the world. During and after the war, at the same time as certain European and other consuming countries were founding or enlarging their own local refining industries, United States imports (also mainly of crude for 'market-centred' refining there) began to increase. In spite of a considerable and continuing export of particular oil products, the United States demand for crude rose faster than the capacity of its facilities for moving crude to refining centres, and there were indeed scares about a shortage of production capacity. The world's largest producer of and market for oil swung over in the late forties from being a net exporter to a net importer of oil. And a new source of cheap crude was now growing in importance on the world oil map. At the end of the forties, the United States as well as Europe began to import growing quantities of crude oil from the Middle East.

The major international companies after the war faced a rapidly rising demand for oil products in Western Europe, which was unable to pay in dollars. They were short of refining capacity anywhere to meet the postwar growth in demand, and particularly of conveniently-located capacity. They were also short of tankers—and the growth of domestic demand in the United States was beginning to make larger demands on the tanker tonnage available. In terms of supply possibilities, political expediency and of dollar shortage, at the time, the solution chosen was logical: to supply Western markets with Middle East oil, and to supply it as crude for refining in Europe, not as products.

Before the war Persian oil was exported, mainly to Near and Far Eastern markets, as products from Abadan. Iraq oil was piped to the Mediterranean and Persian Gulf, was exported partly as products from coastal refinery terminals, and partly as crude to certain countries in Europe such as Italy and France that had already developed some local refineries. Oil had still to be exported in significant commercial quantities from Saudi Arabia or Kuwait. It was not until after the war that two of the largest American majors, Standard Oil of New Jersey and Socony-Vacuum (as it was then) bought their way into Aramco, enhancing the financial resources available for development of Saudi Arabian oil and giving it access to considerably more widespread markets than its original owners, Standard Oil of California and the Texas Company, possessed outside the United States. Large-scale purchasing contracts between Standard Oil of New Jersey and Socony-Vacuum respectively and B.P., and between Royal Dutch/Shell and Gulf, similarly offered Kuwait oil access to world markets.

Before the war, no prices had ever been posted at export terminals in the Middle East, for products or for crude oil. Purchasers of oil from this region, even when they were located close to the Persian Gulf itself, paid the same landed price that they would have done for oil from the United States. This meant that the effective values obtained for any given oil at Middle East terminals varied according to how far away the customers who bought particular shipments were. If the distance to a given market from the Middle East was less than the distance from the U.S.

Gulf to the same point, a 'Gulf plus freight' price to the customer charged him a margin of 'phantom freight', and gave the Middle East supplier a higher realized value at source than the Gulf price. If oil from the Middle East were moved farther to supply any given market than oil from the U.S. Gulf would have had to have been, the Middle East supplier had to 'absorb freight' and accept a lower netback value than the Gulf f.o.b. level. Given the pattern of the world oil markets and of ownership among the international suppliers this system could be considered logical: it bore rather hard upon customers located near, say, Abadan, but these had a low demand and little bargaining power. It can be argued that the international majors, within this basing point system, were prolonging the 'tenure' of the U.S. Gulf as the single basing point. But the Middle East, up to the beginning of the war, was supplying under five per cent of world exports and was hardly significant enough to form the nucleus of any new pricing pattern.

During the Second World War, however, Middle East oil deliveries to Europe were cut for lack of tanker tonnage, and though deliveries east of Suez rose in volume, total sales were held down. Moreover, suppliers in the Persian Gulf had to deal on a very large scale with two 'nearby' customers of very considerable bargaining power, the British and United States navies. The British Treasury, it turned out, was not prepared to pay for bunker supplies at Abadan what it would have had to pay for fuel oil shipped from refineries in Texas: after much argument it agreed to pay f.o.b. prices in the Persian Gulf at the same level as prices published in the Gulf of Mexico. The United States Navy, buying products (and later crude for lend-lease purposes) from Bahrein and Saudi Arabia, was indeed none too satisfied with an f.o.b. price identical to that in the U.S. Gulf; but it did eventually accept this level.

The quotation of specific prices to customers, at Persian Gulf terminals, as against identical delivered prices in every market regardless of where the oil came from, altered the pattern of delivered prices and established a 'natural' market area for Middle East oil—the area to which at prevailing freight rates Middle East crude and products could be delivered more cheaply than oil from the Gulf of Mexico. The westward limit of that area, a 'watershed' between the markets to which it paid the supplier best to ship Middle East rather than Western hemisphere oil, at the level of freights then ruling, was in the region of Italy. With prices equal at each source or 'basing point', it would not theoretically have paid to ship Middle East oil farther west into Europe. But the net cost of this oil, as distinct from its price, was potentially very low providing output could be stepped up; the world was short of crude oil; Europe was short of dollars and was building market-oriented refineries in order to reduce the dollar outgoings on its growing oil imports.

As the European affiliates of international oil companies began to bring these local refineries into commission, their parent companies began to ship large volumes of crude from the Middle East for the first time. On the bulk of their transactions, the quotations in the Persian Gulf were no more than transfer prices to these major groups. While the price at source was identical with Western hemisphere oil, the net integrated cost of moving this Middle East oil to Western Europe was lower, and the dollar element in it—which mattered a lot then to European customers—could be held down. So the majors delivered the Middle East oil as far as it paid them, well beyond the 'watershed' of the market area based on those Persian Gulf quotations, and customers were glad to have it.

This was a period when posted prices in the United States were rising rapidly in a period of shortage after the removal of oil price controls, and Venezuelan postings were being increased in line with them. The Middle East quotations—which were not, in the earliest postwar years, 'posted prices' offered to all comers, but notifications by telegram to existing customers—were raised several times too, but rather less than proportionately. This made the quoted prices of Middle East crude and products steadily cheaper in relation to prices in the Caribbean. The prices quoted in the Persian Gulf were then not necessarily set at the same levels by all companies, or changed simultaneously. But as these prices generally became cheaper in relation to those in the Western hemisphere, the 'watershed' where delivered prices became equal moved westward across Europe.

By 1948, the point of equalization of delivered prices from the two hemispheres was the United Kingdom. During that year the Middle East quotations were cut somewhat, taking into account the lower freight rates from Venezuela than from the U.S. Gulf, which when equalized at the U.K. 'netted back' a rather lower price to the Persian Gulf. But by the end of that year certain majors were in fact moving large volumes of Middle East crude into the United States: once again they were 'absorbing freight' on a significant scale, and selling farther west than their Middle East quotations plus freights would in theory have permitted. The European Co-operation Administration at this time was zealous in its determination not to pay higher prices for the crude oil that it was often financing for West European countries than any other substantial buyer was effectively obtaining for regular supplies. Partly perhaps to satisfy representations from this agency, Middle East prices were again reduced during 1949, in two steps; by September, 1949, the equalization point for 'delivered price competition' between Middle East and Caribbean crude had become the eastern seaboard of the United States.[10]

Middle East prices did not begin to be formally 'posted' for deliveries to all comers until 1950, when Socony began posting prices for 'free on board' sales of oil from Ras Tanura in Arabia, Qatar and Tripoli (terminal of one of the larger Iraq pipelines, then not long completed). Within a short time all the other major companies were doing the same. This shift to publicly posted prices coincided with, and eventually became linked with, a shift in the financial arrangements between these companies and the host governments of the Middle East: the replacement of fixed royalties per ton or barrel of oil by income taxes which were set to give the host governments 50 per cent of the profit shown on Middle East oil. For the first time in most of these countries, the governments acquired a direct interest in Middle East oil prices. So even at the outset, some of the Middle East prices were posted primarily as benchmarks for tax purposes.

The posted prices in which these governments became newly interested, during the fifties, moved parallel with though below those in the Western hemisphere. American crude prices rose in 1953, and the international companies increased Venezuelan and Middle East posted prices in line with them. There were rises in American and Venezuelan prices in 1956–57, owing to the Suez crisis, when deliveries of Middle East oil were sharply reduced because the Canal was cut; and when supplies were resumed, Middle East crude was put up too. This increase, once again, was less than proportionate to the increases that had taken place for Western hemisphere crudes. Anyone still inclined to use the netback pricing formula to explain this in terms of a unified oil market in the free world could argue that the 'equalization point' of delivered prices was being pushed still farther westwards, and that Middle East oil was competing inland, within the oil market of the United States mid-continent. But in practice 'nobody figured it that close'.[11] Oil demand and supply, and the facilities required, were roughly by balance in the mid-fifties, apart from interruptions such as the Suez incident, and it was no longer advisable to push up posted prices upon which there was growing pressure for discounts strictly in accordance with any theoretical formula. The next rise, in Venezuela in late 1957, was not matched in the United States or the Middle East. In 1959, a cut in prices was initiated in West Texas and followed first in Venezuela and later in the Middle East; then there was a further adjustment in Venezuela. At the beginning of 1960, another small cut in Texas was not followed elsewhere, though discounts on posted prices for crude were becoming general in independent deals in the world market. And on 9th August, 1960, a unilateral cut in Middle East prices was made, and followed nowhere else. International oil prices were ceasing to be explainable in terms of netback pricing formulae linking the prices in different producing centres. More and more crude was being moved at discounts off the prices formally 'posted'; and as experience ever since 1960 has showed, the international companies seem understandably uneasy about adjusting posted prices on which government tax revenues depend according to the real circumstances of the world market. They have never formally abandoned their contractual right to set and change these prices, freely and alone. In early 1965 they managed to achieve a discount off these prices for tax purposes—though very modest discounts in relation to those they were in fact having to concede directly or indirectly in the world market. But these discounts were only part of a deal on the expensing of royalties. Achieving them did not reduce the companies' payments to governments. It simply cost them less in tax than they would have had to pay otherwise.

It is difficult for the outside observer to know quite what to make of these 'netback' rationalizations of oil pricing. They have been critically questioned by both oil consumers and oil-producing governments; nor have most of the companies that first advanced them in order to explain the common factors that affect and link up oil prices around the world recently been keen to discuss them in great detail. Originally these formulae were offered to various investigating committees as *post-hoc* rationalizations of the companies' pricing behaviour, rather than as specific explanations of how decisions about prices were in fact made as market conditions changed. Obviously in setting a price any marketer has to consider the cost of supplies from other sources. But posted prices in the world oil market were prices set in markets where arm's-length deals were the exception: and though offered to all comers, in practice they served mainly to set transfer prices between producing and refining affiliates of the same international groups. They were not simply matters of book-keeping, in the postwar era: they determined the amounts of particular currencies that had to be transferred between affiliates of the groups in different countries, and later they became the determinants of taxable income in producing countries. But they were 'administered prices' set by corporate decisions for particular reasons, mainly tax, rather than prices emerging from market bargaining: comparatively few independent bargains for Middle East oil at any rate can ever have been made exactly at posted prices.

Shaikh Abdullah Tariki complained in 1960[12] that the international companies, over the decade from 1949 to 1959, had posted Middle East crude prices lower than was necessary, so that the host countries' share of profits from those prices was unnecessarily depressed. He proceeded from the point that while the Middle East postings for crude were being brought down, in stages, by comparison with the Western hemisphere, product prices in Western Europe and other major markets were not. This was broadly true: the list prices for products in Europe until say the mid-fifties did remain approximately in line with 'Caribbean parity' —i.e., what it would have cost to import them from export refineries in the Caribbean—and discounts off list prices, in circumstances of shortage, were not granted at all generally. When crude postings were brought down in the Middle East, therefore, the refinery margins available to the major's European affiliates—and to independent refiners there—must have widened. Western consumer countries welcomed this because it cut import costs and saved foreign exchange, and gave them a better return on the very heavy investment in new refineries in their countries. To the representative of a Middle East producer government such as Shaikh Abdullah, however, the process appeared as one of siphoning off profits into tanker or refining companies at the expense of profits on Middle East production.

Shaikh Abdullah's main argument about the netback formula was that the equalization point for delivered prices of Eastern and Western hemisphere crudes should never have been changed from London to the United States in 1949. This shift, certainly, was used to explain lower Middle East postings for crude—and to widen markets for this crude. What the shift really signified was that in terms of net integrated return it paid the companies enormously to widen the markets for this crude—which was potentially far the cheapest in the world, once full advantage could be taken of the enormous productivity of the Middle East fields. Shaikh Abdullah felt the relative cuts were never justified, since the American market was absorbing no more, in 1949, than 10 per cent of Middle East crude exports. To the impartial observer, the American market, from 1949 until, say, 1955, could nevertheless have been argued to be—at that time—the marginal market for crude from any source in the world. And the companies used these pricing formulae, after all, to 'simulate' the conditions that might have applied in a freely competitive market, in order to assist the sensible allocation of resources between 'departments' of large international companies in conditions where such competition was largely lacking. To bring published prices into line with a sensible resource allocation in such circumstances—i.e., the movement of oil as far as it paid the companies in terms of 'net integrated cost'—it would be logical to set them the highest prices at which this marginal market, given effective competition, would have continued to soak up all the additional crude on offer, even if it was not yet taking vast amounts from any given source. In a competitive market that price could not have exceeded the price at which domestic crude could be delivered to the U.S. East Coast. There was no need to set published prices any lower, since that would have established a more attractive margin, freely on offer, to refiners competing with the internationally integrated groups. So according to the netback pricing formulae, which Shaikh Abdullah accepted and used, equalization at the eastern seaboard of the United States may have been rational enough.

The United States is still, today, the largest single importer of crude oil and the only one still importing large quantities from both Venezuela and the Middle East. But it is no longer possible to suggest that it remains the marginal market for imported crude, from anywhere except perhaps Canada and Mexico; no other crude is imported freely. For since 1958, the informal American restrictions on oil imports have been made statutory, limiting imports to quotas determined by administrative decision regardless of price (however formed and however competitive). It is effectively insulated from the effects of price in the world market. In these deliberately altered circumstances, Shaikh Abdullah's contention that Western Europe ought to be taken as the marginal market for Middle East crude for the setting of posted prices became more reasonable. But the Western consumer of oil could draw some very different conclusions about the 'right price' of oil from this same set of premises.

For Shaikh Abdullah, in late 1960, suggested that the price to use in London, if this were re-adopted as an equalization point, ought to be the delivered price at which oil from the Caribbean could be landed there. The posted price that he suggested for the Middle East was such a price in London less freights from the Persian Gulf—in practice some

60 cents more than the posted prices ruling there at the time he spoke. A consumer's reaction in Western Europe might be to ask, 'Why base the price on Western hemisphere crude oil at all? The chance of importing it might set a ceiling to crude prices here. But why should we accept it as a floor?' For by 1960, not much Venezuelan crude, apart from cargoes of a few grades specially imported for lubricating oils and bitumen, was reaching the European market. And independent buyers there could already get petroleum products and crude, from the Middle East and elsewhere, at bargain prices quite unrelated to 'Caribbean parity'. Ever since, the bargains have gone on improving; and though by 1965 there were some signs of a slight hardening in product prices, only some very sanguine oilmen were prepared to argue that the downward trend had been more than temporarily checked.

NEED PRICES REFLECT COSTS?

Consumers' criticism of the prices they have had to pay for Middle East crude oil and the products refined from it in the largest market for both of these, Western Europe, have always harked back upon an element that is generally missing from any discussion of these prices among producing interests—the cost of the crude oil. Oil industry spokesmen have tended to scout this approach. And they have objected, often quite reasonably, to calculations of cost from published figures of posted prices, of the volume of exports, and of government revenues, when these are put forward by consumers as the basis from which the final price of oil products 'ought' to be built up—just as they object to the calculations about profits on production that can be made from these. Mr R. A. R. Pattman of Shell once[13] described suggestions that the 'right price' for Middle East oil ought to be based on production cost plus some 'fair and reasonable' profit figure as comparable with 'one of those fantastic arithmetical problems ending with "What was the name of the engine driver?" ' And obviously, consumers cannot expect prices to be set in any industry according to some arbitrary judgment of what profits are 'just'. In any business transaction, prices depend upon the balance of bargaining power on each side of the table, which depends mainly on the alternative supplies or markets open to the buyer and seller.

In the immediate postwar years there were virtually no alternative supplies on offer to buyers of oil in the international market. (There were not in any case many independent buyers of crude; mostly, the customers were buying products.) During the whole period up to the placing of statutory restrictions on oil imports into the United States it could be argued plausibly that if the buyer in Europe did not want to pay the posted prices that the majors asked for Middle East crude and the products refined from it, there were customers in the United States who would. And the customer in Europe, be he one of the few independent refiners in business or, farther removed, the ultimate consumer, could not then get large and continuing supplies any cheaper from elsewhere. The alternative source for large-scale imports was the Caribbean, where costs were higher. Moreover, a customer had to deal there largely with the same set of international suppliers, who had no reason to undercut themselves and logical reasons, set out before, for not undercutting each other. But while the market was tight, independent suppliers from Venezuela would not have supplied oil to Europe any cheaper, either, than they could sell it in the United States—where the level of prices was supported largely by pro-rationing by state authorities.

There is nothing sinister about such a market situation as this, though consumers may not enjoy it. Nor does it wholly arise out of conditions of oligopoly among suppliers, though these conditions probably did tend to delay adjustments of price to changing market circumstances. In any market, however atomistically competitive, any new supplier whose costs are particularly low, and whose circumstances are immune from being matched by competitors, is likely for a time to reap the 'economic rent' of his specially advantageous circumstances. For a time he will obtain whatever price the total supplies available in the market can be sold for. He can reduce his price to increase his share of the market, but would be unwise to do this faster than he can build up output to supply the increase his reduced prices can capture. Until he is in a position to supply the whole of the market if necessary, his costs will not dictate the ruling price: this will be set by the highest-cost producer required to meet total demand. But in a fully competitive market it would pay the low-cost producer to increase output as fast and far as he can, driving the highest-cost producers out. Middle East crude supplies to the world market expanded very rapidly in the postwar decade— as fast, perhaps, as refineries could be built to process the oil. Even so, this area took several years to become the dominant supplier in world trade, and it was never permitted to become the marginal and dominant supplier of the United States market. This was prevented primarily by the United States governmental system, federal and state. But it must be remembered that this protection of the highest-cost production in the United States, in its various forms, yielded the American groups among the international majors very high domestic profits, pretty moderately taxed. Even had the United States market been left open, these circumstances might have reduced their advantage from replacing domestic with foreign crude. Western European governments, too, had indigenous fuel industries to protect; and no great desire to boost too fast imports with a high dollar content. And the few major international companies, who largely controlled the total oil supplies from anywhere in the early postwar years, had no reason to change too fast either.

As the supply of Middle East oil was expanded, bringing its marginal costs down, its prices, in relation to those of higher-cost areas, came down too—but more slowly and less far than competition between many smaller operators in the market might perhaps have brought them. So Middle East producers earned an economic rent—indeed, what might be called the richest economic rent of all time. And by the time the 50:50 deals were finally completed and adjusted, the companies were committed to share the main benefits from this economic rent with the host governments, which gave the lucky landlords an equally strong interest in maintaining the ruling prices of oil. But within a few years, the obvious size of that economic rent was attracting in fresh competitors. And even among the major companies controlling the low-cost oil, some were more tempted than others to cut prices more and increase sales faster. More and more, the rent—for the companies—was being reduced. The very comfortable return earned at this time on integrated oil operations as a whole, though shown mainly at the production stage, had tempted many newcomers to try to break into the enclave of special advantage enjoyed in an area of low-cost oil. And once alternative suppliers arrive on the scene, and begin to achieve access to crude of comparable cost, allowing for freight advantage—for example in Libya —then questions from the consuming end about costs become quite relevant. And the question of what return is 'fair and reasonable' ceases to be a fantastic problem. The return any supplier can secure will be largely determined by what other producers enjoying similar costs will accept.

This competition made itself felt in the late fifties at the point where all oil finally changes hands, in real rather than notional sales—in the market for products. Ultimately, this is where the price of oil is set: the effective value of crude can be no more than whatever can be realized for the range of products refined from it, less the cost and return on capital required for distribution, refining, and transport from the source.

Product prices, in theory, bear a similar relationship to one another in the different regions of the world market to those of crude; but they are not all quoted in the same way. In Western Europe, almost without exception, the only prices quoted are delivered zonal prices; ex-refinery prices are not posted. Relatively and now in absolute volume, the amounts of refined products actually imported to Europe have dropped since the war, as the continent has switched over to local refineries. In some of these countries the schedules of wholesale prices are still set broadly in accordance with landed prices calculated for products delivered from export refineries in the Caribbean (or in some countries from the United States Gulf) assumed to be at posted f.o.b. prices plus long-term averages of freights. But there were no European markets left by the early sixties where such prices could in practice be realized for all products from all customers.

The Caribbean certainly remains the world's largest exporter of refined products, and in particular of fuel oil. Quite a large quantity of products, even after the very low levels of freight in the late fifties had reduced Venezuela's advantage over the Middle East in distance, continue to be moved across the Atlantic to Europe. Middle East refineries, such as Abadan, send some products, though in much smaller quantities, through the Suez Canal to a few markets in Europe; but their main markets are in the countries bordering on the Indian Ocean. The Far Eastern refineries in Borneo and Indonesia supply mainly nearby markets; most of the larger Far Eastern markets, notably Japan, have become large customers for Middle East crude since the war. These export refining centres, therefore, are still relevant in the supply pattern of products for certain markets. Until the mid-sixties, as noted above, actual prices for products in some of these areas did not fall so far below prices posted internationally as in Europe or Japan—particularly when the customers were developing countries without much bargaining power. But that has led to pressure for local refining, to avoid suffering from price discrimination—or the suspicion of it. So more and more markets are becoming broadly self-sufficient in refining capacity. Even their balancing exports and imports move within the same marketing region, for the most part.

It is still possible to argue that the Caribbean could be called on as the ultimate source of supply for some refined products, at times when demand was out of balance with the yield of refining capacity in Western

Europe—though at the beginning of the sixties some people feared or hoped that Russia might later take its place. So the possibility of importing more products from the Caribbean, if necessary, may set a ceiling to the prices that could be charged for all products. But in practice the pattern of market demand upon Caribbean refineries was very different from the pattern of demand in Europe. And product prices related to each other roughly in accordance with what would give a refiner in the Caribbean a reasonable margin do not necessarily do so for the refiner in an area with a different pattern of demand. Over the last decade, in Western Europe, demand has been strongest for middle distillates, at times, for fuel often, for naphtha (at very low prices) occasionally. Growth slackened off most for gasoline—which in accordance with Western hemisphere rules is the high-priced product marking the largest contribution to refining margins. These margins, in parts of Europe, have been further squeezed when price competition in 'dealer gasoline', as well as in all other products, began soon after 1955 and after the Suez interruption became quite bitter. The entry of North African oil in the early sixties has increased the number of producers ready to offer crude at bargain prices to such independent refiners as exist. And in most markets by now, though not all, these independent refiners can get fairly ready access to the final consumer with products cheaper than affiliates of the majors like to sell them.

The effect of this widespread discounting has been that in Western Europe, regardless of the official delivered prices reflecting roughly the Caribbean or United States Gulf prices plus freights, the actual level of product prices can reflect the pattern and strength of actual demand and the extent to which suppliers other than the established marketers have penetrated any given markets. The 'cost of entry'—investment in terminals, storage and the building of stations or financial inducements to dealers—is often high, and in some markets entry is legally restricted in one way or another. But some major companies themselves have been determinedly giving bigger and bigger rebates, either to get a bigger share of the business or to make the competition too hot for smaller fry. The pattern that has emerged reflects European demand perforce better than prices related according to Caribbean formulae could ever do; it has also been far more erosive of refining margins for any refining affiliate that still has to pay posted prices for crude. The wholesale price of gasoline has been pushed down in all European markets, though in some more than others; this one might have expected in a region where demand for gasoline was weaker, relative to other products, than in the

Western hemisphere. But the price of fuel oil, for which demand was rising so much more strongly, did not harden as independent refiners might have wished. In practice large imports of fuel oil have been on offer, at distress prices, from other regions, such as the Caribbean and the U.S.S.R. (partly because this is one of the cheaper markets to penetrate). But fuel oil, in any case, has to compete with other fuels, often while bearing quite heavy duties. And the price of crude sets an effective ceiling to fuel oil prices: if the price went much higher, it would pay to burn crude as such.

COMPETITIVE PRICES EMERGE

Whether any logically unified pattern of actual prices for petroleum products would emerge in Western Europe, and if so what it would be, was a matter of major controversy inside and to some extent outside the oil industry from the early fifties onwards. The number of people inside the industry who are prepared to agree that 'Caribbean plus' or 'United States Gulf plus' no longer make much sense in Europe has been growing as the years go by. But even those most anxious to get rid of this formula have differed about what kind of price structure should replace it.

There was a growing body of opinion in Europe, among the better-informed consumers and some governments, in favour of a structure of published prices in Europe related to actual demand there—as the actual prices paid have perforce become related in most European markets. This might imply the publication of prices at actual refineries in Europe reflecting the kind of realistically discounted price for Middle East crude that large-scale buyers (for example the Japanese) can regularly get and are regularly publishing; term charter freights; and some reasonable margin for a European refiner producing the yield of products that European consumers actually want. Caribbean prices for certain products might certainly continue to set a theoretical ceiling; but the 'low' of the range should come from some such new formula. Indeed, one would expect Caribbean prices to respond to those built up from Middle East going prices for crude, rather than the other way round.

In practice, by the mid-sixties, the new price structure was coming into being, for products as well as for crude. What was still lacking was any systematic reporting of the bargains being made. The petroleum press was picking up quite a number of these. But in Europe, this scattered information could not be cited with any of the authority that the main price reporting services carry in the United States. European authorities concerned with fuel continued to talk of 'price transparency' as a growing need in the market: they were less agreed on how to achieve it. But adequately reported or not, the prices in European bargains reflect Europe's pattern of demand. And this demand for petroleum products is exerted upon European refineries processing imported crude. The prices set by demand, supply and bargaining power in these local markets seem to the consumer more logical than any price reflecting conditions in distant markets, even if all the regional markets in the world oil trade continue to overlap at the fringes.

The development of product prices geared to European market conditions, however, must necessarily reflect back upon the prices of the crude oil from which those products are processed. Indeed, the effective price of crude will be what can be obtained in final markets for the products made from it; less a refining margin including a return based on the opportunity cost of capital at similar risk elsewhere; less tanker freights adequate to cover costs in modern large vessels plus a similar return—say, the long-term charter rate. And this is where the costs of developing and producing crude do come in. For it will presumably pay a producing company with large proven reserves to accept any price that will yield it a return on developing and producing those reserves comparable with what it can get from projects of comparable risk elsewhere. In an arm's-length sale, the price will be a price for crude oil. For an integrated company, the prices it will have to accept are for products. The costs, including return on capital, that it will have to cover will include marketing, refining, and transport. It will have to secure its acceptable return on all the capital involved. But if the final prices in the product markets are the same for all, then the final answer to the subtraction sum, back to the crude, will be the same too (unless the tax burden differs; there are cases where non-integrated suppliers pay more in tax in total than an integrated supplier may). It will not matter, except for tax, where the integrated group shows the profit. 'Downstream losses' are relevant only if they reduce the integrated return below acceptable levels on the capital in each of the stages involved. If these do cut far into the return on capital an integrated group needs—and it is convinced that this is more than temporary—it might possibly do better to sell the crude at arm's length. It is likely to be careful, however, not to sell the crude at such levels to arm's-length buyers who are likely to use it to compete with cheap crude in the integrated supplier's own final markets.

It goes without saying that the majority of European consumers are not concerned with analysing oil prices in this or any other way; they simply want the prices down, and in many parts of Europe they have enough bargaining power to get them down. To them, unlike Shaikh Abdullah Tariki, the profits apparently earned from the posted prices of Middle East crude have seemed too high over the years, not too low: the oil companies and the Arab countries for years seem to them indeed to have shared something of a killing. Between the prices that consumers in one part of the world want to pay and the rents that landlords in another are able to charge, the international oil companies have found it impossible, in recent years, to maintain a balance and earn an integrated return nearly as happy as they did in that halcyon postwar decade—though the return still looks attractive enough to induce them to go on investing in (possibly higher-cost) oil development, and to attract new capital. Nor can it be said that these companies, any longer, retain nearly as much power as they once had to administer prices according to their own judgment. At both ends of this business, the pressures exerted have become more and more political; and in the meantime, commercial competition in the world oil market has become more real and bitter than it had been for many years. This has led OPEC to volunteer to take over the task of administering prices that would suit its members—though probably not oil consumers.

WHO SHALL ADMINISTER PRICES?

It is not surprising that OPEC should have volunteered for the task of propping prices up. For once the net profits companies can make on Middle East and North African crudes begin to be cut by competition, the only element of exceptional economic rent left in the prices realized for crude oil is what its member governments get. The realized prices that have been emerging for Middle East crude—either in arm's-length deals, or in the crude prices that can be netted back from realizations on products—are now being formed by competition. They are probably no longer yielding producing companies, integrated or not, so exceptional a margin of net profit over 'taxpaid cost'; or soon they will not. Taking the Middle East and North Africa as producing regions, much of the exceptional economic rent derived from average prices—for the companies as a group—has gone. (Within these regions, some producers with exceptionally low costs still obtain economic rents at the going level of prices; that is only to be expected.) But the competitive prices that have emerged are still far above inescapable cost, as most other industries and all economists would define costs. This is because the governments are still drawing their share of that original exceptional economic rent. In crude oil prices, Government revenue per barrel is the only part of the margin over costs that remains much inflated.

Since 1965, that government share has been related to posted prices in the Middle East, and now in Libya, by percentage discounts that it is agreed may be reduced, but in no circumstances can be increased beyond the 1966 percentage. It is true that in principle the posted price benchmarks themselves could still be changed. In theory, the companies still insist on their role right to alter posted prices at will without consulting governments. But even in principle that right has been eroded by their agreement to a maximum percentage discount for tax purposes. And in practice, the companies have not ventured to exercise that right to cut posted prices since 1960. Writing during late 1966, it is not easy to envisage future circumstances in which they would dare to do so without host governments' consent.

If so, the boot is on the other foot. It is no longer a matter just of the companies thinking of 'tax-paid cost' as a minimum above which they must decide what margin they will accept. Once the companies are accepting net profit margins on crude—in arm's-length and integrated sales—that are giving them no more than the rate of return on capital they could expect from other investment projects of comparable risk (i.e. an 'opportunity cost' return on the capital needed for oil development), then other concepts begin to matter in pricing. Let us call them 'private development cost' and 'cost-paid tax'. It is now the governments to which these concepts matter, not the companies. 'Private development cost' is what a host government needs to allow an entrepreneur to retain under a concession agreement in order to cover physical costs and attract fresh capital in for continued development. 'Cost-paid tax', to the government, is its own profit margin per barrel. Once the entrepreneur is down to the minimum return he will accept to go on developing oil (in low-cost areas, from already proved reserves), then it is his share, over and above cost, that sets the fixed minimum. Any further bargaining on price—if bargaining there is to be—can only be done in terms of the government's 'cost-paid tax'. And as to that, the decision will rest with the government.

It is some years now since Professor Morris Adelman began to point out[14] that Middle East governments would sooner rather than later have to decide whether to stick unalterably to their minimum revenues per barrel, and if necessary tell concessionnaires to turn customers away; or agree to shade their own tax-alias-profit per barrel in order to sell more oil. Most people in or around the oil business were extremely reluctant to accept the possibility. I was myself, believing for example that the then apparently lowest-cost producer, Kuwait, might find 'government price-cutting' too dangerous a pastime politically to embark upon. In that particular case, I still do: moreover, I believe all of the main Middle East producers would have at least some political inhibitions about beginning on such a course. OPEC, of course, is dedicated to outlawing such dangerous behaviour; and so long as its member governments believe it has a chance of jacking up realized prices towards posted levels by cartel practices, they may well refrain from taking this opposite line.

Nevertheless, I myself feel the last few years have demonstrated that Professor Adelman's suggestion was always an entirely logical possibility. In some circumstances, it could gain individual host governments more advantage than the collective benefits that OPEC hopes it may one day secure for all its members by propping up prices in general. Not in all circumstances. If the National Iranian Oil Company, operating say in partnership with an American newcomer to the Middle East, were by cutting prices to secure business that otherwise would have been secured by a Consortium partner, it would have to consider carefully which sale brings Iran the most benefit—particularly if its marginal sale were to help bring down crude and/or product realizations on all Iranian oil sold. Professor Adelman has calculated, no doubt correctly, that if by investing $500 a Middle East 'national company' could produce a barrel of oil a year, then the company could sell this crude at a dollar a barrel and still make a return of about 65–78 per cent on its investment. True—provided, always, that this sale would not 'back out' other Iranian sales where the government can realize say 80–85 cents a barrel in royalties and tax for no investment at all. But there is always the chance that if an NIOC sale did not undercut Consortium crude and prevent its sale, some other country's crude sold cheap would. So Iran might not have the simple choice between NIOC profit and Consortium royalty plux tax. If it refrained, Iranian oil might not get the business at all.

In any case, several Middle East national companies are now involved in partnership concessions that are likely, over the next few years, to discover sizeable reserves of oil. They will want to sell this oil, not leave it in the ground. It might well be politically sensitive for any host government in the Middle East to 'shade' its own revenue per barrel in order to help a private concessionnaire secure a contract for additional offtake. To do the same to help a national company elbow its way into the market could hardly be as sensitive politically; it could even be politically popular. Some of the sensible technocrats in the national companies, who want to get into business, who understand the cost of leaving oil in the ground, but who still support OPEC's ideal of collective action to harden prices, are in an extreme dilemma. It has left them trying to find markets for their oil outside the ordinary world market—for example, among the Communist satellite countries. But these sales in their turn, if secured by price-cutting, might simply 'back out' sales of Soviet crude—and perhaps back it out, eventually, into that same world market. It is not easy to sell crude oil anywhere—outside the United States at least—without some repercussions in the world market.

Short-term influences in this world market, at the beginning of 1966, were tending to harden prices. First among these was Libya's imposition of a tax formula related to posted prices upon concessionnaires whose agreements stipulated taxation related to realized prices—chronicled at the beginning of this book. Secondly, some further concentration was occurring among the international companies. In some cases, established majors were buying into concessions, or buying into production, that competed with them. In others, majors were buying up independent refiners and marketers whose bargaining had helped pull prices down; or independent refiners were gaining access to low-cost crude produced by the majors on terms that gave both a parallel interest in getting the best product prices possible. Thirdly, some consumer governments' 'cheap energy' policies were faltering. In Germany, possibly in Japan, conceivably in India and Australia too, governments that had logically applauded the decline in prices of imported oil were toying with help for weak enterprise—in both coal and oil—at home. For what OPEC's production programme was worth, its influence—early in 1966, hardly perceptible—was exerted in the same direction. Venezuela, emboldened by Libya, had also managed to push its taxation on to a posted price basis. There were, in short, many pressures—the political much outweighing the commercial—tending to harden oil prices.

It remains questionable how long these could prop up prices so far above inescapable cost. Assume that newcomers could no longer count on more than an 'opportunity cost return' on the capital they plough into exploring new areas. Assume—which goes farther—that established producers with proven reserves could not hope for more than an opportunity cost return on investment simply in developing those reserves. (Put in the time factor: any normal discount rate, or merely the fact that in a given number of years the concession, at best, will be gone: it is hard to see why such producers should leave any oil in the ground which produced now will add to their total net profits.) Assume that we have reached a level of price where even established low-cost concessionnaires refrain from developing new production. Still, the national companies are engaged in exploring for new oil and developing it towards production; already deeply committed. Alone or in partnership, it may well pay them to sell at prices that the private entrepreneurs, with irreducible royalties and taxes, would not find it worthwhile to accept. This might be a powerful downward influence on oil prices beyond the short term, operating against the varied short-term influences tending to hold them up.

Those upward influences are considerable, and for a time at least likely to be effective. (Many high-minded socialists, since the war, have suspected the reappearance of an international oil cartel. It would be ironic if when one did finally emerge, the parties conniving to jack up prices were mainly governments. But perhaps all consciences could be squared by calling it a commodity agreement . . .) But on the other side there is the very large difference between actual cost—i.e. the cost of developing extra capacity to produce oil—and even the discounted price. The profit over inescapable cost—including an acceptable return on the private capital involved—remains a fat one: the fact that it happens largely to be collected by governments does not affect matters. The temptations to shade the profit, cut the effective price, get business a neighbour otherwise might, are strong and logical. (Total demand for crude oil may or may not be elastic to average price. But demand for A's crude instead of B's similar crude is highly elastic to any few cents a barrel that A is prepared to cut.)

This part of this book was designed to consider the economics of oil, not its politics. But separating the two, as we have seen, is often impossible. Host governments of oil-producing countries, for years, have been saying that they wanted to get right into the business. Not all of them, in spite of their pride in national companies, perhaps realize how far they are in, commercially, already. I would not care to predict their behaviour now that they have this new degree of commercial initiative. I believe too many students of this industry in recent years, including myself, have been inclined to predict what they believe to be logically economic behaviour by the governments, only to be nonplussed by the largely political decisions the governments later actually made. Even so, I believe it a shade more likely that the net influence on prices of their incursion into the market will be downward through competition rather than upward—through a cartel.

CHAPTER X

Orderly Competition: As Was

I f you ask a chemist to tell you something of the essential nature of petroleum, he is apt to begin drawing a number of diagrams in which a large number of capital Cs and Hs are joined by lines in criss-cross and latticework patterns are varied by hexagonal 'rings', and sometimes by a few Ss. If the interest that you hasten to express betrays a continuing incomprehension, he may show you the same thing done rather more elegantly with a number of white, red and black plastic balls that can be linked together by springs, or segments of which can be fitted together into variegated clusters, also joined together by these flexible steel linkages. These 'solid diagrams' of the petroleum molecule are of almost unending complexity; any given crude oil contains a mixture of many. The connexions are hard to trace through; the segmented clusters join each other and their 'parent' atoms at many points, but remain a mixture rather than a rigidly connected structure. It was a senior executive of one of the seven major international companies who first pointed out to me how closely this organic mixture resembles the interlinked structure of the privately-owned oil industry outside the United States.

Take these seven companies—or eight with the *Compagnie Française des Pétroles*—which own some 90 per cent, as we have seen, of production, refining and marketing in this industry. They largely control the most important segment of it, Middle East oil, almost entirely through joint producing companies in which all or some of them are associated. All the major companies, together with a band of smaller American companies, are shareholders in the consortium that manages and operates the Iranian oil industry, though actual ownership is vested in the National Iranian Oil Company. Five are shareholders in the Iraq operating companies; four in Saudi Arabia; two—with special contracts involving three of the others—in Kuwait. These are the most important joint operations in producing oil in the Middle East, though there are many others in the area. Quite a number of independent 'newcomers' to the Middle Eastern scene have secured concessions on their own (or in partnership with governments); but Shell's Kuwait offshore concession at the end of 1960 was the first that any of the majors had secured on its own in the region since 1950. The same is not as true of Venezuela—or indeed of new producing areas such as Libya. In these areas the major companies such as Esso, Shell, Texas, Gulf and Mobil operate mainly through separate, single-company concessions or licences in smaller areas than those in the Middle East, and it is the smaller American groups that in some cases operate on a joint basis. In Europe, and 'the franc zone', however, the majors often prospect and produce together or jointly with local companies. For instance, it was a company owned by Jersey and Shell that recently discovered big natural gas deposits in Holland and is developing it with the Dutch state as a major partner, while some major companies have concessions in the Sahara in partnership with semi-nationalized French firms.

In the Middle East, again, since the late fifties, some of the independent groups have secured new concessions by entering into partnerships for the purpose with national companies set up in the host countries (mainly with State capital). First Shell and later other major companies have followed suit. Indeed, this pattern seems likely to become the rule that any private investor, major, independent or newcomer, will have to accept in order to obtain concessions in established producing countries in future. And it seems probable, too, that this same pattern of partnership with a national company may come to apply over large proportions even of existing concessions in some host countries, by the existing concessionnaires. This would follow from the agreement negotiated in Iraq by mid-1965 (though up to the time this book was published, not ratified by the Iraq government or put into practice). Once accepted there, any advantages it might confer would be sought by neighbouring governments. These partnerships may be interpreted as part of government-company relations, or as genuine commercial joint operations. In either case, they further inter-mix the pattern of formal structure.

Joint producing companies, then, are the first clusters linked to the primary 'atoms' of the oil industry: once one goes further into refining and marketing, other sets of cross-linkages, formal and informal, appear. In the United Kingdom, Eire, the Near East, many African territories, and Ceylon, Shell and BP engage in joint marketing operations and occasionally in joint refining as Shell-Mex and BP; Standard of California and the Texas Company do so in most countries of the Eastern hemisphere as Caltex. Until the end of 1960, Jersey and Mobil worked together in Africa and most countries East of Suez as Stanvac; though this has now been generally dissolved, some vestigial joint operations continue. At this stage of operations, the links may be a matter of contracts rather than of joint ownership. Shell buys much of its Middle East crude supplies from Gulf in Kuwait, and shares the eventual proceeds of marketing, wherever and under whatever brand the oil is finally sold; Jersey and Mobil, similarly, have long-term purchase contracts with BP in Kuwait. Gulf, BP and some others have long-term contracts with a number of so-called independent refineries in Italy and other parts of Europe to refine crude for them (which is one way that companies short of marketing facilities can get their oil to the final consumer). Moreover, outside the United States as well as inside it, substantial exchanges of crude and products take place between the major companies as a matter of business convenience. The majors sell crude to their biggest competitors, such as ENI in Italy; their European refineries, again, often supply products to some of their most thrusting independent competitors.

In the ocean transport of oil, joint operation is much less frequent, though the majors, owning large fleets of tankers and controlling the operations of yet larger fleets, sometimes charter out their tankers to other oil companies; and one or two joint delivery arrangements exist. But in pipeline ownership in Western Europe, which began to develop at the end of the fifties, joint ownership by the companies' marketing affiliates is once again the rule: the line from Lavera near Marseilles up to Mulhouse, Strasbourg and Karlsruhe, for example, is owned by no less than 16 major and minor companies.

Any outside observer—particularly the private motorist who is used to buying his gasoline from these companies, in spite of their strongly competitive advertising, at identical prices—may be forgiven for not quite managing to sort them out, and for wondering whether they really are as separate as all that. Most people are vaguely aware that at times in the past, if not today, the major international companies have joined in various business agreements, tending to limit competition. The late Signor Mattei of ENI, who admittedly had few kind words from the major companies himself, seldom referred to the majors as anything but 'the cartel'. The French, and officials in the European communities, have a rather more temperate habit of calling them '*le club*'.

Yet in the original home of the oil industry and of several of these major companies, the pressure of anti-trust legislation and investigation is constant and powerful. Any form of consultation or concerted action between the companies, even in such emergencies as the shortage of tankers after the Suez incident, requires clearing by the United States Department of Justice—which clearing usually tends to reduce or delay the flexibility in logistics that the companies can manage. In the first decade and a half after the Second World War, there were several investigations into the American oil industry by the Federal Trade Commission, Senate committees, or judges in particular anti-trust suits.[1] The very European officials who call the majors '*le club*' are aware that the local *groupements* and oil trade associations with which they broadly prefer to do business are a source of constant anxiety to the headquarters of the American companies represented in them. More than once since the war these headquarters have sent high-level emissaries throughout their European subsidiaries, impressing upon them the undesirability of engaging in just the kind of overt joint action, for example on fuel oil prices, in which European governments have simultaneously been pressing them to engage. (This conflict of government policies has become so real a possibility that American law now specifically allows for it. American companies are now forbidden to engage in cartel practices with one significant escape clause—when foreign governments or supra-national authorities require them to do so.[2])

Oil companies with headquarters in Europe do not live under nearly the same pressure always to be seen to be competing. But nobody in the oil business, especially after the bitter marketing experience of the last few years, would take kindly to the implication that he or it is insulated from competition, or comfortably free to rig prices in some form of conspiratorial international cartel of the type that used to be caricatured by the industry's more sensational critics. Even the domestic consumer in Western Europe, during recent years, has become pretty aware that the members of *le club* are now beset by some complete outsiders, and are not even behaving in a wholly clubbable manner towards each other.

Nobody would suggest that business behaviour in the oil trade is governed by 'perfect competition' in the 'ideal' copybook sense. Even in the United States, which as we have seen, has a far larger number of much smaller independent operators at each stage of the oil business than there are abroad, the predominance of the integrated companies in most stages of the business, and the concentration of these in terms of size makes competition 'oligopolistic', and in the international market competition is yet more so. These are quite real forms of competition, at most times; but they are often not conducive to price competition—particularly when, as in the case of some oil products, demand is generally considered to be 'inelastic' to small changes up or down in price. Oligopoly is not infrequent in the industrial world today, particularly where very large amounts of capital are required for anyone starting up in business. And in other industries, as well as in oil, it is characterized by what is called 'non-price' competition.

Gasoline is an oil product for which demand is generally considered to be inelastic to moderate movements in price; and in some markets, particularly the American, demand for gasoline is what mainly determines the level of general refining activity. It may thus determine whether the production of other oil products in any given region balances demand for them. (But in the large developed markets of Western Europe and Japan, gasoline nowadays plays no such dominant role for the refiner.) Price inelasticity is a phenomenon that tends to hamper the traditional function of 'the price mechanism' in bringing demand and supply into balance. Where it exists, a moderate cut in prices will generally bring about less than a proportionate increase in demand, and much less than a proportionate reduction in supplies. This is generally taken to be true of motor fuels and lubricants. The amount consumed depends on the volume of motor transport and the degree of activity of a vast range of different machines. In the long run, the retail price of gasoline certainly affects the type and size of engine designers put into cars; and in countries where large numbers of motorists are only just over the 'threshold' of owning a small car or a scooter, the price of gasoline can affect the amount of pleasure motoring that they can afford. But this price of gasoline is ordinarily a small element in the total cost of motor transport, and the price of lubrication an insignificant one. Motor transport itself, too, often represents a 'derived demand', being dependent on business decisions to which the transport involved is ancillary. Even in pleasure motoring the high initial cost of a car and its rapid depreciation in value give the owner a certain economic incentive to get as much use out of his investment as soon as he can; the price of gasoline would seldom deter him.

The high taxes on gasoline often levied by governments, moreover, tend to reduce the effect that small changes in net prices by the supplier can make to the total retail price at the pump. One of the few recent cases where any significant increase in gasoline consumption does seem to have occurred *post* if not wholly *propter* a cut in prices was in Italy in 1960–61. But there a cut in net prices was backed up by a large cut in tax and the retail price fell by no less than 25 per cent (more, indeed, than the total net price of the gasoline). (Demand is generally said to be elastic or inelastic according to the reaction to *small* changes in price.) And governments seldom reduce a tax that is so dependable a source of revenue: no product seems to them more suitable for indirect taxation than one for which they can assume that demand is inelastic to price. American taxes on gasoline would seem mild to any European motorist; even so, they are currently adding about 40 per cent to the price before tax.

If total demand for gasoline is fairly inelastic, demand for any particular brand of gasoline is a lot more elastic than marketers would like. Brand loyalty, much as the advertising departments strive to inculcate it, is evanescent (there is far more loyalty to a given service station than to the brand it sells). For any given grade of gasoline, therefore, an established marketer cannot afford to charge any more than the next brand is sold for. In theory, every major competitive marketer has to match whatever cuts are made, and knows his competitors must too. In theory, therefore, to initiate a price war is likely to be not only costly, but relatively ineffective in increasing one's share of the market. For the established marketer, therefore, competitive activity may take the form of financial help for the retailer in rebuilding, advertising, and real estate operations: getting the best located stations and helping them build up their service, rather than price cutting.

Such theoretical reasoning offers plausible reasons why gasoline price wars might never break out. But as in the larger developed markets they pretty often do, it is somewhat inadequate as a rationale of gasoline pricing. Not every established marketer has the same degree of influence on the final selling price of gasoline at stations selling his brand; and on occasion a particular station owner may feel that while prices will eventually be cut everywhere to match a reduction he initiates, a cut may in the meantime pick him up some extra business that he can retain. Nor are all the established marketers equally established everywhere, or always equally in balance in their producing and refining activities. The most statesmanlike of major companies, on occasion, may want to expand its sales in a market where it feels under-represented. And newcomers to any given market—which in recent years, in Europe, have often been 'semi-integrated', local marketers backed by crude suppliers and refiners abroad—are often ready to sell at a loss for a time in order to gain some share of the market with lesser-known brands or 'unbranded' gasoline.

In the American market 'unbranded' gasoline can generally sell at one or two cents a gallon less than branded gasoline of the same grade without generating retaliation from the majors. Certain major companies will argue, on the basis of market research, that these two levels of price often reflect a division between two largely separate markets, hardly overlapping or competitive in price, even in the same town; one set of customers who buy simply on price, and another who patronize a given station for all kinds of automotive service. But once the prices begin to differ by more than an accepted, conventional margin, even regular customers will begin to transfer their allegiance, and competitive price-cutting may begin. It is often said that once price-cutters gain more than about 8 to 10 per cent of a market, estab-lished marketers are forced to retaliate. The retail dealers involved take the brunt of such price wars, though their suppliers will usually make some kind of arrangement to share the cost of price-cutting, and some-times guarantee their margins regardless of the levels to which prices are cut. Such price wars occasionally appear to end in covert agree-ments not to go on cutting each other's prices and throats. More often, however, one leading marketer in the field will take a stand, when margins all round have been pushed too low, and persuade his dealers to stabilize or even to increase prices at all their stations. Providing he has picked the psychological moment when most other suppliers are sick of the price war too, his move is often successful in snuffing out further price-cutting. But it may take quite a time before prices can be edged up to the earlier levels, restoring everybody's margins. And the eventual pattern of shares in the market, contrary to the theoretical arguments against price-cutting, may have altered quite significantly.

'Non-price' competition between oil companies, major or inde-pendent, for the favour of the private motorist is usually concentrated on the dealer, not the motorist. The main competition occurs in seek-ing supply contracts with the favourably-placed service station. The dealer gets special rebates for exclusive dealing; he may get capital assistance when a contract comes up for renewal, or assistance in the re-equipment of his station. Alternatively, the supplying companies may bid up strategic sites to a real estate value well above anything that the site could fetch for any other purpose; make their stations more and more lavish and attentive; and engage in the duplication of their main rivals' stations wherever these are particularly well-placed. At times this has led to the building of far too many service stations, and the reduction of average throughput to an uneconomically low level; but in most countries today some form of licensing has been imposed to limit the number of service stations built. This in its turn gives the licensed site some degree of monopoly value. When there is a lot of competition among gasoline suppliers, the dealer can usually secure the full value of this monopoly. But unless there are price-cutters in the retail market too, he may be under no pressure to pass his advantage on to the motorist. Large oil companies are often accused of monopoly practices in gasoline marketing; but the dealer seems often to get what monopoly value there is.

Though some marketing men in oil profess considerable scepticism about it, the companies spend heavily on another form of non-price competition—with advertising and to some extent with research. They spend very heavily on attempts to implant the brand name in motorists' minds; sometimes mainly through general advertising designed to inculcate goodwill, but often through the steady refinement of claims for new and specialized additives to give improved qualities to the petrol. Over the last thirty years or so, there has been a very marked improvement in the purity and the general fuel qualities of the gasolines sold. Many consumers and some oilmen, however, express more scepticism about particular 'new additives', and about the 'octane race' that has steadily raised the anti-knock quality of gasolines. This has been partly engendered by the motor industry's search for more efficient engines: but it may also by now have outstripped the compression ratios of the engines fitted into many customers' cars.

Quality competition of this kind is one of the characteristic forms of non-price competition. It steadily helps to increase the technical efficiency with which the consumer can use the fuel, though sometimes at a significant cost in the technical efficiency with which the refinery that produces the fuel is run. It gives the consumer higher quality at the same price without offering him the choice of the same quality at lower price; this sets up a kind of technocratic criterion, and tells the customer what is best for him. Wholesale distribution of gasoline and lubricants has probably become a good deal more efficient since the growth of exclusive dealing and one-brand stations increased the amount of gasoline 'dropped' by the road oil tankers of any one company at each of its filling stations. But this has been at some limited cost in the reduction of consumers' choice; there may have been a tendency towards building too many unnecessarily lavish stations and motorists have not necessarily shared in the cost savings.[3]

This kind of competition at service stations is in contrast to a much larger amount of price competition for motor fuels sold to fleet consumers, and in the marketing of the black oils as general fuels, particularly to industry. In Western Europe during the early sixties, newcomers were cutting their way into these bulk markets, where the cost of entry is not so great as with 'dealer gasoline'; and the established marketers have retaliated very sharply at times. This is straight price competition, withoug any indulgence in trading stamps, gifts, or special offers. The absence of open competition in published prices, as we saw in the last chapter, does not preclude very real price competition with discounts and rebates, open and hidden. And finally, price competition does break out occasionally even in markets where the final consumer has no great bargaining power, such as the service station market.

Conditions of sharpened competition have returned to the international oil market only in the last decade, after about a quarter of a century, during which the majors were largely immune from any significant outside competition. Competition since the mid-fifties, however, may not have reached the degree of severity of the bitter international competition of the twenties—in which the attitudes of the majors towards really severe price competition were decisively tested. During the twenties, a number of other American companies, plus the Russians, were also active in the world oil market, while the rivalry of the American and British/Dutch groups for leadership was somewhat accentuated by diplomatic backing for both sides. Many of the other American companies eventually 'retired hurt', selling off their interests to one or another of the few remaining in the world market. The Russians had patched up an armistice with the remaining majors at the end of the twenties, and though this truce was not without its frontier incidents of further dumping at cut prices, development of their own economy during the thirties reduced Soviet interest in the world oil market. The main American and British/Dutch groups, in 1928, reached agreements, which came to be known as the 'As Is' agreements, on the stabilization of company shares in the world market and some stabilization of prices. These arrangements were later paralleled by the 'Red Line' agreements between the main groups in the Middle East for the co-operative development of existing oil-producing areas and controlled development of new ones. The As Is agreements never appear to have worked in a watertight fashion, though undoubtedly, along with the buying up of competitors, they did something to stabilize prices. They were to be abandoned on American initiative at the beginning of the Second World War, partly in deference to growing public and governmental suspicion towards cartels. But one has dispassionately to recognize how logical the agreements were for the major oil companies that engaged in them after almost a decade of potentially ruinous price wars. It was no accident that this attempt to regulate prices in a seemingly bottomless market paralleled the development of plans for state regulation of output in the United States. At the end of the war, the American and British governments toyed with the idea of taking over the control system themselves in the form of the abortive Anglo-American petroleum agreement of 1944. That was thwarted in the American legislature.[4] But the ideas of price stabilization through production control constantly recur. By the sixties, it was the oil producing governments, through OPEC, who had taken up the notions.

Joint operating companies in Iraq preceded the Red Line agreements of the thirties: but these agreements would have stamped the pattern on each new concession and in fact, though not simply as a result, most Middle East concessions are jointly owned. These agreements too were abandoned after the war (causing some litigation between certain of the American companies that were withdrawing and European companies that did not want to see the 'Red Line' restrictions relaxed). But the pattern of joint ownership persisted and was indeed made easier to develop: Standard Oil of New Jersey and Socony Mobil needed freedom from these restrictions, indeed, to remove objections to buying their way into Aramco. For about ten years after the war the international majors were largely without effective competitors in the Middle East, though during the fifties a large number of other concerns had begun to seek concessions in Venezuela and in the Middle East. This was a period of rapidly rising demand for energy, with little expansion in supply of primary fuels. Demand for oil products was rising as fast as the major companies could build tankers, refining and marketing facilities to meet them.

No formal agreements governed the market behaviour of the international majors during this period, and the American companies were particularly uneasy even about the informal arrangements that had to be reached from time to time to deal with political emergencies. But no agreements were needed during such a period to persuade most of them to desist from price competition. There were other, less potentially double-edged ways of raising total revenue and, for some, of increasing one's share of the business. Certain of the relative newcomers to these rich supplies of cheap crude and to the European market, such as Caltex, offered very advantageous terms for products and occasionally crude to independent buyers during this period, to gain footholds in parts of Europe; the the more fully integrated majors had no need to match them. What some of these majors approvingly christened 'orderly competition' was the rule. And though it has since been largely disrupted, orderly competition is what many in the major companies still think can and should be restored. This aim, it may be noted, is shared by some of the newcomers and by many of the governments seeking nowadays to influence the world oil business. These have different ideas, however, about who is going to do the ordering of the competition.

How real was that orderly competition, and is its equilibrium likely to be restored? These are obvious questions for the sixties. It has been noted here that orderly competition did not preclude shifts in market shares. Indeed, the forbearance involved in retaining relative stability in the market probably meant that the largest and most powerful companies exerted less than their full strength, and that 'juniors' among the seven obtained a share in the international market more easily than they might otherwise have done. This orderly development of low-cost Middle East oil, and the huge shift in the pattern of world oil movement that it involved, occupied a decade in which the growth of the total market and the high rates of profit available from oil produced in the Middle East were more important to the biggest of the established companies than maintaining their share of the market. Since the growth of oil demand began to slacken, and thrusting newcomers have arrived on the scene to challenge all established marketers, this forbearance has been largely discarded. But it might not have lasted much longer anyway.

Some people at the top of the major companies, at any rate, argue that these external influences—the slackening of world demand, plus the restriction of imports into the United States, the intrusion of Russian competition, and the arrival of the newcomers—did no more than hasten the time at which competition even among the few would have begun to become less orderly. The interests of the seven or eight great international groups had lain broadly parallel during the first postwar decade, through common interest rather than through any compact, formal or informal. There had been too much work to do profitably for anyone to wish to rock the boat. But any period of forbearance from competition, in any industry, generally tends to be at the expense of the most efficient. And there were signs that these most efficient groups were becoming restive, even apart from the other influences leading towards more competition in the market. As one man at the top of one of the large groups said late in 1960, 'I am not sure that we all still live in quite the same world.' That may be even truer in 1970.

It has to be remembered that the geographical dispersion of interests of these eight major groups around the world, and their relative strength at different stages of the oil business, differs considerably. So does their pattern of net profitability after tax. What on balance may be advantageous to one may not suit another at all.

Ordinarily, this does not matter; there is no reason why their operational behaviour, for example which markets they decide to supply from which source, need always be uniform, or remain so. But as we have seen, in this pattern of 'competition among the few' there is one point on which their policies cannot differ for long—published prices, at any rate where these act as tax benchmarks for oil sold from joint producing operations.

While one accepts a particular price level as given, the essential art of efficient management of an international oil company becomes primarily 'logistic'—the quartermaster's art of arranging one's disposition of supplies from sources to markets to achieve the lowest possible net cost and highest possible net return on new capital investment right across the business. If one were to accept a particular pattern of supply as given, the art would presumably lie in getting the price at each point in the business that offered, similarly, this lowest cost and best return— remembering the significance of tax at so many points in this worldwide pattern. In practice, of course, the two are indivisible: these are programming exercises that call for (and get) the computer, made more complex at each end because of shifts in demand for refinery products, the chance for refiners to use mixtures of crude, and the similar chances for producers to alter the qualities of 'reconstructed' crudes. In practice, the major oil companies have always chosen to change published prices relatively seldom (though of late they may have been using different internal transfer prices, or 'absorbing freights' in between source and market). So over long periods the logistic art, the ability to keep a vast and interlocked network of production, movement, processing and marketing flexibly deployed, and to seek out every advantage that can be sought from shifts in the pattern of cost and return here and there, will predominate. But the balance of advantage and cost, for any single company, changes over time.

One should not under-estimate the powerful common interests of these major international companies. They are all in the business to stay, and they may well regard the competitive activity of newcomers, who may take shorter views, with common alarm. They have had bitter experience of competitive price-cutting across the world. They co-exist in many countries in not altogether easy relationships with the same governments. Nevertheless, their interests, ultimately, may diverge. It may be that the periods when their common interests are so predominant—as for example the decade or so after the war when they were developing the vast potential of the Middle East, to their own and that region's joint and great profit—are exceptional. It can be argued, on the other hand, that this decade of parallel policies on price and on agreements with governments demonstrates the extent to which genuine common interests will generally govern the conduct of this industry whenever participants in it settle down to stay. But that may not be inconsistent with the proposition that at times this common interest is more manifest than at others. Even the prewar period of agreement to limit competition in various ways did not always or universally hold firm.

No cartel agreements survived to clamp conformity on to the business behaviour of the major groups after the war. None was needed, during that first fabulous decade. But the joint operating companies did and do survive; in Iran, indeed, another was added (and a number of smaller American companies were given their first taste of Middle East returns on investment). Now clearly these partnerships, plus the major share-holders' interlocking interests within them, do serve generally to restrain severe internecine competition in terms of development. They also, as Dr Edith Penrose has pointed out,[5] tend to hold down the rate at which output in any area is developed, to that accepted by some form of majority of the integrated shareholders. Elaborate rules for the forward planning of production and 'lifting' (i.e. taking one's proportionate share of oil) govern individual shareholders' initiative in most of these joint operations. These 'offtake agreements' do not wholly preclude effectively competitive behaviour, within these joint operating companies—though this is 'competition' by restricting the opportunities open to other partners, rather than by using one's opportunities as fully as possible. Each partner within them has some room for manœuvre, even where strict rules obtain. There are provisions giving each some freedom to take or not to take the share of output to which its financial shareholding entitles it; and a group with interests in more of these countries than one may choose the most advantageous places to lift the supplies it wants while making it as expensive as possible for its partners to do the same.

The actual operating companies in most of these areas—IPC and Qatar Petroleum Company, Kuwait Oil Company and the consortium in Iran—are non-profit-making companies. They carry out the physical operations but transfer the oil, at cost or a fraction more, at the tanker terminal or the border point on a pipeline, to their shareholder companies or local 'trading company' affiliates of these groups. These companies therefore get their basic share of the profits of the operations in the form of 'cost oil'; and it is these local trading companies, transferring this oil at posted price to other affiliates of the group, that show the profit and pay most of the tax by the host government. In Aramco the pattern is different. This is organized as a profit-making company paying the tax on the oil produced; it sells oil to its shareholder companies at prices corresponding to those they charge (when they resell to affiliates at posted price, they pay Aramco too at posted prices, but when they resell to a third party at a discount, they pay Aramco the actual sale price realized).

As well as differences in formal structure, there are differences in 'offtake agreements' between these joint companies. In Iraq, within the three-company structure that so far has survived the partial expropriation of the concession areas, the constitution calls for programmes of 'offtake' to be settled five to ten years ahead. Each corporate shareholder 'tables' its requirements over a five-year period five years before that period begins—e.g. for 1967–71 in 1962. These forward estimates are totalled and after certain agreed adjustments set the future production programme; this is adjusted to give each 'offtaker' a share of the annual programmes in proportion to its shareholding in the group. Any company that proposes to take less than its proportionate share of the volumes programmed can arrange in advance with another shareholder to take the remainder of its entitlement as 'half-way cost oil'—i.e. at a price halfway between the cost including tax and the posted price. But if it has not made such prior arrangements and when the time comes it has to 'turn back' oil, this oil becomes available to its partners, *pro rata*, at cost, not halfway cost; and it therefore loses all the profit on this oil that it fails to lift.

Details of the Iran consortium rules have never been published, but they appear to operate rather differently. Each partner nominates each year in advance an estimate not of his own requirements, but of the total consortium production for the following year. The figure accepted is the lowest total nominated that will cover the estimates put in by shareholders representing a given percentage majority of the shares in the consortium. This total is then redistributed into entitlements proportionate to the holdings of each shareholder in the consortium. If a shareholder lifts less than his entitlement, there is no penalty, down to 75 per cent of the figure. If he wants to lift more than his entitlement, he will have to buy the excess from any 'underlifters' at full posted price. Over the years, there is often a fairly regular division between those companies that nominate high totals for the next year's production schedule for Iran production—mainly those inherently 'short of crude' —and those that nominate low, because they have more crude available elsewhere, either at lower costs or in countries where they are more concerned to increase total offtake.

In Kuwait, rather oddly at first sight, there are no binding rules at all about offtake. This is a concession held directly by the shareholder companies, BP and Gulf, not by the Kuwait Oil Company, which is simply a managing organization (again non-profit-making) handling the physical operations. Each owner can lift as much oil as it likes at cost (plus one shilling) up to the limit of KOC's physical facilities; there are no rules governing offtake, and hence no 'overlifting' or 'underlifting'. Originally this exceptional freedom of operational action—and of potential competition between the partners—was qualified by some undertakings not to compete in marketing written into the joint concession agreement; but in 1951 a revision of the joint agreement excised these clauses. Gulf's large-scale and long-term supply agreements with Shell, on which it receives half of the profits earned by Shell in getting the oil to market, may indirectly restrain its competition with BP, in that Shell and BP market jointly in a number of European, African, and Eastern markets. But in practice, in the last few years, Gulf has been widening its own marketing in European markets; its inhibitions about marketing

Kuwait oil in competition with its concession partner seem at any rate to be thinning out. At the production stage, both companies reckon the oil taken out as a 'free good', in that they see no chance of running out of it during the concession period (until 2026) even at rising rates of off-take. For each barrel of oil that either partner takes, it pays a requisite amount in the 'cost per barrel' towards depreciation of the physical facilities that KOC provides plus the capital cost of any extra invest-ment required to provide the extra output it wants. And the companies take this as the proportionate contribution towards developing output of Kuwait oil to the levels that their aggregate demands upon it require.

In Aramco, also, there is no set programme of production for the year ahead, though the partners in it have agreed to a programme of invest-ment that steadily increases its capacity. Each partner company normally undertakes to take up to its proportionate requirement of this rising production; there is no penalty for 'underlifting', but a group that takes more than its proportionate share in any year is entitled to lift as high a percentage again the next, at the expense of the proportions avail-able to any who chose to underlift. The rules of this arrangement have been modified over the years; details of the present 'incentive dividend plan' are a nightmare to anybody except a devoted accountant. Broadly, however, each partner gets part of its return from Aramco as a propor-tionate share of half of what the Aramco profit would be if all oil were sold at posted price. This is a dividend on ownership, unrelated to the shareholder's behaviour as an offtaker. The remainder of the actual profits made—which will be somewhat less than the notional 'half' above, since a proportion of the oil will in fact be sold at discounts below the posted price—is distributed between shareholders in proportion to their contribution to Aramco's actual profits, in terms of the oil they lift and the prices at which they take it. The latest change in this offtake arrangement appears to have been carried out in order to make it cheaper for partners to 'lift' more than their proportionate share of out-put. The change, reflecting the 'proving' of even more enormous reserves in Saudi Arabia, appears to have been particularly useful to Socony Mobil; but it may also have reinforced Texaco's growing aggressiveness in European competition.

Under both arrangements, a shareholding group that lifts less than its full entitlement of oil gets some share of profit simply on account of its shareholding (and its proportionate contribution of capital to the development of oil production in the company in question). Against a volume of offtake that is less than its proportionate entitlement, its total profit works out at slightly more than the average number of cents per barrel. Equally, a shareholder that lifts more than its entitlement, by paying an 'overlift price' for the excess or by getting only that proportion of profits on it that is distributed according to offtake, will average across the total volume he lifts rather less than the ordinary profit per barrel. His marginal offtake, effectively, costs him more than his allocated exports under the offtake agreement.

Under various outside purchase contracts, some of the major companies have the chance to get large amounts of oil at less than these overlift prices—i.e. to buy oil outside at lower cost than by taking it from concessions that they jointly own. If one can hold offtake down in a joint operating company and oblige other shareholders who need larger volumes to take more than their share, one may get a higher average profit on one's own annual offtake. And then it may be possible to make up one's own requirements with oil at less than the overlift price. Across the whole operation it is thus on occasion possible to realize a small margin of advantage in terms of net profit per barrel, at other companies' expense if they are less advantageously placed; and a cent or two per barrel, with the huge volumes involved in this business, can soon run into hundreds of thousands of dollars. Companies that are 'long on crude', in general may thus be able to benefit at the expense of their partners in joint companies who are short of crude and are forced to 'over-lift'. In the Middle East there is even a special word for this commercially logical behaviour—'coat-tail riding'.

The main point here is that these partners in the operating companies—which usually dispose of different amounts of voting power in each of them—may be able to influence the total offtake of a country, or indeed the total offtake of one country by their voting on the annual offtake from another. It will be seen that there are quite a number of permutations and combinations of more or less clubbable behaviour in which the members of *le club* can engage. The ramifications of the internecine behaviour of these companies in the Middle East can be quite tortuous. This is not what Adam Smith meant by competition, or what might have occurred if the Middle East had been developed by companies operating quite separately. It has presumably, at different times in different countries, limited the growth of offtake; and has also probably helped to slow the decline in crude market prices. Dr Penrose has emphasized the resultant tendency to slow expansion of output, which is undeniable. But it is hardly what one would expect of some sinister, well-disciplined cartel, either. To me this presents itself as a technique of 'non-price competition', or at any rate of competition not necessarily affecting prices to customers, that nobody could call imaginary.

Offtake agreements including a comparatively new element are becoming the rule in the new 'partnership' concessions between private groups and national companies from the host countries, common since the late fifties. Here the private partner is generally experienced not only technically but commercially in the world market; the national company partner is usually a newcomer to both. The national company might be expected at least to have the inside track inside the oil-producing country itself. But that will not necessarily be true: the host country may already be getting its crude and refined products extremely cheap from an established producer there, so that handing the internal market over may simply back out crude (and government revenue, or perhaps 'royalty oil') what was being produced anyway. These national companies are anxious to do business in the world market too, but aware of their inexperience. Generally, therefore, along with the offtake agreements that govern development and crude 'liftings' by each corporate partner, these agreements provide for 'buy-back prices' applying not only to overlifting, but to quantities that the national partner may require the private partner to acquire from it from its ordinary share of offtake. For example, the private partner may be required to take any proportion, up to the whole, of the national partner's share, at a price say halfway between the cost plus government royalty and tax and the posted price, less some agreed discount. In such circumstances, if the national partner could not sell any of the crude, it gets half of the profit that would have been made on sales at that price; the government gets royalty and taxes on the whole output; and the private partner gets all the crude, though having paid considerably more for it than he would have had to for his own proportionate share.

Even where they were most closely linked in joint operating ventures, therefore, and even before their joint preserve was invaded by outsiders, co-operation had its limits between these major international groups. Whether it would have grown further in any case, over the years, is a matter of opinion. The same pattern of joint operation has not, in general, been repeated in some of the newer areas when oil for export is being developed, so that some of the majors such as Jersey in Libya have enjoyed freedom to operate entirely on their own. The outsider may feel that relations between the major companies would anyway, during the fifties, have come under increasing strain. In practice, however, it was the understanding of the huge potential output available for development well below ruling prices, of the world surplus, and the consequent incursion of newcomers into the business that helped complicate the course of this orderly competition. At first, the majors' attitude towards this invasion might have brought their policies more than ever into line, against the disorderly newcomers. In practice, it fairly soon—once it became clear that some of the newcomers, too, were here to stay—began to uncover points at which the majors' interests were more openly divergent. The disputed cuts in Middle East crude prices, which caused the formation of OPEC, offered one fairly clear example. In its original announcement that it was cutting prices, in August, 1960, Jersey spoke of disruptive influences in the world oil market, and did not mention the Russians alone. It singled out also 'discount sales from marketers with unlimited supplies of crude—which can only have meant some among its fellow majors.

At the same time, even the differently-situated major companies still have more in common with each other than they have with thrusting independents—until these, in their turn, acquire a sufficient size and spread of interests across the world to become concerned with long-term rather than short-term returns. The extent of non-price competition, and how close it comes to merging into price competition, will vary in different periods of the industry's history. But the common interests return—towards the fullest exploitation of oil resources consistent with seeking relative stability of prices and profits; and towards the 'optimizing' of long-term return via steady and not too cyclical expansion. The extremes of price fluctuation to which short-term competitive interest might drive the industry are not generally to the taste of oil companies that intend to go on being oil companies. Flexibility is transferred from prices to logistic behaviour.

So long as these major companies commanded the main sources of oil for export, and demand for imports was rising as fast as transport, processing and marketing facilities were being expanded (by themselves and others), competition in the international oil business remained weak as well as technically imperfect, and consumers had not nearly enough 'countervailing power' to bring prices down more than suppliers reduced them. But the trade was not entirely closed to newcomers; new capital was gradually moving into the international end of it. Various non-economic or not wholly economic decisions, such as the insertion of a number of the independent American companies into the Iran Consortium, followed by American self-insulation from the growth of the international trade and Russian re-entry into it, rather suddenly restricted the growth of import demand below what had been foreseen, added to the number of newcomers, and made it impracticable for the groups already established, even had they wished, to move over and make room for these. Since the late fifties competition has become progressively less orderly. Moreover, it may now have become impossible for purely commercial forces to re-stabilize this market until prices have come a long way farther down. Some buying up of competitive newcomers by the big groups is entirely likely, and certain of the disorderly independents are becoming big and broadly-based enough themselves to value stability. For now neither the consumer of oil nor the landlord governments of oil-producing areas seem prepared to accept market stabilization via survival of the fittest among the companies, even presuming this commercial evolution would be practicable and sufficient to restore orderly competition.

Interposed between consumer and landlord, the oil business can hardly avoid suspicion from both sides; particularly because the two are in different countries, while the business must always seem to them to exist, somewhere, not easily identifiable, in the middle. It looks like either an 'overseas trading corporation' or a 'foreign capitalist'. The economic function of this industry indeed depends upon the concept of the world as a single market, across which resources can freely be traded with benefit to all: it is one of the few genuinely international manifestations of private enterprise. Part I of this book has attempted to stick to the strictly economic and commercial aspects of this industry's operations, mainly to the exclusion of other aspects. Even so, it has been impossible to leave out some of the points at which national policies impinge upon and modify the commercial pattern of these operationss It is the impact of such national policies upon the oil industry, and their importance as facts of life for the international oil operator, with which the remainder of the book will be concerned.

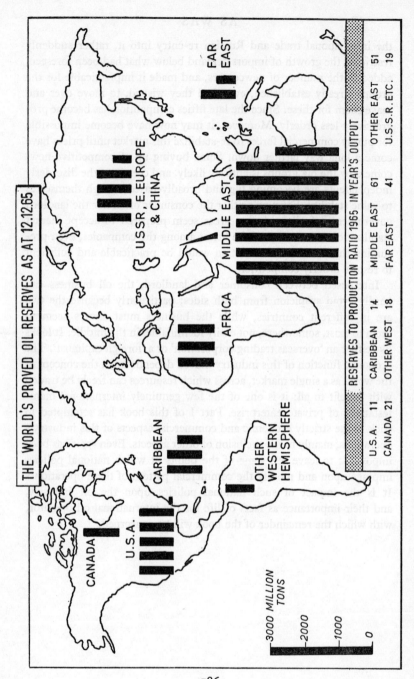

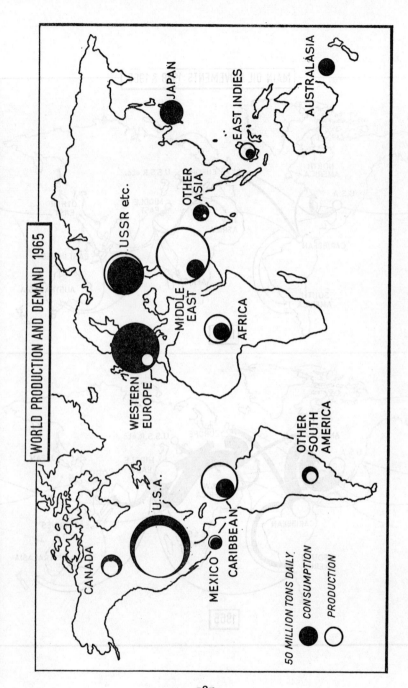

WORLD PRODUCTION AND DEMAND 1965

JAPAN

EAST INDIES

AUSTRALASIA

OTHER ASIA

USSR etc.

MIDDLE EAST

AFRICA

WESTERN EUROPE

OTHER SOUTH AMERICA

U.S.A.

CANADA

MEXICO

CARIBBEAN

50 MILLION TONS DAILY.

CONSUMPTION

PRODUCTION

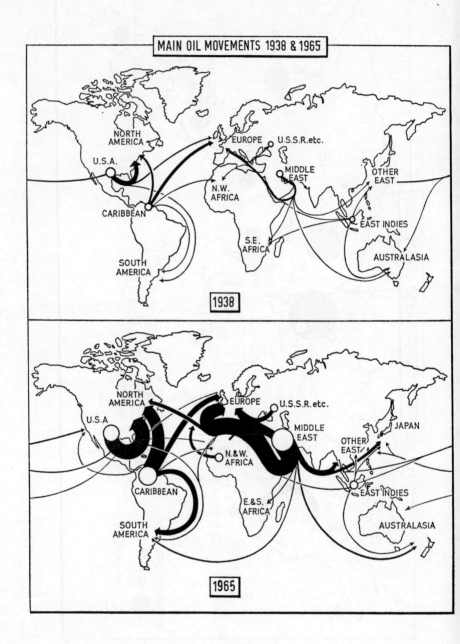

MAIN OIL MOVEMENTS 1938 & 1965

1938

1965

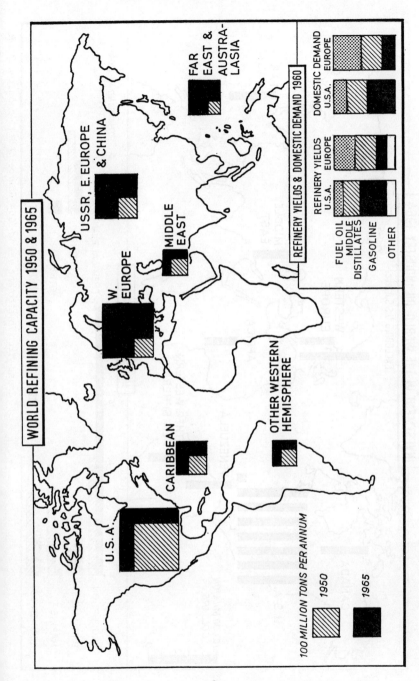

WORLD REFINING CAPACITY 1950 & 1965

USSR, E. EUROPE & CHINA

FAR EAST & AUSTRALASIA

W. EUROPE

MIDDLE EAST

U.S.A.

CARIBBEAN

OTHER WESTERN HEMISPHERE

REFINERY YIELDS & DOMESTIC DEMAND 1960

DOMESTIC DEMAND
EUROPE

DOMESTIC DEMAND
U.S.A.

REFINERY YIELDS
EUROPE

REFINERY YIELDS
U.S.A.

FUEL OIL
MIDDLE DISTILLATES
GASOLINE
OTHER

100 MILLION TONS PER ANNUM

1950

1965

189

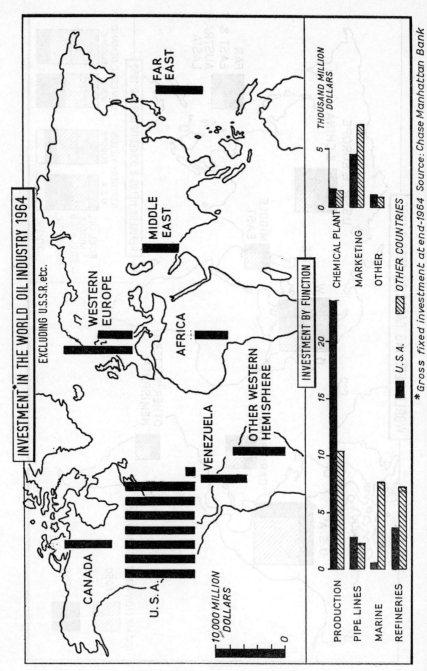

INVESTMENT* IN THE WORLD OIL INDUSTRY 1964

EXCLUDING U.S.S.R. etc.

FAR EAST

MIDDLE EAST

WESTERN EUROPE

AFRICA

OTHER WESTERN HEMISPHERE

VENEZUELA

CANADA

U.S.A.

10,000 MILLION DOLLARS

0

INVESTMENT BY FUNCTION

THOUSAND MILLION DOLLARS

CHEMICAL PLANT

MARKETING

OTHER

PRODUCTION

PIPE LINES

MARINE

REFINERIES

0   5   10   15   20

0   5

■ U.S.A.   ▨ OTHER COUNTRIES

*Gross fixed investment at end-1964   Source: Chase Manhattan Bank

190

Part Two

CHAPTER XI

Oil Companies as Taxpayers

So far as possible, up to here, this book has sketched the behaviour of the oil business in an unreal isolation, as if oil companies lived and worked in a grey, neutral, logical world of economic men without a country. Many oilmen, perhaps, sometimes wish they did; and certainly this is as international an industry as has ever been built up. But for writer and reader the device has been one simply of convenience—to trace some outlines of an industry that is complex enough in all conscience even before one pins the tracing back where it belongs, across a rich and colourful map of nations. Put back in their proper place, the outlines are harder to follow. They are almost lost within a more turbulent pattern, as the colours of nationalism show through.

The international sweep of this industry does not absolve it from living with governments, as every other industry has to; it only introduces the complication, which can have advantages but has disadvantages as well, of living with more governments than one. The oil industry is incessantly engaged in trade by sea and across frontiers, but its movement of bulk cargo around the world is only one of the simpler among its operations. It explores and produces, usually, on land: even offshore, it has not yet ventured far out beyond territorial limits and national governments are clearly bent on extending their jurisdiction out as far as it becomes technically able to explore. It processes and sells its products, increasingly, for use inside the national frontiers of the country where the processing is done; but still engages in a sizeable balancing export-import trade in these manufactured products. Its relations with the governments of the lands where it does business vary according to the kind of society concerned and with oil's importance to any given economy. But the fact that an oil company is often not operating in one country alone, and may have a world-wide scatter of interests, tends to complicate the industry's relationship with each individual government.

Primary in every such relationship is the oil industry's role as a tax-payer of each country of which it is a commercial citizen. This is indeed the point where discussion of the industry's economic behaviour in isolation breaks down: many things about this industry simply cannot be understood without some idea of its tax situation. And tax is of such pervasive importance in the financial reckoning of this industry that even the least financially-minded oilman, asked for his opinion of any unexpected move by any major company, immediately tries to figure out the 'tax angles' that may have affected its decision. The tax treatment of oil profits in the country where any international company has its head-quarters is likely to condition its industrial strategy all over the world. But such a company has also to fit into the tax formulae imposed by most of the other countries. These taxes may be used to implement deliberate national policies regarding oil: or they may simply reflect the fact that wherever so rich an industry does business, local treasuries are usually anxious to find a formula that entitles them to a cut of the take. In either case, the situation of the oil company operating internationally will also depend upon the treatment that its parent government and perhaps other tax authorities too, apply to income already taxed by other governments.[1]

This incidence and interaction of taxes in each country where it operates inevitably modifies the considerations of cost and final price that affect an international oil company's decisions on issues large and small. Its decisions whether to do business in one country as against another, for example, will be affected not merely by comparisons of cost or market potential, but by comparisons of the taxation there, and by consideration of the treatment of 'double taxation' between these countries and its own domicile. In the last few years a number of the biggest oil companies have begun to use electronic computers to 'simulate' their circumstances in certain kinds of operation, particularly the logistics of matching demand at many points with supply from a number of possible sources. Taxes have to be fed in as one set of variables: for the ultimate purpose will not be simply to minimize cost, but to maximize 'the integrated net profit after tax' that will arise from the company's mixture of interests across the world. And the answer varies with the company mix. That is one of the reasons why one can never assume in this industry that what suits A, except by chance, will remain permanently satisfactory to B.

Its tax system at home, and the tax treatment it applies to taxes paid abroad, set the basic frame of reference for each oil company. In the United States and Britain, headquarters of the largest international companies, taxes paid abroad can be 'credited' against tax liabilities on this foreign income at home, and royalties paid abroad are excluded from home tax consideration as expenses of doing business. Their tax codes differ considerably in detail (mainly perhaps because the United States has a large home oil industry and Britain has not).

The United States gives very favourable tax treatment for oil exploration and development, by allowing losses, dry holes, and 'intangibles' (i.e. the costs of oil development not embodied in salvageable equipment) to be applied to reduce American taxable income—regardless of where the exploration takes place, or what activity in the United States the taxable income was earned from. These 'intangible' costs of finding oil can thus be 'expensed' against current income at home; the embodied capital equipment can be written off through depreciation, the United States also gives a 'depletion allowance' against tax in respect of the wasting oil reserve in the ground (at 27½ per cent of gross producing income, or 50 per cent of net producing income, whichever is the lower). As to relief for foreign tax, it allows income taxes paid abroad, so long as these apply generally in the country concerned and are not simply specific taxes for oil operations, as a credit against U.S. income tax liability on the same foreign income, and may apply this to U.S. tax liability on the income underlying dividends from subsidiaries or share-holdings in joint companies, down to a shareholding as low as 10 per cent. Britain has virtually no specific tax legislation affecting oil; its treatment of exploration, in particular, is relatively ungenerous. But it does have a flexible system of foreign tax relief. The British government allows taxes similar to income taxes to be credited against U.K. income tax on foreign income where no specific treaty exists. Tax treatment of oil exploration in the Netherlands is more generous than in Britain—which presumably affects the operating pattern of Royal Dutch/Shell; but the Dutch version of credit for foreign tax gives roughly equal results to that of the British. (Holland credits tax paid abroad by reducing its own tax in the proportion that the foreign income bears to the total, not by the absolute sum paid in foreign tax.) In France and some other European countries company tax is not usually payable on profits earned abroad; this 'income exemption' method is sometimes considered more advantageous, but since 1965–66 France has been offering the option of a tax credit system *à l'Americaine* as an alternative.

Most of the American tax rules specifically affecting oil exploration and production were specifically designed for the purpose, though usually for the domestic oil industry first, then extended on similar lines to oil ventures abroad. Most of the British oil ventures abroad were in train before company taxation in the country became fully codified; but on occasion account has probably been taken of the particular circumstances of British oil companies in making amendments to the tax rules affecting all British investment overseas. The effect for both countries is that, effectively, international groups based there generally manage to pay no home country tax at all on their foreign income from operations overseas. In neither country is tax paid abroad allowed to be credited directly against profits made by the company inside the home country—though the inquirer can always find British oilmen convinced that various loopholes do make this possible for American oilmen, and American oilmen convinced of just the converse. Britain certainly, up to 1966, was considerably less generous than the United States—and most European countries—in its treatment of exploration expenditures incurred before oil was found and developed taxable income. On the other hand, the possibility of making 'subvention payments' between subsidiaries of an international group based in Britain possibly made it easier for British oil companies to contrive not to 'waste' foreign tax credit than for American. Just which tax system offers the international oil company more advantage is perhaps a question for scholastic accountants (the answers always being temporary, since the company tax structures may change as radically as Britain's did in 1965-66). What is perhaps more important is that, rightly or wrongly, other developed countries less strongly placed in international oil believe that the Anglo-American dominance in its ownership derives partly from the tax advantages their systems give. During 1965 and 1966 a number of European oil companies began to argue this; France decided to change over to a tax credit system more like the American and British; and the European Economic Commission began to study possible 'Community tax incentives' to exploration for oil, at home and abroad.

At the other end of the business, in 'host countries' the liability of oil companies to tax differs rather more than might appear. At any time, some 'general principle' such as 50:50 may be accepted in most countries: but its effects can differ a great deal. When 50:50 was the principle applied in Venezuela, from 1948 to 1958, it meant that royalties and tax together amounted to at least half the profit achieved at the price actually realized in selling the oil—though this was never written in as an integral part of the concession, as it was in Middle East countries. 'Realized prices' again were stipulated as the tax base in the concessions granted in Libya from 1955 to 1965. By 1958, Venezuela had increased its take to close on 70 per cent of the profits realized: and late in 1966 the country changed over to fixed 'tax-reference prices', similar to those now applied in the Middle East. Libya in 1965, as we have noted earlier, in applying the 'OPEC modifications' to its 50:50 concessions, also managed to oblige all its concessionnaires to change over to profits reckoned on tax reference prices, whether such prices are realized in all bargains or not. Such prices are still well above those paid in most oil transactions. Up to 1964, it was roughly reckoned that this kind of 50:50 tax meant in practice that the governments received at least 56–57 per cent of the profits actually realized. Since 1964, their share has increased further. But even under the 50:50 formula with tax reference prices, the profits shown may not always mean quite the same thing. Much depends upon the 'ground rules' set down in the different concessions. The income tax has always to be a general tax, even if the oil company is in practice the only substantial taxpayer in a state; otherwise it might not be accepted by the company's home government for the purposes of relief. But what items are accepted as allowable costs before computing profits in the host country, and whether certain items of expenditure are 'expensed' against current earnings in the year concerned, or 'capitalized' and amortized over a longer period, depends on the original terms of each 50:50 agreement, as later worked upon by government and company accountants and lawyers over the years.

The origins of 50:50 in the Middle East offer an example of the way in which the inter-action of tax systems can facilitate—though it may later obstruct—the amendment of financial relationships between oil companies and governments. Following what it believed to be the Venezuelan example, Saudi Arabia in 1949 decreed that an income tax should be imposed: this would have entitled it to 50 per cent of Aramco's income *after* payment of United States tax. Negotiations between the government, the company and its corporate shareholders, and the United States Treasury ensued: eventually the law was drafted to give Saudi Arabia 50 per cent of profits *before* payment of American tax. The Arabian government received considerable help in the drafting of its tax legislation from the American government, which was concerned to ensure that this should be generally applicable and not a special tax, and hence admissible for foreign tax credit against the companies' American tax liability on this income. The result was quite a considerable increase in the Arabian revenue per barrel of oil, over and above the fixed royalty per barrel chargeable before: this royalty stayed at about 21–22 cents per barrel, but was credited against the tax in the final accounting. But the sizeable increase in host government revenue did not bring about a corresponding reduction in the net income of Aramco and its parent companies. Indeed, most non-American oilmen operating in the Middle East would question whether the acceptance of 50:50 cost the American companies operating in Arabia anything at all in net income—on the argument that the whole increase in Arabian tax, eligible for tax credit, was in practice offset by reductions in American tax on the same income.

At the same time, comparison between the companies' situation before and after 50:50 was blurred by the fact that the income on which the Saudi tax was charged originally differed from that on which American tax was. Aramco submitted to Arabian tax in 1950–51 on profits calculated on transfer prices to its parent company 'offtakers', who received a substantial 'cost of sales' discount below the price at which Arabian crude was available to outsiders. This reduced the turnover and hence the profit on which Arabian tax was charged. It probably meant that the Arabian tax and royalty, which worked out at a higher total rate than American tax plus Arabian royalty had done but was applied to a lower profit, amounted in absolute terms to about the same payments to governments, leaving the companies roughly as before. In 1953, however, these special discounts to offtakers were abolished: the Arabian tax was reckoned on profits on sales at posted prices to parent companies (and for a time at the actual prices realized in sales to third parties). When 50:50 deals were made in other Middle East countries, cost of sales discounts were applied in some cases; in others, such as Kuwait, the offtake contracts at low prices between the companies producing there and other major companies purchasing and marketing large volumes of the oil complicated matters for a time. Moreover, the companies that produce the oil are generally not the ones that sell it at posted price and submit to tax. But in many cases, nowadays, the same result holds good: the tax plus royalty in the Middle East more than offsets American (or British) tax on the same income. It has been one of the arts of every integrated group's accountants, dealing with the whole of its widespread international operations, to try to make sure that on the average, over the years, it is not left with 'excess tax credit' of which it cannot take benefit. (Britain's change to a 40 per cent corporation tax, in 1965–66, however, seemed to baffle such artistry, in that almost all other countries' rates of tax are higher. It seemed virtually impossible for British oil companies with overseas income, from then on, to avoid being left with excess and unusable tax credit.)

Effectively, therefore, the shift to 50:50 a decade ago represented largely a transfer of tax revenue from the American and the British treasuries to those of the Middle East. The companies became the channel for this transfer—which was admittedly a transfer of tax levied on the proceeds of selling Middle East oil—adding in some cases a little extra out of their own income. When these deals were made, no double taxation treaties existed between these Western countries and the Middle East nations concerned: nor do any now. The initiative of the American Treasury, therefore, was in extending unilateral relief to income taxation levied in those countries. Although in effect it was handing over (or handing back, as Arabs would probably prefer to put it) a very large slice of extra income to the whole Middle East, it was not radically altering the provisions of its own tax law for the purpose. French tax law, at that time, excluded profits made abroad by their nationals' operations abroad, and Dutch tax was reduced by the proportion that foreign income bore to total income regardless of the foreign tax actually paid: so in the Middle East the French and partly Dutch companies did not have as much tax liability on foreign income to credit the Arabs' new 50 per cent taxes against. For a time, some people in CFP and Shell will argue, the shift to 50:50 cost these two groups more than any other. Since they had been paying less tax at home before on this income, they had not the same cushion to offset the increase in tax abroad.

It so happened that the 50:50 formula came eventually, almost incidentally, to tie the revenues of Middle East countries to the prices posted for crude oil there. That, as we have seen, has become inconvenient in the present period of surplus in the oil market. The posted prices have to be kept up, regardless of the discounts increasingly available in actual bargains, and the companies, submitting to a '50 per cent' income tax, pay taxes that are in practice closer to 60 per cent of the profits actually realized. How long the treasuries of the parent countries of all oil companies would continue to accept this higher rate of tax, reckoned on a price now admittedly fictitious, as still being a general income tax fully creditable against home tax on foreign income, was a matter for speculation in more companies and countries than one.

It is worth noting that the unilateral reliefs for double tax available in the United States and Western Europe could be used to facilitate the transfer from a fixed revenue per barrel in the Middle East to a tax and royalty system fluctuating with selling income—or later with posted price and the volume of offtake. But once the foreign tax credits equalled or exceeded the home tax liability against which they could be credited, no further help for changes in the international oil companies' tax situation abroad was available. It seems doubtful whether many of these companies were able to obtain much offset in home tax to help them pay the most recent increase in the government revenues of some Middle East countries, from 1964 onwards. This was the payment of royalty on oil produced separately from tax, as an expense chargeable against the Middle East taxable income (instead of offsetting the royalty due against the Middle East tax, which left the government take at 50 per cent of notional 'profits' reckoned at posted price). Under the Western tax systems applied to the same income royalty already was 'expensed' before computing taxable income, not credited as a foreign tax can be against home tax liability on the income.

'Excess tax credits' may be of use to a company that has foreign income from other countries to take home on which it would be liable to some further tax in its parent country; in the United States a company can opt to be treated for tax purposes either on a one country or an 'overall' basis, and a British company can make subventions between different subsidiaries. But these credits cannot be used directly to offset tax liabilities on income earned in operations at home, which for the American groups are likely to be very sizeable. In Britain excess tax credits cannot be carried forward to later years; in the United States they can, but the chances are that a company with excess tax credit in one year may be in the same position in the next.

However, income earned in oil production by American companies anywhere, though not in later operations, also qualifies for the 'depletion allowance' mentioned above of $27\frac{1}{2}$ per cent of gross (or 50 per cent of net) income. Moreover, it is possible to 'expense'—i.e. to write off against income in the year it is incurred—all 'intangible' costs of drilling as well as other expenses of exploration, anywhere in the world, against domestic income before tax. These 'intangible costs'—i.e. those that do not remain embodied in physical assets on which depreciation can be charged—amount to about 75 per cent of drilling costs. And an American corporation, registered say in Delaware, may be responsible directly for all the international exploration of the group. Britain does not grant any depletion allowance on income from production at home or abroad (which derives, perhaps, primarily from the fact that oil production has never represented a significant domestic industry); some European countries do. And these countries, like the United States but unlike Britain, can expense drilling and other exploration costs in countries where production has not yet begun against income from companies where production has begun and there is taxable income to offset these expenses against.

It may well suit an American oil company, therefore, operating at home and abroad, to use any spare tax credits it has available after paying high taxes in producing countries abroad to offset American tax liability on any not 'fully offset' profits from other overseas activities; or, alternatively, to carry on through an American company a high rate of exploration abroad, the cost of much of which can be offset against profits at home. Within the United States, again, a judicious degree of drilling and a sizeable proportion of its income at the point of production, on which depletion allowance is available, can minimize its home tax liabilities. But European oil companies' income originating inside European countries is not comparable in proportion to that of the American international majors inside America. (Nor is it generally inflated by a comparable degree of protection against imports.) As a result, foreign tax credit is liable to bring down their total home tax liability to nil or a negligible percentage more easily than it can the home tax due from American countries. But the Americans, after all, have their home profits, after tax, to strengthen them financially.

Any such bald summary becomes a caricature in its over-simplification of what is a vast and complex pattern of operations, where tax is only one of the factors motivating decisions, though one seldom wholly ignored in any decision. Tax circumstances in between these end points, the producing and the parent countries, are obviously of importance in the commercial strategy of an international company. The physical movement of oil from well to terminal, into the tanker, out into a coastal refinery the other end, and from refinery product storage out along the channels of distribution to the final consumer, may be simple and highly economical. One constant exercise in oil management is to keep it flowing from a number of As to a myriad of Bs with the lowest possible expenditure of time and resources, and as few halts on the way as possible. But on paper, at least, this oil may take a very much less straightforward route to market; the notional itinerary being chosen to get the oil home with the least possible subtraction of tax from the price eventually paid for it.

From a joint, non-profit-making company in the Middle East, for example, the ownership of the oil, or of the right to take the oil, or of the right to a depletion allowance on the oil taken, may pass to several other local trading companies in the country concerned. These companies—which in practice are sometimes no more than a brass plate in the entrance of a local bank—exist for the purpose of buying oil at cost from the jointly-owned producer, selling it at posted price to an international trading affiliate of the same group, and submitting to tax on the profits shown. In certain circumstances, there may be more than one rank of these: A.3. and A.2. companies, as the phrase goes, as well as the A.1. that actually produces and despatches the oil. Moreover, some of these various affiliates of the same major company, under the umbrella of whose eventual ownership the oil may be produced, moved, processed and finally marketed, may possibly be owned at different levels by different intermediate holding companies. The purpose of these transfers of ownership along the oil's route to market may be partly to settle foreign currency transfers, but partly also for it to confer profits or losses upon a succession of affiliates along the way. The integrated groups are usually able to marry some of these losses with some of the profits that come out on other deals. Sir Henry Deterding is credited with the formulation of the 'straight line', by which the oil moved along the most economical possible route to market. Physically, it still does: but in terms of title and tax liability, the best financial way home may often nowadays be much less direct.

No sensible business firm anywhere arranges its affairs for the benefit of the tax collector; or, particularly, for the purpose of paying tax twice on the same income. The international oil companies differ from those in most other industries only by having to operate within so many tax systems that their perfectly legal arrangements to avoid leaving most of their shareholders' profits in the hands of tax collectors, by comparison, have to become somewhat three-dimensional. Other liabilities to tax— and other collectors' pressures to maintain the amount paid in taxes— again occur in between producing government and home government. Another complication arising since the fifties from the political fixity of posted prices for crude oil while discounts are in practice having to be conceded on the sale of products has been that this has tended to squeeze refinery margins down. Refining affiliates that invoiced crude oil at posted prices, but which could not sell their products at prices that would give a reasonable return on their investment after paying for the crude, could be forced into a loss—even though a group profit was being made on the crude oil they process and sell.

At the end of the fifties, the governments of some countries where such refining was done began to ask awkward questions about these losses and the local taxes that these affiliates of apparently rich international companies were therefore not paying. If these were not viable entities, it was acidly inquired, why did not their owners close them down? And if they were vital links in a chain of international movement, manufacture and marketing, ought they not to bear a commensurate share of taxation with other individuals and enterprises in the countries where their owners still seemed glad to go on selling? The question, to a consumer country, seemed a perfectly fair one—particularly a consumer country not getting much in the way of dividends from integrated international oil companies. Faced with this pressure, since the beginning of the sixties, certain of the major companies have quietly helped their affiliates in some of these countries at least to break even, if not to show large profits. This may have meant writing down certain current debts to other affiliates from their books: it could mean 'discounting to affiliates' on crude as well as to independent buyers; it might involve subvention payments. Occasionally the international deployment of the oil business, it will be seen, involves it in contriving to pay more tax here and there, not less.

American tax law bulks large in any consideration of the effect of tax on international oil operations, mainly because it was the original home of the modern oil industry, remains the domicile of most of the largest companies, and is one of the only highly developed countries in which some of the tax law has been largely shaped with oil in mind. It has been said above that an American oil company can moderate its home tax liability by engaging in a fairly large degree of production and an intensive programme of drilling, at home and overseas. But it should be added that this hardly amounts even to tax avoidance, if one defines that as ingenious manœuvring within the tax laws. It is simply a matter of doing what the American government wants oil companies to do and rewards them for doing.

These provisions in the tax law were specifically enacted to encourage a high rate of drilling and to maintain a large oil producing industry inside the United States and elsewhere under American management. To the extent that American oil companies take advantage of it (to reduce their tax liability), the object of the provisions is achieved. Not all interests and politicians in the United States approve of the opportunities that this network of general and specific tax legislation offers the oil enterprise to reduce and offset its liability to American income tax. But none of them question that it is entirely proper for the companies to take advantage of the opportunities offered. Some of these critics would be prepared to advise complete reconsideration of the purposes for which the United States offers oil these tax incentives. Others argue that the purposes might be achieved even if certain of the incentive provisions in the tax laws were pruned back somewhat. All that the outsider needs to note is that significant alterations in these provisions might considerably affect the balance of factors in many decisions for the international companies based in America. And such changes could therefore have consequences for oil deals and government revenues far outside the borders of the United States.

Taxation policies designed mainly to bring about oil developments considered desirable inside this one country, therefore, have a very powerful effect upon oil development in the rest of the world, when the country concerned plays so pivotal a role in the industry as the United States does. Consider this chain of consequences and side-effects, sought and unsought. Income from the production of oil inside the United States, rather than its later transport, processing or marketing, receives special tax treatment in order to maintain a strong producing industry there. 'The profit,' in the phrase that many American oilmen use, 'is made on the crude': and certainly it will bear less tax if it is. The prices of American crude oil on which those profits are made had for many years a logically dominant effect in setting the prices on crude oil produced elsewhere. Tax arrangements facilitated originally by the American Treasury allow all of the tax paid on income from the production of crude overseas to remain in the hands of host governments: and these governments' taxes have become tied to the advertised, not the actual, prices paid for that foreign crude. Other incentives in the American tax system (matched by their foreign competitors) meanwhile promote an extremely high rate of exploration and development drilling, everywhere in the world as well as in the United States. This adds to the temptation for American oil companies, both international majors and independents, to pre-empt the chances of possible future bonanzas that are inherent in the high risks but high winnings associated with oli exploration. Where oil is discovered in this worldwide effort, governments anxious in their turn to begin to latch on to the tax revenues available from oil-producing income press for its rapid development to the stage of production. And the high rate of oil development has helped inevitably to uncover and exacerbate the potential surplus of oil in the world market. There is no simple pattern of cause and effect here; the surplus is basically engendered by the extent to which ruling prices exceed the cost of new oil. But the economic and fiscal factors probably do interact. Tax incentives introduced to develop the American oil industry in a 'healthy' fashion may have contributed to developing and rigidifying some quite unhealthy economic and fiscal distortions in the working of the oil industry outside America.

Taxes are often the chosen instruments of national or nationalist policy towards oil, though not the only ones used: the remaining chapters of this book are devoted to sketching the wide variety of policies affecting oil now developing around the world. But it would be unreal to mention here simply the company taxes that affect the production of oil and the businesses concerned with it. A vast sum in taxation of petroleum products, levied occasionally for reasons of deliberate 'oil policy' but more often simply as a very dependable way of raising revenue, is paid every year by petroleum consumers in most countries. Gasoline and other road fuels are expendable goods with a demand that is fairly inelastic to price: just what any finance minister would and does pick for indirect taxation. These taxes, over the long run, have major effects upon the pattern of relative demand for products in different consuming nations. The rates of tax applicable to road fuels, for example, may either enhance or offset the technical advantages of using diesel oil as against gasoline in motor transport. They may also have a considerable effect, over time, on the types and sizes of engine and motor vehicle used in different countries. But these taxes, huge in amount as they are, are often fairly 'neutral' in motive and effect, because the motor fuels are not as easily open to substitution as are say the fuels used for general heating. Excise taxes on petroleum products used as general fuels, which have been imposed in many countries in the last few years, bring us back however to the sphere of policies deliberately applied towards oil, towards imports, or towards all kinds of fuel.

The content of government policies towards oil varies according to their national circumstances. Some have it at home, or are hopeful of finding it. Others have not, but may have command, through national companies, of large supplies of it abroad. Others have not, but have large national fuel industries that cannot produce as cheaply as oil can be imported. Other nations have neither, and want the cheapest oil they can get anywhere. And some nations have virtually nothing but oil. In addition to these attitudes reflecting national circumstances as regards oil, two other elements are reflected in the attitudes of governments towards the industry. The first is a set of varying social attitudes towards private property, towards foreign enterprise, towards bigness in industry: all, springing from different philosophies and motives, may be applied to bridle the freedom of action of international oil companies. The second is the desire, again common in countries enjoying very different circumstances, for 'conservation' of ultimately exhaustible natural resources.

Emotionally, people and governments in countries that possess oil are for 'conservation' somewhat in the way that everybody is against sin. The trouble only begins when they have to decide what they mean by the term. In principle, everyone can agree in condemning extravagance in the development of any natural resource. Puritans may apply this to the extravagant consumption of oil and other minerals—though even puritan ideas of what rate of consumption is excessive vary over time and between different societies. Geologists apply the term to the use of methods of taking the oil out of the ground that may over time maximize the amount that can ultimately be extracted from any reservoir—and to the prevention of methods that do the opposite, such as letting wells run 'flush' that are liable to dissipate the gas or water pressure in the reservoir. There is no doubt at all that in the past much oil has been lost by techniques that worked out the pressure drive in oilfields long before it need have done, and reduced the recovery rate—i.e. the proportion of the oil *in situ* that can be got out—below what could have been achieved even then, let alone today. Improved techniques of secondary recovery can increase that rate, hence 'stretching' the economically recoverable amount of oil from a reserve. But in general 'conservation' is used simply to mean the prevention of wasteful exploitation of reserves in the first place.[2]

Economists are somewhat cautious about the employment of this concept of conservation.[3] 'Waste' to them is production which it would pay to postpone or do without altogether. In order to identify this waste, and hence to decide the point at which one should restrict production, you might theoretically estimate the future value of all the oil liable to be extracted from any given reservoir, on whatever assumption about prices and recovery you thought best: then discount this value according to an interest rate reflecting 'the cost of waiting'; and finally compare this value with the marginal cost of producing and using less oil now. If the discounted future value of oil exceeds the cost of doing without it today, restricting output would be economically logical. But to state such a proposition is not to be able to apply it (nor would the discounted future value to an international oil company be necessarily the same as to, say, an underdeveloped country). Such a calculation also requires the uncertain assessment of the future course of technology, both in the extraction of oil and of possible alternative fuels and in their future use. Admittedly, the period of prediction required may not be as long as might appear. Apply even a low rate of discount to any estimated value 30 to 40 years ahead, and the present value comes rapidly down towards nil; so mistakes in estimating the future value matter less and less the longer ahead one looks. But governments, for the most part, have not yet accepted the economists' criteria here; engineering concepts of conservation are more usual.

No country that possesses oil is yet within striking distance of running out of it, though the world's greatest oil producer and consumer, the United States, has already perhaps some grounds for caution, if one extrapolates its recent increases in capacity against the recent increase in consumption. Some expert estimates of the time by which domestic production there may pass its peak rate of oil extraction have put this no farther off than the seventies.

At the other end of the scale of countries that possess oil come those where vast increases in national wealth have been built purely upon the exploitation of recently-discovered oil reserves. For such countries, these reserves represent a treasure chest, the opening of which has transformed their whole ways of living—but by definition not a bottomless treasure chest. These reserves are 'neutral stuff' of no more than potential value, *in situ*, until the technical resources and capital supplied by 'visiting' oil companies have transformed them into realizable value from marketable oil. Nevertheless, to the governments of these countries, the huge incomes that these visitors have been able to draw up and share with them from these reserves still appear as drawings upon a national store of capital.

Different governments have adopted different attitudes towards this extraction of wasting national riches. Some have built conservation policies into the very system of granting the original drilling leases, such as Alberta. Others have ploughed back the oil revenues into education and technical training of their people and the fostering of any other practicable industries inside their borders, against the time when their rich revenues of oil must be expected to decline—or to be devalued by lasting reductions in the cost of alternative forms of energy, such as nuclear power. A few have invested the huge funds that oil has gathered them in industry abroad, upon the argument that local investment offers too limited a return. Markets in the places where oil has developed outside the United States have been generally too small and too underdeveloped for oil to attract industries to cluster around it. But the limited opportunities of 'replanting' industrial capital in some of the countries that are now growing rich by taking out their oil must condition those countries' attitude towards the rate of return that they hope to get on the oil taken out. Among such countries, only Venezuela has so far evinced practical interest in the limitation of output for purposes of technical conservation. But other members of OPEC, along with it, have certainly considered the limitation of output to 'market demand' at high and stable prices—that is, something on the lines that the state regulatory agencies carry out in the United States. Predictably, this was a theme to which OPEC returned in 1965, as soon as it had gained some success from its pressure to get royalties 'expensed'. Its 'programming' of production began much more modestly than the American states' regulatory agencies operate; and had no initial effect at all. But its ambitions are certainly no smaller.

Government intervention in the oil industry of the United States to regulate the volume of output has of late been buttressed with the regulation of imports of oil, as a more open measure of protection for domestic oil—and other domestic fuel industries. This is a kind of government intervention matched in one or two countries that rely almost entirely upon imports for their oil, and are increasing their dependence upon oil as a general fuel. In one form or another 'fuel policies' of one kind or another, overt or covert, are to be found in most of the countries of Western Europe. The coal industries of some of these countries, after a decade of inadequate attempts to increase output to meet increasing fuel demand, were during the late fifties suddenly left stranded as consumers who had turned to oil simply as a freely available alternative were followed by those who preferred its convenience, reliability of supply, and of late, its cheapness. These industries very soon sought, and gained, protection.

As well as these short-term problems of structural adjustment within their economies, the continuing shift to oil and the further possibility of relying somewhat on imports of natural gas pose some longer-term problems for the governments of such consumer countries. Europe has enough memories of postwar balance of payments difficulties not to

OIL COMPANIES AS TAXPAYERS

shrug off too easily questions of the rising import costs of petroleum in future.

There remain uncertainties about oil prices in the medium run. Though few people expect them to rise for cost reasons as much as the price of coal, many note that the producing governments are now increasing their 'take' and whether companies can avoid passing this increase in 'tax-paid cost' on in prices. There are uncertainties for the longer run about how much a country can afford to run down its capacity for producing coal. The costs of getting coal out of the ground seem certain to grow more than those of oil, but there may ultimately be much more of it there. The world has never been prospected for coal with anything like the intensity that it is now being explored for oil. But even so most oil geologists would agree in guessing that the world's ultimate resources of coal, however big, seem likely so far to be several times bigger than those of oil. This may however in the meantime become irrelevant. Once economic nuclear energy begins to set the ciling price for all fuels, what will matter for the fossil fuels is not the ultimate total reserves, but the amounts obtainable at that price or less. The weight that can or should be given to such considerations by countries in different situations *vis-à-vis* oil must be a matter of argument. Nobody is more interested in such arguments than the oil business itself and of late, some of the other fuel industries with which it competes.

Attention to what is often called 'the impact of nationalism on the oil industry' tends to be focused simply upon the growing interest of host governments in the oil production of integrated companies— primarily the major international companies—within the borders of countries remote alike from the main markets and from the countries in which these oil companies' headquarters are domiciled. Sometimes the term is used scornfully, too, of underdeveloped countries' pressures to develop local refining or otherwise cut foreign exchange. This attitude represents a blinkered view and sometimes an unconsciously 'colonialist' one. Governments in most countries, developed or undeveloped, nowadays are intervening in the affairs of the oil industry, and seeking to bring its activities into line with 'national policies': and perhaps they inevitably must. This is not to say that all their policies are sensible, or likely individually or in concatenation to lead to the optimum development of oil and other energy resources. But this industry cannot escape a large degree of political involvement; this is a 'penalty of greatness' for it in the economies that it supports, serves and enriches.

In the remainder of this book an attempt is made to outline some of the ways in which such national policies impinge upon the oil industry, and some of the ways in which the policies of particular countries may soon impinge upon each other. National policies in the wider sense, rather than under any blinkered definition of nationalism, are considered with some attempt at assessing their influence upon the industry in the immediate future. So are the 'supra-national' policies that organizations of governments, both at the producing and the consuming end of the business, may soon be pressing upon this industry.

It may be that such policies are part of the facts of life for any industry of comparable importance in our increasingly organized world. One can argue more convincingly, perhaps, that energy industries are peculiarly subject to such governmental concern. 'Nationalism' as regards energy, at any rate, seems almost universal today. Its nature varies according to the country's situation, from producer to consumer. In the following chapters, as case studies of different approaches to oil, a small selection of countries in differing situations are considered in detail. They range on the one hand from the relatively self-sufficient in oil to those that are large consumers but produce practically none, and on the other hand to the large-scale producers with far more oil than they could ever consume at home. The various categories, chosen for convenience, are inevitably arbitrary, over-simplified and often debatable. Some countries ought strictly to be considered under more than one heading on this scale; and the situation of others is changing quite fast. But these countries have been chosen and classified to show how varied and complex governmental pressures on this industry are becoming; and to emphasize how liable the policies that different governments press upon it are to conflict.

CHAPTER XII

Self-sufficiency in Oil: I. The United States

Once a month—often on a Friday morning, in one of the public rooms of the Commodore Perry Hotel in Austin, Texas—three professional public servants of the State of Texas decide roughly how much oil the world's largest single private industry shall produce during the next month. Their decision is not concerned with prices, but it is based partly on estimates of market demand, defined as 'demand at existing prices': as such, indirectly, it does provide a powerful though not absolute support to the level of crude oil prices charged in the American oil industry. The Texas Railroad Commission, again, is concerned with the 'proration' of crude oil output according to the maximum rate of efficient production and to reasonable market demand only inside Texas: there are other regulatory bodies to set output rates in other oil-producing states, and a number of states in which production is not controlled at all. But Texas is the largest producing state, with about 30 per cent of current output in the United States and close on half of the country's proved reserves. And experience suggests that Texas, as the fully-regulated largest producer, acts as the stabilizing balance-wheel for total American oil production. When demand goes down, Texan output goes down most; when demand rises, Texan output follows upward too, but less sharply. This last point does not please Texas producers, who feel they benefit less on the roundabouts than some less self-disciplined oil-producing states. But with their larger production, they would stand to lose much more heavily on the swings if total production were allowed to rise much above market demand and prices were to collapse.

To the foreign observer, who is frequently lectured by American oil companies operating overseas about their utter and immutable opposition to anything approaching state control or the protection of indigenous fuels against low-cost imports, it is somewhat paradoxical to find that in the United States these companies, and a host of smaller, even more rambunctiously 'free enterprisers' in the domestic oil business there, get on very comfortably thank you with state agencies telling them how much crude oil they can produce, how much they can buy and who from, and of late, federal agencies telling them how much crude and products they can import. Even the last of these, statutory import control, which dates only from 1958, and was originally sharply opposed by some major companies, seems now quite cheerfully accepted by these bitter opponents of 'statism'. Talking inside the American industry during the early sixties, such a foreign visitor could find some companies still prepared to argue about details of the way in which these restrictive import quotas were set and allocated. But none, even those with the largest and cheapest foreign oil reserves, were prepared to argue against protection of the American oil market in principle. Most of the restricted importers are domestic producers too; and considering the decline in prices and rise in government payments abroad, they must find profits per barrel a good deal easier to earn inside the American imports fence.[1] Taxed with a degree of doublethink here, some American oilmen confess it disarmingly: 'It all depend on whose ox is being gored.' Others do not. An ability to profess and act upon several mutually contradictory propositions at the same time has its convenience in business, as in many other spheres of social activity.

To recognize from the beginning that the privately-owned oil industry, in its own home, is subject to a very large degree of governmental influence, is not to deny that there is some logic in the purpose that the different elements of government influence there are fitted together to achieve the maintenance in being of a large domestic oil-producing industry in the United States. Some would define the purpose of government influence here as absolute national self-sufficiency in energy, which is probably more than any American government now aims at. Others might say it is the maintenance of an efficient and commercially competitive domestic oil industry, which is certainly more than these measures achieve. But once given such a purpose—and though it has the obvious danger of making energy costs in the United States higher than they need be, protection from foreign competition is one of the principles behind which American industries grew great—and given the legal pattern of property relationships in the United States, then a system of regulations and incentives probably had to be devised for domestic oil development. It can indeed be argued that given the inherent nature of oil production some such system needs to emerge everywhere: the OPEC governments have so argued. But a glance at some of the details of one outstanding element in this regulatory system may be useful in illustrating the complexity of the whole system's workings in the United States—and may indicate how efficiently or inefficiently regulation serves its protective purpose.

A monthly 'hearing' before the Texas Railroad Commission (which was set up in the nineties to regulate railway operations, and proceeding via the supervision of bus and truck transport, gas utilities and pipeline regulations, was in 1919 first set the task of oil and gas conservation in the State) often takes less than half an hour, though once every year there is a regular full-dress hearing at greater length, and at any monthly hearing argument or cross-examination may lengthen the proceedings. Held before the three-man commission, it is attended by representatives of the major refining companies that buy crude oil from independent producers in Texas oilfields (to balance out their own requirements and supplies), by representatives of producers, truckers, and other people interested in Texas oil production. The commission is armed with statements showing the 'nominations' put forward by each of these crude buyers to say how much it would like to purchase in the coming month, its actual and desired levels of crude and product stocks, and the rate at which each has been operating its refining capacity during the month before. It is also supplied by the Federal Bureau of Mines in Washington with that agency's estimate of market demand for Texas crude during the next month, and with estimates of stocks and refinery runs throughout the United States. And because its own investigators have estimated and are checking as constantly as they can the 'MER' (maximum rate of efficient flow) of every different oilfield reservoir in Texas, the commission also knows how much oil will be produced from any given percentage of capacity operation of the 90,000-odd wells in the State that are 'prorated', i.e. have their output adjusted up and down according to the percentage of their 'schedule allowable', or theoretical 100 per cent producing capacity, that the commission sets for any given month.

Though the nominations have in fact been put in writing to the commission before the hearing, it is usual for a number of the major crude buyers to repeat these verbally there, saying how much oil they want to purchase and the percentage 'producing pattern' that they think would be advisable for the coming month. Members of the commission may question them about their estimates: representatives of producers or other interested parties can put in their views. The commission briefly deliberates: then it announces the 'total state allowable' for the next month and the percentage of their own 'schedule allowables' that all prorated wells will be permitted to produce during the month.[2]

This is not as simple a process as it sounds, though most people at these Austin hearings have it down to a fine art. Relying mainly, perhaps, upon its assessment of crude and product stocks throughout the nation, the commission decides approximately how much crude will be needed from Texas wells in the coming month to accord with the demand they foresee. It has then to deduct from this total certain large elements of Texas oil production that are exempt from variation from month to month in their rates of output—in the jargon, exempt from percentage proration. These comprise first the huge East Texas field, which in order to maintain pressure and hence flow from the reservoir is operated at a rate of efficient production much lower than its proportionate share of Texas oil reserves; secondly, fields producing on provisional 'discovery allowables' during their first two years of operation, before their 'MERs' can be properly determined; thirdly, 'stripper wells' in the later stage of their producing lives, which when producing less than 20 barrels a day are assumed to be produced at efficient rates and are not controlled; and fourthly, wells being produced by certain 'secondary recovery' methods.

In mid-April, 1963, to take an actual example, these exempt wells accounted for nearly 1,220,000 barrels a day out of the total 'schedule allowable' in Texas—i.e., the aggregate of maximum rates for efficient production of oil from all the wells there, as reckoned by the Railroad Commission—of approaching 7,000,000 barrels a day. This left a possible 5,580,000 barrels a day or so of production theoretically possible from 'wells subject to proration'. Some crude buyers' nominations early in March of their requirements for April 1963 were as high as 2,850,000 barrels a day, or just about 1,630,000 barrels a day over and above the output exempt from control. The commission in fact set an allowable for April of some 2,820,000 barrels, which meant that the wells subject to proration were each allowed to produce 28 per cent of their individual 'allowables'. This total rate of output for the month from production liable to variable control is in practice allocated between fields according to their share in proven Texas reserves, and within fields between wells according to rules specifically though rather arbitrarily worked out for the regulation of each field. But in practice, as a House of Representatives committee was told in 1957 by Lt.-Gen. E. O. Thompson of the Railroad Commission, the grand old man of oil proration in the

United States, 'each man knows what his allowable is for each and every well.'

That allowable tells each producer how much he can legally supply from each well each month: and his output is liable to be checked against the throughput of the refinery to which he sells to see that he produces no more. He is forbidden to produce and sell oil in excess of this: a federal law, the Connally 'Hot Oil' Act, which prohibits 'exports' of oil across state lines to escape the scrutiny and jurisdiction of state regulatory agencies, seals one possible escape route. On the other hand, control of the producer is accompanied by regulation of the purchaser. The principle of the 'rateable take' requires every buyer to take oil in equal proportion from all the wells connected to his gathering pipelines, even if for one reason or another he should be forced to reduce his total offtake below plan and to practise 'pipeline proration'. Therefore a big integrated company will generally be taking much less of its requirements from its own producing capacity (on which it gets full producing profits as well as any profits on later operations) than it might economically choose; and much more than it would choose from independents to whom it has to pay posted prices and hence gets only the later 'downstream' profits. This factor was one, in the immediate postwar years, that made many majors with overseas operations plan growing imports of crude from overseas for their United States refineries. Such crude was not merely cheap oil; it was their own 'cost oil'.

Proration of oil production is not universal in the United States, and the statutes and rules in different states are constantly being revised.[2] California, for example, is now a net importer of oil among other fuels and is hardly concerned to regulate the volume of production at all. Some of the significant oil-producing states, such as Wyoming, do not authorize proration to market demand, but control output only to maintain efficient production in their reservoirs. Louisiana sets its 'allowables' by rather different methods from those of Texas—and it gives its increasing offshore production rather better allowables than comparable onshore wells, since this costs more to develop. In Oklahoma, which early this century became the first state to engage in the proration of oil according to market demand as well as physical conservation, the production from each lease rather than each well is controlled, which enables each producer to take his permitted output from his most convenient or efficient wells. This state, also, was ahead of most others in legislating for compulsory 'unitization'—i.e. the management of production from all wells in any given reservoir according to the characteristics and needs of the whole field, provided that a given proportion of lessees and royalty owners approve. Most of the other producing states also now provide for unitization of fields; but the agreement of a large percentage of the producers concerned is often impossible to achieve. In New Mexico, proration takes place under a new law that has been regarded as a model. In Kansas, a fairly elaborate proration system has been largely nullified by a law setting the minimum 'allowable' for any well at 25 barrels a day for every well, which leaves the state's Corporation Commission little chance to grant the better wells more than that minimum: only a small proportion of Kansas wells, therefore, are effectively prorated. In Mississippi and some other states, proration is prohibited from taking 'market demand' into account; and Illinois has no proration at all.

Though oil is now produced in more than 30 states of the Union, some 90 per cent of it comes from the nine named above: and the country's spare capacity to produce oil is concentrated in six of them, which together produce about 75 per cent. Texas has long been overwhelmingly the biggest producer. Its proration to market demand is the main factor bringing production in 'Districts 1–4' of the United States oil market—i.e. the United States East of the Rockies—into line with the demand that its Railroad Commission and other experts forecast.

This predominance of Texas, and its consequently greater incentive to stabilize the market, have probably a much greater 'automatic' effect in co-ordinating the effect of state regulation than any direct efforts of the Inter-State Oil Compact to Conserve Oil and Gas ever have. This is an agreement signed in 1935 between six oil-producing states, to which twenty-nine now adhere, and to the meetings of which certain federal departments and agencies, plus the government of Venezuela and the Canadian oil producing provinces of Alberta and Saskatchewan, now send observers. An Inter-State Compact Commission organizes conferences and co-operation between these different state regulatory bodies, which may enhance the like-mindedness anyway to be expected among them. There have been occasions in the past when critics of proration have alleged that action to cut back production had followed upon specific agreement within this commission to keep prices up. Such collusion has always been hotly denied by the members of the Compact; nor does it ever appear to have attempted any form of 'higher-level proration', i.e. sharing out production equitably among the oil-producing states of the Union. The Texas Commission, indeed, would probably argue that what happens is inequitable, and that Texas is nearly always left to take alone the brunt of the cuts in output necessary to hold total American production down to market demand. This may easily happen under any proration system: the biggest producer may feel it has the most to lose from market instability. On the other hand, the proration commissions cannot control the bids of demand that integrated companies and other pipeline operators put in. Although in any state the integrated companies have to buy crude 'rateably' from all comers, they decide themselves how much they will buy from each state.

In addition to the setting of production allowables, the prohibition of sales of 'hot oil' across state lines, and the 'rateable take', conservation in Texas and elsewhere lays down many rules regarding the technique of production in actual oilfields. There are rules laying down the minimum 'spacing' between wells—which in Texas has been adjusted upwards, though fairly slowly, from one well per 10 acres to one per 40 acres, with exceptions for some special cases. There are in certain circumstances extra allowables for the introduction of pressure maintenance techniques. In Oklahoma, for years, and more recently elsewhere, state regulatory agencies encourage the unitization of whole fields. Many of the worst and most stupid technical abuses in oilfield development have been outlawed by these commissions, and in certain major fields such as East Texas it seems clear that the ultimate quantity of oil recoverable has been considerably increased by measures of pressure maintenance undertaken as a result of their influence. Yet technically, as well as economically, the real effects on productive efficiency of all this regulatory activity are highly debatable.[3]

'We have nothing to do with price,' said General Thompson to that same committee of the House of Representatives in 1957. 'We are forbidden to consider economics; purely physical waste. I know nothing about price.' Behind his disclaimer—and General Thompson spoke as a brilliant administrator, trained as a lawyer, but with a grasp of economics to which many Texas businessmen would testify— lay the experience of years of controversy over the motives of proration and its effects. In Texas that controversy had at times in the past been taken to courts which had reversed the proration decisions of the Railroad Commission. In some states proration agencies are still enjoined—as that of Texas was for many years—from overtly taking market demand into account when setting production allowables.

Texas is no longer so enjoined: and market demand (*pace* the General) clearly takes one over the fringe into economics. 'Although no state oil regulatory body gives consideration to price in determining market demand,' said Mr. William Murray, one of the General's then colleagues on the Railroad Commission, in an address in 1960, 'it would be naïve not to recognize that market demand proration does affect price. But the effect is to stabilize price and eliminate the rapid and extreme fluctuations from ruinously low prices to the consumer in times of over-supply to disastrously high prices to the consumer in times of scarcity.' Mr. Murray agreed that it gave the producer a higher average price over the years, protecting the independent by a 'rateable take' of his crude output, making his operation 'bankable' by ensuring him a proportionate market outlet, and making wild-catting worth while by promising 'discovery allowable' production for any well brought in. He argued, further, that the economies proration makes possible in above-ground storage, pipeline capacity and working capital, and the denial of exaggerated profit margins to the speculator, reduce the margin between what the producer receives and what the consumer pays. That may be true too: but where the balance of advantage from stabilizing prices works out over the years depends upon which are the longer—periods of over-supply or of scarcity. There seems little doubt that in oil's history so far the times of surplus, in aggregate, have been longer. And to that certain features of the pro-ration methods used, along with other elements of governmental policy affecting United States oil, have themselves contributed.

The original need for discipline, both technical and economic, in oilfield development in the United States, arose from the pattern of property rights in land ownership there. The 'rule of capture' which has been mentioned earlier was first adumbrated in American petroleum development in a natural gas case in 1889. Relying on the analogy of water percolating into riparian owners' land and of game lured to a neighbour's land, the Pennsylvania judges told plaintiffs who accused neighbours of 'stealing' the oil beneath their land by drilling wells just across the fence that they could suggest no remedy except, 'Only go and do likewise'. This ruling legally justified the drilling of 'offset wells' as close as possible to wherever a nearby landowner had found oil, and the sub-division of land where oil was discovered into tiny lots, on each of which as many wells were drilled as could physically be put together there. Technically, such overdrilling meant the dissipation of gas-cap and other pressures below ground, rapidly reducing the rate of flow from wells and ultimately the proportion of the oil *in situ* recoverable from any given field. Economically, the pressure upon landowner and oil lessee to get all the oil they could out of the ground as soon as possible led to production without regard to what the market could take. That softened prices; and often instead of reducing the incentive to produce oil, this merely spurred on yet higher output in order to make up the total income of the parties dependent upon production. Even recently there have been cases in which new techniques of 'directional drilling' have been used not merely to 'offset' other wells, but to drill at an angle under the ground right into a neighbour's 'pay zone'. So the temptation clearly remains a real one.

Nobody can fault proration in principle where its aim is confined to limiting oil production to the maximum rates compatible with a high rate of recovery from each oil reservoir, while at the same time protecting the property rights of individual surface leaseholders, by preventing the dissipation of gas pressures and the like—though it must be realized that any estimate of the maximum practicable recovery from a reservoir involves economic as well as engineering considerations. But even putting on one side this estimation—which is a matter of choosing the 'right' rate of discount to compare future with present values—the actual proration rules used might lead to waste even in engineering terms. The 'discovery allowables' that new wells are offered—along with some American tax rules—encourage an exaggerated level of drilling activity. Although the regulation of well spacing, to reduce this effect, is being improved, it has not yet checked a higher rate of drilling in most American oil-producing areas than would seem justified in terms of new reserves discovered, or of efficiency in reservoir development. Some American oil experts will point with pride to the fact that when effective proration began in Texas in the mid-thirties the state had 60,000 producing wells: today it has about 200,000 and well completions continue in the state at the rate of 13,000 a year. But statistics that are more sobering show a steady decline in the rate of reserves discovered per foot of wells drilled. And it is a matter of argument how much of this drilling represents the genuine search for new oilfields, as against an exaggerated rate of development drilling, aimed at the acquisition of a guaranteed right to produce even a trickle more oil from known fields.

However, the incentives that promote a greater rate of development drilling in American oilfields than undistorted commercial interest would justify arise perhaps more from taxation than proration. The depletion allowance upon producing income, but not upon other kinds of oil income, makes oil production a particularly advantageous kind of investment to engage in, both for established oil operators and for speculators from outside who are in high tax brackets for marginal income. The right to set off, for tax purposes, the 'intangible' costs of drilling and development—i.e., those other than the cost of equipment that can be amortized, amounting to say 75 per cent of total drilling costs—against other income in the year that they are incurred means that the costs of looking for oil are lightened and indeed may, on occasion, become a positive advantage to incur. There are cynical statisticians inside the American oil business who will point to the surge of drilling activity that seems regularly to take place in the second half of each financial year, and to link this with the point at which entrepreneurs begin to get fairly firm estimates of what their final income, and hence their prospective tax liability, may be. There is even a phrase for it—'drilling up one's tax'. That applies to oil producers as a whole. For the speculator from outside oil, who has of late been supplying quite a large amount of venture capital for oil drilling, this form of gamble with dollars on which he is otherwise liable to very high rates of tax gives the chance of finding property against the revenue from which his unsuccessful exploration costs can be written off and upon which an eventual capital gain may be realized, with a consequently lower rate of tax liability. That is one reason why the odds so often quoted from American experience against finding oil by wildcatting, and the percentage of dry holes even in development drilling, do not bear any real relationship to the risks in exploration and drilling elsewhere. They reflect real problems of finding oil in the most mature oil-producing country in the world, and certainly the most intensively explored. But they also represent incentives offered by tax and proration that promote an exaggerated rate of drilling.

Output regulation and special taxation treatment together certainly make for a big American oil-producing industry; the particular forms chosen did not make for economic efficiency in all its operations even before import restrictions were added to complete the charmed circle for domestic oil producers. Both systems are designed deliberately to encourage a higher rate of drilling than would otherwise occur—and by keeping up exploratory activity, they have encouraged considerable technological improvement in its methods over the years. The actual rate of drilling undertaken is still largely dependent upon the level of prosperity in the crude producing industry and in the American economy generally: after 1956, the number of wells completed tended to fall somewhat and the total footage drilled also to decline (though not as much as the number of wells, because the average well completed continues gradually to get deeper). The discovery of giant oil reservoirs is still too random and unpredictable a business to say how much of this drilling effort is wasted. Every dry hole at least develops knowledge for the next explorer, even if only negative knowledge of where not to drill. But the additions to American reserves of late have not grown in proportion to the footage drilled or the expenditure on exploration. In terms of feet drilled or of dollars spent per extra barrel of proven reserves, the 'cost of replacement' of American crude oil has been rising. It would be unwise, perhaps, to accept these trends as utterly irreversible. New techniques of multiple drilling, on the one hand, and of secondary recovery of much higher proportions of the oil *in situ* in reserves already proven, on the other, offer impressive possibilities of bringing down the cost of making extra oil available for the future. If they can, governmental backing given to drilling and the improvement of reservoir engineering in the United States will have contributed to both these hopeful lines of development.

But even accepting a big American oil-producing industry with a high rate of exploration to replenish its reserves quite uncritically as a Good Thing, regardless of comparisons with the cost of alternative ways of supplying America with its oil, there would appear to the outside observer many weaknesses in the ways state and federal governments go about this there. Within the proration system these derive largely, perhaps, from tensions between what Professor E. W. Zimmermann[4] has defined as the two basic objectives of the regulatory programme:

(1) the prevention of waste of oil and gas, through which the ultimate recovery of these products from their reservoirs might be greatly increased; and

(2) the protection and adjustments of correlative property rights appertaining to each owner of land in an oil or gas pool.

And this second objective of protecting individual property rights has a good deal to do with basic social attitudes towards small property owners and big in the United States.

The guarantee of a rateable take to every property owner or lessee, combined with inadequate supervision of well spacing, must surely reduce the technical efficiency of output from most fields as well as provide a constant incentive to obtain further entitlements to output, at the expense of the average rate of offtake for established producers there. Texas, for example, guarantees a minimum rate of gas production even to wells drilled down to tap a gas-cap which may be the (declining) driving force of flow from a whole oilfield. Again, the maintenance in being of some 20 per cent of national production in 'stripper' and other wells of very low average output, by exempting them from the production control applied to more productive wells, must substantially increase average costs. There are limits, throughout American political thinking and legal practice, to the extent to which the pursuit of economic or technical efficiency, particularly via bigness or co-operative organization, is ever trusted to override the rights of the individual. When large integrated companies are denied the right to produce all the oil they want from their own wells, or to produce even their own allowable output all from those of their own wells whence it would be most technically efficient, their potential efficiency is held down. Similarly, when reluctant individual oil producers refuse to co-operate in the unitization of a field where secondary recovery organized on a large scale is becoming vital, technical conservation may be prejudiced as well as economic efficiency. But in America the recalcitrant individualist can always be pretty sure of sympathy: and the integrated company frustrated in its economic logic can always be sure of suspicion.

No foreign visitor to the environment of large corporations in the United States in general, and of major oil companies in particular, can avoid realizing the degree to which anti-trust legislation and departmental practice condition their behaviour in a surprisingly wide range of circumstances. Considering the history of the industry, and the extent that the oil industry figured in the circumstances out of which 'trust-busting' sentiments and legislation arose, the Department of Justice's continued interest in it is understandable. But its effect is to make oil executives in major companies lean over backwards in order to maintain postures of exaggerated apparent competition, and to refrain from overt consultation on many issues upon which it would be logical to expect collective views for different sections of the industry to crystallize through open argument. Such companies often spend a good deal of time trying to make management decisions that they decided to take because of their realistic assessment of circumstances and probabilities appear 'right' according to a quite distinct and largely archaic set of 'perfectly competitive' rules abstracted from market circumstances that no longer exist, if ever they existed anywhere in pure form. This may have its incidental benefits as a form of intellectual discipline for business (rather as the learning of dead languages is alleged to develop all our minds) but it has the danger of being expensive as well as irrelevant. It would perhaps be surprising if the intense collective concentration on private advantage that characterizes management in big American corporations, and not least in oil corporations, were not sometimes to collide with considerations of the public interest. And the knowledge that circumstances of wholly unfettered atomistic competition are entirely foreign to most parts of this industry, might well justify the Washington vigilantes in keeping a close watch on how it does behave itself in its own peculiar circumstances. But it might be better for all concerned if this industry (and others in America) were not judged, and had not always to explain its practice, in the terms of an early nineteenth-century produce market.

It has already been argued, in earlier chapters, that the influence of American anti-trust legislation and tax practice upon the behaviour of American oil companies has had repercussions upon the conduct of oil business outside the United States. The same, indirectly, is true of the effects of regulation of oil production there. The repercussions of all three have been complex: and even a pragmatic observer, setting aside any ideals of untrammelled free enterprise and free trade, may conclude that these repercussions have not always been advantageous. Within an American national context, any foreign observer has to be careful in passing judgments upon these governmental influences on the oil industry: for they are after all deliberately applied with ends in view that most Americans, including most American oilmen, approve. One may doubt whether they achieve these ends efficiently: that is one question. Whether the ends in themselves are desirable is another question. Some philosophical liberals (in the European rather than the American sense of the word) dislike nationalism in itself, wherever they encounter it. Most liberal economists dislike economic nationalism. But their particular competence as economists is surely confined to assessing what extra costs may follow for a country that adopts such a policy—and also for other countries with which it might otherwise trade more freely; and also, perhaps, to assessing the costs of different ways of doing it. This is perhaps particularly necessary for an Englishman to bear in mind, coming from a country where a brief but impressive tradition of free trade, long discarded, has left us automatically sanctimonious about economic nationalism anywhere else, and trained us not to be really conscious of it when we practise it ourselves. There is something slightly shocking, if curiously stimulating, for an Englishman to hear anyone say bluntly, 'Of course we have to maintain a strong domestic industry', without an apologetic note in his voice.

Economic nationalism in the world's largest oil industry cannot but affect the whole oil business outside it. American oil companies own more of the international oil industry outside their borders than those of any other nation; and while other American industries frequently rank as the largest in the world, few have a comparable grip on foreign production. As we have seen, state regulation arose because the American oil producers, unrestrained, were liable to produce far too much oil; and in spite of anxiety about maintaining the national level of reserves, American companies are always ready to produce as much more oil as they are allowed. Until the late forties, the United States, on balance, was more than self-sufficient in oil, exporting more products than it imported crude. Since then it has been a net importer; and while its refiners were free to seek the lowest comparative costs for supplies to their markets, it seemed likely in the early fifties to import a steadily growing proportion of its requirements. Since the early fifties, it has imposed first voluntary and later administrative restrictions on the volume of its imports, holding these down now to around 20 per cent of its total consumption. But it still imports more oil than any other single country. Only one other industrialized area in the world boasts a comparable degree of self-sufficiency, though at a far lower level of production and consumption: the U.S.S.R., apart from supplying the bloc of Communist nations, is still a net exporter of oil, and also impinges somewhat upon the world oil market.

Until the fifties, as outlined in earlier chapters, customary rather than simply competitive patterns of pricing linked the prices of crude oil and products in the rest of the world, directly or indirectly, with prices inside the United States. To the extent that the state regulation of output reduced over-production there and guaranteed remuneration on investment in relatively high-cost home production in the United States, therefore, it offered support not only to the level of prices there, but also in some degree to oil prices everywhere in the world trade. But the lower cost of oil production in other oil-producing regions, particularly the Middle East and Venezuela, gave the companies with concessions abroad a growing incentive to bring this cheaper oil into the United States market. And in the middle and

I. THE UNITED STATES

late fifties the growth in imports that could be foreseen in future sent many important American companies without foreign interests abroad to seek concessions, particularly in Venezuela, but to a growing extent in the Middle East. Venezuela, with leases over smaller areas and with a number of new fields being opened up, was easier to enter than the Middle East, where the companies already established had concessions covering huge areas. Some newcomers were allocated a small shareholding in the Iran Consortium; others gained footholds in odd corners such as the Saudi-Kuwait Neutral zone, offshore areas, or some of the tinier shaikhdoms of the Persian Gulf. These were well worth exploring (Kuwait, after all, is tiny enough). They looked the more attractive in view of the expanding markets for oil that such American companies commanded in the United States. It was not simply that this foreign oil was cheap. What was almost more important was that it was free of output regulation. The integrated refiner did not have to buy some of it from all the other producers in the field to which he had a pipeline, pay posted price for this, and keep an equivalent amount of his own oil shut into the ground.

Growing imports of low-cost crude, for a time after the war, made it necessary to hold American domestic production level and eventually restrict it further (in Texas). This in its turn brought political opposition from producers whose interests were entirely in domestic oil. For a time these protests were allayed by voluntary import restrictions on the volumes brought in by the major importers, on the principle that imports should 'supplement but not supplant' American supplies. But both these importers and the new ones bringing in production abroad had invested heavily in the prospect of bringing in increasing amounts of foreign crude. And no sensible businessman can be expected voluntarily to deny himself crude supplies which he has invested to bring into being. It takes a government to decide that in the national interest a nation should accept more expensive supplies than it need. The voluntary restrictions were not effective enough to satisfy the vociferous domestic producers of oil; and in 1959 the American government decided to make import restrictions mandatory.

In the framework of existing oil policy in the United States, this action could be regarded as logical enough. It can indeed be argued that it was essential to keep that policy effective—if one takes the purpose of policy as protecting the American oil industry and keeping its productive capacity growing, and not simply as promoting technical conservation. Some American experts are persuaded[5] that continued restrictions on imports will enable the growing needs of the United States to be met for the next twenty years or so from domestic sources, without significantly raising the real costs of oil inside the United States. Such a policy, on that analysis, would not necessarily mean any absolute increases in American energy costs—though it certainly would mean continuing to pay higher prices for energy than America might have to pay for it in the meantime from abroad. There is no doubt that considerable increases in domestic oil production in the United States are technically practicable. It can be argued that developments in drilling and reservoir engineering, allied to more sensible methods of controlling the exploitation of oilfields such as unitization, could offset the increases in cost to be expected over time in any extractive industry, and even in the apparently high cost of 'replacing' the oil one takes out of the ground. The technical advances in drilling may well occur. Whether the more sensible management of oilfields will, given the present ideology of proration, is much more doubtful. But even assuming import restriction goes on unchanged, there may be a growth of internal criticism of present proration and tax incentive methods, on the ground that they will make the protected industry an unnecessarily inefficient one.

Any country that deliberately decides to protect and stimulate any domestic industry inevitably faces this dilemma of seeking still to keep it as efficient as possible without competition from outside. Some critics such as Professor Adelman, who support a degree of protection for American oil on grounds of national security, would complain that long before import restrictions began the combined effects of proration and incentive tax advantages had ensured that the domestic industry would be a wasteful and inefficient one, not a strong and efficient one. The cost of protecting a margin of American oil production, higher-cost than imports but still as low in cost as internal efficiency could make it, would in any case be high, since it must mean higher energy costs throughout the economy. (Even so, American energy costs are not high in relation to most other developed economies.) But to inflate costs within this industry—and its size—by the protection of a wide margin of tiny high-cost producers from the internal competition of more efficient American operations would hardly seem to add to national security. Nor, necessarily, does the stimulation of an artificially high rate of drilling by tax and the chance of preferential allowables for new wells. If one takes into account the tax and proration advantages of drilling new wells, the exemption from proration of wells with a very low rate of output, and the comfortable price now ensured by protection from imported oil, it might well be worth while now for certain entrepreneurs to concentrate on drilling cheap wells where the chances are high that the successful ones would produce so little as to rank as strippers. Preferential treatment of largely exhausted wells, approaching the end of a long and profitable life history, can perhaps be defended, on somewhat sentimental grounds. The encouragement of newcomers to develop capacity of low productivity simply to enjoy these 'retirement benefits' seems a less praiseworthy result of public policy. These unsought effects of tax incentives and proration must vastly increase the cost of maintaining the American oil industry at its present rates of output One official inquiry in 1963 estimated the cost of protecting American oil production (at a crude price of about \$3 a barrel) against imports (which could be landed for \$1 a barrel less) at \$3½ to \$4 billion dollars, simply by multiplying total United States oil consumption by this extra margin of price.[6] But Professor Adelman would argue that this same output of American oil could be achieved at a price of little more than \$2.25 billion, if wasteful producing capacity were abandoned and the output concentrated on to the efficient wells. That would mean an 'internal' saving of say \$2 billion to \$2½ billion a year:

'The difference between two and a half billion dollars and four billion is essentially the additional saving on getting genuinely cheaper oil from abroad than can be produced non-wastefully at home. This is where the security problem enters.'[7]

None of this figuring can do more than suggest orders of magnitude. But what it does suggest is that the United States, which has chosen to support home oil production on grounds of national security, could probably obtain the same amount of security a good deal more cheaply.

This choice was the United States' own business. Its effect upon the rest of the world's oil industry, however, was profound. It was arguably quite as important as any other single factor in precipitating the potential surplus that was accumulating in the world market from the mid-fifties onwards, though that surplus would soon, in any case, have made itself felt.[8] The first effects upon the world price structure of insulating American supply and demand from the rest of the world market were discussed in the chapters on pricing. The longer-term consequences have still to be seen. No other single policy decision of protective economic nationalism anywhere in the world was directly as important to the oil industry as this one. And it has also been significant as an example to other governments, of more kinds than one.

Confident prophecies that Europe could depend on cheap imported oil as its main marginal source of energy in the future by diversifying its potential sources of overseas supply, as Dr Sam Schurr has pointed out, perhaps depend more than is generally realized upon the assumption that the United States continue to maintain in being a large excess capacity to produce oil, capable of being drawn upon in emergency (Texas Railroad Commission permitting). This is not to argue that a freeing of American imports, if decided on now, would necessarily harden prices in the world market. It would raise demand; but also bring in some very large, hard-bargaining buyers. On the other hand, European ideas about putting quotas on oil imports, which are again becoming stronger in some countries, can point to a Transatlantic example. And the arguments about proration of world oil supplies in accordance with world 'market demand' that were long put forward by such spokesmen of petroleum-exporting countries as Shaikh Abdullah Tariki and Dr Perez Alfonzo and have now been followed up by OPEC, draw fairly logically upon the experience, and the arguments in justification, of proration in the United States.

It can be argued persuasively, indeed, that the development of state regulation in the home of the oil industry and the stronghold of private enterprise suggests that there is something about this industry that positively invites regulation. This is not a view that would be popular with the private businessmen concerned in this industry. On the other hand, one seldom finds any American oilman who is prepared to condemn all aspects of this powerful and pervasive system of government intervention in private business. Thoroughgoing condemnation of government interference in oil is confined to the interference of governments outside the United States.

According to its own spread of interests, the American oil company with large international ties may be sceptical about the judgment of the regulatory agencies or even about the system itself, in that this gives what it considers relatively inefficient companies handsome rates of return. Some began by being positively indignant about import restrictions; but after a year or two, few were inclined to do more than complain about quotas on fuel oil imports, and the ways in which all import quotas were allocated. Import quotas were still valuable assets, which very soon acquired a definable market price: but the restriction of imports had made profits easier to earn at home than in the chilly international market. A major international company is apt to attach more value to tax allowances for foreign depletion than, say, an independent producer in Texas; but both will argue equally firmly for the absolute economic necessity for the depletion allowance on domestic oil to be 27½ per cent of producing income. Many more oilmen are critical of the actual ways in which output is regulated than of the principle of regulating output: on the other hand, proposals for compulsory unitization, which from the outside looks a more rational system, have generally foundered upon the opposition of the industry itself. Federal regulation of the price of natural gas, again, has brought much justified criticism of the formulae that the government agencies suggest. But not many people inside the industry have been prepared to offer logically convincing alternative formulae for pricing gas. The industry generally argues with some justice that the whole current machinery of regulation, incentives, and protection in American oil, despite the different origins and original purposes of different elements in it, now hangs together. One might be unable to change one part of it without changing all the rest; and understandably, the industry would be very uneasy about some entirely new structure of protection-cum-control, with all the new side-effects this might bring. There have been relaxations from time to time in the restrictions. Few oilmen inside or outside the United States, for the present, seem to be expecting any reversal soon of the American industry's administrative isolation from the rest of the world oil market. The control over oil imports, in particular, does not preclude further growth of the actual volume of imports into the United States; but how much more imports may be allowed in will be settled by administrative decision, not according to market prices or net integrated costs in the world oil business. This isolation partly conditions the behaviour of major American companies operating in the world market, and affects the extent to which they could act to reduce the surplus of oil in the rest of it. It has also become a potent factor in oil companies' decisions, all over the world, about the scale of investment in production and transport for the future. It was in a sense ironic that this final twist of protective state regulation of the largest private enterprise industry in the world, by governments believing firmly in private capitalism and acting reasonably in the American 'national interest', probably did as much, initially, to soften the world market as the deliberate re-entry into that market, at about the same time, of the state-owned industry of the only other great nation that produces enough oil for itself, Soviet Russia.

CHAPTER XIII

Self-sufficiency in Oil: II. The Soviet Bloc

During 1960, a team of American oilmen visited the Soviet oil industry, and on a return trip a team of Soviet oilmen visited the American oil industry.[1] The reactions of each might be selectively summed up in remarks said to have been made by the two leaders. The leader of the American team asked, 'Why do you employ so many people?' The leader of the Soviet team asked, 'Why do you drill so many wells?' Both questions were telling; they brought out basic differences between the legal and economic circumstances in which managers of the oil industry conduct their business in these dominant countries of world capitalism and communism. To the third party who has to depend on imported oil, however, the oil industries of two rival colossi have at least one thing in common: they can supply broadly enough for their own needs. In this they are, so far, unlike all other industrialized societies.

For three to four years at the turn of the century, Russia was actually producing more oil than the United States. It drew level and passed in 1897–98; but by 1902 its brief spell in the lead was over. Russia did not experience the revolution of mass motor ownership that took place in the United States during the first two to three decades of this century. So far, it never has. And Mr Khrushchev, during his eventful visits to America in 1959 and 1960, was ready to say that he thought it never should. The statements of statesmen about technological and social development, over the years, have a way of rebounding upon themselves. Nevertheless, gasoline consumption by the private motorist is certainly not one of the ways in which the Russian government proclaims the ambition of surpassing American standards of living. However, the Soviet production target for oil by 1980, set at 14 million barrels a day, is more ambitious than almost any forecast ever made for the United States.

The present level of Russian output—nearing 5 million barrels of oil a day and about 130,000 million cubic metres of gas a year in 1965—is only about half of that in the United States, and its consumption, for a much larger population, is only about a third as large. And even if one counts production elsewhere in the Communist bloc, which can be classed with Russia though nowadays split in its loyalties (how much petroleum China produces remains a mystery to Western observers), the total only comes up to about $5\frac{1}{4}$ million barrels of oil a day and just over 180,000 million cubic metres of gas a year—while consumption per head taking the Communist countries as a whole, is less than a fifth of that in America. Russia's proven oil reserves, however, are now not much smaller than those of the United States, and its natural gas reserves, though much less developed, are about a third as large. And during the last decade production and consumption of petroleum in Russia and the East European countries have been rising far more rapidly than in America or the rest of the free world. By 1961, Russia was already the second largest producer in the world, passing Venezuela: its output was about two-thirds as large as the whole of the Middle East. But both America and the Middle East were producing much less oil than they could readily have done. This may not have been as true of Russia.

Government control of the oil industry in Russia is not a matter of interference with the owners, who no longer exist; it is simply how industry in a Communist country is run. In practice, it does sometimes seem to be regarded as interference by the directly responsible Soviet management: their Russian opposite numbers told the American oil team in 1960 that some of the direction from the centre was too remote from the real facts, though the various successive experiments in decentralization that have gone on in the last five or six years may have improved matters somewhat. But the criteria that affect management decisions in a Communist economy differ considerably from those that concern a Western manager. Both are concerned to improve their technical efficiency and to reduce the cost of specific operations. But the relation between labour cost and capital charges in the two kinds of economy, for example, differs radically.

Russia no longer has any general surplus of labour. But it has a tradition of fairly lavish manning of its plant, partly in order to give green labour 'on-site' training, and nowadays it seems to be applying much the same principles in staffing, to habituate its college-trained engineers to actual industrial operations. By contrast, it is extremely short of capital: at least, its economic planners have to withdraw what they decide it shall invest from a limited national output that still leaves only meagre standards of living to its citizens. But it is not easy for the Westerner to understand how the concept of capital charges is taken into account in planning Soviet investment. And it still appears that major decisions about large-scale investment, at any rate, are taken somewhere in the administrative hierarchy well above the level of the director of any actual operating unit in the Soviet industry. Price hardly enters into the operating manager's calculations; transfer prices at the various stages are set at cost plus a given level of 'profit', but turn-over taxes, at various levels, are then built into each price to influence the pattern of consumption (and incidentally to provide the Soviet government with its main formal source of revenue). It might perhaps be said that in practice the manager of any given Soviet oil enterprise may silll have as much power of independent decision as say the local manager of a non-profit-making operating company owned by several foreign parents in the Middle East. But the ultimate managers who take the really important decisions in the West are at least slightly more identifiable, and accountable in principle to shareholders somewhere.

Some of the key decisions of these unidentifiable Soviet managers, however, are made public from time to time; and there is little doubt about their performance. Over the past ten years Russia appears to have been expanding its crude oil output at about 12 per cent a year; there has been a considerable growth in refinery capacity and in pipeline transport. During its 1959–65 seven-year plan, Russia proposed to increase its use of crude oil and natural gas from 26 per cent and 6 per cent respectively of its total energy consumption to 32·7 and 17·0 per cent; in fact it slightly exceeded this, the two together reaching 51·7 per cent of total fuel production. Coal, which in 1960 supplied over 50 per cent of the energy used, supplied less than 40 per cent by end-1965, though even this represented an increase of more than 12 per cent in its output. During the postwar years, in which the great international companies were opening out production in the Middle East, Russia was doing the same in a smaller way for its newer oilfields in the Volga-Urals area, which now supply over 70 per cent of Soviet crude production. Since then, it has been opening up further oilfields in Central Asia and exploring others in Siberia. By 1970, the Russians plan on an output of about 7 million barrels a day of oil and 240,000 million cubic metres of natural gas. Their percentage share of fuel will not rise much further, however; over this five years Russia is planning to increase coal output faster than of late, even though this is costlier.[1] Few oilmen who have visited the Soviet petroleum industry doubt that it will be able to achieve this huge effort of development.

This geographical shift of Russia's main areas of oil supply has significantly altered not only its pattern but its methods of transport. Baku, in Azerbaijan, formerly the dominant area (upon selling whose oil it will be remembered the original Shell oil business was founded), was fairly well situated for tanker shipment to its markets, across the Caspian Sea, up the Volga, or across the Black Sea to European Russia or to the outside world. Nowadays the bulk of the output comes from the Ural-Volga area; and Russia is opening up vast new reserves in Siberia and Central Asia. The new inland oilfields, however, have had to be served by pipeline—mainly to refineries situated in consuming areas. Russia has had to lay a substantial new network of pipelines throughout its territories and beyond them to feed its satellites and perhaps other customers. An even larger pipeline network is being developed to make use of natural gas from Central Asia and West Siberia to the Urals industrial region and European Russia. These developments, and particularly the line which now carries oil some 2,800 miles into Central Europe, were initially hampered by shortage of capacity for making large-diameter pipe.

The apparent centralization of decisions in the Russian oil industry, and the absence of recognizable criteria for decision, have been mentioned. It would be churlish not to recognize that such centralization can have some possible advantages for an industry that has had to accept state regulation even in America, that stronghold of private enterprise. Under state ownership, there has been no room for argument about how oilfields should be developed and what constitutes wasteful exploitation of resources. 'Mandatory unitization' has been the rule in the older Russian oilfields ever since the Bolsheviks gained control, and the newer fields have been developed under such principles from the start. Russian oilfields, as their team leader observed, have not for years been faced with the problems of 'over-drilling' that still affect American fields even under proration. Oilmen there pay strict attention to what would be considered in the West technical rather than economic conservation principles. One result of this difference in approach is a matter of technique; they begin water injection to maintain reservoir pressure as soon as production from the field begins, bringing in pressure maintenance to reinforce primary production as soon as this is done partly because pressure in the fields is not as high as in some rich fields elsewhere. But it also results in about 70 per cent of all Russian wells continuing to produce by this form of 'primary recovery'. A smaller proportion appears to be 'on the pump' than in the United States, the only other area where oil production on an industrial scale has been carried on for any comparable length of time (Baku began producing in 1873, only about ten years after the Appalachian fields in Pennsylvania).[2]

This use of assisted recovery on so general a scale illustrates another strength of Soviet centralized decision that the West has been recognizing in other technical spheres since the war: the ability to get any new technique applied really rapidly and widely once it is accepted.

For the third time in the history of this industry, Russian oil exports began in the mid-fifties to become a significant factor in the international oil market; and the state ownership of the Russian industry naturally made other traders ask whether these exports ought to be considered in economic terms or in political. Russia had been one of the major exporters in the first twenty years or so of the world oil trade, but its importance had faded before the First World War. It became a very significant oil exporter indeed between the world wars, its sales on the world market reaching a peak of 120,000 barrels a day in 1932. Its attempts to force a way into various markets in Europe and the Near East—after the major Shell and Jersey Standard groups, both of which handled Russian oil for a time after the revolution, had ceased to buy it—contributed to the slump in prices in the late twenties and early thirties which occasioned the various attempts of the major groups to restrain competition through their 'As Is' agreements. During those years the Russians were aggressive sellers, but not averse to market-sharing agreements. (Rumania, in practice, was a much more aggressive price-cutter.) They appear to have reached various agreements to restrain competition with the international companies during the period. As their first five-year plans began to take effect, their own internal demand for oil products began to increase. At all events, they reduced their exports of petroleum very sharply within a year of the prewar peak in 1933; and from then until the beginning of the Second World War, they tended to withdraw from the international market, selling the marketing facilities they had built up abroad to Western companies. Mr. E. P. Gurov, chairman of Sojuzneftexport, the Russian oil export organization, claimed at the Beirut oil congress in 1960 that during the

II. THE SOVIET BLOC

decade 1925–35, Russia had supplied 14·3 per cent of all the oil imported by Western countries, and that during the peak years of 1930–33 its share reached 19 per cent. About 14 per cent of Soviet production, he added, was exported during the thirties; its peak exports reached 30 per cent of its annual output.

The Russian industry began to export once again after the war, though in the early immediate postwar years it was at the same time importing products from Rumania, and may at one time have been a net importer. But later its production began to develop faster than its internal demand; its exports rose, to its partners among the Communist countries but also to countries outside the Iron Curtain. In 1950, it sent overseas about 22,000 barrels a day, but only 4,000 barrels went beyond its own sphere to the importing countries of the West. By 1960, its total exports had grown to nearly 30 times as much; and of this 60 per cent or more was going to non-Communist countries.

The absolute figures of exports are not as large as that rate of growth might suggest when they are set against the total of world oil exports. Russia's own 1963 figures of Russian oil exports, some $48\frac{1}{2}$ million tons or 1,000,000 barrels a day, amounted to about 20 per cent of Soviet oil production and to about 7 per cent of world oil exports in that year (most Western estimates of these exports were far lower, 35–45 million tons). Of these, less than half a million barrels a day came to countries outside the Soviet sphere, amounting to only about 4 per cent of the imports of all other countries. However, in oil it is often argued that it needs only a few more barrels to make the market overflow; and Russian exports had been among the influences that helped to soften the world market during the late fifties. For a year or two Russia had then become a less active seller; and there were suggestions in the world outside that its own demands for fuel of all kinds were simply rising so fast that it had not enough extra oil to spare to go on increasing exports. But in 1965, again, its exports to the outside world rose significantly, to about 35 million tons, or 750,000 barrels a day. They had certainly widened the range of their salesmanship throughout the world. The National Petroleum Council in the U.S.A.—whose estimates of Soviet exports outside the Communist bloc were fairly well borne out in 1965 —thinks that by 1970 Russia will have 69 million tons a year, or 1,380,000 barrels a day, to export to the free world.[3]

About half of the postwar Soviet oil exports, so far, have been in the form of products, mainly residual fuel oil (some of low-sulphur content), diesel fuel, and low-grade gasoline. (Russia's own biggest demand is for the middle distillates such as diesel oil; with its growing use of natural gas, it may well have surpluses of fuel oil to dispose of, and with its small private car population it has gasoline to spare. It markets only one grade of gasoline from its refineries, with a relatively low octane rating by Western standards. As the American oilmen's report on the Russian industry commented, 'it needs to be no higher than practical', a remark that could have more meanings than one). But the proportion of crude in Soviet oil exports has gradually been growing.

A good deal of this oil, products and crude, has been sold at prices significantly lower than the generally scheduled prices in the markets outside. It would hardly have found purchasers if it had not been available at some sort of discount. But obviously different marketers, in periods of developing surplus, have different ideas about how much discounting is legitimate, how much represents 'distress sales', and how much might be regarded as 'dumping'. During the very sharp period of price-cutting between 1958 and 1961, the Russians do not seem always to have offered the biggest discounts off scheduled prices—the deepest price cutters seem to have been certain independent producers with surplus crude in Venezuela and in the Middle East. But the Russians were sometimes prepared to cut as far as was necessary to gain a particular sale. In 1960, making a four-year contract with the Italian state oil company ENI, the Russians, for example, sold it crude at a very low price indeed—roughly $1.40 delivered in Italy, which meant something of the order of a dollar a barrel f.o.b. Black Sea terminals. This deal, like many others in which the Russians engaged, was not simply a straight sale; there were elements of barter in it, involving Italian steel pipe and petroleum chemicals produced from ENI's plant built to process Sicilian oil.

Many Russian offers in the late fifties seemed neatly selected to offer the major companies the maximum of embarrassment—quite often to markets where the majors were entrenched with practically no other competition, and therefore markets likely to attract any independent seller looking for an opening. Cuba was one such market: Ceylon was another; here, Soviet oil (and influence) was followed by expropriation of the Western companies. There are large Russian sales, too, to some other underdeveloped countries, short of foreign exchange, strong nationalists and nursing some suspicions of price discrimination by their established suppliers as a relic of 'colonialism' or 'dollar diplomacy'; for example, India, Egypt, and Ghana.

But of late Russia's export salesmen seem to have been concentrating quite as much on a quite distinct and very important group of customers for Soviet oil, led by Italy, Japan and Scandinavia. These are among the most cold-blooded of all oil importers, without the least interest in the ideological flavour of the oil: Switzerland and Spain are two of the latest. Such customers have always had a sharp eye for a bargain and a reluctance to tie themselves to any single group of suppliers. Moreover, independent refiners and marketers have always given the major companies more competition there than elsewhere. Businessmen in these countries, moreover, have a natural eye to the possibilities of reciprocal trade with Russia and the East European countries. Russia may be geographically and commercially an attractive alternative source for them. For example, Japan in the late fifties had become accustomed to some of the lowest discounted prices for crude that any customer could obtain anywhere. But in the early sixties, it saw its own crude prices levelling out while discounted prices to Western Europe went on down. The reason was simple: Japan did not have the benefit of Libyan production expanding nearby. Japan was already a steady buyer of Russian crude on a moderate scale; but in 1965 it began talking with the Russians about doubling its imports, to perhaps 10 million tons a year by 1970—when this amount would still be only about 10 per cent of its enormous total imports of crude. The Russians were naturally interested: guaranteed 10 million tons a year over a long-term contract, they would be prepared to extend their trans-Siberian pipeline 2,750 miles to the Pacific—using, of course, Japanese pipe . . . Whether this particular deal ever comes to pass remains to be seen. But there are obviously many growing oil markets in the world that would become natural markets for competition from Soviet crude if strategic and political tensions should lessen over the years. And Russian oilmen who are tending to think more and more commercially in their own internal management and accounting are likely to be more interested in these long-term markets than in political possibilities for Soviet oil in marginal underdeveloped markets—growing fast, but tiny in terms of volume for the time being.

Complaints about Soviet 'dumping' of oil began to be made as soon as large-scale exports of it began again during the late fifties, and indeed formed part of the arguments upon which some governmental organizations in Europe, in particular, considered imposing quotas on imports of Soviet oil. It is always wise for the consumer to regard any such arguments with a certain amount of caution: essentially, they are appeals to his government to help someone charge him more than he need pay. The definition normally offered of dumping is selling abroad at a lower price than one sells in one's own home market; (it may be added that on a strict application of it, most exporters of most manufactured goods do, and are usually dumping). Quite certainly the Russians go on charging other Communist countries much more for their oil than customers in the free world. But as between a capitalist importer and a Communist supplier, it is not clear whether this phrase 'dumping' has much significance at all. Certainly few of the accusers have been able to offer much in the way of estimates of Russian costs. And since the mid-fifties, quite a lot of oil has been sold by very respectable companies at prices below those Soviet prices that used to be cited as evidence of dumping.

The international oil industry's complaints about Soviet exports, whatever the terminology, do however reflect a genuine difficulty in meeting competition from this entirely different kind of economy—which is also an entirely closed one. The oil companies are used to price cutting by 'distress sellers' without marketing facilities in times of surplus. They are equally prepared to meet competition from more substantial newcomers who are prepared to pay the cost of entry—that is the investment needed in storage, distribution and retailing outlets—in the markets where they are established. But between established international marketers, they can usually expect price competition to be limited by the knowledge that if A undercuts B in one market and gains a larger share, there are always markets where B can gain a similar edge on A.

Sojuzneftexport is among the most substantially established marketers of all in the world oil market; there is nothing 'here today and gone tomorrow' about Russian competition. But in two ways it differs from all other established marketers. Its own market is almost entirely closed to competition from any other group; and since World War II, in contrast to its efforts in the twenties and thirties, it has managed to sell without paying the normal cost of entry. (In doing so, it has chosen wholly to forgo marketing profits; but these, during the decade that Russia has been back in the market, have not been particularly attractive anyway.) The kind of deal it has preferred, that is to say, is one between governments, in which an important government can be induced to buy oil from Russia. What the government does with the oil from then on is not Sojuzneftexport's affair. What some of the governments to which it has sold oil have done in fact is to require marketers already established in the area to distribute or even to refine this Russian oil in their own facilities. An alternative is to set up a state oil distribution company to sell the Russian oil at cut prices—possibly giving it power to expropriate the established marketers' facilities. This was the issue over which the established oil companies pulled out of Cuba in 1960, and over which they later came under pressure—to handle Soviet oil or meet its prices with their own oil sales to local affiliates—from the governments of India, Ceylon, and Ghana.

It was notable, during the late fifties, that some of the European-based international oil companies professed to feel much more menaced by the growth of Russian exports than others. Some were ready to argue that Russian exports could still be interpreted largely in terms of commercial competition, and that on the whole the Russians, while never missing a trick, were not out to upset the whole game. Most of the American companies, by contrast, professed much darker suspicions about 'political competition'.

Some of the reactions, European and American, have been political too. Member nations of the European Economic Community have accepted an informal limit on their imports of Soviet oil, at 10 per cent of each country's imports. A number of American companies, some years ago, boycotted tanker operators that did business with Russian oil. This obliged the Russians to build their own tanker fleet up much faster than before (which was as happy a windfall for European and Japanese shipbuilders as it was a cold draught for independent tanker owners). By 1965, Soviet oil exports were almost independent of chartering tankers in the outside world. Not that this had been convenient; the growth of the fleet and of tonnage under construction had involved about twice as much investment in tankers as Russia had postulated in its 1959–65 plan. The ban on exports of large-diameter steel pipe imposed by a number of Nato countries and their allies in the early sixties, again, did put the Russians in real difficulties, for lack of their own pipe mill capacity. And their large programme of refinery construction, again, depends significantly upon Western help—which the United States until recently wanted withheld.

It seems probable that Russian motives in this export drive for oil are mixed; a Russian, indeed, might consider the suggestion that commercial motives can ever wholly be separated from political as quite naïve. There has been ample commercial justification, in the terms of Soviet commerce, for selling this oil abroad for whatever it will fetch.

In the rapid development of the Soviet oil industry, local surpluses of crude and products will inevitably be built up from time to time, as they are in any oil industry; sold abroad, they can be worth more than at home. Oil exports may at first have been incidental to the massive development of petroleum in the Soviet economy—though one of Russia's most saleable exports to pay for their own vast import needs of raw material and specialized equipment. It is true that if consumption should from time to time swing ahead of production, exports might in turn be cut off without too much regard to Russia's long-term position in the market or the goodwill of its customers. It may be significant that so far the Russians have refrained from setting up any marketing organizations in Western Europe to handle the sale of their products, as they did between the wars—though they have talked, occasionally, about setting some up again. On the other hand, they have pushed their pipelines deep into Central Europe; and they now own a number of much larger tankers than they have ever possessed before. There seems little doubt, either, that their economic planning is now allowing for sizeable margins of oil exports, as a continuing commitment of fairly high priority.

Guesses about their future policy in the West, depend to a great extent upon how successful one expects them to be in developing and supplying internal consumption. Some arguments have been voiced in recent years that Russia's incursion into the world market may be entirely temporary; that their rapid growth in home demand may soon outstrip their productive potential, turning them into net importers; and that by the end of the century, quite apart from political ambitions, they may need to expand their influence in the Middle East simply to lay their hands on sufficient petroleum. This speculation is so far away in time as to be beyond proof, disproof, or even sensible argument. The only factor within the Soviet sphere—not within Russia—that once offered any support for such an argument is the potential growth that theoretically could materialize in Chinese demand for petroleum. This vast area and population is largely unexplored in terms of oil, but its proven reserves are relatively insignificant. Any rise in its tiny consumption of energy per head, however insignificant, could represent a big addition to its total demand. But great efforts are being put into seeking self-sufficiency; politically, China is now trying to reduce dependence on Russia for oil or anything else; and as a result Russia may not always remain its Communist rival's chief supplier. In any case, China's standards of living are not rising as fast as all that.

II. THE SOVIET BLOC

In practice, Russia has not appeared anywhere as a prospective customer even for marginal amounts of Middle East crude—though in 1965 it did arrange to buy very large quantities of natural gas from Iran. A number of other Communist bloc countries, however, have been bargaining with the new national oil companies of these countries for crude. New commercial relationships such as these have some political logic too.

The Communist countries accept oil from the Middle East countries in return for some of the technical aid that they seem anxious to press upon these countries; and the deals might present the Soviet bloc to these countries in a more favourable light than simply the cut-price competitor that it must sometimes appear at present.

The Russian oil industry has appeared nowhere except Spitzbergen as an explorer seeking concessions; but it has sent prospecting teams to certain countries such as Afghanistan and Pakistan, and has built refineries for Egypt and India. In all cases it is working purely as an agent of the local government, lending money but not investing 'capital'. The activity may cement its relations with such countries and secure further outlets for its crude. And it apparently hopes to avoid the jealousy that the private oil companies' presence in such countries has often aroused. (This approach was not necessarily what the countries concerned might have preferred; Pakistan, it is said, originally proposed a normal concession with Russia putting in the risk capital.) But the offers of help are widespread and diverse: for example, the offer of help in developing and processing local oil shales in Brazil. (In Estonia, the Soviet Union has one of the only shale oil operations in the world operating on a fully commercial scale.)

National policy, in this second great area of present self-sufficiency in petroleum, is therefore largely indistinguishable from the business behaviour, be this economic or political, of its oil industry. It seems clear that Soviet oil exports will rise over the next five years, perhaps quite rapidly. This may help to maintain and to exacerbate softness in the international oil market. Consumers in some countries, indeed, may look to Russia as a marginal supplier of oil, and logically the supplier that ought to set a ceiling on all prices; the rest of the world's suppliers would not like this but might possibly have to lump it. It seems equally clear that Russian political pressure will be deployed in politically unstable oil-producing countries, as well as in politically unstable markets such as Cuba, so as to cause the maximum possible embarrassment to the Western oil companies. It is not clear, however, that Soviet objectives such as its competition in rates of growth with the West will necessitate actual penetration into the Middle East. Commercially, the Russians do not appear anxious to push oil prices down to impossibly low levels. There might still be some possibility of a deal with the Western oil interests to hold the line such as they have made before; compare their agreement to market diamonds via de Beers. Moreover, if OPEC's 'production programming' were to harden prices, the Russians would seem unlikely to try to puncture such a cartel. Politically, however, there is as yet little sign that they desire any accommodation with Western companies, or Western companies with them. Moreover, could the Western companies themselves agree? In the meantime the oil business offers pretty ready foreign exchange, and a highly convenient range of points at which to pinprick the West.

To the outside observer, it seems surprising that the international oil companies chose to accept this manifestation of 'Soviet economic competition with the West' wholly within their own preserves. By the sixties, certainly, they were combating it fiercely in certain markets, quoting prices that were sometimes too low for the Russians in order to hold or to recapture customers: the Russians were by no means the only marketers on the offensive. But very severe price cutting to hold one's share of the market, in the areas where they had much to lose and the Russians had nothing, was a somewhat sacrificial business. Was there no ground whatever for more direct counter-attack?

Offers of very cheap crude or products in some Communist markets to which Russia does not find it too easy to deliver oil cheaply migth have been a possibility. It is perhaps not quite certain that the state import organizations of these countries would have been ready to turn down cargoes of really cheap crude or products even from Western sellers—particularly as Russia is not offering its Communist partners in Comecon anything like the discounts that it does to penetrate Western markets. Like other oil marketers, it engages in price discrimination where it can: its satellites have so far constituted effectively a captive market. Even if the Western companies did not get the business, they might have a chance of embarrassing Russia where its prices are high. Some of these companies were inhibited more than others by embargoes on trade with the Soviet bloc. But Western governments that inhibit them from countering the Russians in a way that commercially might hit them 'where they live' are not necessarily helping the West. It is said that one international group, during the fifties, seriously considered an attempt at large-scale penetration of the Chinese market with cheap oil, but that American opposition to 'trading with the enemy' dissuaded it. (By the mid-sixties, some European suppliers appeared less inhibited about this.)

Some American and European companies would prefer a diplomatic or strategic counter to Soviet exports: they have frequently argued to European governments that quotas on imports, although they oppose these as a general principle, should be tightened up against Russian oil. They are in danger, too often, of appearing to seek government intervention on their own commercial behalf—which seems unwise for an industry so generally opposed to government intervention of any other kind. More commercial forms of counter-attack, attempting to compete with the Russians 'where they live', might be better suited to the competence—and the dignity—of international private enterprise. And by 1965, with a new interest in trade with Eastern Europe spreading even to the United States, there were signs that some of the international oil companies may be preparing a new competitive strategy towards Russian oil.

CHAPTER XIV

Seeking Their Own Petroleum

Nations that are self-sufficient in oil, as we have just seen, generate and may export their own *embarras de richesse*. But self-sufficiency in oil, to nations that do not possess it, appears a most enviable condition—both to the less developed economies that visualize a new dynamo of cheap energy and even perhaps a commodity for export to bring them riches overnight, and to the developed economies whose dependence upon petroleum is inevitably increasing, and which may well yearn to secure command of adequate supplies. Governments usually take a hand in this search for self-sufficiency. Many offer tax incentives and some subsidies to private explorers for oil; some go into the exploration business directly. The countries that one picks out to illustrate such circumstances must be chosen arbitrarily. Canada is a case where government policy, applied as directives to a privately-owned industry, has revived a success story that seemed to have gone wrong in the late fifties. In Brazil the government went into oil exploration itself; found little for many years; and after reorganizing its efforts has now achieved some success. In Argentina a government oil company invited in private oil companies as 'contractors', and for a year or two touched self-sufficiency; then evicted foreign oil, but has not managed to retain its autarchy. Then there are countries such as Mexico and Austria, which have at times produced as much oil as they consume, but have been unable to take full advantage of their virtually complete self-sufficiency; and Australia, which after a huge exploration effort is only just beginning to find a little oil.

Exploration for oil or gas is going on, today, in most countries in the world; and most countries can boast at least a trickle or a puff of their own. The continuing demand for new concessions or even for areas that other explorers choose to relinquish demonstrates to governments everywhere how worthwhile a gamble exploration seems to experts, even when oil isn't scarce. There are few other economic sectors where international capital can be attracted so easily. Most countries afford to any production that they can develop some degree of protection against competition from imported fuels—and equally insert into concessions or exploration licences specific obligations to develop without delay any oil that is found. Most of the industrialized countries other than the United States and Russia have had to resign themselves to overwhelming reliance on imports. Some countries where oil has been found in impressive quantities, for lack of local markets, have quickly graduated into the ranks of the exporting countries. But in between there remains a handful of countries where supply is in balance, or is expected soon to be with demand. Demand and supply, of course, seldom develop at the same rate; so self-sufficiency, even if once achieved, may be a temporary phase, as an economy grows. Nevertheless, developing nations often look to the prospects of oil to help them achieve their economic 'take-off '.

In terms of untapped resources, Canada might think of itself as a developing nation; but it already has a high standard of living even in Western terms. Among those resources, until just after the war, was petroleum. Few countries in recent years have had a more dramatic discovery and development of oil than Canada. When the Leduc field in Alberta was discovered during 1946, it seemed to open up the possibilities not only of self-sufficiency in oil for Canada—or at any rate, a balance between exports and imports—but even of the country's becoming a significant net exporter.

The oilfields, admittedly, were in the far West, while Canada's largest centres of consumption were in the East, using imported crude oil and products. But with support from the Canadian and the United States governments, pipelines were laid from Edmonton to Ontario and onward to the American Middle West (the Interprovincial pipeline system) and to Vancouver and the U.S. West Coast (the Trans-Mountain pipeline) which gave this landlocked oil access to coastal and mid-continental refineries. And prominent among the foreign oil companies that poured capital into Canadian oil—over $9,000 million between 1947 and 1965—were large American companies and certain of the international majors. These were also the most important owners of refineries in Montreal, serving the markets of Eastern Canada with products from imported crude. Whether or not Canadian crude could be expected to replace foreign crude in Montreal, these companies were counted upon to export a corresponding volume of Canadian crude to United States refineries.

Canada's oil boom in the early fifties lived up to all these expectations; production rose to nearly half a million barrels a day by 1957, and exports to the United States to 156,000 barrels a day. During the Suez emergency of the winter of 1956–57, the Trans-Mountain pipeline was running at its full capacity of 200,000 barrels a day. But after Suez came a sharp readjustment—not only for oil but for the Canadian economy as a whole. The country's rate of growth slackened. Its balance of payments deficit worsened (epitomized, in oil terms, by the fact that within eighteen months after Suez the flow through the Trans-Mountain line was down to 11,000 barrels a day). The total volume of exports fell away in 1958 to about 90,000 barrels a day. After a dip in 1958, total Canadian oil output did go on rising slowly, but between 1957 and 1960 it rose by only 5 per cent, to 524,000 barrels a day.

As to self-sufficiency, the volume of imports had been held at about 300,000 barrels a day up to 1955, with the Canadian crude supplying the growth in consumption. From 1955 onwards it had begun to grow again, but this had been more than offset for a few years, by the dramatic rise in Canadian crude exports. But from 1957 to 1960, domestic production rose by only about half as much as Canadian consumption. In 1960, Canada's productive capacity amounted to well over a million barrels a day, against a national consumption of some 850,000 barrels a day; yet more than half of its productive capacity was idle, and imports of crude and products amounted to about 425,000 barrels a day. The industry was still putting more cash annually into exploration, development and production than it earned as income.

This flattening out of fortune was largely due to developments in the world market, but elements of governmental policy were involved alike in the disappointments of the Canadian oilfields and in the nation's reactions to them. Exploration and development in Canada are not cheap, and the respectable amount of reserves that have been discovered (7,700 million barrels by end-1965, after eighteen years in which 4,800 million barrels had been extracted) are not of the massive order of the Middle East. So this is not particularly low-cost oil.

The provincial government of Alberta, moreover, from the beginning of its oil development, imposed a system of relinquishment of parts of leased areas in the interests of conservation; and in 1950 it imposed a form of prorationing. Both policies made sense in terms of the efficient exploitation of the oilfields. Unfortunately, when it came to exports, the large integrated producers who could have found this oil markets in the

United States were faced with the fact that all producers had the right to share in whatever extra output was produced. This reduced the profits they could gain from prorated Canadian oil in comparison with using their own crude from Venezuela or the Middle East. It did, in fact, reduce the growth of output in Alberta relative to that of Saskatchewan, where no prorationing system was in force.

Canadian oil was given the privilege of exemption (along with Mexican) when American import restrictions came formally into force in 1959, as 'overland oil' able to enter the United States by pipeline, motor carrier, or rail. But this still did not persuade American importers to take up less of their import quotas for the cheaper foreign crudes from Venezuela and the Middle East. And the decline in tanker freight rates, plus the growth of discounting, has made those imports from distant areas, in comparison with Canadian oil overland, cheaper.

With the share of imports in the Canadian market tending to grow, and a large proportion of domestic capacity idle, clamour for economic nationalism was inevitable. The then government's eventual response was indeed nationalist, but not impracticably so. It did not follow the example it had been set from south of the border, and impose import restrictions. What it did was to lay down that by the middle sixties the Ontario market—border of competition between Canadian and imported crudes—ought to be supplied completely from Canadian production, which should reach a given level by 1963. Most of Canadian crude production was controlled by American companies, which also controlled the refineries in Eastern Canada that were importing Venezuelan and Middle East oil. By setting the output target but not imposing import restrictions, the Canadian government left it up to them. What it assumed they would choose—and what they did—was to increase Canadian exports south to the United States at a faster rate than they increased imports into Eastern Canada. Canada would thus approach self-sufficiency 'net'—in terms of exports rising to equal imports—rather than in the simpler terms of meeting all home demand with domestic supplies. The sheer geography of the country, with Canadian crude sources far nearer American markets to the south than Canadian markets far to the east, made this solution better sense.[1] This governmental nationalism was thus permissive: but it was backed with the potential threat that if it did not work the government could order construction of the much-disputed pipeline to serve the Montreal refineries with Canadian crude. Faced with the choice of using more high-cost Canadian crude in one set of markets or another, the international companies chose the least uneconomic course—increasing imports to the United States.

By the mid-sixties, it seemed that Canada's 'National Oil Policy' had succeeded. By 1964, crude oil output reached 750,000 barrels a day, plus 100,000 barrels a day of natural gas liquids; effectively, this was the target that the government had set, though achieved about a year late. Exports had accounted for almost all of this: the amount of Canadian crude reaching the Canadian market had increased very little. Nevertheless, 'net self-sufficiency' was well on the way to achievement: by 1964 production was about 80 per cent of the total consumption figure, and still expanding somewhat faster. This moderate economic nationalism has worked effectively so far, perhaps, mainly because it fits into the 'Continental Concept'—i.e. taking as little account as possible of the 49th Parallel and supplying all areas of North America as economically as possible from the cheapest—North American—sources. There are limits to the competitiveness, in these terms, of Canadian crude in the United States. Alaskan crude production is beginning, with a duty advantage; Venezuela has continued to lobby for equal treatment in terms of United States import restrictions, and informally, the United States government in the mid-sixties was urging some moderation in the growth of American imports from Canada. In terms of ownership, again, this economic nationalism had succeeded partly by encouraging Canadian independent producers to be bought up by American groups. Nevertheless, by the mid-sixties Canadian oil was in a far happier state than five years before, and looking forward with some confidence, if hardly with the boundless enthusiasm of the early years after Leduc. Producers were continuing to explore and develop on a sizeable scale, spending something of the order of $850,000 a year. And in contrast to their first fifteen years, they were drawing an annual turnover significantly greater than this, so that the industry was beginning to 'get money back'. But it would still be a long time before they had got back all of the enormous amounts they had drilled into Canada to build this industry.

Not many of the other countries in which governments are putting their influence behind the search for self-sufficiency in oil began with the initial, heady success that Canada enjoyed. And others adopted 'national policies for oil' at earlier stages in the development of their oil industry. In Brazil, for example, exploration was begun by the state between the two wars: little oil was found in the early years, and after 1953, when Petroleos Brasileros (Petrobras) was formed, there were more substantial additions to reserves. By the end of 1960, the total proved reserves amounted to some 700 million barrels, against 50 million barrels in 1954, and output had reached about 80,000 barrels a day. In 1954, when Petrobras began operating, that volume of output might have been a national achievement, for domestic demand was only about 150,000 barrels a day: but by 1960, demand had doubled. Local crude production, from Petrobras wells and others, was still equivalent to about a third of local consumption; but the actual amount of oil that still had to be imported, about 230,000 barrels a day, had grown too. By 1964, production was still only about 90,000 barrels a day; and in spite of some significant discoveries of oil in the meantime, there had been no net additions to reserves.

Moreover, the output achieved was almost all from one field, the Reconcavo basin in Bahia; and in 1960, Mr Walter Link, a geological consultant engaged by Petrobras, submitted a very pessimistic report on the possibilities of finding commercial oil anywhere else. Brazil has 1·3 million square miles of sedimentary areas, and between 1954 and 1960, spent some $300 million on exploring various among apparently promising areas: but this latest expert suggested the abandonment of exploration of many such areas, and a reduction of effort in others. Since Mr Link himself had formerly been optimistic about oil to be found in the Amazon area, his pessimism was denounced. But up to the middle sixties, not much oil had been found elsewhere. Not enough, indeed, to replace the oil extracted in the meantime.

Petrobras is owned mainly by the state, with some municipal and private capital in it. When it was founded in 1953, it had a monopoly of petroleum production and the sole right to build additional refinery capacity; in 1963, it had added to its powers a monopoly of refining, and the then government decided also to nationalize the other six privately-owned refineries. The succeeding government renounced this nationalization decree, but the import monopoly was confirmed. Petrobras was already one of the largest single buyers of crude in the world market. It has only a limited direct share in marketing, but the international companies marketing in Brazil are obliged to distribute the oil that it refines; and locally-refined oil products are protected by a preferential rate of excise duty. Its obvious main weakness, at the beginning of the sixties, lay in not having found enough oil. One might put this down simply to the fact that Brazil's terrain, in spite of superficially favourable characteristics, simply did not contain commercial oil.

Certainly one could not complain that too little effort had been put into exploration. The oil business, across the world, has had to write off some sustained and very expensive exploration ventures. But few single ventures in any other country have quite equalled the $300 million that Petrobras put into exploration (apart from development) between 1954 and 1964, with fairly disappointing results. And a state company, spending the resources of a fairly poor state, has not the spread of operations elsewhere, some of which offer far easier rewards, to offset its bad luck in the one chosen territory.

Some other countries that had begun by seeking self-sufficiency on their own account have gradually, over the years, conceded a somewhat large place to the major oil companies—though they have generally retained very considerable privileges for their nationalized or nationally owned 'chosen instrument'. The Turkish government looked for its own oil from 1933 to 1954, and found some; but after twenty years, short of capital for refining and for further exploration, with its imports increasing much faster than its production, it decided to grant exploration concessions to private oil companies. Bolivia, which in 1937 expropriated the Jersey Standard subsidiary that first developed oil there (paying in compensation about a quarter of Jersey's valuation) and handed the properties over to Yaciementos Petroliferos Fiscales Bolivianos, kept all oil operations in the hands of this state-owned corporation for fifteen years. The state corporation discovered fresh reserves, and built refineries and pipelines: it did eventually achieve self-sufficiency in oil for Bolivia. But this partly reflected the slow development of the economy and of internal oil consumption; oil did not stimulate economic growth in the company as much as had been hoped. Moreover, YPFB was short of capital, and this hampered its development of crude production for export, to earn foreign exchange. From 1952 onwards, the government began to offer concessions to certain foreign oil developers; and in 1956 it adopted a new petroleum law that opened most of the country's territories to development by private foreign capital. About a dozen foreign groups took up concessions; but after five years only Gulf had made significant discoveries, and most of the others pulled out.

The state corporation continued to develop in its own areas in Bolivia—hampered by government policies of economic stabilization that involved cutting oil product prices down to an artificially low level, and obliging YPFB to supply other government departments without payment. It produces enough crude itself to supply the country's limited international oil requirements (about 8,000 barrels a day in 1965) and export a few thousand barrels of oil a day. It retained a monopoly of refining and marketing; but Bolivian Gulf has already found a large oilfield at Caranda, in the Santa Cruz area of the country, and has plans to export some 50,000 barrels a day. Both YPFB and Gulf, too, have gas for export.

Argentina, again, is another example of a Latin American country that has shifted emphasis in oil development from a State corporation to the private capital invited in from abroad—and then back and forth again. Its state oil corporation, Yaciementos Petroliferos Argentinos, was founded in 1922, but was not given any formal monopoly of oil in the country, and oil has continued to be produced by private companies there through YPF's history. From the mid-thirties, however, the government began to restrict the expansion of private development, and private oil output began to decline. After the war, oil consumption in the economy began to rise rapidly, while domestic production, which in 1946 had supplied about half of this consumption, did not at first keep pace. But by 1963 crude output totalled 270,000 barrels a day, of which YPF produced 125,000 barrels a day. Through a fairly large-scale drilling programme, which was mainly however development as against exploratory drilling, the country had trebled its estimate of proven reserves to 1,550 million barrels and was on the verge of achieving its goal of self-sufficiency.

It had run, however, into the same financial difficulties that other state corporations in Latin America had encountered, basically through shortage of local capital; and in mid-1958 the country had altered its oil policy. It confirmed YPF's monopoly of oil development in Argentina, but provided for YPF to make arrangements with private oil companies to explore, develop and produce oil under contract to it. The forms of contract differed as between different foreign companies. Some were simply drilling contracts at a fee per metre drilled; YPF was entitled to the whole value of the oil. Others, classed as 'development contracts', provided for these companies to sell any oil eventually produced to YPF at prices related to world market levels, giving the 'contractor' companies a return in that way. A third type, which involved exploration as well as development, provided for recovery of the foreign venture capital through a percentage of the value of any crude produced, plus 'benefits' of a given percentage on all oil produced over a given period.

This form of contract, in which title to the oil was retained by YPF but the foreign contractors would effectively 'self-finance' their exploration from any oil discovered, was a fairly new one to the international oil industry. The Argentine government and public may have exaggerated the difference that they could make; and in the event, they did not last. The government of Dr Frondizi, which concluded most of these contracts, was deposed in March 1962, and after the Illia administration took over in 1963, all the contracts were decreed null and void. By early 1966 compensation terms had been agreed with most of the companies involved, and a later government has again talked guardedly about co-operation with foreign capital in the development of Argentine oil resources. But both sides appear to be extremely cautious about the terms on which any future co-operation could be agreed upon.

During the few years of co-operation under these contracts, Argentine output did rise considerably, and the country did achieve broad self-sufficiency. Between 1958 and 1963, the country's oil output was trebled. The main increase was in the output of YPF, itself, assisted by drilling contractors. But the development contractors did achieve production equivalent to about a third of the national total, though little production was ever achieved under the exploration contracts. By 1964 Argentina's output and consumption were both of the order of 14 million tons a year, or 275,000 barrels a day. But consumption was rising and output tending to lag; it remained open to question whether YPF could manage to maintain this national self-sufficiency without outside assistance.

It is not easy to classify Mexico in any book about the oil business. It presents object lessons in the history of relations between the host governments of oil exporting countries and the companies operating there, which will be considered in Chapter XVIII: it has, in the twenty years since it nationalized its oil, been an exporter, a net importer, and again a self-sufficient supplier; and it is also the home of one of the outstanding 'national companies' of the oil world. Petroleos Mexicanos, or Pemex, the state company to which the expropriated company installations were handed over in 1938, took over an oil industry that was perhaps past maturity: it had been the world's second producer at the beginning of the twenties, but production had fallen away, and limited exploration in the thirties had added little to the country's proved reserves.

When Pemex took over Mexico was producing about 128,000 barrels a day, and refining about 118,000 barrels a day: since local consumption was less than half the total output, it had been a large exporter (at the time as big as Venezuela). It lost export markets for products from coastal refineries; it was short of equipment and trained men and could not get either easily from a naturally hostile oil industry. After the war, with Mexican internal demand for petroleum growing, Pemex initiated a substantial exploration programme, with growing success: it was able to keep its output rising, for a while, slightly ahead of internal consumption and to modernize its refining capacity (and to find large gas fields). The Mexican economy, however, began to grow faster as a whole in the middle fifties; and from 1957 to 1959 the country was a net importer, with imports of products exceeding its own exports of crude and products. During this period Pemex was less successful financially than operationally, mainly because, until 1959, the Mexican government held product prices artificially low. In that year the government finally allowed prices to rise, and Pemex was reorganized; its financial situation immediately began to improve. By the sixties Mexico had achieved effective self-sufficiency, with a small flow of net imports to the United States (where, like Canada, it is exempt from import restrictions). Pemex was managing to keep pace with the oil—and gas—demand of a booming economy. It had, moreover, developed the basis for a powerful petrochemicals industry. The government had sought aid from the World Bank; Pemex had employed a number of American drilling contractors and, in limiting its petrochemical effort to the production of base feedstocks, claimed that it believed there was room for both private and public enterprise to work side by side. But Mexican oil was still a public monopoly barring private enterprise. Mexico was proud of it[2]; and a number of Latin American countries looked to it as an example both of national enterprise and of self-sufficiency.

One further example of the country seeking self-sufficiency in oil might be taken from within Europe—which is not even today wholly the importing market that it is sometimes taken to be, and may in future develop considerably more indigenous oil and gas production. In Austria oil came under government ownership essentially as a result of anschluss and war, rather than of nationalist or ideological pressures.

In 1938, the RAG group, a joint subsidiary of Mobil and Shell, had its exploration rights in lower Austria, from which most Austrian production of oil came, expropriated under German law. After the war these fields fell into the Russian occupation zone of Austria; and when the occupation ended in 1955, the Russians handed them over to a state-owned corporation, the Austrian Oil Administration, OeMV, but retained the right to reparations deliveries of a million tons of oil a year until 1965. From 1958, onwards, however, the Russians effectively reduced the burden of these deliveries, first by sending Austria half a million tons of Kuibyshev oil a year cost-free, and later by cutting the rate of reparations deliveries to half a million tons, and agreeing that reparations deliveries should end in 1963. These reparations turned Austria from a self-sufficient country into a net importer rather earlier than this would have happened anyway. State and private development of Austrian oil and has has continued fairly amicably side by side. But local production has levelled off while Austrian consumption has gone on growing. Since 1959, imports have exceeded exports (including up to 1963, reparations): the country cannot avoid greater dependence on imports. To a land-locked market, oil imports must come by pipeline: with one terminal of the Comecon line from Russia at the Czech border, and a Western-owned line planned from Trieste, Austria is now able to buy either Western or Soviet oil fairly cheaply.

The search for self-sufficiency in oil in the countries which we have examined, does not necessarily involve the participation of state companies; and these when set up have not necessarily been able to maintain monopolies conferred on them at least in the field of production and exploration. But it often does mean 'nationalized' oil development; and in countries where it does not it often means other forms of governmental pressure upon private companies engaged in oil development there to conform with 'national policies' in oil. Mr. Walter Levy, the American oil consultant, in a study that he prepared for the World Bank in 1961, argued very powerfully that exploration and development, at any rate, are usually too expensive and risky an operation for the governments of underdeveloped countries to engage in on their own. With the limited capital resources they usually possess, he thought they might well concentrate on investments offering a more guaranteed return, since the international oil industry was prepared to put in the risk capital. Many governments, however, remain tempted.

Nations seeking self-sufficiency for their growing oil markets, again, have the chance to benefit from a tendency in the exploration effort of the world oil industry that has become obvious in the last few years. This is the readiness of international companies, established majors or newcomers, to explore for oil in countries where there is a developing market—which offers a likely, and even perhaps protected, outlet for the oil if they do find it. Oil—and gas—is worth a great deal more on the spot where it can be sold than in areas remote from markets, where its development may be much harder to command.

CHAPTER XV

Consumers Commanding Oil

'If we cannot secure the access to this island of oil ships, we cannot secure the access to this island of the whole of the great volume of our trade on which we shall depend in war as in peace, if we are to maintain ourselves effectively,' said Mr Winston Churchill in the House of Commons on 7th June, 1914. 'The proposition that the Navy should be able to keep our ports open and to keep our trade routes safe in time of war for all the vast merchant fleets which traffic with this island, and yet should lack the power to bring in the comparatively few but, from our point of view, specially interesting oil cargoes, is a proposition which is naturally, inherently and, if need be, demonstrably absurd.'

These were perhaps not the obvious terms for a First Lord of the Admiralty to use in justifying the purchase, originally for £2,200,000, of a controlling interest in the Anglo-Persian Oil Company. But Mr Churchill was emphasizing the commercial, as against the strategic, significance of the government's purchase of a stake in oil. 'Nobody cares in war time,' he went on to say, 'how much they pay for a vital commodity, but in peace—that is the period to which I wish to direct the attention of the Committee—price is rather an important matter, and as we hope that there will be many years of peace to every week of war, I cannot feel that we are not fully justified in taking up the time of the Committee in considering how, in years of peace and in a long period of peace, we may acquire proper bargaining power and facilities with regard to the purchase of oil. The price of oil does not depend wholly or even mainly on the ordinary workings of supply and demand.' Mr Churchill was concerned with the question of supplies for the Royal Navy, which was becoming, in the interests of efficiency, more dependent on oil; a long-term contract for naval supplies was, indeed, one of the corollaries of the share purchase. But he was setting out in this debate more than half a century ago exactly the mixture of motives, not

entirely strategic but not entirely commercial, with which the governments of many countries who have to rely on imports for their oil regard
their increasing dependence upon it, and with which some are seeking
command, or assurance, of supplies. Sir Edward Grey put it more
bluntly in the same debate, 'What you want is an independent source of
supply which is, as far as possible, uncontrolled by any agency which
can exact undue prices or what the customer considers undue prices.'

In the long run, the consequences of this decision were momentous
and complex. It certainly assured oil supplies for the Navy; it also
assured governmental backing for the development of Anglo-Persian
(later Anglo-Iranian and finally British Petroleum) throughout the
Middle East. It incidentally must have proved perhaps the most profitable investment of British public money in any industrial operation in
our time. Less happily for Britain, there is little doubt that this identification of government and company had more than a little to do, over the
years, in forming political attitudes towards the company in the Middle
East, which eventually culminated in the nationalization of Iranian oil
and may also have had something to do, ten years later, with the drastic
and unilateral abrogation of the Iraq concession. One thing that it did
not do, as matters turned out, was to ensure the British consumer
particularly cheap oil.

This move represented the first open manifestation of the vital interest to the government of a country lacking indigenous oil supplies of
securing a source of supply that it recognized as strategically vital. It
was to become a prototype. Britain sought and gained command of
securely 'tied' supplies of oil from a promising source that later turned
out to be part of the richest oil-bearing region yet discovered. Over the
years it extended that command in the region, though its chosen instrument was not able to obtain exclusive rights anywhere except in Iran,
and later lost them there. Nor was BP its only lien upon international
oil. The 40 per cent British interest in Royal Dutch/Shell, in spite of
hard words about that 'combine' when Anglo-Persian was being bought,
has linked this group's interests with Britain's almost as firmly as those
of BP.

The Netherlands, alike, had its own oil needs guaranteed through
ownership of the other 60 per cent of Royal Dutch/Shell. Victory in the
First World War gave the Allies the chance to cut Germany out of the
stake in Middle East oil that it had invested in Iraq; but this, in its turn,
cut France in. France had already begun seeking some control over its
supplies of oil products, at least, by developing a refinery industry

behind tariff protection. Access to Iraq oil, for which it created CFP, gave it command over growing supplies of crude, though not enough to cover all its needs.

These three major industrialized consuming countries, which until recently lacked petroleum resources within their own frontiers, have thus large enough strategic and financial interests in petroleum elsewhere for their governments, very often, to behave more like producers than consumers. Through CFP, France has somewhat enlarged its Middle East interests over the years, though not nearly as much as Britain has through BP. The Royal Dutch/Shell group widened its interests with the Iraq Petroleum group, was allotted quite a sizeable share in the Iran Consortium, and has recently begun developing oil from Oman; but up to now this group, and hence the Netherlands, have had much larger interests in the Western hemisphere and the Far East than in the Middle East. France, since the war, has invested heavily in developing oil production in one of its own spheres of interest, Algeria, and other parts of the 'franc zone'. Though all these have now attained independence, it has paid Algeria, in its early years of oil exporting, to maintain a specially close relationship with France.

This command of oil, eroded somewhat though it continues to be by the emergence from tutelage of the oil-producing states, significantly modifies the commercial stance of the British, Dutch and French governments in dealing with the oil business. Their oil policies are not identical. Britain's 'invisible' income from international oil profits was for years believed to have outweighed its foreign exchange disbursements on buying oil supplies for international consumption; this is no longer true, but the large invisible income of the two 'sterling oil' groups still greatly reduces the net foreign exchange cost of the country's growing oil imports. Holland still probably is a net earner of foreign exchange on oil account, since it has a sizeable entrepot trade and large export refineries, apart from its invisible income from production overseas. These two countries favour liberal import policies (though not so liberal as to make oil too cheap). France has a smaller financial interest in international oil; only recently has it had the prospect of its tied or associated oil production exceeding its internal demand; its approach is *dirigiste* rather than liberal. But all three countries share this mixture of interests in general energy policy. They are somewhat less concerned than other industrialized consumer countries with protecting their domestic coal industries. France and Britain, at any rate, are also less concerned that their home consumers should get oil cheap.

The BP group does not behave like the semi-nationalized or 'national' companies of the kind that other countries have created recently. Commercially, it behaves like one of the international majors (which it is) controlled by private ownership (which it is not). But the decision that Churchill took affirmed a policy that was acted upon consistently throughout the interwar period: that British diplomatic interests in the Middle East were inextricably tied up with oil. About 40 years later, this was the principle upon which Britain risked its whole influence in the Middle East, in the Suez affair. From Sir Anthony Eden's memoirs of that time, one gains the impression that Britain's impending shortage of fuel, and its utter dependence upon getting Middle East oil through the Suez Canal, were perhaps the two economic 'facts' that ever became firmly implanted in Sir Anthony's mind. That neither happen to be a fact did not alter their importance in that odd and damaging aberration of British foreign policy.

British Petroleum has never enjoyed any privilege in the British market, though it and the Shell group, marketing together in this country, still have the largest 'single' share of sales of refined products. Britain did not develop a significant home refining industry until after the Second World War, Although the government gave some support to the experimental development of oil from coal, by hydrogenation at Billingham, its prewar view, endorsed by a committee in 1939, was that home refining made little difference to the strategic security of oil supplies, and was uneconomic. Dollar shortage; doubts about political stability in the Middle East; growth of the British market to a size where it could absorb large enough quantities of a wide range of products to fit refining yields without burdensome surpluses; and the development of petrochemicals—all these after the war reversed its view. Its refining capacity amounted at the end of 1965 to 1,470,000 b/d (72 million tons a year), third in Europe behind Italy and Germany; this is still expanding. It has a sizeable export trade to Europe in products; also higher product prices than most, and more comfortable refining margins. In 1964, 73 million tons of oil (1,500,000 barrels a day) were consumed in the United Kingdom, and only a trickle, about 0·2 per cent of consumption, was produced. The only fuel Britain really has at home is coal, produced by one of the world's largest mining industries; and since the late fifties this coal has been suffering severe competition from oil. Yet the British government never displays quite the same attitudes towards these imports that the governments of certain other coal-producing countries in Western Europe do—being conscious that though the country commands no oil, it commands considerable oil profits.

Admittedly, though they accept a decline in the output of coal, successive British governments have given the industry a good deal of transitional protection. The Suez affair heightened the fears of an energy gap (though in fact supplies of fuel were already becoming larger than could be sold). The government, during this short period of 'oil shortage', trebled its nuclear programme and committed itself to heavier investment in nationalized coal. When oil became abundant again, and estimates of the cost of nuclear electricity began to mount, the government for a time cut back its nuclear investment. It also reduced the amount of oil that would be used in power stations. The electricity authorities had found that oil at coastal stations in the South of England was becoming cheaper than coal at pithead power stations in the Midlands.

Nor had the professed liberalism meant entirely free imports of fuel. Until 1961 Britain gave no formal protection to coal through taxes on fuel oil, as many other consuming countries did. But it also did not allow private consumers—or the nationalized electricity industry—to import coal, which could have been had very cheaply from America or Poland during periods of low ocean freights. Equally, it has granted almost no licences to import Russian oil. There were always, therefore significant hidden elements of protection for established interests—both in oil and coal—in British energy policy.[1] But in the Budget of 1961, the protection became admitted. Until then, only petroleum products used as transport fuels had been taxed: but in the 1961 budget, the government re-imposed an excise duty of 2d. a gallon on other products. This meant nearly £2 a ton on fuel oil, of which consumption had been rising at a dramatic rate. Yet the British energy policy remained mixed. Within six months of the imposition of this fuel oil duty, the Ministry of Power was promoting petroleum imports to compete with coal: it authorized imports of a technically unproven and initially at any rate more expensive form of petroleum, liquefied natural gas, and arranged for an import duty to be remitted. In this the nationalized gas industry, formerly largely dependent on coal, was associated with an importing group in the ownership of which figured one of the oil companies that Britain considered utterly dependable, the Royal Dutch/Shell group. Moreover, owing to an anomaly in the existing legislation on to which the fuel oil duty was grafted, the 2d. a gallon applied only to oils that were burned, not those chemically converted. As a result, the electricity industry had to pay duty on the fairly limited amount of oil it used in power stations; but the gas industry enjoyed exemption for the rapidly growing amount of naphtha that it chemically converted into gas in its oil gasworks. In the domestic market, again, the oil duty tended to reduce the rate of growth of oil central heating; but the biggest beneficiary among its competitors was gas, which for additional sales was largely relying on oil gasification.

By the middle sixties, with 'planning' all the vogue in Britain, the government was planning a further moderate decline in coal, from 65 per cent of total energy supplies in 1964 to only 52 per cent of a larger consumption in 1970. It was not reducing its restraint upon oil in the general market: the oil duty continued, the electricity industry was instructed to continue to give coal preference, and the coal industry was allowed to write down its capital and thus reduce the interest charges that bore so heavily upon its declining output. At the same time, the government accepted that the main growth would be in oil consumption; it was welcoming newcomers to the British market—so long as they showed willingness to set up refineries as soon as their sales reached a substantial level.[2] But two elements emerging in the British energy situation seemed likely to hasten more radical change from the seventies onwards: cheap nuclear power and the development of natural gas from under the Continental Shelf of the North Sea. Following upon American developments that radically cheapened nuclear costs at the beginning of the sixties, the British designers had done the same: stations were being ordered in 1965 that by 1971 were expected to generate nuclear electricity markedly cheaper than coal-fired ones, and probably about as cheaply as oil-fired stations without the fuel oil duty. Whatever the merit of the precise costings, nuclear power had emerged as the generation system for base load power in Britain. Natural gas was less certain and perhaps less of a lasting asset; nevertheless, early discoveries, within a year of the first drilling, suggested that very large contributions to the British market might come from this new source too. It was entirely in keeping with the traditions of British oil policy that the Government threw exploration rights in the North Sea open to all comers, 'taking into account their contribution to the British fuel economy'; and that it was BP that made the first commercial discovery of gas late in 1965.

Holland is the home of Royal Dutch, the senior (60 per cent) partner in the Royal Dutch/Shell group; and though until recently the Dutch government had no shareholding in any petroleum operations, it has a natural concern with an industry that bulks so large in the economics of the home country and its associated territories. Holland lost much of its sovereignty over Far Eastern oil with the accession of Indonesia to independence after the Second World War, but the output of the Royal Dutch/Shell group was already widely spread elsewhere. In the Netherlands Antilles the refineries of Shell at Curaçao and Esso at Aruba, processing Venezuelan oil, make these Dutch islands one of the most important export refining centres in the world. In Holland itself the great refining and petrochemical complex round Rotterdam is a very substantial exporter of products to the rest of Europe, though the pipelines now running from Rotterdam to inland refineries around Karlsruhe and Stuttgart are tending to limit the marketing area for products refined coastally there.

The Dutch government, to the oil industry, acts as a very friendly neutral. Holland has a smallish coal industry, which has encountered the same difficulties in competition with oil of recent years as have others in Europe. Beyond ceasing to issue licences for imports of American coal since the fifties, and putting on regulations about keeping minimum stocks by oil marketers, the government has taken no measures to protect coal or limit the switch to oil. Its coal mines supply only about a third of its energy requirements, and it has no hydro-power: so reliance on imported energy for the majority of its consumption is neither new nor frightening to it. However, in the early sixties it opened up huge new reserves of fuel at home. Shell had explored in Holland since the thirties, originally with an effective monopoly: after the war it took Esso in as a partner in prospecting. Their joint subsidiary Nederlandse Aardolie Matschappij, NAM, developed some small oil production in Holland and after a number of minor natural gas finds, in 1960 it discovered a field at Slochteren, in Groningen province, that is among the largest petroleum reserves ever located in the world. From estimates of 150 milliard cubic metres, the reserve figures were rapidly revised up to 1,100 milliard cubic metres; this was the published estimate in 1963, though unofficial Dutch guesses have put it at from 2,000 to 6,000 milliard cubic metres. Under Dutch mining law, no concession had to be granted until petroleum was found: so the government could dictate its own terms to NAM. Through its state mining organization, it took a 40 per cent shareholding in the company that will develop the gas, and formulated a sales policy that will discipline the rate of expansion of sales of this gas at home, though it hopes to promote home exports.[3]

In a sense, Holland began by protecting imported oil, as well as home-produced coal, against this new source of indigenous energy. Could liberalism go farther?

Within the European Common Market, the Dutch government has been one of the strongest advocates of a liberal policy towards importing energy. At the end of 1960, it did concede the principle of a limit to duty-free imports of petroleum products from the Netherlands Antilles into Europe as part of the price for association of these Caribbean Islands with EEC; without this, its partners in the Six would not have agreed to association. This minor concession to restrictive policies towards energy imports demonstrated that Holland has to temper its liberalism for the sake of its special interests. Nevertheless, there are few governments whose professed liberalism in energy policy is as unadulterated; its European partners, as the Dutch gas is developed as a massive new energy supply for North-West Europe, will be watching to see if unearthing this buried treasure of new indigenous energy in any way dilutes that liberalism.

Self-sufficiency in oil production is a new postwar aim of French governments; but it was not the first interest they had shown in self-sufficiency. After the First World War, France had imposed various forms of protection to encourage refining within the country. The measure that finally did bring about a significant development of French refining, the oil law of 1928, laid the foundations of a considerably greater degree of State supervision for oil companies operating there than exists in most of Western Europe. Refining and marketing has remained largely in the hands of local affiliates of the major international companies; but these are subject to strict licensing. Refiners and marketers are licensed, and new permits are not freely granted; licensees have obligations to maintain reserve stocks of a given size, are allotted quotas of imports of crude, and are subject inside the market to price controls on their products.

The creation of CFP, with its share in the Middle East, resulted from a diplomatic rather than a commercial French initiative. The Treaty of San Remo, after the First World War, transferred to France German rights in the Turkish Petroleum Company, which in 1929 became the Iraq Petroleum Company, and CFP was founded in 1924, to exercise these rights. Today it is also a participant in the Iranian consortium, and is a partner with BP in the offshore Abn Dhabi concession; and it has played a part, though hardly a dominant one, in the development of the Sahara. Its Middle East production is larger than it can sell through its 'Total' distributing subsidiary, which operates in a number of European countries and at the end of the fifties was extending its interests into others, such as Britain; but it sells considerable amounts of crude to other major companies and to independent buyers. Its refining associate Compagnie Francaise de Raffinage is one of the largest refiners in France. Since the end of the fifties it has been processing a growing proportion of Saharan oil—as other refineries in France have also been obliged to do.

Few potential oil-producing areas in the whole history of the oil industry have ever been explored and developed with the single-minded intensity that France put into the Sahara after the war. Up to Algerian independence in 1962, expenditure on exploration and development there had reached about NF 6,000 million, or $1,200 million since exploration began in earnest during 1947; and France was investing heavily in exploration and development in other parts of the 'franc zone', such as Gabon and the Middle Congo. At the end of 1964 there were about 40 drilling rigs in operation in the Sahara alone, and another 90–100 were active in France itself and the rest of the franc zone. Oil began to be discovered from 1954 onwards, and very important finds of oil were made in 1956 at Hassi Messaoud; all the significant discoveries were hundreds of miles from the coast, and involved vast investment in pipelines to bring this oil, and the gas from the Hassi R'Mel field located in 1957, to the coast of the Mediterranean. By 1965, output had reached 550,000 barrels a day ($23\frac{1}{2}$ million tons a year): it could not grow until the third pipeline from the fields to the sea came on stream in 1966. It was not until the end of 1959 that oil began to be exported. But by spring 1962 Algeria had achieved independence and France's links with Algerian oil had become strictly economic.

These Saharan finds represented one of the most important single additions to major oil-producing areas made during the fifties—second only, perhaps, to the adjacent finds, in rather more favourable circumstances, in Libya. But they were still small in comparison with the 180 billion barrels of proved reserves in the Middle East. Even Iraq, which has the lowest total of proved reserves in the four major Middle East producers, had nearly four times as high a figure as the Sahara at the end of 1964. In this industry one tends to think of proved reserves as to some degree proportional to the scale of effort in exploration. It may be worth noting that the huge reserves of the Middle

East have been located by the drilling, over many years, of perhaps 2,000 wells; the far more concentrated effort in the Sahara, in the space of a dozen years, has not compared in its rewards. And the money spent has been even more, in proportion, than the physical effort of drilling; for drilling in the Sahara, owing to the even worse physical and climatic conditions there, is more costly than in most parts of the Middle East.

But the most significant difference between the exploration and development of the French Sahara and that of most other oil-producing areas outside the United States was that it was initiated strictly by nationals of the country then ruling the area, backed by their government. Shell was associated with CREPS, one of the companies in the Sahara, from the start; other major companies later accepted the French government's invitation to take leases in the area. But all had to operate in partnership with French (later partly Algerian) semi-nationalized companies. This Saharan success was the crown of a community-wide exploration effort organized by the French government after the Second World War, as one of its dogged national efforts to restore *la gloire*; it was a more constructive and fruitful effort than some.

No sooner was this particular contribution to glory brought to fruition than France agreed to hand it over to a new, nationalist Algeria. The new Algeria succeeded to the 50 per cent governmental share of profits on Algerian oil, to a sizeable share in the ownership of S.N.Repal, the main French operating company in the Sahara, and to smaller shares in other companies developing Algerian oil and gas. But it needs French co-operation—and capital—to get the full benefit of this costly inherited national oil industry. An initial *modus vivendi* on oil was reached in a protocol to the Evian agreement of early 1962. Many other countries attaining some degree of independence had been left with oil companies that had entered the country under the previous régime. No other one has ever had to deal with companies that were so tightly linked by ownership with the colonial government that seemed at last to be relinquishing sovereignty. But the Algerian government showed no inhibitions about doing so. The more substantive agreement for the continued oil development that it reached in July 1965 was again with the French government: indeed, this was one of the first deals between governments for the exploitation of the natural resources of one of them ever concluded. And the Algerians drove a fairly effective bargain. The Accord provided for upward revision of the tax rate, and other adjustments of the financial terms of existing concessions in Algeria (which had not been generous). It provided the Algerian Government with first rights to the disposal of natural gas. And it provided for the future development of a large part of Algeria's prospective oil territories under a joint 'Association Co-Operative', with Algeria taking a full part in the operation as well as the ownership of oil ventures there. Algeria obtained, moreover, as part of the same deal, sizeable long-term credits for the development of the rest of its economy.[5]

Its location alone would have secured Saharan oil a significant place in the French market and probably elsewhere in Southern Europe; its only immediate competition from nearby is in Libya. But the initial French state backing of Saharan oil guaranteed it privileged entry into the French market at least; and the degree of control the state possessed over refining and marketing companies in France has enabled it to require all refineries to handle a quota of oil from the new source. Indeed, it may still seek some preference for the Saharan oil elsewhere in Western Europe. This was one of the main market tangible economic benefits that France had to offer the new Algerian state.

Introduction of the Saharan crude posed some technical and commercial questions, regardless of its political backing. This is a light crude, giving a higher yield of gasoline and a much lower yield of fuel oil than is suited to the French market, where, like most of Western Europe, it has been demand for fuel oil and the middle distillates that have grown fastest. But apart from pressing Saharan oil upon the major companies that refine and distribute there, the French government, in 1959, bought its way into the refining and marketing business. A new company, Union Générale des Pétroles, was set up and purchased a 60 per cent interest in the Caltex refinery and marketing system in France. When it set up this marketing company the government offered some reassurances to the existing marketers that it would not receive preferential treatment. But in 1963, in allocating its next batch of import quotas, it did 'make room' for UGP at the expense of the other refining companies—who were left, if they chose, to make up their demand with further Saharan oil. France's policy at home was to retain control over foreign oil refiners and marketers—while keeping prices up and profits comfortable. Abroad, it wanted to fortify its oil partnership with Algeria. Doing both involved something of a tightrope act.

Another fresh supply of 'franc petroleum' has been a few years behind Saharan oil in crossing the seas to Western Europe—Saharan natural gas. The projects to supply this liquefied in ocean tankers to Britain have already been discussed in Chapter VI; as was also mentioned there, it may alternatively cross the sea by undersea pipeline, or in 'trains' of refrigerated barges. Large supplies of natural gas, incidentally, may make up for the low yield of fuel oil from Saharan crudes. France has already a sizeable market for natural gas, developed on the basis of its own Lacq deposits near the Spanish border; but these are not enough alone, and by the mid-sixties it was buying from Holland as well as Algeria.

While France controlled Algeria, the international companies that obtained concessions there had the unusual experience of dealing with a 'host government' whose economic experience was as industrialized and as sophisticated as their own. They also had to deal with something they generally distrust elsewhere: a government with substantial share-holdings in most of the oil operations in the area, and in any case requiring more than 50 per cent of ownership to be French. Since Algerian self-determination, moreover, they have had to deal also with a new and at least radical Arab 'host government' which can draw on Middle East experience, has a powerful ally in marketing its oil in the still-financially-interested French government—and which has also, by political succession, inherited without monetary investment certain direct shareholdings in the oil business of a kind that most companies were reluctant to concede to longer-established 'hosts'.

The chance of 'tied' oil supplies through national ownership of countries operating abroad attracts other industrialized countries in Europe and Asia. Portugal is now seeking what it hopes may become 'self-sufficiency' through development of oil in Angola. It may get sufficient from there to cover its needs. But how long Angola will remain 'part of' Portugal is perhaps less certain. Italy and Japan, however, are both anxious to command supplies of oil through their own companies—though for the moment, in circumstances of oil surplus, the main role of both is as 'arm's-length buyers' of oil using all their bargaining power to get it as cheaply as they can from anywhere. Italy's chosen instrument, a thorn in the side of the international companies, is a fully-nationalized concern, not one with partial government ownership such as BP or CFP. The Japanese company now producing part of the Middle East oil that Japan imports is privately owned. But links between the government and this group of banks, utilities and other Japanese businesses are close: the company seems to obtain some preference for its crude, and it now appears that the Japanese government is developing an 'oil policy' that might facilitate this. These countries, like France, would seem likely to offer special privileges to their own companies in competing with other supplying companies. But for the moment, their ambition to gain a stake in production in no way inhibits Italy and Japan from thinking, and behaving, primarily as single-minded consumers.

CHAPTER XVI

Consumers in the Market Place

O n 1st February, 1964, the Gelsenberg Benzin AG of Gelsen-kirchen posted a price of $2.21 per barrel f.o.b. Es Sider terminal for crude oil from the Hofra concession in Libya. There was nothing remarkable about this price: it was the same as Esso and other companies were already posting for Libyan crude. What was remarkable was the nationality of the producing company. Gelsenberg, operating this concession jointly with Mobil, was the first German company ever to post a price for crude oil in the international market. It was some years behind Japan. But it had been inevitable that both would arrive some time.

Until the last few years Germany has had no significant financial interest in the world oil business, except as a customer. It played a part in the initial bidding for Middle East oil concessions before the first world war; but after defeat in 1918, its claims to Turkish concessions over what became the nation of Iraq were taken from it by the Allied powers and eventually handed over to France. So German capital was shut out of the Middle East during virtually the whole history of oil development in the region; nor had it any part in Western hemisphere oil. The Federal Republic, by the middle sixties, had overhauled Britain as Europe's largest consumer of oil: Japan was a considerably larger consumer than either. But unlike Britain or the United States, these two huge developed consumers had no major international oil companies based at home to command supplies and invisible income from the world oil trade. Germany remains a consumer in the market place, bargaining—though not quite singlemindedly—for the cheapest oil it can get. During the current years of surplus, this role has given first Japan and later Germany some of the lowest oil prices anywhere. But few countries are content to accept complete dependence on imports, through foreign companies, as wholly comfortable.

Germany has one of the largest coal industries and the largest domestic production of oil in Europe; both need and receive protection from imports. It took rather longer than in most other West European countries for the switch over to oil to develop in the Federal Republic: but once it began, the rate of change was explosive. During the fifties, oil consumption rose in most years by 20 per cent or more, with consumption of the black oils that compete with coal growing fastest; in 1964, it reached about 77 million metric tons, against 4 million tons in 1950. The rate of growth was moderating, but between 1964 and 1965 it was still over 15 per cent. Total energy consumption in Germany was not growing nearly as rapidly: here as elsewhere in Europe, oil had accounted for more than the absolute growth in total demand during recent years, causing some decline in the consumption of coal. And virtually all the growth in consumption of oil came from imports: domestic output remained fairly level at about 7–7½ million tons a year.

In the late fifties West German coal production suffered heavily from competitive imports—first of American coal, when Transatlantic freight rates dropped, and later of fuel oil when prices began to soften. An import duty of DM 20 per ton on imported coal, apart from a duty-free quota of just under 6½ million tons a year for traditional importing areas, broadly offset the price advantage of imported coal. Most of the large-scale import contracts for American supplies were cancelled. But a surge of fuel oil imports into the country, brought in by newcomers to the market and by coal dealers seeking to keep their trade up through oil, generated intense competition in the German market. Prices were slashed; and the imposition of excise duties of DM 25 a ton on heavy fuel oil and DM 10 a ton on light fuel oil failed to stem the inroads of oil into coal's traditional markets. Oil marketers were soon absorbing this tax, and selling fuel oil at discounts that made it as much cheaper than coal as before. Moreover, a certain amount of Russian oil flowed in to sharpen price competition for general fuel in the German market. There was much more independent competition, moreover, among the filling stations selling gasoline to the German motorist than those selling to his British counterpart; independent stations reached 15–20 per cent of gasoline sales. And when profits on dearer gasoline are squeezed, it has a severe effect on the refining margins and total profits of any marketing company. Some of the major companies' refining and marketing affiliates in Germany, in 1959 and 1960, showed losses. And the West German tax authorities began to ask some questions about accepting these financial results for tax purposes.

Traditionally, Ruhr coal wields considerable political influence in

Germany. Governments committed to the *Sozialmarkt* economics of Dr Erhard, first as Minister of Economics and later as Chancellor, disliked protectionism, but could not wholly ignore the coal lobby. They toyed with other measures to ease the plight of the mining industry, over and above the duties on the black oils. In 1959 there was an abortive attempt to arrange a coal-oil 'cartel' to moderate competition in the oil industry; but this soon broke down.[1] In 1963 came a rationalization law for the German coal industry, in which a fund of DM $1\frac{1}{2}$ billion was set aside to assist rationalization and concentration plans, compensating collieries closed down, and giving the industry a degree of open subsidy. (Various forms of concealed subvention were nothing new to German coal; but open subsidy was, since the Ruhr lobby had always advocated protection by duties or quotas on imported energy.) Not even this was enough to prevent a further decline in coal sales. In 1964–65, with an election to win, Dr Erhard's government went as far as imposing another 'voluntary' cartel upon the oil companies, with limitations upon the growth of sales of fuel and heating oils, legislation permitting (but not immediately imposing) quotas upon oil importing, and the 'licensing' of further German refinery construction.

The country's first wave of refinery building after the war was designed strictly to meet home demand, mainly in the lighter products, with a minimum yield of fuel oil; no 'export refineries' were built. The product pattern reflected the form of tariff protection. Unlike most other European countries, Germany after the war levied an import duty on crude oil to protect its relatively large indigenous production; but a remission of part of the duty in respect of the black oils produced gave refiners of German crude an incentive to concentrate on output of the lighter dutiable products to gain the maximum protection available. (In passing, it may be noted that products hydrogenated from East German brown coal enjoyed the same protection inside the Federal Republic as from West German production, since the Bonn government does not recognize any separation of the country.)

But the latest expansion of German refining capacity has altered the product pattern as well as the geographical pattern of this processing industry; and the fiscal influences specially affecting refiners' yields have disappeared. Much of the capacity coming on stream in the early sixties has been in the south-west and south-east of Germany: in the Upper Rhineland, with refineries from Frankfurt to Karlsruhe, and Bavaria, with a number of new plants around Ingolstadt. This continues a migration of refining inland from the original centres at Hamburg and Bremen; first to the Ruhr refineries fed from Rotterdam, first by small tanker and later by crude pipeline, and now to the new southern centres fed by pipelines from Mediterranean terminals. For Bavaria, in particular, the new refineries offer a base for delayed industrialization; they also offered, when they came on stream in 1963–64, a fresh surge of cheap black oils to compete with coal on price too now as well as on convenience. A peculiarity of the German market is its very high proportion of demand for light fuel 'heating' oils, accounting for about a third of total sales. Refinery expansion will supply an increasing share of this; but the need to import a sizeable volume of these oils may persist.

The change in fiscal influence upon the refining pattern came at the end of 1963, with the abandonment of West Germany's import duty on crude, in accordance with a protocol to the Treaty of Rome. Under the Treaty, which listed crude oil among the products upon which the eventual common external tariff of the European Economic Community would become nil, Germany was permitted to retain its duty on crude to the end of 1963. It was then obliged to change its import duties on petroleum products to the final levels set in the List 'G' common external tariff for all E.E.C. countries. Germany replaced the financial effect, and yield, of the former crude duty on products refined from imported crude by a series of corresponding excise duties on products. So far as supporting high-cost German crude production was concerned, the Government decided to pay subsidies on a degressive scale—from DM 50 per ton in 1964 and 1965 down to DM 20 per ton in 1968 and 1969—related to a basic production of 6·2 million tons a year. (The country has still no depletion allowance.) During the same year, the excise duties on black oils were renewed; these too were given a degressive timetable, being extended at the full rate until 1967, and for two further years at half rate.

High-cost German coal and high-cost German oil, in the early sixties, were thus both given a further lease of protection, but not indefinitely. A second element in its revision of mineral oil legislation in 1963 showed that the Bonn government was more concerned to encourage German enterprise in oil exploration than to ensure that the exploration should occur inside Germany. The new law provided for government loans totalling up to DM 800 million to German oil companies exploring outside the country's borders (North Sea exploration for gas being eligible for such loans). The loans were not formally discriminatory. But they were to be granted at the discretion of the Ministry of Economics, and were designed for ventures for which finance would not be forthcoming through ordinary commercial channels. If the Ministry chose, it could interpret these principles as precluding overseas ventures of German affiliates of the international major companies, who were not short of their own finance (or in the case of American companies, of tax advantages for exploration).

The German government leans over backwards from overt economic nationalism. Nevertheless, it is not difficult to find in the Ministry of Economics in Bonn some reserve about undue dependence upon the international or 'Anglo-American' oil companies for almost the whole supplies of the form of energy upon which the country is becoming so dependent. This uneasiness varies in degree: you can find open and vociferous opponents of *'Uberfremdung'* in all forms of business, or on the other hand suspicion of the way in which some of the major international oil companies, after driving German-owned marketing competitors to the wall in bitter price competition, have managed to buy some of them up. Some kind of Government-backed 'German solution' seems possible—perhaps a coalition of the remaining German companies (with their coal interests) into some kind of national combine. There is certainly the wish to encourage German enterprise in the exploration and production field; allied, perhaps, with some impatience about the too comfortable existence, as it may have looked to Bonn, of these German producing companies inside their protected homeland. A number of the German-owned groups, to do them credit, were already engaged in foreign ventures before any question of Government loans arose—though they continue to argue that German taxation offers inadequate incentives, in terms of foreign tax credit, to encourage them to compete against the allegedly better-placed American and British companies. German firms have been among the eager bidders for new concessions in any of the relinquished areas re-offered in the main Middle East producing countries. Several of them, for example, are jointly concerned in one of the off-shore concessions let out by the Iranian government in 1965 and now in new Libyan concessions. German entrepreneurs are not likely to be deterred by suggestions that oil exploration there, at any rate, involves great risks and vast amounts of capital. They have the Japanese example to ponder.

Japan impinged upon the international oil market in the fifties, quite simply, as about the toughest big customer of the lot. It was achieving a phenomenal rate of general economic growth that remains something of a mystery to the Western observer. Moreover, it was at the time a highly protected economy, with a partnership between government and private capital in the forced re-expansion of industry that was working wonders. In the business of importing oil, this government-industry relationship worked with peculiar advantage in bargaining to secure ever larger discounts. The less a Japanese oil importer then paid for his oil, the more foreign exchange he could get to buy it next time. Japan had a tight control on foreign currency for imports, as a result of continuing balance of payments difficulties during postwar years. It also had the fastest rate of growth in oil consumption of any comparably developed industrial country. Up to 1962 its Ministry of Trade and Industry (MITI) allocated foreign exchange for the purchase of oil, mainly from the Middle East, partly in relation to how much each importer had spent in the previous three months, and partly in relation to how much oil he managed to buy with this money. Moreover, freight charges did not affect this: foreign exchange to finance transport seemed to be granted automatically. As a result, every Japanese importer was under extra pressure to get the lowest f.o.b. prices he could—which meant the biggest possible discounts off posted prices. Moreover, the redoubtable Ministry of Trade and Industry made public, regularly, details of the bargain prices actually received, *pour encourager les autres*. This was fairly embarrassing for the oil companies posting oil prices, who had to justify them as realistic to the governments of some countries where their own associated refineries were invoiced at posted prices for the oil they imported.

Publicity did not necessarily push these discounts down farther. The heaviest price-cutting usually takes place when it can be kept secret from all but the favoured few customers. Indeed, publication of these 'MITI reports' may possibly have helped to stabilize the level of discounts in the Persian Gulf for a time. Companies supplying Japan with crude then took to offering special 'non-price' inducements such as loans to importing firms, rather than concede bigger, better publicized discounts. Many Japanese importers are associated with Western companies: most of the international majors, in particular, own stakes in Japenese refining, which by 1965 had a capacity of 90 million tons a year, of 1,840,000 barrels a day. But, until 1962, the law precluded foreigners from owning more than 50 per cent of any Japanese concern. So the international companies were not in a particularly strong position to counsel moderation in bargaining to these associates. Moreover, the cheaper one could invoice the oil, the more chance one had of expanding one's share of an extraordinarily buoyant market. This particular incentive to hard bargaining has since disappeared. But the tempting Japanese market has gone on helping to soften world oil prices.

Commitments to the International Monetary Fund to remove Japanese foreign exchange restrictions, in 1962, resulted in some changes in this governmental encouragement to bargaining. But 'liberalization' does not, in Japan, seem to guarantee liberalism. Under the nation's 1962 Oil Law, MITI gained more power over its oil industry, not less. Though this power was no longer operated through the foreign exchange control, the ministry was required to lay down a five-year oil plan, to be revised annually, which would govern local production and imports of both crude and oil products. The construction or expansion of Japan's refining capacity, which has been growing at a tremendous rate, became subject to ministry licensing. Moreover, MITI kept the power to fix 'standard selling prices' for oil products. This legislation is permissive; it will not necessarily be administered to the limits of MITI's new powers at any one time. But the Japanese government, understandably remaining careful about its balance of payments, has reserved very considerable powers to 'assure the stable and cheap supply of petroleum'.

During the early sixties, to Japanese dismay, some other buyers of oil began to get better terms than they could. Between 1957 and 1962 the average f.o.b. prices Japanese importers paid in the Persian Gulf came down by 17–18 per cent; between 1962 and 1964 this price (excluding Soviet crude) rose slightly. This was rather surprising when discounts were increasing for independent buyers in Western Europe. The upturn after 1962 does not seem to have been due, at any rate wholly, to the end of the MITI incentive system of exchange control for oil buying; it seems to have been mainly that Western Europe had access to a nearby source of cheap crude in Libya, which Japan did not.

This did not exactly please MITI: it occurred at a time when Japan was suffering from a limited setback in its rate of expansion (though still booming along more merrily than any other developed economy). The ministry, on the one hand, was trying to help improve the level of product prices for marketers inside Japan. This did not stop it beginning to discuss with the Russians a very large long-term contract for crude supplies, which would have made it worthwhile for Russia, using Japanese pipe, to build a crude pipeline to its Pacific coast. Japan, like most other developed economies, was in the middle sixties earnestly discussing a possible 'energy policy'.[2] Westerners might have been excused for assuming that it had one already—a fairly uninhibited pressure to get its oil imports as cheaply as possible.

Japan has an oil partnership with Indonesian national companies in North Sumatra; and if all Western oil companies were to leave Indonesia it is possible that the Indonesian government might consider Japan the only capitalist partner that it might be prepared to trust. So far, however, Japan's main impact at the producing end of the business has been in the Middle East. Its Arabian Oil Company, which obtained concessions offshore from Kuwait and Saudi Arabia in 1958, was formed by a group of Japanese financial interests and oil consumers, including electricity utility companies.[3] It had no experience whatever in oil and no established interests elsewhere to protect; hence, no inhibitions about agreeing to a government 'take' of 56–57 per cent, plus the option of participation, at a time when established companies there were still sticking religiously to 50–50. Moreover, this company found commercial oil with its first well, after investing only about $10 million. By 1961 it was exporting its Khafjhi crude back to Japan. This has not become an enormous operation; but the successful foray into exploration, with minimum mystique, must have whetted aspirations elsewhere. As Professor Adelman has remarked, 'In the world oil market since Suez, the Japanese have been the real revolutionaries, not the Russians.'[4]

Japan, however, was only the best-publicized—save perhaps Italy—among a growing selection of consuming countries, in East and West, industrialized and underdeveloped, that were bargaining really hard for cheap oil. Some were among the industrial nations of Western Europe that needed large-scale imports but commanded no significant share in ownership of the world oil business, such as Germany, Sweden and Italy. Others were developing nations that so far had been unsuccessful in finding sizeable oil production at home: short of oil, short of national income per head, and very short of foreign exchange, such as India and Ceylon. Others, barely significant consumers at all, were new nations seeking to bargain for national refineries and foreign investment as the price of access of entry to their nascent markets. Some of the newly independent African nations, seeking a government shareholding in refining and marketing, were setting foot on a road earlier taken by such European nations as Spain and Portugal. Certain of these consuming countries, incidentally, are inhibited in their bargaining for the cheapest energy possible by compunction for ailing domestic coal industries that cannot really compete: but not all of them.

Competition is rumbustiously free in certain of the highly industrialized markets that depend most heavily on imports. Sweden and Switzerland, for example, have hydropower but no other significant home production of energy. They rely on imports of oil and coal for 55–65 per cent of their fuel supplies—which are high in relation to their population, as both countries enjoy high standards of living. Hydroelectric capacity, once installed, offers power at almost nil running cost, so it needs no tariff protection against imported fuels. In neither of these countries, therefore, does the government exert much influence upon the free choice of fuels—except to encourage customers to bargain hard. In recent years, both have been receptive markets for price-cutters. Consumers' co-operative movements play a considerable part in petroleum marketing in both countries. The Swiss organization, Migros, founded by a remarkable businessman who disliked profit, the late Herr Duttweiler, did indeed extend its activities into Germany. In Sweden every petroleum consumer, down to the individual motorist, expects a discount. Motorists collect receipts for every tankful, send these vouchers to their suppliers, and are nowadays paid cash discounts not only by the co-operative movement and individual suppliers but by the major marketers too.

Sweden, it may be added, is quite a significant buyer of Russian oil, under two-way trade agreements with the Soviet Union. It has not become deeply dependent on Soviet oil, nor is ever likely to put all its eggs in this or any other basket. But it is not moved by arguments about Western strategy to deprive itself of this source of cheap energy, which also serves to lever down the prices Western oil suppliers charge. This nation has price-cutting independent traders who regularly get large discounts on crude oil and products. Switzerland, landlocked, did not go in for refining until the sixties, but even before this price-cutting was the rule in its very competitive market. In 1965, Esso sought to buy up the country's first refinery (and to terminate its contract for Soviet crude). Whether this would make the Swiss market more orderly remained to be seen.

Another group of Western consumer countries displays more mixed attitudes towards cheap energy imports, because of solicitude towards uncompetitive domestic fuel industries. Belgium, for example, has a market for petroleum products where discounts and price-cutting are now very pronounced. Its best known oil company, Petrofina, is an international refining and marketing group with only limited integration back into production, and is credited with the aphorism: 'Only fools and affiliates pay posted prices.' Yet the Belgian government has intervened in oil-coal competition with a sizeable tax on fuel oil. It has the weakest coal industry in Europe, which early in the sixties had had to be granted a temporary insulation from the competition even of other European coal suppliers, with restrictive quotas on all coal imports and subsidy of the weakest mines. This need to protect weak domestic fuel tempers its appetite for really cheap oil.

In considering the policies of governments in these coal-producing countries, such as Germany, Belgium, and to some extent also Britain, in spite of its financial connexions with the world oil industry, one has to recognize the importance of their indigenous fuel industries. These industries, in the ECSC countries and Britain, employed at the beginning of the sixties some two million men and produced about 400 million tons of coal a year. They were the original foundation of the prosperity and industrial advantages of these countries. Politically, neither coal miners nor coal owners are without some weight. Moreover, the coal-producing countries of Western Europe, since the end of the last war, have ploughed very large amounts of capital into the modernization of their mining industries. And though these industries nowadays earn comparatively little in exports, they supply fuel without making any claim on a country's balance of payments.

Such considerations regarding their own indigenous fuel industries were reinforced with continuing uncertainties about petroleum. Politically there remain memories of the crises over Abadan and the Suez Canal. In both crises, supplies of oil to Europe were in fact fairly well maintained and quickly restored, largely through the managerial flexibility of the major companies. But both were reminders of a certain vulnerability in the main supplies of cheap energy for Europe. Commercially, as well, these governments have other doubts about running down indigenous supplies of energy in the confidence that imports would remain cheap. When oil began to be offered at big discounts, the governments were told by the major companies that the extremes of price-cutting in 1958–60 were simply 'distress sales'. Not until 1961, when the chairman of the German subsidiary of Jersey Standard predicted low oil prices for 10–15 years, did any of these major companies commit itself to a guess about how long the surplus and these soft prices would last; and this, it was later made clear, was an individual and not a company view. European governments, moreover, keep an uneasy eye upon OPEC.

Occasionally, in countries that have a growing demand for oil and large reserves of increasingly unwanted coal, enthusiastic engineers discuss the possibility of making the one out of the other. Germany did develop processes for making oil from coal between the wars, and operated a number of plants during the war when it was cut off from peacetime sources of oil; but the economics of these plants made sense only in a siege economy.

There are places in the world, with far cheaper coal, where these techniques make more sense, though whether they could anywhere at present be fully competitive is very doubtful. A South African state corporation, Sasol, built and is operating the largest synthetic oil plant in the world near Johannesburg. This is now an impressive piece of chemical engineering (though its early history was marred by the failure of some new items of plant that were 'scaled up from the drawing board' without any pilot plant stage). But the synthetic motor spirit, diesel oil, and other products that it produces are protected both by a preferential excise duty and by extremely high rail and road costs of moving oil products from the coastal refineries at Durban to the Rand; proposals for a pipeline were held up for many years; and in the one completed in the mid-sixties railway interests appear to retain considerable influence over the charges. So even Sasol, getting coal at roughly five shillings a ton from its own highly mechanized 'captive mine', can hardly be considered a genuinely competitive proposition. In such areas, where vast reserves of coal, or perhaps of lignite, can be had really cheaply, synthetic production of oil may eventually become a commercial proposition; but the costs of producing oil have to rise considerably before it will.

In Italy, by contrast, imports of cheap energy are welcome, except at one point. The government has never had any compunction about allowing purchases of fuel at the cheapest prices that could be found, since it has neither oil nor coal production at home. But when fuel oil prices began to be cut heavily they affected sales of natural gas, and reduced the earnings of ENI, the state hydro-carbon combine. Italy already had a high tax on fuel oil; ENI began to attack the oil companies at the other end, by cutting the prices of the gasoline sold through filling stations. The government supported ENI's price cuts by cuts in taxes on gasoline, and the resultant large reductions in price, as mentioned before, were followed by a much greater increase in sales than anyone (including ENI) had expected. Such cuts must certainly have reduced total refining margins in Italy: ENI's reasoning appears to have been that it might stop its competitors cutting the price of fuel oil as savagely as before.

This kind of co-ordinated operation in the market between the government and the nationalized energy combine is just the kind of thing that the privately-owned oil industry fears must happen with state enterprise in the oil business. It was, however, only one of the mixture of reasons why they came to dislike and fear ENI. The state combine's founder, the late Signor Enrico Mattei, chairman, never troubled to conceal that the dislike was mutual. He constantly argued that the major international groups acted like a cartel. He suggested that their operating margins, in between oil product prices that he considered too high and payments to host governments that he called too small, could easily be squeezed further. And he was responsible for the doctrine that dealings direct between governments of consuming countries— through organizations such as ENI—and those of producing countries could give both a better bargain than complete reliance upon the international companies as intermediaries.

Signor Mattei, who died in 1962, was a man of great dynamism; he gave one the impression, rightly or wrongly, that he had more in common with the ruthless private oilmen who built up this business than some of the men at the top of its smooth and mature bureaucracies today. He was appointed, after the war, to handle a small and ailing state-owned company that possessed the natural gas monopoly in the Po Valley in Northern Italy. Instead of winding it up, he saw its possibilities, developed the gas on a very large scale and sold it with some rather imaginative marketing techniques, and then built up the ENI group into a powerful oil refining, distributing and marketing company serving the Italian market. Here again his marketing was imaginative— and lavish. He led the way in competition to woo the Italian motorist with elaborately equipped petrol stations—relying for finance, it would appear, upon the surplus from his gas sales. The price of ENI gas is fixed in accordance with fuel oil prices, though slightly lower; as fuel oil nowadays bears a substantial tax in the Italian market and ENI pays much less tax on its gas, this gave the group a sizeable 'economic rent' to offer financial backing for its other ventures.

ENI's power in petroleum marketing in Italy, and its political connexions, have so far largely insulated it from the effects of criticism in Italy, of which there is plenty from other people as well as the oil companies. Its main vulnerability has been its failure—after years of fairly intensive search in promising areas—to find any significant oil in Italy. It has brought in some production in Sicily, where Gulf Oil also had producing wells; but the majors stopped exploration of the Italian mainland after the passing of a new petroleum law in Italy in 1958, which gave ENI peculiar privileges in any area where any oil was found, regardless of who found it.

Criticism of ENI for not finding oil in Italy has become less cogent since the world oil surplus gave independent consumers without oil so much bargaining power to get it cheap. Basically, Italy is an importer of energy interested in keeping world market prices as low as is consistent with the continuance of supplies. But ENI policies displayed rather more mixed motives. In the late fifties, ENI obtained concessions in various countries of North Africa and the Middle East in order to seek the crude supplies it could not locate at home and had to buy from the major companies with which it was on bad terms. But by the late fifties, for the meantime, it switched to bothering the international industry, much more practically, as a cold-blooded independent refiner and marketer buying the cheapest oil it could. It made sizeable long-term contracts with the Russians for oil at prices which could have been matched in the Middle East only by savage cuts in the companies' profit margins on production.

From its exploration overseas, ENI was beginning to get growing supplies of its own cost crude from Egypt and Iran. This appeared to be setting it some commercial conundrums. After paying an income tax and royalty amounting to 50 per cent of profits at whatever price it posted for such oil, plus a half share in the commercial profit—which was the apparent effect of its concession terms off shore in the Persian Gulf—is ENI's 'cost crude' from the Middle East a better bargain than the Russia and Libyan crude it has been buying at whacking discounts?

Shortly before Signor Mattei's death in an aeroplane accident late in 1962, he had negotiated an agreement with the most powerful of the 'Seven Sisters' he loved to deride, the Standard Oil Company of New Jersey, for another long-term contract for crude oil supplies. This was comparable in size to the Russian contracts; also, it is rumoured, in price. Jersey had new low-cost production arising in Libya far closer to Italy than the Black Sea; this gave it some margin to quote comparable c.i.f. prices to ENI. In 1963 Signor Cefis, one of Mattei's successors, negotiated a renewal and extension of the Russian crude contract; shortly after came another long-term deal with Gulf Oil Corporation. Gulf had huge potential supplies of low-cost crude from

Kuwait, more than the marketing network it was trying to strengthen throughout Europe could accommodate at the time; in the deal with ENI it also passed over its Ragusa production in Sicily, and its financial backers in Pittsburgh, the Mellon interests, gave ENI some financial assistance.

Since Mattei's death ENI has continued the policies he set in train, rather less flamboyantly in terms of argument but still pin-pricking the international companies at many points around the world, notably in bidding for African refineries. Its aims are still to develop its production abroad; but by 1970 it will need luck to have much more than 6–7 million tons of its own 'cost crude' against a requirement of perhaps 30 million tons a year for its widespread marketing commitments. Financing its investment programme, in which a large proportion of projects can at best bring only a long-term return and some others, such as petrochemicals, matured at a time of surplus, is no longer proving as easy as in its earlier years. The Italian capital market, from which it raised its government-guaranteed loans during the Mattei era, was by the early sixties no longer a very fruitful source of funds. With an obsolete and top-heavy capital structure that Italy's uncertain governments took a long time to reform, the group was forced into much heavier self-financing. But the most serious emerging problem for the new management was in ENI's supplies of gas, upon which the whole empire had been founded. By the early sixties, reserves in the Po Valley seemed adequate for no more than about 15 years' supplies, allowing for rising rates of consumption during the sixties. Ample gas reserves, however, were not far off, across the Mediterranean: in 1965 ENI concluded another contract with the Jersey group, for large-scale supplies of liquefied natural gas at extremely low prices. Whether or not ENI's five-legged dog had ceased breathing fire, the group was certainly doing more and more business with one particular Sister out of the seven that Mattei had been accustomed to be so rude about.

Most of the group's new foreign investment, in the late fifties, was understandably shifted towards marketing and refining—in Western Europe, in newly independent Africa, here and there in Latin America and Southern Asia. This was logical for ENI: it was not necessarily logical for Italy. The country had other claims upon its available capital that were at least as pressing as foreign investment in oil marketing. Even among its critics in Italy a foreigner occasionally encountered a grudging admission of the contribution that the ENI group has made to Italy's current economic *resorgimento*. But even among ENI's friends, one often heard doubts whether one nationalized group should be committing the country to so much foreign investment; and in 1965, there were signs of retrenchment in some of its overseas ventures. Nor was ENI always confident of getting *cheap* oil from these foreign ventures. In 1965, it was arguing that such oil found by community companies would deserve an import preference.

Many of the same elements—the reluctance of governments short of foreign exchange to accept posted prices that independent customers do not pay, the purchase of cheap oil from anywhere that might break prices that are considered artificial, and the setting up of state companies to squeeze the established international majors—are appearing among the emergent underdeveloped countries. Mixed with this, in most cases, there are elements of anti-capitalism, red or pink, and of anti-Westernism: but the ideological mixtures vary.

When the Indian government in 1960 and 1961 threatened to buy Russian oil unless the international companies would sell it their products cheaper, history was repeating itself. In the early years of the century, Shell had sold Russian oil in this market to compete with Standard Oil. In the early twenties the roles were reversed: for a time the Americans sold Russian oil in India against Shell, which had lost investments in Russia and was boycotting Bolshevik oil. In the first postwar decade and a half oil supplies in India came almost entirely from the major European and American companies. Price competition between them was as orderly in India as elsewhere. But the Indian government has never been slow to learn such Western techniques, technical or commercial, as it considers of advantage to it. It is also brutally and chronically short of foreign currency to finance the imports it needs for development. And it had never enjoyed the currency dispensations in paying for oil imports that some more favoured European customers did in the years just after the war.

India was developing its own 'public sector' oil, but this would take time. It was prepared to do business with foreign 'private sector' oil companies—but not at their prices. Its pressure upon the refining and marketing affiliates operating there has been tenacious and continuing. In mid-1960, its pressure upon these companies to obtain discounts below posted prices plus freights for the crude their parent groups supplied played a part in breaking the Middle East crude price structure. In 1961 and again in 1965, governmental committees, after examining the state of the world oil market, suggested that oil could have been had much more cheaply—in scarce foreign exchange—in India. The companies denied this, arguing that products, in markets east of Suez, were in fact not moving at large discounts; but in fact they later did concede discounts on crude for India. The Indian government, already committed to building its own refineries (for its limited indigenous crude production), extended these plans to add refineries that could bargain for crude supplies in the world market and brought in new partners, such as Phillips, who were prepared to give it better deals on crude. More immediately, it held down its allocations of foreign exchange allocations for oil purchased by the major companies' refining affiliates, and set up its own importing marketing company to bring in and distribute petroleum products from Russia, and forced further cuts in landed prices. Later, it established direct contacts with groups in which the National Iranian Oil Company and the Kuwait National Petroleum Company were partners.

The same difficulties over foreign exchange for oil brought collisions between the companies and governments in Cuba and Ceylon. Cuba's reaction, in 1960, had been to 'intervene in', or in plain language seize, the oil refineries of international companies that could not supply oil except for payment in convertible currencies, and naturally refused to process the Russian crude President Castro thought he could get for blocked currency. This expropriation was so largely political, in the process from 'anti-gringoism' towards a Caribbean version of Communism, that it is probably a case apart. And the marketing company set up by the Ceylon government in 1961 to sell Russian petroleum products cheaper than those of the international companies' marketing affiliates—it was given almost unlimited power to requisition these companies' facilities in the process of undercutting them, and in spring 1962, seized about a third of their facilities, which handled about half the island's sale of oil products—was again the instrument of a party rather close to Communism, though the companies were not deprived of the whole of their business.

Various other mixtures of state ownership with private enterprise in oil refining and marketing, arrived at more peaceably, were coming into being in the early sixties in the newly independent states around Africa, in South-East Asia, and in the Philippines. There was quite sharp competition between international major companies—and ENI—for marketing rights in these countries. To get them, and the consequent outlet for his crude oil, the successful bidder had often to agree to build a refinery—and usually to accept some state or national participation in the ownership of it. Where major companies succeeded, they had to swallow their dislike of state enterprise. Some of these refineries gained monopoly or preferential supply rights for the country concerned; processing rights were usually granted to other marketers, though this sometimes involved a certain amount of horse-trading with others who had been successful in the bidding elsewhere.

Many of these underdeveloped markets for oil—generally small in volume, though with possibilities of rapid growth—are therefore taking advantage of a buyer's market for oil to exact a share of ownership, to save expenditure of foreign exchange on oil, and to secure cut-price oil. Few have gone as far as one or two European countries did in a similar buyer's market between the wars. In Spain, for example, there is a government monopoly of wholesale marketing inside the country though the management of this is delegated to a privately-owned group. Spain has recently allowed foreign private capital in as minority partners in refining groups; but it remains one of the only markets outside the Russian sphere effectively closed to marketing competition by the international companies with which it has to bargain for oil supplies. Refining and marketing in Portugal, too, is reserved to national companies and dominated by a state concern. Neither is ideologically opposed to private enterprise. But they represent prototypes of an attitude, recently spreading, with which the international oil industry has to reckon—that the government may find it profitable, ideologies aside, to take a hand in bargaining for oil.

CHAPTER XVII

Consumers: Common Interests

After the Organization of Petroleum Exporting Countries was formed at Baghdad in Autumn, 1960, the question was often asked whether it would be matched by an Organization of Petroleum Importing Countries. The possibility does in fact appear soon to have been discussed, seriously or not, in some of the deliberations of consumer governments in Western Europe. For the time, no rival firm was in fact set up; it might have appeared deliberately obstructive. Many people in the West believed that OPEC could have a useful role to play, and should be given every chance to establish itself. But even without an OPIC, it might perhaps be said that there were sufficient organizations of oil consumer governments already—as the board of OPEC perhaps realized in locating its headquarters in Geneva. Within five years, indeed, the Organization for Economic Co-operation and Development—taking in, by 1965, North America and Japan as well as Western Europe—did set up an inner group that looked quite ready to become an OPIC, a sort of consumers' 'fleet in being'.

The international or supra-national organization is no stranger to the problems of energy—including oil—in Western Europe at least, though oil remained detached from the central interest and influence of such organizations longer than any other fuel. From the end of the war onwards, and particularly during the rebuilding of the West European economy with large-scale aid from the United States, the governments of the region engaged in fairly continuous consultation upon their common economic interests. At the beginning of the period they were engaged fairly seriously in the 'rationing' of energy. Actual rationing between countries was never carried out on any international scale—except, as it happens, for the semi-formal rationing of oil supplies during two periods of emergency when first oil supplies from Iran and later supplies through the Suez Canal were cut off. But during the early years there was consultation over, for example, the amounts of coal exports that producers could make available to meet the total demands that the coal-importing countries set out. And a good deal of discussion went on over 'the dollar element' in imported oil and in the operations of American oil companies in Europe, during the years in which dollars were so scarce a currency there. These consultations took place mainly within two bodies—the Organization for European Economic Co-operation, which was originally an organization of governments receiving Marshall Aid, but which lasted after aid ceased (and eventually became OECD), and the Economic Commission for Europe, a section of the United Nations secretariat concerned with the whole of Europe, including nations from the Soviet bloc.

Oil companies operating in Europe have often been concerned with the deliberations of these bodies (as indeed from time to time they are with logistic arrangements under the North Atlantic Treaty Organization). They were mainly concerned with OEEC in oil and energy discussions, though on occasion they had to deal with ECE, and encountered its rather different, characteristically independent, approach to economic matters. It was ECE, in a study of the development of the demand for the black oils in Europe, that first singled out for comment the problems that this rapid rise in demand might pose in European refining. In 1954, it had a brush with the companies when it published a fairly critical report, purely from the point of view of the consumer, on the price of Middle East oil.[1] After that report, ECE seems to have been more or less 'warned off' oil. This became from then on the preserve of the somewhat 'safer' OEEC, which had a specialized oil committee publishing periodical, uncontroversial, but expert and useful reports.[2] Its general reports on energy, moreover, were significant documents in setting the background against which other European groupings began later to formulate more ambitious and 'positive' energy policies. At the end of 1961, OEEC became OECD, the Organization for European Co-operation and Development.

Perhaps partly because its own reports, which needed approval line by line from nineteen governments, were of necessity more cautious in approach, OEEC twice in succession in the mid-fifties appointed commissions of independent experts to study future demand for energy in Western Europe and the way in which this demand might be supplied —matters of great concern to the oil business among other fuel suppliers in the OEEC area.

The first commission, led by Sir Harold Hartley, a distinguished fuel scientist and industrialist, was appointed in 1954 and reported in May, 1956.[3] Following its suggestion in this report, OEEC decided to repeat the exercise. A second commission of experts (with some members in common) was set up in 1957, and reported at the beginning of 1960.[4] The statistical projections about European demand for energy, looking, four years apart, forward to 1975, produced practically identical results. The two groups' conclusions from the statistics could hardly have been more diametrically opposed. Both marshalled intrinsically impressive arguments; but it is possible that in retrospect they will be considered primarily as indicative of the sharp change in the European fuel market between the dates when they came to report, and the change in the intellectual fashions of thinking about fuel. As the second commission sensibly remarked, 'the probable errors in our forecasts stem from the sort of mistakes of general optimism or pessimism that are likely to affect at a given moment all who attempt such forecasts, rather than from errors that may be involved in particular approaches to the problem'.

The Hartley report was published just before the Suez crisis, but well suited the mood that soon resulted from that crisis. Sir Harold frequently described it, frankly, as 'a coal report', which hardly did it justice. It made projections of total energy demand, and reckoned the amount of imports of fuel that might be necessary to satisfy this demand if the total output of indigenous fuels, mainly coal, could not be raised faster than it had been of late; and recommended very heavy investment to step up the rate of expansion in these domestic fuel industries, in order to moderate the growth of oil imports. The commission was apprehensive about the cost in foreign exchange that large scale imports of oil and American coal would impose on Western Europe. It was deliberating, one may note, during a period when Europe was having to import American coal very expensively indeed.

Three and a half years later, reaching virtually identical conclusions about the amount of energy that Western Europe would need in future years, the report of the second commission headed by Professor E. A. G. Robinson showed not the least concern in accepting that a large and growing proportion of this expanding demand should be met from imports. In the three years since the Hartley report, even though these included the Suez crisis and a short-lived oil shortage, it had become hard to sell all the coal that could be produced in Europe. This second report, accordingly, was concerned more with what consumers wanted than what it would be possible to let them have. Consumers were switching to oil on a very large scale indeed: unsold stocks of coal were mounting; and imported fuels (including American coal) were far cheaper than indigenous supplies. So far the Robinson commission could see, imported fuel seemed likely to remain cheap; and it could see no justification for any measures likely to bring about the production of fuel that would probably not be able to compete.

The commission was not worried about the effect of growing imports of fuel on the balance of payments, since it held that a prosperous European economy could export enough to pay for whatever range of convenient imports it chose. It scouted arguments about the security of oil dependence on the Middle East, on the grounds that potential oil sources were since being greatly diversified. (This was true to some extent: but the Robinson committee, happily, was reporting before OPEC had come into being.)

Oil, up to that time, had never been one of the fuels that came under more positively co-ordinating international organizations in Europe. Coal, from 1953 onwards, had come under the European Coal-Steel Community set up under the six-country Schuman Plan, and producers in each of its member countries were subjected to a growing degree of supervision, plus the obligation to publish and abide by price schedules (at least inside the community), and to follow other rules of competition. Oil, as an imported commodity, did not; and this became a source of growing irritation to coal industries in the Six as its competition began to bite deep into their markets. By the time that the Robinson Report was published, the European Common Market had come into being. While ECSC had worked on fairly cordial terms with OEEC, the new community in which its members were now joined by the Treaty of Rome was not originally enamoured of the nineteen-country organization in Paris. Moreover, the common market was founded upon a customs union that involved some degree of protection against imports; and it had no limits to its purview of economic affairs. The Common Market, moreover, happened to have come into being during a period of drastic change in the pattern of energy consumption in Europe. Some of the older coal industries were at the time in a state of what the High Authority of the European Coal and Steel Community in Luxembourg was inclined to call 'manifest crisis'. This immediately raised the question of unified energy policies for the European Six. No such policies, up to the time of writing, have been agreed upon. But eventually, some probably will be. And

288

already preparations for a common policy have begun to affect the oil industry significantly.

Some of the national energy policies inside these six European countries, which have already been discussed, are sharply discriminatory against imported energy and becoming more so. Others that are less directly discriminatory, such as the French, involve a large degree of *dirigisme* that is liable to be directed increasingly to serving 'national petroleum' of one kind and another. Many cross-currents, economic and political, affect both the policies that are being discussed and the three communities—ECSC, the Common Market Commission, and Euratom—which since 1959 have had the task of formulating a co-ordinated energy policy. For a time it seemed possible that what emerged would be a lowest common denominator of agreement—in which case one would not expect any joint energy policy to be very positive in its impact on the different fuel industries. But in fact, while no policy at all has yet emerged, it would be unwise to assume that none will; or that when it does it will prove nugatory. Brussels and Luxembourg are full of enthusiasts for the European idea who are naturally anxious that it should engage in positive rather than passive policies. At the end of 1965, when this began to be revised, dispute over financing of a common agricultural policy had paralysed progress in the development of the European communities. But in practice what had happened was that the Common Market has survived, with its practice informally modified to the satisfaction of the French; and that the 'fusion' of EEC, ECSC, and Euratom, agreed upon in 1965, might take place during 1967–69.

A common energy policy for the Common Market need not inevitably mean protecting indigenous or 'associated' sources of fuel, but the oil industry has been understandably worried that in practice it will. Indeed, the first idea that was put forward for discussion by the inter-executive group set up by the three community secretariats, early in 1960, could easily have been interpreted as implying protection for coal. This was the idea of a *prix d'orientation* for fuels in Europe.[6] Essentially, this was to be a price, or range of prices, suggested by the energy planners after consultation with all concerned, as a reasonable level to aim at for a few years ahead: a competitive price at which indigenous fuel industries would be able to aim in planning their forward investment. In a market open to imports, this would obviously mean some form of import parity price. Indigenous fuel industries could not expect to invest in output at a higher cost than the long-term marginal price at which energy could be brought in from abroad, be this oil, gas, or American coal. The danger was that this price might soon be converted from a guidance price into a minimum price, to which fuel importers might be expected to adhere. The first range of prices suggested was based on estimates of the landed price at which American coal could be imported into Europe on a long-term basis, and not merely at times of very low freights: it would have given coal industries in Europe a range of say $16-17 a ton to match. This might have left a smallish amount of coal to be produced within the community. But a price based upon the figures in the early sixties at which fuel oil was actually being sold inside Europe—far below the landed price of American coal, though even that had come down—would have been one that practically no mine in Western Europe would be able to match.

The second time that the executives of the European communities concerned with energy came up with proposals for a common energy policy, in July, 1962,[7] the open proposal for a *prix d'orientation*—though not necessarily the idea underlying it—had disappeared. So, on the face of it, had the basic principle of protection for indigenous energy. This was a policy that accepted as a certainty the growing dependence of these six European countries—which Britain might later join as a seventh—upon imported energy. The executives reckoned that coal, which in 1960 provided 52 per cent of the total demand, could not by 1970 provide more than 35 per cent. Allowing for local crude oil and natural gas production, and for a rapid development of nuclear power, the bulk of the increase would have to come from imports—primarily from imported oil.

Accepting this, the common energy policy these executives proposed was based on two principles: cheap energy, and security of supplies. The ruling price of energy in Europe, they held, should be the price at which energy could be imported from outside; it would be locally-produced energy that would have to adapt itself to this price level, not imported energy that should in some way be brought up towards the price levels of home production. Crude oil should remain free of duty; there should be a low level of customs or excise duties on oil products competing in the general fuel market and on imported coal; and there should be no general system of quotas upon imports of energy. The only quotas on imported fuel they proposed were upon oil and coal from the Soviet bloc, which they considered an insecure source on which Europe should not become too dependent; here they proposed that a community quota should be imposed to keep these imports down to a given percentage of total energy consumption. These executives had calculated that bereft of all support, coal production in Europe might well have fallen under this policy from about 230 million tons in 1960 to perhaps 90 million tons by the seventies. They allowed for the support of some production of coal—and of crude oil—over and above such a core of competitive output. But they proposed that anything over and above this competitive level that the governments wished to keep in production should be kept going by subsidies, not by protective import or excise taxes on competing imported fuels, or by quotas on the imports brought in.

Technically, the weakness of this calculation was still the one that had bedevilled ideas about a *prix d'orientation*—that the price of 'imported fuel' is not uniform. The calculations about the tonnage of European coal that could compete with this 'ruling price of imported energy' were in practice based upon estimates of the long-term landed price of imported coal. In the meantime, fuel oil, in terms of calorific equivalent, was much cheaper than this. So a given subsidy, designed to keep in being a given tonnage of coal against the competition of imported coal, would have been unlikely to be enough to protect that much home production against imported fuel oil. True, these proposals about subsidies were based upon forward estimates about import prices, and home production costs, in the seventies. By then, some of the economists in Luxembourg and Brussels were prepared to argue, fuel oil will have reached parity in price with imported coal.[8] This could be true; it is one of the possible developments in the European fuel market that in some ways might suit almost everyone concerned, from local coalowners to Middle East oil-producing governments, except perhaps the consumer. But it seemed unlikely then, and has become more so since, considering the landed prices of fuel oil and their trend, and the new possibilities of cheap nuclear energy and natural gas.

In many ways, these 1962 proposals represented a more liberal energy policy for Europe than the oil companies that supply Europe might have feared would emerge. Some of its liberalism, however, went farther than they would have liked: in particular, its emphasis upon the principle of non-discrimination, which is central to Common Market thinking about commercial policy. This was reflected in the proposals for energy policy by a suggestion that certain of the rules of the competition that the coal industries in ECSC have to follow—in particular the publication of the actual prices they charge, and the obligation not to give any customers special discounts that they do not offer to all customers—should be applied, in one way or another, to oil. It was suggested that oil marketers should be obliged to publish, *a posteriori*, details of the prices at which they sold all their products to all their customers. Even without specific rules against discrimination, this would invite all customers to press to get the same prices and discounts that the customers with most bargaining power had been able to exact privately. These are conditions of competition under which coal has to operate; moreover, the coal industries concerned are enjoined by national law and the rules of ECSC from price discrimination, or giving some customers special treatment. Even though this inter-executive memorandum was never accepted by the governments, the pressure for 'price transparency' seems likely to form part of any common energy policy that ever is adopted. Some degree of price transparency—comparable, say, with that which price reporting agencies provide in the United States—seems certain eventually to come into being. Up to 1966, energy policy in the European Community continued to evolve in two parallel streams. The High Authority of the European Coal/Steel Community in Luxembourg concentrated mainly on coal questions—though its knowledge of fuel oil prices was as up to date as that of many an oil company. In spring 1964 it managed to achieve agreement from the governments of the Six to a protocol on energy policy that was mainly designed to give an ECSC imprimatur to the various forms of coal subsidy that all its coal-producing member countries, in different ways, were giving, although these were formally contrary to the Treaty of Paris.[9] It found a formula, under the Treaty, that could regularize, and conceivably limit, what the governments were in practice doing. (Finding formulae under treaties for what governments will agree to do is one of the main preoccupations of the European executives. Since in so doing one usually stretches paper theory a lot but alters actual practice a little, only a fool could consider this an unworthy exercise.) The European Economic Commission, in Brussels, concentrated on certain measures affecting oil that have to be completed, common energy policy or not.[10] It managed to achieve agreement on a common external tariff for the Community on refined oil products: formally, the levels of duty written in were fairly high, but in practice they were suspended and the effective levels accepted by the member countries were quite low. It recommended minimum levels of stocks to be held, compulsorily, by oil companies supplying the Community. The figure recommended, 65 days' supplies for each country, was roughly in line with that which the Oil Committee of OECD had suggested that all its member countries should enjoin upon suppliers. In spring 1964 the Six governments committed themselves to bringing these parallel efforts closer together, by 'fusion' first of the executives and later of the European Communities. Uniting the energy divisions of the executives may obviate some of the divergences of opinion that have quite often been noticeable between a coal-oriented High Authority and a Commission concerned, in the fuel context, mainly with oil and natural gas. Depending upon the terms that could be arranged, fusion also offered chances to the executives of persuading their member governments that a European energy policy would finally be necessary; perhaps, indeed, of writing a time-table for its completion into an eventual, similarly 'fused' Treaty. So far, the governments are not committed. Indeed, at times the very range of different and partly conflicting interests of the six members of these communities have seemed liable to preclude any form of agreement on a positive energy policy. Germany, France, and Belgium are major coal producers. France has interests in Middle East oil and other interests, growing steadily more important, in Saharan oil and gas. Holland is one of the parent countries of the Royal Dutch–Shell group, and could become important as a large exporter of natural gas inside North-West Europe. Italy relies for its fuel mainly on imports from the cheapest bidder, and the organization that exploits its only significant indigenous fuel, natural gas, is a thrusting competitor in the world oil market. If Britain, despite the 1963 rebuff, is again approaching membership of the Common Market, that may introduce another country to these arguments, which generally professes liberal policies towards importing energy, even if it does not always behave with liberalism.

One among these diverse national interests, however, seemed liable to provide the oil companies marketing in Europe with more embarrassments than the others. The French government has not seemed particularly inclined, during the sixties, to offer its state coal mines much special protection—beyond the fact that its imports of coal were entirely in the hands of a state agency, and the rather tight control that it already possesses over the marketers of oil inside France. What it has seemed interested in was to press Saharan petroleum not only into the French market but into the whole of the Common Market. A proposal that it aired from time to time during the discussions on fuel policy in Brussels—and later during discussions on the external tariff of the

Common Market—was the possibility of giving some preference by quotas, import duties, or excise duties to oil products refined from 'Community oil'. This oil could be variously defined. It would certainly include Saharan crude; it was liable to be widened to include CFP's crude from the Middle East; and it might even be stretched to include products refined from other oil produced by companies with headquarters in the Common Market—under which Shell might qualify. This proposal could obviously be developed to extend to the rest of the Common Market countries the same kind of *dirigiste* régime under which the oil companies have to do business in France. Moreover, it would obviously make a considerable amount of difference to the prospects for Middle East crude if Saharan petroleum should be guaranteed more than its natural degree of access to the markets of Europe. These French proposals were not pressed; but nor were they discarded.

Governmental attitudes towards energy policy in these supranational communities of Europe, up to the mid-sixties, have remained shifting and uncertain. So have the attitudes of the major oil companies towards European governmental policies regarding energy. The American companies, in particular are as loth as ever to become involved in any formal conferences or arrangements that could later be interpreted by their anti-trust authorities as some form of conspiracy not to compete. On the other hand, it is possible to argue that if the oil industry is to gain as effective a hearing for its point of view as the other fuel industries, it may have to have some continuing form of representation in the discussions of these organizations, rather than the occasional individual informal discussions that did in fact take place. It is easy to argue that the oil industry ought to make more positive contributions; less easy to see, however, what it would have to contribute except concessions that it would find most distasteful.

For their part, the European executives display somewhat ambivalent attitudes towards the international oil companies. This is not to any large degree a matter of anti-Americanism or suspicion of 'Anglo-Saxon oil', though both prejudices are apparent in some of their member countries. It is an uneasiness about dependence for oil, now Europe's main fuel, upon organizations ultimately outwith European control which themselves draw supplies from areas where other governments are themselves seeking a greater degree of control over oil. M. Robert Marjolin, vice-president of the European Commission, expressed it clearly in November 1964:

'I recognize that the big international companies have done good work, but they must understand, and I believe they do understand, that the European and national authorities cannot avoid taking an interest in what happens in such a vital sector of their economic life.'

And Signor Corradini, of the ECSC High Authority, was even more specific a month or so later:

'As regards the oil companies, obviously the more numerous and the more different in structure and capacity (and hence very possibly in interests) they are the better the chances of a continuing lively market. . . .

. . . Europe cannot achieve security of supply, short-term or long-term, unless it can count on making use of these tried and tested organizations. But the fact remains that the majors, even though their outlook is gradually changing to a greater awareness of their public responsibility, are still not all sufficiently attuned to the needs and concerns of European consumers. . . .

The European Commission, in particular, puts great importance upon continued exploration to increase the diversification of Europe's sources of oil supplies. It appreciates the extent to which the major companies go on doing this (though perhaps not sufficiently the commercial pressures that make it logical for them to go on doing so). But it is never quite confident that they will go on doing enough, or that they will always be in a financial position to explore as much as Europe needs to rely on oil remaining cheap. Hence its studies of financial incentives of one kind and another that might persuade oil companies—particularly, perhaps, European ones—to engage in a high rate of exploration. The ECSC view is a little more cold-blooded. Signor Corradini is clearly interested in the diversification of companies in, for example, Middle East oil, producing greater competition to press prices downwards, as well as in the diversification of supply sources in the hands of the established major companies.

During 1964, as it became clear that the major companies and Middle East member governments of OPEC were moving towards agreement, these European executives, along with a wider circle of consumer governments, began to take a slightly more anxious interest in the circumstances of their oil supply. M. Marjolin, for the EEC Commission, sought rather closer consultation with the top management of the oil companies supplying Europe than he had had at all regularly before. The Oil Committee of OECD, after considerable internal negotiation, decided to set up a small inner group of governmental representatives (with the EEC Commission represented as an observer): initially to set in train a study of oil demand and supply probabilities over the rest of the decade, but also to facilitate regular consultation between the governments involved, on behalf of Western Europe. Britain suggested this; the United States, after some initial misgivings, supported it. The European Commission, which had at times appeared envious of the special relationship that it believed the British and American governments had with their oil companies, strongly supported this initiative too, at the same time as pressing for its own talks with the oil companies. The Commission remained extremely chary of any ideas of seeking contacts, over the heads of these companies, with the governments of oil-producing countries, for example with OPEC; the ECSC High Authority significantly less so. Signor Corradini, for example, in the same speech quoted above, went on:

> . . . it is clearly necessary to intervene in the present State/company set-up in order to obviate, or at any rate reduce, the risk of conflicts, the main sufferers in which would be the consumers. From the political angle, comprehensive co-operation arrangements would certainly be the best, with a view to stabilizing the revenues of the countries concerned. The Treaty of Rome offers numerous possibilities in this regard. . . .

His views were not official; but in 1965 there were signs that the High Authority was itself toying with attempts to establish contact with OPEC and its member governments. It had, after all, ambitions to take the major part in formulating an energy policy for the Communities, once fusion should be achieved.

The question of how dependent Western Europe could afford to become upon imported fuels, and how far it could safely run down its own indigenous fuel industries while doing so, was one thing. An equally important question for the businesses supplying those imports of fuel was whether the decision was to become a matter of supra-national policy, rather than a myriad of individual decisions representing market choice. Circumstances in which the world's main commercial imports of oil might become largely controlled by governments or associations of governments would tend further to whittle down the flexibility in operations that is perhaps the main talent of the international oil industry. It would, moreover, tend to increase pressure upon them from the other end of the business—their host governments in the exporting countries. Some of these, too, have already begun organizing more direct contact with the governments of some of their consumers—trying to bypass the industry that works in the middle.

CHAPTER XVIII

Producers for Export:
The Western Hemisphere

All kinds of governments, this book has argued, are nowadays intervening in the oil business; but when you say 'the governments' to any oilman, he thinks of one kind first—the 'host governments' of the countries from which his industry exports oil. The oil industry is more important to these governments than to any others, and its relations with them are centrally important to it. These relations are always formally governed by legal contract: but even the most binding contract cannot guarantee goodwill, and more than once in the history of this industry the contracts themselves have not turned out in the long run to be binding either.

In its effect, the oil concession can be almost a revolutionary instrument, quite transforming the economy of any country where really rich deposits are found and developed. And the social pressures that this economic development can generate in turn may bear upon the whole structure of established relationships in such a country—including, ultimately, the concession agreement itself. An oil concession, until recently, at least, has generally been designed to hold one economic and social relationship in such a country stable for usually very long periods —yet success in its fulfilment necessarily implies accelerated change. This paradox is not always amusing to either party to the agreement.

Some of the nations into which this international industry took the idea of developing oil commercially already possessed established legal systems governing the exploitation of their mineral resources. The first mining law covering Venezuela, for example, was a decree of 1784, making over to the Spanish crown 'whatever fossils, juices or bituminous substances from earth' were found, regardless of who owned the surface, and the same principle was retained after Venezuela attained its independence in 1811. One or two countries where foreign capital ventured to develop oil, such as Mexico, began with individual land-owners' rights to oil tapped from their land, as in the United States.

Politically, however, most of these bargains with the government have put the oil company into an anomalous position inside the country where it is developing oil. Of necessity, its closest relationship must be with the established government and ruling groups. The relationship can be and indeed has to be shifted when these alter, but not until then. Yet its own impact on such a society must generally be to widen the ambitions of people below the ruling groups, by bringing greater riches, education, and professional training to some. This need not mean social unrest; it depends on the wisdom of the government concerned. But it often does, particularly when oil wealth merely seems to widen the difference in standards between rich and poor. And if it does, the big foreign oil company, as perhaps the country's largest employer and tax-payer, may well become the butt of criticism from both above and below.

As an 'overmighty subject' that has arrived to tap the country's wealth and carry it away, it is anyway an object of suspicion. Any government, royalist or revolutionary, will be tempted to canalize popular discontent on to so convenient a scapegoat. Moreover, many of the original con-cessions were made years before anyone in the countries concerned quite realized what oil wealth could mean: some of them must have been among the first commercial contracts that the governments concerned had ever entered into. There were, often enough, items in the small print that they regretted later. Moreover, once any company finds low-cost, highly profitable oil it is difficult for the government concerned to remember—if it has ever appreciated—the amount of risk originally involved in what has turned out to be a successful venture.

Squeezing the oil company a bit more, then, is nearly always likely to be a convenient course with any government facing popular unrest. But neither giving up more to 'the old régime' nor refusing it will necessarily earn the company any popularity with the radical groups pushing from below. To the radical nationalist—who need not have the least leaning to Communism, though local and foreign Communists may well try to lean on him—the foreign capitalist, particularly in an extractive industry, begins as an object of distrust. It happens, more-over, that from Mexico to the Sahara, a large proportion of the places where oil exploration has struck it rich happen to have had either memories or the present reality of colonial tutelage preying on their minds. And the colonial rulers, even those of yesterday, were often of the same nationality as some of the oil developers of today.

These countries where oil has been produced primarily for export, however, are far from identical in their circumstances—or their attitudes. Apart from Rumania, on one side of the world, and Indonesia on the other (with the oil industry in the first now nationalized, and in the other hanging on, but under threat of the same fate), all the significant oil exporters have come from Latin America, the Middle East, and now Africa. Development of the first two started at much the same time, but Latin America moved into the lead, in terms of volume, in the early years of this century and held it for nearly half a century. The oil industry had encountered most of the governmental attitudes that it is ever likely to—from any single host government at least—before the Second World War, and before certain of the present largest oil exporters from the Middle East had ever loaded a barrel of oil into an ocean-going tanker. And it is in Latin America, also, that we have already begun to see problems of 'maturity' in oil development in countries that have never managed to build up much other large-scale industry on the spot, but have remained essentially dependent on a wasting natural resource.

By the time that commercial production of oil in Venezuela began on any significant scale, in 1917, from the Mene Grande fields close to Lake Maracaibo, Mexico was already the world's second-largest producer and exporter of oil: it had, moreover, begun upon the revision of its legal attitudes towards oil development that were to lead, twenty-one years later, to the expropriation of the oil companies operating there.

Drilling for oil in Mexico had begun about the turn of the century: British interests founded Compania Mexicana de Petrole, 'El Aguila' SA, better remembered as Mexican Eagle, and many American companies came south of the border to explore for oil. Production began in 1901; in 1910 came the fabulous 'Golden Lane' near Tampico, a line of fields 300 yards wide over a length of about fifty miles, one of the most prolific oil areas ever discovered. Mexican oil was developed by a large number of foreign producers who either bought the land or worked it on the basis of fragmented oil leases roughly similar to that of the United States. Some of its fields do seem to have been wastefully exploited, in those years when techniques were relatively primitive, without regard to technical conservation.

After years of revolution, two provisions in the country's new constitution of 1917, one bringing all land and subsoil rights under state ownership and the other establishing labour's 'rights' to what were then revolutionary hours and conditions, there began a long period of legal dispute with the oil companies. These rumbled on for about a decade at the diplomatic level between the United States and Mexican governments, with the British government occasionally taking a not necessarily helpful interest. (Most of the private oil interests concerned were American, but the Shell-controlled Mexican Eagle company was among the largest operators, and the early twenties were a period of most bitter British-American rivalry in the international oil industry.) In the meantime, Mexican production reached a peak of some 500,000 barrels a day in 1921, and thereafter began to decline. Physically wasteful exploitation of the fields had had something to do with this; but the political turmoil of the time, and the companies' continuing dispute with successive governments about their title to the areas from which they were producing oil, cannot have encouraged very adventurous further investment. After an agreement was reached at the diplomatic level in 1928, by which oil rights acquired after 1918 were exempted from the constitutional 'nationalization', production rose somewhat. But by this time the world was in depression and oil was in surplus: the rate of drilling, everywhere, went down. And there were richer oil prospects elsewhere in Latin America.

During the same year, private oil development in Mexico came to an abrupt end. A government under President Lazaro Cardenas had been pressing for a change in the legal status of the operating companies' oil rights there, and for sweeping improvements in the pay and conditions of their 25,000 Mexican workers, who were already the highest-paid in the country. The companies offered alternatively an excess-profits tax, or very large increases in pay. But in November, 1936, the trade unions presented demands that might effectively have taken away the companies' power to run their own business (quite apart from an extra $80–85 million a year in labour cost). The dispute dragged on for a year or so, with strikes halting production: in November, 1938, the Mexican government passed an act expropriating the companies.[1] (Eventually, it agreed to pay compensation amounting to $180 million by instalments, and has kept its word: payment of this compensation, which the companies argued at the time would cover only about 60 per cent of the value of their properties, was completed in 1950 to the American companies concerned and to the British, Dutch and Canadian interests by 1963.)

All that remains of Mexican Eagle today is the 'Mex' in the name of the Shell-Mex distributing organization. The fortunes of Mexican oil under state control, which took a long time to come up to nationalist hopes, but have certainly given Mexican development indirect benefits in national self-confidence, were reviewed briefly in Chapter XV. But it is a salutary reflection for all concerned that at the time of nationalization, the Mexican government was getting a royalty of 14 per cent of the value of oil produced, plus a small tax payment. Within ten years, the international oil companies were paying host governments 50 per cent of their profits, and professing at least to like it.

It was the Venezuelan government that pressed them to do so—and has since pressed on regardless. Venezuela had its first oil boom in the twenties: it took no more than a dozen years from the beginning of production to become the world's second largest producer of oil. And though output dropped for a few years after 1930, it picked up again by 1934: by the end of the thirties, producing 520,000 barrels a day, it was almost equal to Soviet Russia, the world's second producer. The Venezuelan government, dominated for many years after oil production had begun there by one dictator, Juan Vicente Gomez, obtained a flat-rate royalty on all concessions granted prior to 1918, and a percentage royalty on those granted later. The valuation of the oil for this purpose, until the early forties, was based, by a netback formula, on the prices for products, first in New York and later on sales from the island refineries of Aruba and Curaçao, off Venezuela, where a large proportion of crude from the Maracaibo area was refined. From a modest 163,000 bolivars (about $54,000) in 1917, government revenues from oil rose to 20,866,000 bolivars in 1925, and to 112,756,000 bolivars ($44 million) by 1938. At the time, this revenue represented about 13 per cent of the total declared value of the oil: it incidentally accounted for 35 per cent of Venezuela's total tax revenue.

At the outbreak of the Second World War, the danger of submarines reduced tanker shipments of products from the Caribbean refineries. This not only reduced the volume of Venezuelan exports and output; because throughput at the Caribbean refineries was reduced, their overhead costs rose, and the Venezuelan revenue per barrel fell too. In 1942, the companies operating in Venezuela, Creole (Jersey Standard), Mene Grande (Gulf), Shell of Venezuela, Mobil and Texas, agreed to value Venezuelan offtake according to the prices of similar crudes in the Gulf of Mexico, not according to the products yielded. In the next year, for the first time, Venezuela began to charge the companies a small income tax, and gradually this element in its oil revenues began to grow in relation to the percentage royalty. For all companies as a whole—but not each one individually—the tax was claimed to make the government revenue from oil equal to the net profits of the companies. In 1948, the law was amended to provide for a 'surtax' of 50 per cent on any sum by which any company's net income in any year exceeded the government's total revenue derived from the company's oil operations. This formula set the 50–50 pattern for particular co-panies by which the major international companies, ever since, have set so much store. But it may be noted that these taxes were never part of the concessions, or in any way tied by them, as the income taxes imposed on oil in the Middle East, for example, formally are. Moreover, taxable income in Venezuela, in principle at least, was at the time based on the prices actually realized, not posted prices.

Politically, this was a period in which the Gomez dictatorship ended in 1935 with his death. Some years of democratic government ensued, and then the army, under Colonel Perez Jiménez, seized power in 1948. From about 1944 onwards, moreover, the country's oil industry was in a boom again. Output doubled between 1943 and 1946; by 1955 it had doubled again, and in 1957, the annual output topped a billion barrels. Venezuelan output did not rise as fast as in the Middle East in the postwar years, but in absolute volume in the middle fifties total Caribbean exports were not far short of the Middle East's. Moreover, its future prospects looked excellent. Venezuela was the area favoured by most of the American 'big independents' that in the fifties began to search overseas to gain command of sources of imports into the United States. These groups paid large bonuses for concessions in the Lake Maracaibo area, frequently well offshore into the middle of this great lake, and in the Gulf of Paria in Eastern Venezuela, close to Trinidad. Apart from Jersey, Shell and Gulf, there were about a dozen groups of American companies established in the country by 1956–57. Their large exploration commitments offered the likelihood of boosting Venezuela's proved reserves—which were beginning to need this.

The oil revenues of the Venezuelan government in 1957, reached nearly $1,240 million—about 85 cents a barrel on regular production, plus about $370 million in 'occasional taxes'—mainly bonuses for the grant of the new concessions that were auctioned off in 1956–57. This amounted to about 71 per cent of the country's total tax revenues. The next year, the Jiménez régime was overthrown, and after an interim during which a provisional government was in power, a democratic government under President Romulo Betancourt took power. One of its first significant financial measures, under an expert and ambitious petroleum minister, Dr Juan Perez Alfonzo, was to seek a bigger share, Dr Perez Alfonzo had once estimated, in 1943, that in the first twenty-five years of their operations in Venezuela the split in profits had been 77 per cent for the companies and 23 per cent for the nation's revenues. He was determined to tip the balance, from its nominal 50–50, the other way.

In 1958, the military junta increased the progressive-rated part of its corporate income tax from 28½ to 47½ per cent for companies in the top bracket of income and the later Betancourt régime put this new tax régime into practice. Along with royalties and other taxes, this brought the government's total take from oil from 52 per cent of profits in 1957 to 65 per cent in 1958, and 69 per cent in 1959. Surplus, however, was again appearing in the world oil trade; America was restricting oil imports; and since their profits in every oil-exporting area of the world were coming under pressure, the oil companies were naturally disinclined to increase output in an area where the government was increasing its share of whatever profit they did make. In 1958, Venezuelan offtake dropped by about 6 per cent, and though it recovered in 1959, growth since has remained slow. The government's oil revenues, from regular taxes per barrel, however, rose significantly, in spite of a reduction in crude oil prices in 1959, reaching about $1·03 a barrel in 1959, and yielding the government about a billion dollars, as against $866 million in 1957, the peak under the earlier tax formula.[1] In 1959, also, the local trade unions secured very substantial increases in wages, with governmental backing for the oil workers who already had by far the highest wages in the country: this increased the actual costs of Venezuelan oil. By 1965, Venezuelan output was only about 25 per cent above the 1957 level, while Middle East output had risen by 130 per cent. It was inevitable that low costs in the Middle East would give it the greater growth; but the increase in the Venezuelan revenue per barrel, to the integrated company, had also increased the difference in 'tax-paid cost'.

Up to 1966 Venezuelan tax, as noted above, was based on the actual prices paid, not on posted prices. So if the company was obliged to accept a discount in order to sell the oil, the Venezuelan exchequer, in theory, bore 65 per cent or more of the cut. But in practice, like other governments that charge tax on 'realizations', the Venezuelan government did its best to discourage heavy discounting. It has a Co-ordinating Commission that demands the right to be told, theoretically in advance, of the prices agreed for every oil export contract. And this commission, if it believes the price is unduly low, can recommend the income tax authorities not to accept the taxable income declared as a result of it. Oil companies, like most other businesses, are accustomed to governments arguing years in arrear over their exact liability for income tax. But in Venezuela there had built up a backlog of dispute over taxes, arising largely over discounted prices, that was longer than most.

Increases in taxes had been only one of the factors checking growth in Venezuelan exports—and causing the discounting. Venezuelan oil imports into the United States were held down by import restrictions, since Venezuela enjoyed no preference of the kind Canada was given. The decline in world tanker rates cut down the limited chance Venezuela had of selling to Western Europe. This made competition, particularly between its 'newcomer' groups, very bitter in markets still within reach, such as the rest of Latin America, Canada, and the Pacific archipelago. The producers' reaction was predictable—to hold down output inside Venezuela, so far as they could, and to reduce drilling activity drastically. By the early sixties, there were only about 30 drilling rigs working in the country, against about 90 at the end of 1958; this was the lowest level of exploration since the war years.

In 1966, this tax dispute came to a head—but as suddenly, was resolved by an agreed settlement. First, Venezuela announced that it would refuse to recognize more than fixed levels of discount on fuel oil and later on crude, in settling exporters' tax liability. Next, it threatened an 'excess profits tax'. The dispute seemed likely to become even more bitter; but in September 1966, after lengthy pourparlers, agreement was reached on a quite new basis. This was costly enough for the companies; the basic income tax rate was raised from $47\frac{1}{2}$ to 52 per cent, on profits reckoned according to fixed 'tax reference prices' instead of those actually realized, and the companies agreed to pay some $560 million in settlement of back taxes for the period 1958–65. The government's total take from oil profits went up to an estimated 72 per cent (though companies increasing investment or output significantly had a chance to get reductions of up to 2 per cent in the basic tax rate).

A slowdown in the rate of growth of Venezuelan output had been expected and accepted by the Venezuelan government, but the slowdown of 1957–66 was more than it would have chosen. Dr Perez Alfonzo, in October, 1959, had said that he was prepared to see the rate of increase slip to about four to six per cent a year, enough to cover the budgetary deficit, and to let oil remain in the ground for future generations. During the Second World War, he had opposed the passing of the country's Law of Hydrocarbons of 1943, which in return for somewhat more favourable oil revenues had extended existing concessions for forty years. In the short period of democratic government between 1945 and 1948, before Jiménez seized power, the policy of 'no more concessions' was originated. This did not stop the Jiménez régime granting a large number of new concessions during 1956 and 1957; but when the Betancourt government returned in 1959, this was part of its oil policy. Dr Perez Alfonzo blamed the Jiménez régime for letting in the smaller newcomers, which he rightly identified as 'soft sellers' following the imposition of import restrictions on the American market. He said he would prefer to deal with a few big companies; and to develop the rest of Venezuela's oil through the state petroleum corporation that was set up in 1960.

The Venezuelan Ministry of Mines and Hydrocarbons is one of the best-informed oil ministries in the world, technically and commercially. Technically, it developed an effective supervision of technical conservation, and the *Corporaçion Venezolana de Petroleo* has carried out a certain amount of exploration. But in 1965, for example, the country produced about 12 per cent of the world's output while it had officially only 5 per cent of the world's reserves.

Opinions may differ about the relative value of producing oil now or leaving it in the ground. Nobody doubts that Venezuela has a very large amount of it left in the ground; but the proven reserves are limited, and some of the rest could be particularly expensive to produce. This is the very heavy oil of the Tarbelt—an oil-bearing region stretching across the country north of the River Orinoco, which is so viscous that it might have to be assisted to the surface by special means. But even apart from this, oil companies in Venezuela argue that reserves producible by conventional means could be developed to allow an increase in Venezuelan production to say 225 million tons a year (4,450,000 barrels a day) by 1980, against the 175 million tons of 1965; and still leave 15 years' production in hand at that rate. If that were the limit of the reserves, production would probably begin gradually to decline after 1980; but if the Tarbelt could be produced economically, output of that 1980 order of magnitude could be held until around the end of the century. The trouble, in the mid-sixties, was that not even the extra reserves producible by conventional means were being proven by a really substantial exploration effort. The state company CVP was financing a good deal of drilling; but not nearly enough to locate the reserves that the country needed.

Various factors were causing this. The companies had indeed cut exploration sharply after the income tax increase in 1958. The market for residual fuel oil, of which Venezuelan crudes generally provide a high yield, was restricted in the United States; growing fairly rapidly in Europe, but at very low prices that did not 'net back' much profit to Venezuela. The private industry had not found the governments' constant argument over back income tax very comfortable: and it resents having to hand over service stations to CVP without full compensation. But there was no need to go beyond the simplest reason. Most of the concessions under which oil is being produced in Venezuela end in 1983. And the companies had no idea whether, or under what formula, they would be in business in the country after that. The Venezuelan government still believes in 'No more concessions'; and it had not up to early 1966 revealed what, if any, other kind of future arrangement it believes in for the private companies in the country's oil future.[3]

Venezuela has been considering some kind of contractual arrangement; but looking south, it has no taste for the kind of contracts that made, resented, and then cancelled within a few years. Its government appreciates the problem of making a contract in which you want the contractor to carry most of the inherently high risk. Late in 1965, it appeared that it was considering some kind of sliding scale that would give the contractor a reasonable return on his risk capital, but under which the government or Venezuelan partner would get a bigger proportion of the extra proceeds as and when output passed certain defined levels. But it also wanted some improvement on its current rate of government revenue per barrel—which at the time was still the highest in the world for any producing country, over 90 cents a barrel. This was probably about twice the net profit that the companies were getting— though these averages concealed a wide range of fortunes, since even in the last decade or so some of the oil discovered in Venezuela has been cheap by standards anywhere. Providing that the Government can find a practical formula for oil 'contractors'—and if any producing government ever does, this is likely to be the one, through sheer expertise—Venezuela still looks a profitable producing area for the international companies, if its latest agreement on tax works ont.

Venezuela was a leading spirit in the formation of the Organization of Petroleum Exporting Countries, and has been equally anxious to deal with American import restrictions, one of the strongest government interventions of recent years, on a diplomatic basis. It has consistently argued that Venezuela ought to be given a favoured and irreducible quota of American oil imports, on grounds of 'hemisphere security'. From time to time, it has been given reasons to hope by the American government. But these hints or promises, up to 1965, had never come to anything. American restrictions on residual fuel oil have in fact been lifted since. But it is understandable that it is among exporters that Venezuela is most interested in promoting government co-operation.

Several of the other countries that produce oil in Latin America are following different 'national policies' in search of self-sufficiency: one or two of them export oil. Commercial production and continuing exploration has gone on in Colombia for nearly forty years, without its ever emerging as a large-scale producer. So far, about 1,400 million barrels of reserves have been discovered; just over half of these have been tapped already, leaving reserves of some 650 million barrels. Five of the world's major companies operate there, Texaco on its own and in partnership with Mobil; Gulf; Shell; and Jersey (on a small scale, one of its concessions having reverted to the state in 1951); these produce about four-fifths of the country's output, which in 1965 was about 200,000 barrels a day, only about 6 per cent of Venezuela's. There are ten other independents looking for oil, but so far producing practically none; and the state concern *Empresa Columbiana de Petroleos* (Ecopetrol), which has production from some relinquished and declining fields, and has engaged in a number of partnership contracts for secondary recovery and further exploration with private groups. The country's two refineries, one owned by Ecopetrol but both operated by the Jersey Standard subsidiary, have enough capacity to supply Colombia's internal market, which only takes about 50,000 barrels a day, leaving three-quarters of the country's crude production for export.

Colombian taxes at present take 40–50 per cent of oil profits. But in 1961, it passed a new petroleum law enabling it if it chose to increase this share beyond 50 per cent, increasing surface rents and royalties and limiting depletion, cutting concession areas by half and requiring relinquishment of half of the original concession area each year. Both the country and the oil companies have waited patiently for bigger developments in oil; some promising finds of oil and gas have been made, but economic and in particular currency difficulties have made development there difficult. Little of the money ploughed into oil in

Colombia has yet been got back. Bolivia, as noted in Chapter XV, is on the verge of becoming an exporter, once its landlocked oil from the Santa Cruz area can be moved to ocean terminals. Exploration has proceeded for a long time in Peru without developing more than miniscule production. Trinidad possesses one of the earliest-recorded deposits, or seepages, of petroleum, in its famous pitch lake; oil drilling began there as early as in the United States, and at present there is an output of some 150,000 barrels a day. But the island is of greater importance as one of the refining centres of the Caribbean.

Latin America was the first great oil-producing area developed by foreign enterprise. It has also been over the whole period, an area of political instability, with social revolution following upon the establishment of nationalist independence. The oil industry has been one of the few lasting economic institutions in some of the countries where it was developed: but it has received a good deal of nationalist dislike for the foreigner, mingled with envy from the landless poor. It has also tended to be identified, through its own fault or not, with reactionary governments. It is unfortunately perfectly logical for foreign enterprise to prefer the 'strong hand' in government of such a troubled area: dictators often mean stability. Over the years, the oil companies have managed to reduce this identification with particular régimes, and in general to establish their independence of local politics. That, in its turn, may merely cause them to be identified with their own parent governments, and to acquire a new vulnerability as symbols if these parent governments, in turn, become objects of envy and dislike or are pilloried by leftist régimes as supporters of reaction. To have learned the object lesson of Mexico did not make it possible to live with Cuba.

CHAPTER XIX

Producers for Export:
The Eastern Hemisphere

'We have no legal department in the Kuwait Oil Company,' said Mr William Fraser, then managing director of that company, in a discussion of the nature of oil concession agreements at the Second Arab Oil Congress in Beirut in November 1960, 'and we practically never need to refer to the text of the concession.' Mr Fraser, himself a Scottish lawyer, was commenting upon the argument of Mr Frank Hendryx, an American lawyer then working for the Saudi Arabian government, that sovereign governments had the right and even the duty to alter these contracts with private companies if and when circumstances changed and the concessions no longer served the needs of their citizens but operated against them.[1] This is a thesis that tends to incense the concessionaire companies; there had been some elaborate legal attacks upon it, tinged with rancour, from some of their spokesmen. Mr Fraser, characteristically, spoke in human rather than legal terms: and his hearers were aware that in Kuwait the working relationship was perhaps the best in the Middle East. He ended by saying, 'If we have a point to raise, we go to the government. If the government has a point to raise, it comes to us. We talk it over as friends, and settle it as friends. It is only then that we call in the lawyers and bring out the agreement.'

About two months later, it is said, an American visitor was talking with Shaikh Jabir, whose responsibility for financial affairs in the government of Kuwait at the time included petroleum. She was asking about the functions of the new Kuwait National Petroleum Company, which had been financed with government and private Kuwaiti money to take over, as a beginning, the distribution of oil products inside this small and fantastically rich little country. Shaikh Jabir mentioned that the new KNPC might possibly take up the 20 per cent interest to which the government would be entitled in offshore oil production from Kuwait, as and when this began under an agreement recently concluded with Shell. He added that it might later take over exploration and development inland in Kuwait, in the areas to be relinquished by the Kuwait Oil Company. 'But Your Excellency,' asked his visitor, whose knowledge of oil concessions in the Middle East is prodigious, 'I was under the impression that the Kuwait Oil Company's concession did not make any provision for the relinquishment of unexplored territories, as for example those in Iran and Saudi Arabia do.' Shaikh Jabir smiled. 'You are right,' he answered. 'It does not. But I believe you attended the oil congress in Beirut. Did you not hear Mr Fraser say that when we have something to discuss as friends, we are not concerned with what is or is not in the agreement?'

Within twelve months, this retort was a fact. The government of Kuwait—which in the meantime had achieved complete formal independence, had been threatened with annexation, and had withstood this threat partly by the support of British arms—did in early 1962 ask for the relinquishment of part of KOC's concession area, regardless of the terms of the concession. And though the company seemed successfully to have resisted some rather exuberant versions of this request, in May, 1962 it did agree to relinquish 50 per cent of its concession acreage straight away, and 5 per cent more in five years' time. And the national company KNPC was in a larger way of business, looking much farther afield.

Whatever is or is not in it, the oil concession agreement is at the core of the unique relationship between host governments and paying guest companies in the Middle East. Partly because these have often been nation-wide agreements, or at any rate have reserved huge territories to single operating companies, in contrast to the smaller 'mining leases' under mineral laws in Latin America, the terms of each concession have been of far greater importance in the Middle East than in that other great area of oil development by foreign companies. In the Middle East, again, these concessions have from their beginnings been the concern not only of the countries concerned but of the parent governments of the foreign companies concerned, to a greater degree than those in Latin America ever were. Some of the joint operating companies now operating major concessions in the Middle

East evolved as the result of considerable diplomatic negotiations between these parent governments as well as with the governments of the actual countries. To the Middle East government, 'the companies' appear as homogeneous an entity, politically as well as economically, as 'the governments' do to any oilman.

The concessions, too, tend in effect though not in form to appear all of a piece. In spite of many differences of detail between even the main agreements covering oil development in the Middle East nations, the layman may perhaps reasonably consider them as one body of contractual doctrine for the governments and companies concerned. Not all explicitly include a 'most favoured nation' clause requiring any further advantages conceded by the companies concerned under later agreements elsewhere in these countries to become operative under this one too. But in practice any improvement in terms granted by the major companies to any government will pretty soon be granted to all. Not the least important activity of the departments of oil in these governments, already, is the comparative scrutiny of each other's agreements, to make sure they are not missing something other governments get. It is, moreover, one of the declared intentions of OPEC to facilitate such comparisons.

If one can consider these main concessions in the Middle East together, then, it should also be noted that the body of contractual doctrine that they form is in practice a constantly evolving one. The thesis frequently argued by their lawyers—that in this unusual form of contract between a government and a business enterprise operating within its borders the government has an implicit right to change the deal to suit changed circumstances—is obviously not one that companies that are parties to such contracts could ever admit. Whether international lawyers would admit it is doubtful, though there are obscurities in the law covering legal agreements between governments and private 'individuals'.[2] In practice, however, the concessions and the working relationships they govern do change over time. None of the major concessions in the Middle East today lays down the same terms as it did when it was originally made.

Considering the huge changes in relations between industrialized and underdeveloped countries that have taken place since certain of these contracts were negotiated—and the very long periods, often 60–70 years, and in one case 90, over which they run—the layman will not find this surprising. The law, we are told, cannot recognize the argument that when these contracts were made the rulers of the countries concerned were unused to any such binding commercial documents, with their appendices in fine print—or that the agreements, many years ago, could not suit the present interests of these developing nations. But the layman may find some force in them. These are the arguments most engagingly and saltily presented by Shaikh Abdullah Tariki when he says, 'We are the sons of the Indians who sold Manhattan Island. We want to change the deal.' The companies might fairly retort that, as purchased, Manhattan Island was worth virtually nothing. But repartee aside, the fact is that in the real world, whatever the fine print says, the deal is—constantly—changing.

A history of the oil concession in the Middle East, as a legal instrument, seems never to have been written. It appears, even to the layman's cursory inquiries, to differ in kind from the mining codes under which oil has been developed in some other countries and under which, for example, the great British and American metal groups operate overseas. It was in 1872 that the Shah of Persia granted to one Baron Julius de Reuter, a British subject, a seventy-year concession to construct railroads and street-car lines and exploit all mineral resources save gold, silver and precious stones—a concession that Lord Curzon later called 'the most complete and extraordinary surrender of the entire industrial resources of a kingdom into foreign hands that has probably ever been dreamt of . . .' But that concession was cancelled after Russian objections; nor was any oil found by a search in the nineties under a later concession to de Reuter.

The d'Arcy concession signed on 21st May, 1901, did not cover railroads or tramcars (though it did include more relevant transport facilities, pipelines). But it gave William Knox d'Arcy, a Devon man who had become a gold millionaire in Australia,

'a special and exclusive privilege to search for, obtain, exploit, render suitable for trade, carry away and sell natural gas, petroleum asphalt and ozerite throughout the whole extent of the Persian Empire for a term of sixty years.'

This agreement was to become economically and politically one of the most momentous ever concluded in the history of the oil·industry and of the whole Middle East. It was revised, denounced, revised again and the area reduced but prolonged, broken by nationalization, replaced by a different kind of agreement and different signatories. But the development that it set in train has produced oil ever since 1908; and as present agreements go, it is likely to go on producing oil until 1993.

That original d'Arcy concession, it may be intriguing to note, provided both for profit-sharing and for a government shareholding in the operating company to be set up, features we tend to think of as postwar innovations in the Middle East oil business. It was altered, in 1919, to provide among other things for government participation in all net profits arising from the 'mining, refining and marketing of Persian oil' through subsidiaries 'inside or outside Persia', which no major company offers in any present concession. In 1933, after a lengthy diplomatic dispute and hearings before the League of Nations over a Persian proposal to cancel it, the concession was re-negotiated to substitute for profit-sharing a fixed royalty on oil produced plus a share in dividends over and above a given amount, with an annual minimum. In 1949, it was to have been revised to provide for a larger royalty per ton of oil, a larger minimum payment in respect of dividends (which had been held down through the Labour government's limitation of dividends policy in Britain), and a payment in lieu of tax, from which the company (by that time Anglo-Iranian) had until then been excused. Later, while the new draft agreement was being considered by an oil committee of the Iranian Majlis (under the chairmanship of one Dr. Mohammed Mossadegh) a proposal came from the company offering a 50:50 sharing of profits. It could indeed be said that most of the variants that have ever been proposed for the major agreements between oil companies and governments in the Middle East that we have ever seen were put into or proposed for that Iranian concession at one time or another. The Persians in 1950–51, as it turned out, did not like any of them. There followed nationalization, three years of effective boycott of Iranian oil throughout world markets, and eventually the Consortium Agreement of 1954. Under which Iran accepted back various of the things that it had rejected by nationalization—including Anglo-Iranian, now renamed British Petroleum, as the largest consortium partner— but retained title to the ownership of all oil produced inside its frontiers.

The consortium agreement provides, as today do the concessions covering the main oil production of Kuwait, Iraq, and Saudi Arabia, taxes amounting to 50 per cent of profits made on the production and export of oil. It provides for the management of oil operations in a defined area of southern Iran by two operating companies, the first covering exploration and production, the second responsible for operating the Abadan company. These are non-profit-making companies, somewhat on the lines of the Iraq Petroleum Company, carrying out their activities for a fee. They transfer part of the oil in kind or in value, to the National Iranian Oil Company, which incidentally has operating rights throughout large parts of the rest of Iranian territory. The rest goes, for a fee of a shilling a cubic metre, to trading companies in Iran representing the members of the consortium, in amounts corresponding to their shareholdings in the consortium.

The other major operating companies, like the original Anglo-Persian Oil Company and eventually the Consortium, came into being as a result of commercial initiative more or less liberally admixed with diplomatic influence.[3] Control of Anglo-Persian, as originally formed to take over the d'Arcy concession, was taken over early in its history by the British government. One result was that its oil concession inside Persia itself, until after nationalization, never had to be shared by any other commercial or national competitor; Anglo-Persian, however, gained extensive interests elsewhere in the Middle East over the years. What eventually became the Iraq Petroleum Company in 1928 has been the subject of commercial enterprise since 1904, with concessions sought, gained and challenged by German, British, Italian, Dutch and American interests. After the First World War the German interests were dropped out (being eventually handed over to France in consideration of other claims on the Near East). British and American manœuvring continued, with use on the one side of much argument about Britain's responsibility as mandatory power for Iraq, and on the other of the 'open door' doctrine for all foreign (but particularly American) capital. In 1928, a group of British, Dutch, American and French companies (with the assistance of M. Calouste Gulbenkian) signed an agreement that allowed for the creation not only of IPC but also of joint companies to exploit oil in a large area of the former Turkish empire. Not all of Iraq was covered by the 'Red Line' agreement, or originally, by IPC; other concessions were granted later to other companies for the Mosul and Basra areas, but in the late thirties these were abandoned and taken over by IPC.

Conclusion of these agreements did not end competition from Americans in the Middle East; it meant only that the American shareholders in IPC, Jersey Standard, Socony, and originally Gulf, refrained from competing for concessions within the 'Red Line'. Gulf, for example, abandoned a concession in Bahrein that had been offered to it by a British syndicate formed to seek concessions, allowing it to be taken up by Standard of California, at that time a newcomer to the Middle East. When Gulf did later withdraw from the agreement, selling out of IPC in order to negotiate for a concession with the

Ruler of Kuwait, it found that the British government invoked a prior agreement by the ruler not to grant a concession to any but a British company. The upshot, in 1933, was that Gulf joined with Anglo-Persian in setting up the jointly-owned Kuwait Oil Company to sign a seventy-five-year concession from 1934 (it was later amended to run until the year 2023). In 1933, also, Aramco was formed, on the grant of a concession by Saudi Arabia to Standard of California; Anglo-Persian competed for this concession, but was apparently unwilling to match the £50,000 in gold that Socal's negotiators deposited within forty-eight hours of the offer of a concession. In 1936, the Texas Company bought half interests in Socal's concessions in Saudi Arabia and in Bahrein, allowing the California company a half interest in its own Far East marketing network, under the name Caltex.

These negotiations between the wars effectively drew the original map of the main Middle East concessions of today; but there were changes to come first in the ownership and later in the territorial limits. During the war, with development in Saudi Arabia necessarily reduced and delayed, Saudi Arabia was in difficulties, seeking subventions from the British government; eventually, at the instance of Aramco, the United States brought Saudi Arabia within the sphere of Lendlease. The American government appreciated the companies' insistence that British influence was growing over Saudi Arabia to an extent that they did not like at all; at one time it proposed to buy all or part of Aramco's concession itself. This fell through. Nor was an offer by Aramco to sell the government large quantities of oil very cheap ever taken up. But the refinery at Ras Tanura was built, in 1943–45, as an American military project; and it was with considerable backing from the American government, particularly in respect of export licences for scarce steel pipe, that the TAPline to carry part of Saudi Arabian production overland to the Mediterranean was eventually built just after the war.

In 1946, however, Standard of California and Texaco, which up to then had been outside the 'Red Line' group of companies, obtained extra financial support—and access to far wider marketing facilities—from two of the companies inside. Jersey Standard and Socony purchased a 30 per cent and a 10 per cent interest, respectively, in Aramco and TAPline. (This was the end of the 'Red Line' agreement too, in effect; but to end it in form took much argument and some litigation.)

These American partners in Aramco, in 1950, brought the 50:50 profit-sharing principle to the Middle East. It had originated in Venezuela, as described during the last chapter, at a time when a series of governments there were pressing the oil companies for a larger national interest in the oil industry. It was brought to the Middle East at a time when governments were beginning to show an interest in gaining their oil revenues through taxation rather than through various kinds of royalty income. The first Saudi Arabian income tax law, enacted in 1950, and covered by an agreement in December of that year between the government and Aramco, provided for a tax that would bring the government share, including the existing royalty, up to 50 per cent of the operating profits of the company. These were originally operating profits net of American income tax; the next year, with the assistance of experts from the U.S. Treasury, this was revised so that the Arabian tax was charged before U.S. tax.

At this point the implicit 'most favoured nation clause' that we have mentioned in these major concessions in the Middle East came into play. It was not necessarily convenient for Anglo-Iranian and the European partners in IPC, operating under different tax laws, to match this 50:50 pattern of sharing; but matched it had to be. Anglo-Iranian, whose proposals for a revised agreement were at this very time before the Iranian Majlis, promptly offered to reconsider them, in the light of the new Saudi agreement; this offer did not come in time. Although IPC in December, 1950, had already agreed to a higher royalty on oil production for the Iraq government, it agreed to the new basis; an agreement was finally signed early in 1952. The Kuwait concession was revised along the same lines in 1951; those in Bahrein and Qatar were converted to 50:50 in the following year. And in 1954, when the Consortium Agreement brought Iran back into the oil business, it too provided for income tax on the same pattern. This pattern included the 'crediting' of the 12½ per cent royalty against the income tax, so that 50 per cent of taxable income was the total government take. It also safeguarded the companies against any increase in their tax rates. To qualify for double taxation relief, these had to be general income taxes. So in theory, the 50:50 agreements bound these countries' general tax rates for many years ahead.[4]

The move to 50:50 transformed the basis of the relationship between the oil companies and their host governments, in more ways than one. Immediately, it gave the governments a vast increase in revenue; this was at the expense more of American and later of European tax revenues than of the companies' own income, but that made it no less of a benefit to the oil-producing states. It also, however, gave them an interest in the maintenance of the posted prices for crude oil, and it also meant that any reduction in posted price bore directly upon the governments' revenues per barrel. It is said that during discussion of the American companies' initiative over 50:50 in New York, at a time when the European companies were not wholly enamoured of the new proposals, a representative of one of the British groups said to his opposite number in an American group, 'Calculate how far the crude price has got to drop before you're paying them less than they were getting on the old formula.' That was subtle in market terms; but it assumed that the prices on which tax would be based were part of the market. In fact, they have turned out to have more to do with company-government relationships.

Nor did the cornucopia of 50:50 sate the oil countries' appetite for wealth from their treasure chest that these ingenious foreigners had opened. Within a few years, attracted by the riches accruing to all concerned, there were other foreigners arriving, offering even bigger shares—at least on paper—to be allowed to find and tap new treasures. In 1957 and 1958, Iran granted offshore concessions to three foreign enterprises—including Agip Mineraria, an offshoot of the nationalized Italian group ENI, and Pan-American Petroleum, two groups of American independents—on an entirely new basis. These provided for operating companies to be owned by half the foreign groups and half by Iran's own NIOC, while operating companies would share profits 50:50 with the Iranian government. The concessionaire companies were to bear all exploration expenses until the discovery of oil in commercial quantities; in effect, therefore, these concessions on the face of it offered Iran, through its shareholding and its taxes, 75 per cent of the profits on any oil that might be found. Concessions were to run for twenty-five years with options of renewal; they contained specific most-favoured nation clauses; they provided for the relinquishment of unexplored areas within time limits; and they guaranteed 'Iranization' of given percentages of staff, and in two cases promised preferential treatment for Iranian flag tankers. In 1958, Saudi Arabia and Kuwait granted separate concessions to a Japanese company for exploration in the Arabian Gulf offshore from their jointly-controlled Neutral Zone. These concessions provided for payments of royalties, rents and taxes representing 56 per cent of the profits from oil to Saudi Arabia and 57 per cent to Kuwait; they promised the construction of local refineries once a certain level of throughput was reached; and the governments were given options to purchase 10 per cent of the stock of the company once production began (which the governments exercised during 1961). Moreover, the Japanese Arabian Oil Company was to exercise its concession rights through an operating company which would engage in refining, transport and marketing; and the government's tax share of profits could extend to all these integrated activities.

How far these new and different types of concession would offer the host countries more money remained to be seen: it was not until the early sixties that any of them began to deliver crude from the Middle East to market. Offshore costs are generally higher; the market into which they were beginning to put this crude had grown much softer; and some of these companies had limited marketing facilities in the Eastern hemisphere. So the revenues per barrel that the governments and national companies received under these agreements were not necessarily larger than the share some were getting under 50–50 agreements. Even so, it was the form of participation, rather than the unit revenue, that interested the host governments; and by putting 'buyback' clauses at defined prices into such deals, they could in fact arrange to get more money per barrel as well. The first major company to accept such a partnership formula was Shell, in the concession offshore from Kuwait, signed in January, 1961. Among other provisions, this agreement allowed the state to buy its way into the operating company—at cost—though its offer of extremely favourable terms for any Kuwait share of oil perhaps sounded a better bargain to the government than trying to sell the oil independently. It provided for relinquishment of unexplored territories, and for the possible establishment of a refinery in Kuwait. It was, moreover, a concession of somewhat shorter term than any in which any other major company was engaged in the Middle East—forty-five years. And Shell, unlike any other major company in the area, had the chance to operate on its own, without corporate partners who would have to be persuaded to agree with anything that it chose to do. Up to 1965, this agreement remained one of historic interest. But, unfortunately, not much more: Shell had found no oil under it.

From being a novelty, partnership did not take long to become a customary formula in letting out new concession areas or relinquished acreage. There were variants: in 1963 the United Arab Republic, which had a tradition of toughness towards foreign capital but was a comparative newcomer in oil, granted a number of concessions to American independent companies and to ENI which stipulated partnership but at the same time left the private partners a good deal of freedom, plus relatively easy financial terms. But that was what had to be offered to attract oil companies into a relatively unpromising area. In 1964 the Itanian government, after requiring would-be new concessionnaires to help finance a preliminary investigation of new areas offshore in the Persian Gulf, found a number of bidders ready to pay large bonuses for concessions there on very stringent terms indeed. These involved acceptance of NIOC as a 50 per cent partner, and a well-protected one. These were nicknamed '75:25' concessions, but the government-company division was in fact variable, depending on the price that could be obtained for the crude. The combined Iranian take was not fixed; but there was a fairly high minimum to underpin it. And in 1965 a Saudi Arabian concession granted to a French semi-nationalized company went further. Its financial terms were a little better for the government, though not much; its main innovation was to remove the clause almost every other Middle East concession to date had contained, which put a limit to the tax rate that could in future be charged on the concession. In 1966 Iran however once again took the lead: it made a deal with the French state company ERAP under which the company became a 'contractor' to NIOC, risking the cash for exploration simply against the chance of buying some of the crude it might find from NIOC at a low price.

At the end of 1943, a mission headed by Everette Lee DeGolyer, a well-known geologist, had reported to the Petroleum Reserves Corporation that had been set up by the Roosevelt Administration, that the centre of gravity of world oil production was shifting from the Gulf-Caribbean to the Middle East-Persian Gulf area and was likely to continue to shift. It reckoned, at that time, that in Kuwait there might be reserves of 9 billion barrels, in Iran 6–7 billion barrels, in Saudi Arabia 5 billion barrels, and in Qatar a billion barrels.

Nearly twenty years ago, that was prescience. Today, the shift it envisaged is taken for granted by everyone, and the reserves it guessed at have been proved many times over. In the whole Middle East, at the end of 1965, proven reserves totalled about 215,000 million barrels, or close on 29,000 million tons, which was about 61 per cent of the world's total; and though the Middle East in that year produced only about 27 per cent of the world's oil, it was overwhelmingly the largest source of the crude oil moving in international trade, supplying 7 million barrels a day out of the total of 11 million barrels traded. It is generally held to contain the areas of lowest-cost petroleum output in the world. Though net profits after tax on oil have rivalled it in the past in Venezuela and certainly do nowadays in Libya, in none does the enormous reserve-production ratio impose so little obligation upon the oil developer to invest in further exploration and make the cost of producing more, i.e. development plus production costs for new output, so low. Production from most areas in the region, moreover, could rapidly be stepped up if the need arose, without significant danger of depletion of any major reservoir. Exploration costs in the major producing countries were never high, in terms of reserves discovered; and are at present largely irrelevant.

If the development of Middle East oil since the war has been virtually explosive, its impact upon the traditional societies within whose lands it was found has not been much less so. It has, first, arbitrarily divided the region into three groups of countries, the great producers, the oil transit countries, and the other have-nots. These divisions cut across the political and tribal linkages within Arab nationalism—and to some extent across the traditional spheres of interest of the former tutelary powers, though these between the wars had substantially adjusted their pattern of interests in the Middle East to take account of where the oil happened to lie. The access of riches to some parts, but not others in the region—and often within countries to some groups but not most people—has begun to influence the political structure and connexions of the Middle East countries. Oil happened to be produced in countries ruled by different absolutisms, benevolent or not. The republics of the region, with their differing brands of democracy, are for the most part countries without oil exports to make their fortunes, though General Qasim in 1958 moved Iraq from one of these rather uncertain categories to another. Political turbulence, since the war, has affected the big exporters as well as countries without much foreign income from oil: Iran and Iraq as well as Egypt and Syria.

The great producers of oil—three of them Arab countries, and one not—vary both in political stability and in their attitudes towards the industry that has unlocked their wealth. Kuwait, which up to a few years ago seemed the most stable and contented, is a tiny country of immense wealth. It covers only 5,800 square miles and the majority of these are empty. Its 470,000 inhabitants, of whom only about 150,000 are Kuwaiti nationals, live in the seaport that is its capital city, or in the 'company town' and oil terminal of Ahmadi twenty miles along the coast. In 1955–66 its oil and other government revenues, 90 per cent derived from oil directly or indirectly, must have been of the order of $650 million, about $4,000 a year for each Kuwaiti national. Its other inhabitants, largely expatriates or transients from elsewhere in the Middle East or from Europe, are well paid for their specialist services, but can hardly be said to partake of the national wealth in quite the same way as the country's own citizens.

Kuwait up to 1965 was the largest producer of oil in the Middle East, though Saudi Arabia and Iran, not far behind, were expanding their output far faster. Its lead was not simply due to the fact that enormous reserves plus closeness to tidewater make its oil the cheapest. Its initial spurt into the lead occurred during the years when Iranian oil could not be traded to the world, which the Iranians do not forget. Its neighbours share a certain jealousy of the tiny state's good fortune.

In the twenties the shaikhdom of Kuwait had to establish itself against the house of Saud. From 1899 to 1961, Kuwait was under some degree of British protection; in 1922, its boundaries, including the neutral zone with Saudi Arabia, were delineated by treaty. In 1961 the British government formally withdrew all its reserved powers and recognized the absolute sovereignty of Kuwait: this was immediately followed by claims from Iraq's General Qasim that the state was an Iraqi province. First British troops, and later a force from other Arab countries, had to be sent to Kuwait to support its independent status. Under the then Ruler (who died in 1965), the small state established a national assembly, giving it significant powers to review or delay actions by the ministers (appointed by the Ruler and largely members of the ruling family). The assembly's powers were real—as was shown when it refused approval and was able to delay acceptance of the 'OPEC settlement' on royalty expensing, which ministers had agreed with the oil companies.

Under the Gulf/Anglo-Iranian concession granted in 1934, drilling began in 1936; but the wells were plugged in 1942, and it was not until June, 1946, that commercial shipments of crude oil began from the first terminal installation at Mina al Ahmadi. During the whole of 1946, the country produced just under 800,000 barrels of crude oil. By 1950, this had risen to 7 million barrels a year. During the three years of the dispute over Iranian nationalization it rose to 47 million tons a year; and by 1965, it amounted to 108 million tons a year or 2,170,000 barrels a day, the daily rate being two and-a-half times the year's output in 1946. Two other producers have producing concessions from the state. The American Independent group, Aminoil (owned by a group of sizeable American companies) produce oil from the Neutral Zone between Kuwait and Saudi Arabia under a concession from the Ruler: the Getty group operates in the same area under a concession from the King of Saudi Arabia. And in the area of the Gulf offshore from this neutral zone, a Japanese company is now producing under concessions from each ruler. These concessionnaires were among the first to breach, openly, the generally ruling 50:50 principle.

For some years now, Kuwait's proven reserves have been publicly estimated at 60,000–70,000 million barrels. Whether this means simply that the published figures are notional and not revised, or that the companies involved have been proving simply sufficient extra reserves to make up for the production taken out every year, is not clear; the totals are so large that it does not matter much. But it is worth noting that the growth of output there is now very low, running in the mid-sixties at about 2 per cent annually. Many oilmen in the Middle East are indeed predicting that output in Kuwait is approaching its 'ceiling'. No outside opinion, in the nature of things, can be worth much on such a question. Unless it can be established that technically Kuwait's fields are approaching some 'maximum efficient rate' of operation (itself a vague concept, as noted in Chapter XIII), then the rate of output there would appear to depend upon the likely 'tax-paid cost', and the rate of profit obtainable for this oil to British Petroleum, Gulf, and Shell (which takes a large amount of Gulf's production on a basis involving the sharing of net profit)—in relation to comparable tax-paid costs and net profits on all the other crudes available to these companies. These are obviously hard enough for these companies to predict themselves, let alone anyone else. But the slowdown in rate of growth is a fact. The best company-government relations in the Middle East, which were formerly enjoyed in Kuwait, developed during a period of rapid growth to unimagined prosperity. The prosperity is there; but the oil wealth in it is not growing as fast. These excellent relations are being put to the test.

A very large amount of this small state's revenue has been invested in education and in medical services; there are seventy superbly-equipped schools, a secondary school and technical and commercial colleges. The state finances higher education at overseas universities for all young Kuwaiti nationals who it believes can benefit from it. In the last decade the first sprinkling of these graduates has been returning— to a rather bewildering profusion of important jobs in the civil service, local commerce, or the oil industry. Kuwait's national oil company,

KNPC, is now effectively established at home and venturing abroad. Large amounts of Kuwaiti capital have flowed overseas to finance, in particular, construction in Beirut and Cairo, and it is now offering low-interest loans to less fortunately placed Arab countries.

Saudi Arabia, in 1965, was the second largest producer in the Middle East; in area, though not in population, the largest country, with probably about a million square miles within its partly undefined frontiers. The ruling Saud family provides religious as well as temporal leaders. The nation is an absolutist monarchy with a considerable tinge of xenophobia; local Aramco employees, for example, live under fairly strictly isolated conditions. From an oil production of 1,860,000 barrels a day in 1965–66, the state received revenues amounting to about $650 million a year; its wells have been producing for more than a generation. The Dhahran structure was the first developed, followed by the Qatif and Abqaiq fields; since the war a huge structure known as Ghawar, some 150 miles long, has gradually been mapped out with the drill. Aramco has also offshore fields, Safaniya and Manifa, in production; these were among the first in the Middle East. According to the statistics, Kuwait has the largest reserves in the Middle East, with the Arabian figure not far below it; but most oilmen believe that Saudi Arabia's are probably already known to be even larger. About a quarter of Aramco crude leaves the country via TAPline to Sidon in Lebanon; the remainder goes out from ocean terminals, or via a sub-marine pipeline to Bahrain Island, a refining centre with some limited production of its own.

Under the prime ministership and since 1964 the rule of King Feisal, the Saudi kingdom too has been investing a major part of its oil revenues in general social development, while for its own part Aramco has developed social services to a considerable extent for its fairly large local labour force. Education and technical training, however, tend to separate these Arabian workers to some extent from the rest of the population, which is widely scattered, partly nomadic, and (by Western standards) a good deal less prosperous. Much of the country's budget goes on subsidies to the many nomadic tribes under Saudi tutelage; large sums, also, on maintaining the numerous royal family in what Arabs may think of as Occidental luxury; and in recent years a growing proportion on defence. Saudi Arabia supported the Yemen royalists against the Republican forces backed by Egypt: in many ways, King Feisal is a balancing force to President Nasser in the Arab world. In Arab politics, certainly, a conservative force, against President Nasser's

'Arab Socialism'; but inside Saudi Arabia, King Feisal has been a modernizing force as well as a paternal one.

In rather the same way, Saudi Arabia has sometimes been considered one of the conservative elements in OPEC, when it comes to pressing for change in oil dealings with the companies. But friendly relations with Aramco have not prevented it from being a determined and highly successful bargainer for change in its oil terms at home. In 1963, for example, it secured agreement from Aramco to large-scale relinquishments amounting to 64 per cent of the company's concession area (bringing the relinquished acreage up to 75 per cent of that originally granted); considerable improvements in its income from TAPline; changes in the methods of charging costs against taxable income that increased its 'take'; and an acceleration in the timing of income tax payments. These were very considerable, though not revolutionary changes, in the concession terms; other countries in the Middle East achieved comparable benefits later. The point is that 'conservative' Saudi Arabia achieved them first.[5] In bargaining about terms with newcomers on parts of this relinquished acreage, again, the Arabian government managed to secure, on paper, the most advantageous terms of all: an agreement with a French state-backed company Auxirap, in partnership with the Arabian national company Petromin. This agreement could give Arabia 80 per cent or more of the profits realized; it provided for 'integration forwards' of the Petromin interest into refining and marketing operations 'downstream'; and it did not include any provision protecting the French company against possible later changes in Saudi income tax rates. (It was not quite as specific as recent Iranian deals about the 'buy-back' price for crude between the partners, and it committed Petromin to rather more cash investment. But that may merely have meant that Arabia was more interested in serious participation in the oil business than in protecting its total revenues.) This kind of conservatism seems in no way backward in asserting—successfully— the country's Arab nationalism.

Iran, the oldest-established and, until nationalization in 1951, the leading producer in the Middle East, was, in 1965, only the third with an output of 93 million tons a year or 1,860,000 barrels a day. This nation has a population of 16 million, by far the largest in the area; though Muslims, the majority are not Arabs. Iran is a monarchy, today much more stably established than in the early fifties; but its government has still to deal with undercurrents of political unrest. Formally, Iran owns its own oil, and its National Oil Company takes part in the exploitation even of the area controlled by the international consortium. In practice, oil operations are still wholly managed by the consortium, though a large proportion of the ancillary 'non-basic' operations are handled directly by NIOC. The national company has done a certain amount of exploration in the remainder of Iran; in 1956, it brought in a spectacular discovery at Kum in central Iran, but did not establish any significant field worth developing. In the consortium territory, the longest established field is Masjid-i-Sulaiman, still producing some 55,000 barrels a day; but by far the largest of the area's 14 producing fields is Agha Jari (some 800,000 barrels a day), while output from the relatively new Gach Saran field is now increasing rapidly. Iran's proved reserves, at end-1965, totalled 40,000 million barrels. Abadan, with a capacity of about 430,000 barrels a day, is still one of the largest refineries in the world; with the switch to refining in market areas since the war, even east of Suez, its products now go mainly to balance demand in Eastern markets.

Iran often openly expresses dissatisfaction with the limited growth of its output in comparison with such states as Kuwait, which has 15–20 per cent more output and no more than an eightieth of its population. During the early sixties its output was, in fact, increasing much faster, and narrowing the difference (Kuwait output had been 40 per cent greater as recently as 1961). Nevertheless, the Iranians still feel entitled to achieve once again their historical primacy in Middle East oil production. In the initial 'production programme' agreed upon by OPEC in mid-1965, Iran stood out for an increase of 17·5 per cent, well above the average planned for all OPEC members. And it showed no sign of applying this to limit production; indeed, it used this projected increase, which was more than the Consortium companies were at the time planning, to ask them to step their output *up to* the increase that OPEC had agreed for Iran. During autumn 1965, again, the Shah of Iran himself emphasized that by 1970 he expected the country's output to reach 200 million tons a year, 4,000,000 barrels a day; the onus being on the Consortium, in particular, to achieve most of this enormous increase.

This attitude is not simply a matter of political aggrandisement. More coolly than some of their OPEC fellows, the Iranian authorities appear to have decided that oil produced now, surplus or not, is worth more to them than oil left in the ground for tomorrow. To the extent that it is produced by the Consortium, they can presume, their revenues per barrel from it cannot effectively fall. In the various partnership operations that NIOC is now engaged in with several foreign groups, total Iranian revenues depend to some extent on the state of the market; but the 'half-way price' arrangements in these, requiring the private partner to take as much of NIOC's crude as NIOC requires, may have laid a floor under Iranian revenue there too. (Whether if it suited Iran these minima would be relaxed remains to be seen.) Today, NIOC has a more practical stake in the world oil market than any other national oil company from a producing nation.

This attitude, again, is not too easy to fit into an OPEC policy of restricting the total amount of cheap oil on offer in order to harden prices. Iran is a founder member of OPEC, having welcomed this as an oil grouping representing the countries that really mattered. (It had been extremely cautious in its attitude towards the interest taken in oil by, for example, the Arab League.) It once defined its role in OPEC as that of a 'catalyst', though it was under Iranian leadership that the organization originally developed its secretariat and services. Its relations with Arab neighbours and OPEC fellow-members are not always particularly easy. But other OPEC members besides Iran may have mixed feelings about restriction to harden actual prices—while their own unit revenues are fixed anyway.

In July, 1958, when the former royal régime was overthrown in Iraq by a military revolution, the next government, under General Qasim, inherited some outstanding negotiations with the Iraq Petroleum Company. The new government claims, somewhat elaborated from those of the old, were for a very substantial change in a concession covering an oil industry that was producing, at the time, roughly 35 million tons or 725,000 barrels a day, which was then practically as high a rate as Iran's, with the capacity to increase output a good deal more rapidly. Eighteen months later, Qasim 'nationalized' most of Iraq's oil. In July 1965, negotiators for the companies and for the government that had succeeded (and killed) Qasim initialled an agreement for a new *modus vivendi* in Iraq. By that time, Iraq output was about 64 million tons, or 1,280,000 barrels a day; up by about 80 per cent over 1958. But Iranian output had grown by 125 per cent. And even in 1965, the latest Iraq government did not ratify the treaty.

The famous Kirkuk structure of IPC, which was first discovered in 1927, has been one of the most prolific fields in the history of the oil industry; by 1965 its cumulative output exceeded three and a quarter billion barrels. Its disadvantage is in location; it is 500 miles from tidewater, along the pipelines to Tripoli and Banias. The Mosul field in northern Iraq is on its way towards exhaustion, and must be the only field in the Middle East where oil is produced (to meet the minimum required under its concession) at a loss. In the south, the Basrah Petroleum Company, also owned by IPC, has comparatively rich fields at Zubair and Rumaila, these fields having the advantage of proximity to the Persian Gulf. Iraq is only about half as large as Iran, with a third of the population; its proved reserves of 25,000 million barrels, at end-1965, were the lowest of the 'Big Four' Middle East producing countries, but IPC had been forbidden to explore since 1961.

The issues in dispute between the Iraq government and the three grouped operating companies preceded and outlasted General Qasim. His 'Law 80' of December 1961 restricted the companies to their operations in well under 1 per cent of the original concession area. Following governments were certainly not prepared to abandon this principle.

From 1961 until 1965, therefore, the international oil companies that own IPC were deadlocked in dispute with the Iraq government, as Anglo-Iranian had been with the Iranian government ten years before. The deadlock, however, was comparatively peaceable. The government had cut off, in outlining IPC's 'unexplored areas', some 40 per cent of the group's proved oil reserves, mainly in the northern Rumaila field of the Basrah concession. This did not, however, leave IPC remotely short of oil for current output. Nor, except in Mosul, was the ban on further exploration immediately inconvenient (and even there it saved money on what had in recent years been an expensive, contractually necessary, but fruitless form of investment). The shareholders of IPC did not slow down their 'offtake' of oil though, as we have seen, the group's output did not rise as much as it probably would otherwise have done. The Iraq government, in 1964, passed another law setting up an Iraq National Oil Company, and requiring would-be concessionaires in the areas sequestrated to put in bids accepting INOC partnership (and effectively recognizing Law 80). The IPC group did not so apply; but from 1963 onwards cautious contacts, later becoming full negotiations, were resumed.

The agreement that was initialled in July 1965 by company and governmental negotiators in Baghdad had not, up to the time that this book was revised, been ratified by the Iraq government or published. But its main outlines had become known: and if these terms were accepted, they could produce a further twist of the screw all round the main Middle East concessions. It appeared that the IPC group would receive, in addition to the half per cent or so of its original concession area that it had been left in 1961, roughly as much territory again—but that this might include the prolific proven reserves of the North Rumaila field. (It could be expected, from this, that IPC and the government would then discuss an 'OPEC settlement' on royalty expensing; but that was not in the general agreement.) On a further large acreage—some 8–9 per cent of the original concession area, but evidently the best-assessed and most 'prospective' parts of it—a new joint venture company would be set up by certain of the IPC shareholder companies in partnership with the Iraq National Oil Company. These private companies—BP, Shell, Socony Mobil, CFP and Partex, but *not* the Jersey group—would jointly own two-thirds of the joint venture capital, and INOC one-third; its operations would be governed by the usual form of offtake and buy-back agreements, rather more complicated than most. The Iraq government-and-national company's likely income per barrel from this joint venture should be well above that from the main existing concessions, even after royalty expensing. They would not necessarily have all the fancy features of some of the latest participation deals with newcomers. But those deals were on uncommitted or already relinquished acreage; the Iraqi innovation was to have achieved such a deal with existing main concessionnaires on a large, highly prospective area out of the existing concession. This agreement was not ratified by the government to which it was presented in August 1965; indeed, it probably played some part in the break-up of that government. Three governments later, at the end of 1966, the agreement was still under consideration—by a government determined to stiffen its terms—and not to lose through IPC's dispute with Syria. Other member countries of OPEC were watching the Iraq government's deliberations with considerable interest. It would not take long from the signature of such an agreement in Iraq for its neighbours to be pressing for any elements in it that they thought better than their own existing terms.

Such an Iraq agreement—clearing up in its train a wide range of outstanding points at issue between the IPC group and governments all the way back to Nuri Said—would leave INOC free to engage in further concessions with other partners in the remaining 90 per cent or so of the original IPC concession area. This particular national oil company, headed by some of the ablest 'oil technocrats' in the Middle East, should be an extremely interesting one to watch. Iraq's former oil Minister, Dr Wattari, during whose term of office INOC was set up, was a strong advocate of the production programming that OPEC later adopted. Iraq was among the least likely OPEC members to let out concessions or rush oil to market if the result would be simply to soften prices further. Yet its staff were well aware of the cost of waiting, and of technical trends as well as rates of discount that are liable to reduce the value of oil left in the ground for production some time in the future.[6] The contradictory pressures on OPEC member countries would nowhere be more clearly appreciated—and faced—than in this one major producing country committed to 'Arab socialism'.

These along with the Persian Gulf peninsula of Qatar, which produced in 1965 215,000 barrels of crude a day, from reserves of 3,000 million barrels, are the longest-established producers in the Middle East. But production is being developed rapidly in some new areas of this prodigious oil region. By 1965, after only four years' production, Abu Dhabi had passed the level of output in Qatar, producing close on 15 million tons, say 285,000 barrels a day. Onshore, the concession is held by the IPC group; and during the years of stalemate in Iraq a good deal of investment may have been channelled from there into this tiny, barren sheikhdom on the Trucial Coast. But Abu Dhabi is 'big oil' even by Middle East standards; once the Murban field onshore and the Umm Shaif field offshore (held jointly by BP and CFP) had been proved, development was inevitable.

In the early years of production in Abu Dhabi, its former ruler, Shaikh Shakbut, became world famous as one of oil's few forbearing hosts: he steadily refused to change from his prewar pattern of a flat royalty (some 8-10 cents a barrel) to the 50:50 basis his concessionnaire companies were urging upon him. This was often publicized as *naïveté*. It could have been rationalized as subtlety. It was in fact probably no more than suspicion and disdain. In the first few years of any concession where the government charges income tax, the company can usually write off against taxable income the accumulated costs of exploration over past years. So the government is lucky if it gets more than the bare royalty anyway, and Shaikh Shakbut would have been no better off with a concession charging income tax. It was probably well worth waiting until his income from oil exports reached a level where the amortization of past exploration expenses inherent in an income tax deal bore a little less heavily upon the Shaik's income. When he finally did conclude 50:50 deals, in 1965, the Shaikh accepted what might be called the classic 50:50 pattern, with income reckoned according to posted price but the royalty credited against tax. By this time, it is fair to say, there were almost no others on that classic pattern left. But there can still be sense in accepting terms that give the concessionnaire some preferential advantage, during the initial growth phase of any producing country: look at Libya. The Westerner should always beware of rationalizing the behaviour of responsible Arabs according to his own logic: he had better accept them as they come.

Other nations in the area touch oil as transit countries. Vast amounts of oil move through the United Arab Republic, via the Suez Canal and the pipelines from Iraq and Saudi Arabia. Nationalization of the Canal in 1956 did not arise specifically from a desire to get a bigger revenue from this oil movement, but as a result of the refusal of Western finance for the High Dam at Aswan. Egypt could be classed in various of the categories of government exerting influence on oil that have been used in this book, from that of the nations seeking self-sufficiency to that of the consumer country putting pressure on its refining and marketing companies. It has a number of minor deposits, producing about half of its oil requirements, and in the early sixties granted a number of new partnership concessions offshore in the Gulf of Suez. In 1965, under one of these, Pan American UAR located a prolific field called El Morgan, which by 1970 was hoped alone to produce nearly double Egypt's 127,000 barrels-a-day output of 1965. This might allow 'substantial exports', and qualify Egypt for membership of OPEC. It has also been offering new concessions, generally for rather small areas by Middle East standards. But its main influence on oil in the region has been as a present leader of Arab nationalism.

The influence of the state that has been built up by President Nasser's authoritarian military government is very considerable throughout the Middle East. Egyptian teachers, from the largest reservoir of educated Arabs in the whole area, have influence in other Arab countries, particularly in Kuwait, which in periods of political emergency in the area has shown itself reluctant openly to dissociate itself from UAR policies. The Suez affair of the mid-fifties was not, on the whole, calculated to weaken Egyptian influence in the region. It emphasized the bargaining strength—up to a point—of a transit country athwart the main oil trade route: but also the logistic ability of the Western oil companies to make good supplies in the West and to move a large proportion of exports from the Persian Gulf by other routes. This odd trial of strength devalued Egyptian military pretensions, yet showed that President Nasser, over a few years, could get much of his way politically and economically despite defeat. It showed the Arabs, once again, the alarming strength of Israel. And the affair of the Suez

Canal pilots demonstrated that some of the claims of the West to a monopoly of technical competence were arrant nonsense. That point, politically unimportant in itself, might in the medium run be as important as any other implication of Suez for the oil industry in the Middle East. Egypt did not come as paradoxically well out of the Yemen war, where in backing the republicans it collided head-on with Saudi-Arabian backing of the royalists. This small, bloody little struggle was a drain both on Egypt's military manpower and its reputation in Arab counsels.

Syria and Lebanon, the other two important transit countries, affect oil exports from the Middle East mainly by their efforts to get full value for their geographical position. Effectively, the maximum price of such a transit position is the difference in cost to the operator of making use of the short cut or doing without it. This is very considerable for Iraq oil from the key Kirkuk field: the ban on access to the sea via Israel robs the oil producer of much of his bargaining power here. Late in 1966 the Syrian government, pressing IPC for higher pipeline dues, showed itself very conscious of this, pushing its demands to the point of 'nationalizing' the pipeline.

These Muslim countries of the Middle East form the greatest centre of oil exports in the world, with the largest reserves and—in spite of high government revenues—the lowest costs on crude production anywhere. But they are not the only significant oil exporters in the Eastern hemisphere. There are two other major exporting areas (both as it happens, also, largely Muslim by religion), North Africa and the East Indies.

During the early sixties, a number of substantial new oil-exporting areas were growing in importance as suppliers to Western Europe—at the same time, incidentally, as the newer Japanese, Italian and American ventures in the Persian Gulf area have begun to offer their production at full rate on the international market. The French effort in the Sahara has been discussed already: its oil has been followed to Europe, and passed, by much larger quantities of Libyan production. These new exporting areas—which were the only two of major significance to be opened up for oil in the late fifties—are very often discussed as 'alternative sources' to the Middle East, and it is obvious that to expand production they had to compete in the main markets of oil from the region. But it should also be recognized that Libya, at any rate, is an Arab country that welcomes private enterprise in oil, but is no longer inclined to accept less favourable terms for the development of it than other host governments receive. And the Sahara, developed largely by French efforts, has been transformed overnight from a French, largely nationalized, enterprise ready to accept low prices from Algeria in order to pump this oil into new markets in the European Economic Community into a foreign enterprise operating in the territory of another Arab government, not far away from the Middle East. Algeria will no doubt continue to co-operate with France—so long as both need each other.

Both these areas enjoy a very large freight advantage to Europe. But Algerian oil, in the Sahara, has high transport costs to tidewater: much of the Libyan output is nearer the coast. When Libyan output, in commercial terms, began in September 1961, Saharan output had already reached 320,000 barrels a day. By 1965 Algerian output was still only about 26 million tons a year, 550,000 barrels a day; Libya was producing more than twice as much. Even for a producer like Jersey, moving most of its oil at not far below posted prices (and paying tax in 1964 at about 90 cents a barrel), Libyan output appeared more profitable than almost any other. For independents who up to 1964 paid little more than the bare royalty of about 27 cents a barrel, Libyan crude offered bonanza profits even at heavily discounted prices.

Much has been said about the probable extent of the reserves of the Sahara: very little, by comparison, about the oil resources and possibilities of Libya. The reserves of 10 billion barrels published for 1965 represent pretty meaningless estimates, with output rising rapidly and many new concessions only just beginning to operate. By the same token, it is hard to guess at costs, while one has some idea of the amount of oil to set against investment. Drilling began in Libya in 1956; shows of oil were recorded in 1957, and in June, 1959, Jersey Standard brought in its 'Zelten No. 1' in an area about 200 miles south of Benghazi, reporting an initial flow of 17,500 barrels a day, which is a big find for anywhere. Other companies, particularly Oasis, a joint subsidiary of certain big American newcomers to international oil, had very rich discoveries not long after. Jersey is on its own in Libya (as Shell is off Kuwait). This partly reflects the concessionary circumstances: Libya in 1955 enacted a petroleum law (with the assistance of the oil companies) that cut up the country into a fairly large number of exploration areas, with limits to the total acreage for which any company can hold permits in each of four major zones of the country. In 1961, as relinquished acreage from the first of these began to come up for re-letting, the Libyan government in its turn amended its legislation, ending the possibility of a 25 per cent depletion allowance provided in its 1955 law. The initial terms were generous; in 1961 they were made rather less so; and in 1966, after threats to stop exports and help from other OPEC members, Libya forced through the revision to a posted price basis mentioned at the beginning of this book. Some companies in the oil industry—whose interests were not, this time for once, affected—were inclined to approve.

Even this sharp 1965 rise in government demands did not necessarily make Libya a bad bargain for the companies producing there. And other African territories, where oil search had been stepped up after Suez, were paying off. When this book was first being discussed, in the late fifties, Nigeria ranked as one of the industry's bad bets: millions had been drilled in there to no result. Since then, success has transformed it. By 1965, it was exporting about 13,300,000 tons a year, and surging ahead. During that year, there were half a dozen companies drilling on or off Nigerian shores: every one of them struck new finds of oil or gas.

Oil production in the East Indies, from Borneo, Sumatra and Brunei, formed part of the foundations of both Shell and the Royal Dutch companies that later came together; the original Standard Oil interest continued as Stanvac; and Caltex has considerable interests in the area. Originally a large-scale net exporter, the Far East as a whole was broadly self-sufficient up to the Second World War. Its oil producing industry, in most parts of the area, was very largely destroyed by retreating Allied and, later, Japanese forces. The physical rehabilitation of the industry took time. But it took even longer to approach political calm after the withdrawal from the area of its former colonial rulers; and though the oil companies operating there were able to achieve a considerable increase in production, and discover large new reserves, they found it hard to achieve any lasting *modus vivendi* with the government of the main producing country, Indonesia.

The Indonesian government was then committed to nationalization, though it soon appeared the word could mean many different things. A law nationalizing the operations of the foreign companies was in fact enacted in 1960; but after lengthy discussions, in late 1963 the government agreed to settlements under this law which left the companies able to work out their concession periods as contractors to it, on not particularly stringent financial terms. This could have been an advantageous working arrangement for both sides. But continued political turbulence in the area—complicated by the 'confrontation' of minor frontier warfare between Indonesia and the newly-formed Federation of Malaysia—continued to make business operations there precarious. At the end of 1965 one of the companies involved, Shell, decided to sell its interests to the government, partly for cash down and partly for instalments over a period that might be taken in crude oil. Whether the other companies would carry on was uncertain; yet the area remained attractive, Caltex in particular having developed very large-scale production from fields located since the war. And production continues to rise, with new foreign capital—notably Japanese—being attracted into the exploration possibilities there. In 1965, output was nearly 26 million tons, or about 520,000 barrels a day; and explorers were reporting significant new strikes. Indonesia, too, has interests as a future market as well as a producer—providing it can achieve political stability and economic advance for its 100 million people.

Sarawak, one of the former oil-producing territories of the East Indies, joined the Malaysian Federation; Brunei, the main oil-producing state of today in the British sphere of Borneo, did not. Actual production has dwindled to very little in Sarawak, though it remains a significant refining centre for the region; Brunei's output, which had been sinking from its traditional fields, is now growing from new offshore fields; in 1965 the total was about 3,750,000 tons, or 75,000 barrels a day, refined in Sarawak or Singapore or shipped to customers in Australasia.

During the middle fifties, when the upsurge of world oil demand seemed unlikely to weaken, and countries expected prices to stay firm, the pressure of host governments upon the oil companies operating in the Middle East was mainly for bigger shares than the established 50 per cent of an income they expected to go on growing. As the market slipped into surplus, the emphasis changed. The governments became more cautious in proposing changes in their concessionary relationship with the companies, and their pressure shifted towards the maintenance of posted prices on which profit shares are paid regardless of the actual prices realized, and increases of export offtake. So far, in spite of price cuts in 1959, and again—though the countries have not yet officially recognized them—in 1960, a continued rise in offtake has maintained their income and indeed kept it rising somewhat. The cuts in posted prices were, however, recognized in one way at least. They triggered off what had long been discussed as a possibility on both sides of the Middle East oil business—a compact of the governments of oil-exporting countries.

334

CHAPTER XX

Producers: Interests in Common

After Dr Mohammed Mossadegh nationalized the Iranian oil industry in 1951, he made many speeches. I have not managed to discover, in extracts published from them, whether or not he asked for the support of other oil-producing nations in his dispute with the 'Western oil imperialists'. But if he did, his appeal was unsuccessful. The other oil-producing nations benefited from the shutdown in Iran through very sharp increases in their own output. The dispute was, in particular, the beginning of the meteoric rise of Kuwait oil production. And its legacy lasted long after the dispute was resolved and Iranian output resumed in 1954; indeed, to the mid-sixties. Early in 1966, in pressing for a faster increase in planned output in Iran, the Shah and his government were continuing to cite the extent to which Iran had lost its rightful place in the forefront of Middle East output in the fifties and deserved to regain it.

The late General Qasim, when he decided on nationalization in Iraq, bore that example in mind. One of the first public statements from Baghdad, after his Iraq government in December 1961 produced legislation seizing 99 per cent of the concession areas of the Iraq, Basrah and Mosul oil companies, was to ask the co-operation and support of its OPEC partners. In particular, they were asked not to benefit at its expense. These countries, at the first meeting of OPEC in 1960, had agreed not to benefit in this way at the expense of any fellow-member in dispute with an oil company: Iraq was only seeking implementation of this resolution. In practice, the issue never openly arose in quite this way. The countries concerned were in any case expecting continued increases in production, and achieved these. The companies operating in Iraq never had to interrupt, or reduce, output. But in fact these companies did put more of their group investment into non-Iraq areas such as Abu Dhabi during the period of deadlock. Iraq output rose only slowly from 1961 to 1965; and output in other Middle East OPEC

335

countries rose much faster. These countries did not choose to benefit at Iraq's expense. But some of them can hardly have avoided doing so indirectly.

The Libyan government, in the threat of unilateral action chronicled at the beginning of this book, by which it compelled recalcitrant concessionnaires to accept more onerous financial terms, was even more careful. Its amendment of its petroleum law was designed to allow it to take full advantage of an agreement reached with certain oil companies after lengthy negotiations on demands originally formulated by OPEC. No doubt it had the benefit of advice from OPEC as to just how it should implement this agreement. Quite certainly, it cleared in advance with OPEC what it finally decided to do. During the final arguments with the companies holding out, OPEC held one of its regular conferences. And though its member governments are generally enjoined to secrecy about their deliberations until all resolutions have been ratified, a month or so later, OPEC lost no time in letting it be known that it would offer Libya practical support. Its conference recommended that member governments should not grant any new oil concessions to Libyan concessionnaires who had refused to agree to the new Libyan law—or indeed to any groups in which such companies had an interest of 10 per cent or more. This was not idle support; some of the OPEC countries had concession acreage on offer, and some of the Libyan concessionnaires holding out were interested. How important it was, nobody outside can ever know. But it was the first clear example of an OPEC member country, in dispute with oil companies, seeking and being afforded more than formal support from fellow-members of the organization. OPEC has often been compared to 'a host government's trade union': in this case, the 'industrial action' was being 'made official'.

More frequently, of course, OPEC has been compared to an oil producers' cartel. If it succeeds in becoming one, it would not be the first—nor even the first contemplated between governments. But the others either did not last long, or never got off the ground.

Concerted action among the people in control of the oil supplies entering into world trade is not a new idea, as we have seen in earlier chapters. Some degree of agreed limitation on output and marketing between major companies, American and British, existed during the thirties, though it was not perhaps entirely effective. That was not resumed after the end of the war, partly in response to public and governmental attitudes towards restrictive agreements of this kind. But sometimes the idea of concerted control had come from governments. During the Second World War the governments of the United States and Britain reached agreement to promote an international pact that among other things would have provided that

> 'supplies should be derived from the various producing areas of the world, with due consideration of such factors as available reserves, sound engineering practices, relevant economic factors and interests of producing and consuming countries and with a view to provide full satisfaction to all. . . .'

and

> 'that the adoption of these principles can best be promoted by an international agreement among all countries interested in the petroleum trade, either as producers or consumers.'

The two governments agreed to set up an International Petroleum Commission with 'partly fact-finding and partly advisory' functions. Oil producers inside the United States suspected that its vague wording implied some form of government-sponsored international cartel; their suspicions, and some opposition in Washington, were understandably aroused by a proposal that action under it should be exempted from the provisions of the anti-trust laws. The agreement was re-written, and signed once again; but even in this revised form, the American Senate would not have it, and it disappeared into that limbo to which so many other 'plans for the post-war future' also found their way.[1] The signatory governments had emphasized the need to conduct the world petroleum trade 'in an orderly manner'. For the next ten years, the major international companies took the responsibility for that.

On many occasions during that next decade, proposals were put forward for the 'international control of oil resources', or for the 'regional development of the Middle East'. They came, in the first place, mainly from the West, which did not improve their reception among the nations actually concerned. Some came from private theorists or semi-political bodies; one or two actually from governments, as in 1957 when the Italian government proposed that a financial pool should be created to back economic development of the whole region, with contributions from the United States and Western Europe. In August 1958, following the American landings in the Lebanon, President Eisenhower actually put forward a proposal for an Arab development institution. This was discussed in the United Nations, which invited the Secretary General to confer with the Arab countries on the point, but nothing came of it either.

Nor were similar ideas lacking in the Middle East itself, among politicians and among Arab personalities concerned with oil. The Arab League first took a direct interest in oil at the time of the Palestine War in 1948: it prevailed upon the government of Iraq to force the suspension of shipments through the pipeline to the Haifa refinery at the time, and later, over a period of years, put pressure on oil companies marketing in Israel to withdraw. In 1951 it set up an 'Oil Experts' Committee', and in 1954, it decided to establish a permanent Petroleum Department. It was this department, under the directorship of Mr. Mohammed Salman, an Iraqi engineer, who organized the Arab Oil Congresses in 1949 and 1951; after the second, Mr. Salman became the petroleum minister of General Qasim's government in Iraq, and held this position at the time of the 'forced relinquishment' of the undeveloped areas of the concessions there. It was within the Arab League's committees that most of the ideas concerning pan-Arab policies for oil were first formulated. Although its membership includes some states that have little effective say in oil, and it could never hope to wield so direct and concentrated an influence as OPEC aspires to, the League's intellectual influence on 'Arab economic aspirations', which are largely aspirations regarding oil, has been and may remain significant.

Its committee of oil experts includes a number of the 'Arab technocrats', but their influence extends beyond it and is one of the strengths of OPEC. The group is real, recognizable, and among the more dynamic elements in the social and governmental pattern of the Middle East. These youngish men differ rather significantly, to the casual observer at least, from the similarly aspiring intelligentsia of other developing societies. Their education is sometimes technological rather than legal. Their ladder of advancement has not been primarily political, but within the semi-technical administrative departments that each of the host governments has necessarily created to handle its contacts with its tenant oil company. They have benefited, within these departments, from the absolute shortage of Arabs educated to understand this industry. The rise of some of them, within these departments, has been meteoric, so that able young men not long out of their twenties are at the heads of departments that deal with the companies, and in some cases are government-appointed directors to their boards.

In some ways, the careers that have been so open to the talents of these young men have possibly made for political stability in certain of these countries. The surplus of briefless advocates and other unemployed intellectuals which has so often featured in nationalist politics in other developing (and developed) countries, seems less evident in the oil-producing Arab countries; and where violent political change has come, it has come mainly from military circles. The graduate, in the oil states, need not lack advancement. Educated 'technocrats' may or may not be, as one of them once suggested, 'well placed to enforce, in the long run, practically every point they mean.'[2] Their personal isolation, in some cases, from the feudal social structure of the states they serve, may be uncomfortable and is certainly vulnerable. But they are entrenched in, and while they are in such short supply often essential to, the absolutist governments of these states. Some of them are radical in temper, which in countries of such glaring contrasts between riches and poverty is not surprising. But their radicalism does not need to express itself in politics. They already have the positions of influence that in other countries political radicals might dream of attaining.

These positions, however, do not guarantee them political influence inside their countries. Their political influence is likely to depend upon their success in dealing, on behalf of the host government, with the oil companies. This in itself might tend to canalize their radicalism into seeking always to improve the bargain that the government gets. The better that bargain, the better their chance of achieving, say, the economic development that they believe their country needs. But the tenant oil company, as a nexus of economic power controlled from outside, is liable to be an affront to their patriotic ambitions anyway. In a sense, therefore, nationalism, radicalism and the favour of the ruling families may all press the 'technocrat' in the same direction—towards seeing what more can be gained from the companies. Moreover these young men, whose position rests largely upon their talents and their scarce technical competence, are certain to see possibilities in common action by at least the oil-producing states; also, perhaps, personally but not unworthily, the strength that their own positions can gain from participation and recognition on a larger than national stage. Their training will help them to appreciate the possibility of joint economic and technical action among host governments. It was inevitable that some of these Arab technocrats should have been among the founders of OPEC. And since the same relationship towards foreign oil, though not the same social or political background, exists in Venezuela, it was inevitable that radical intellectuals there, too, should have been ready to co-operate.

The pipe-line project, much discussed in 1957, was avowedly to be based upon the profits available then from TAPline; one of the points made, at a time when the pipelines from Iraq to the Mediterranean were in course of repair, was that if it were owned jointly by Arab countries no one of them would ever be prepared to cut the line. Within a year or two, however, there was a world surplus of tankers and even TAPline alone was working well below capacity: Arab investment in pipelines looked less attractive.

The formation of national oil companies in each producing country, again, was one of the recommendations of the first Arab Petroleum Congress, and the Arab League has long advocated fuller participation by the governments in the later stages of oil operations.

Venezuela was represented, by observers, at the first Arab Petroleum Congress; for the first time, all the great oil exporting countries were sitting down together. Eighteen months later, it was one of the founder members of OPEC. Venezuela had been the leader in unilateral action to increase its share of oil profits, by its new income tax in 1958; but the results, as other oil-producing governments were already noting, were not turning out to be quite what it had hoped. This action did increase its revenue per barrel straight away; but with access to its main United States market limited, and oil available at much lower 'tax-paid cost' to producers elsewhere, both its growth in output and the spending on exploration in Venezuela began to dwindle. Logically, it joined the governments of the Middle East when they protested against cuts made in posted prices, and hence their oil revenues per barrel, without their consent. For these governments, the cuts meant lower unit revenues with no confidence of any larger growth in output than they expected already. For Venezuela, the cuts further reduced the 'tax-paid cost' of the oil with which its own had to compete. And any cuts made in the price of Venezuelan oil to meet this competition— even occasional discounts—affected Venezuelan government revenue. For Venezuela, unlike most Middle East oil countries, then taxed oil profits according to the prices actually realized, not according to posted prices. The motives of Venezuela in helping to found OPEC, therefore, may not have been quite identical with those of the Middle East governments involved. But the overriding common interest was real.

When these producing governments came together to join OPEC, and during the first five years of its existence, the direct concern of the organization was practically concentrated on Middle East oil. It began with a joint refusal to recognize the cuts in posted prices of August 1960 which had been made without these governments' consent.

(These cuts had been made throughout the Middle East; but not in Venezuela.) In 1961 its resolutions mentioned studies of international proration schemes, but these remained studies, for the time. Its first positive demands, in July 1962, again concerned its Middle East members: it called for the restoration of posted prices to their pre-August 1960 levels, for the abolition of the marketing allowances against tax given in some Middle East countries, and for the expensing of royalties. Posted prices do not affect Venezuelan oil revenue; its tax rules allowed only the charging of actual expenses incurred in marketing; and royalties there were already expensed for tax reasons. (Its royalty rate, incidentally, is higher than in the Middle East; in OPEC's mid-1962 arguments there was some discussion of increasing the rate of Middle East royalties, but no action was ever taken to press for this.)

The 1962–64 discussions that ensued between representatives of OPEC governments—in some stages but not all involving officials of the organization itself[3]—did not therefore directly affect Venezuela. Nor did they affect Indonesia, which became a member of OPEC in 1962. Libya, which also joined in 1962, did not have identical tax rules to the Middle East founder members of OPEC; but as we have seen, it did participate in the negotiations and the eventual agreements, and later took its own action to bring itself into line with these other governments in reaping the benefits.

The demand for restoration of posted prices to the levels before August 1960 was hardly, in practice, discussed between the governments and the oil companies concerned: eventually, in a 'quit-claim' clause to the royalty expensing agreements, the governments gave tax clearances on the reduced price basis up to the end of 1963, with the royalty expensing formula taking effect from the tax year 1964 onwards. The marketing allowance was reduced by the companies to a flat half-cent per barrel; for some countries during 1963, and eventually for all those agreeing on royalty expensing back to 1963. The expensing of royalties was eventually agreed; but in doing so the companies were able to stipulate discounts off posted prices, for tax purposes only, of $8\frac{1}{2}$ per cent for 1964; $7\frac{1}{2}$ per cent (for a 'base crude') for 1965; and $8\frac{1}{2}$ per cent (for the base crude) for 1966. (For the two later years, the actual discounts for any given crude were varied according to its gravity, as discussed in Chapter IX.) For later years, variation of the discount was left formally to the companies, but these agreed to consider any representations the governments might make about the level of actual market prices. This negotiation took a fairly long time, though $150 million a year, to the governments concerned, was probably worth waiting a couple of years or so. There does not appear to have been unity, at all times, among the OPEC governments concerned; nor for that matter among the companies on the other side of the table. On the OPEC side, at one point, the governments were asked to face the possibility of taking unilateral action to compel acceptance of their demands. At that time, late in 1963, not all the members were prepared to go so far. The final offers of the companies, at the end of 1964, were eventually accepted by the governments of Iran, Kuwait, Libya, Qatar and Saudi Arabia. (Kuwait was later unable to get its governmental acceptance ratified in its National Assembly; and in Libya, deciding how to implement acceptance took a year.)

Iraq, which had been one of the governments concerned ready to urge unilateral action to achieve these demands in 1963, did not accept the companies' final offer. It complained that two of the conditions they stipulated—the 'most-favoured company clause' and a provision for automatic arbitration on disputes in carrying out the supplementary agreements—infringed the sovereignty of the host governments. (Two of the governments agreeing, Iran and Saudi Arabia, accepted these provisions in principle, but in practice, when making the supplementary agreements, were able to weaken them considerably in practice; so much so that the companies had later to moderate the stipulations that Kuwait and Qatar had accepted to bring the four countries into line.) Iraq, in any case, was already in dispute on fundamental issues regarding its own concession acreage with the companies which had offered these supplementary agreements: and another thing it objected to was that these companies, in making it the offer too, had stipulated that its provisions should remain in abeyance pending agreement in the larger argument. Even later in 1965, when its representatives initialled a draft agreement on the internal questions of its own concessions, it wholly excluded any acceptance of the 'OPEC settlement'; and in public at any rate showed no signs of withdrawing its own objections on the issue of sovereignty.

As an organization, OPEC never gave its collective approval to the acceptance of these royalty expensing settlements by the five member governments concerned. The debate over approval of the companies' final offer, at Djakarta at the end of 1964, appears to have been a heated one and turned out to be irreconcilable. Iraq, the member government concerned that opposed acceptance, was supported in its opposition by

Venezuela and Indonesia, two member governments that were not directly concerned—and to whose problems OPEC had never, up to that time, practically directed its attention. Eventually it was agreed to leave the question of acceptance to the governments directly involved, each for itself; and to pass on to questions concerning the whole OPEC membership.

It could be argued that all OPEC had achieved had been on behalf of its Middle East members, not the others. Alternatively, you could rationalize it a little sourly by saying that anything which increased the tax-paid cost of Middle East oil helped Venezuela by making its oil to some extent more competitive. (No easy rationalization about how OPEC's actions have, or could, help Indonesia, is possible. Indonesian oil policy is individualistic, and generally inscrutable; it shows no sign of needing anyone's help, though it has an instinctive readiness for solidarity against the Western companies and a taste for unilateral action by legislation rather than protracted negotiation.) In its deeper effect, however, the OPEC settlement, as eventually applied, was of significance to all host governments in the oil business. For the first time, OPEC member governments gained an admitted right to consultation before changes in tax reference prices. Moreover the supplementary agreements facilitated, and almost encouraged, Libya's shift from taxation on the basis of realized prices to a basis of posted prices.

This, in particular, was not lost on Venezuela. At an OPEC conference in December 1965, the Organization's Economic Commission (set up that year to study the problem of production programming) was instructed to study the implications of applying posted prices for tax purposes in all member countries. Venezuela and Indonesia were the only two where this system, by the beginning of 1966, still applied. Venezuela for some years had been putting pressure on concessionnaires to limit the discounts off posted prices that they accepted in export sales. At the end of 1965, it proposed to apply a maximum discount of 10 per cent for tax purposes on sales of residual fuel oil—mainly to the United States, where restrictions upon these particular imports were in process of being removed. In autumn 1966, as noted in Chapter XVIII, it did also move its crude oil, for tax purposes, on to a 'tax reference' price basis—characteristically raising its basic income tax rate in the process. But the margins of net profit on Venezuelan oil are already thinner than in the Middle East countries. Unless actual prices in the market can be raised as well as Venezuelan government revenues per barrel, such a shift could simply result in Venezuelan oil losing more ground to competing oil—from members and non-members of OPEC.

One kind of measure that would be considered of unquestionable advantage to all OPEC members alike—to say nothing of the oil companies on the other side of the table—would be anything that could raise the actual prices paid for oil in a world market dominated by potential surplus. It was not surprising, therefore, following upon the royalties settlement—a gain for OPEC, but not one acceptable to all members—that the Organization should have turned back once again, in 1965, to the idea of production control. This was a mild form of international proration designed to arrange things so that the potential surplus simply did not, in any given year, actually materialize and depress prices in the market.

OPEC insisted, when it formulated this production programme at its conferences in spring and summer 1965, that it was not trying to control the total exports of crude oil from its member countries. It analysed the surplus—in my own view correctly—as arising from the availability of proven reserves capable of being brought into production rapidly at additional costs low enough to offer comfortable profits even if sold at prices cut yet further. What it proposed was to control the access to these reserves, by limiting the increase in output from each of its member countries so that the total would rise no more than it estimated world demand would rise during the next twelve months. Its method, in detail, was to estimate the increase in demand likely over the next twelve months, and revise this estimate every three months. Given this percentage increase for the OPEC producing countries as a whole, it then sought to reach agreement between them on the percentage increases to be allocated to each individual country. From its three-monthly revisions of its demand forecasting, it would be able to revise its 'production programme' for each country. And in the last three months of each twelve-month period the OPEC member governments should instruct their concessionnaire companies not to produce or export more than enough to bring the yearly percentage increase up to the amount allotted under the finally revised programme.

If the OPEC royalties settlement had informally encroached quite a little further than before upon the companies' prerogative of setting their own prices, this production programme encroached quite openly and formally upon the companies' right under their concessions to decide how much oil they should export from each country in which they had production. It is true that the first programme, which was 'leaked' though never officially published by OPEC in mid-1965, was a generous one. The percentage increase for the total OPEC area was more than would necessarily be achieved in the twelve months to June 1966. The percentage increases allotted individual countries, for the most part, were also higher than seemed likely to be achieved—in most cases. (The percentages allotted varied widely, from increases of 32 per cent for Qatar and 20 per cent for Libya down to 6·5 per cent for Kuwait and 3·3 per cent for Venezuela.) In some cases, the figures were well above what the country could ordinarily have expected: Iran, indeed, lost no time in asking its concessionnaires to arrange to increase their output enough to hit its production target of an increase of 17·5 per cent.

If the actual figures set raised no problem for the companies, should they have raised no objection or even ignored them? They decided that they should not—because this might have been interpreted, at least in OPEC's publicity, as acceptance of their host government's instructions or of the OPEC programme on which these were based. By the beginning of 1966, in certain OPEC countries, the concessionnaire companies were rejecting any such communications from the host government, and insisting that the issue should be taken to arbitration. This raised problems within OPEC. Some of its member countries, notably Saudi Arabia, were unwilling in the circumstances to accept any production programme for the second half of the initial twelve-month period; these could argue, also, that some other countries were doing their best to raise output without any regard for the percentages designed to stabilize prices. Shaikh Yamani of Saudi Arabia felt 'The main target is price, now. . . . If the present price programme does not work, we must try something else. Stop taxing on a realized price basis.'

Nevertheless, the logic of OPEC's situation will drive it towards perseverance with the idea of production control—unless prices come to be stabilized in some other way. In the United States, as we have seen in an earlier chapter, proration does effectively control the volume of domestic oil coming on to the market and keep prices up, even if it works untidily and with many wasteful side-effects. Since import restrictions were imposed in the United States, total supplies from home and abroad are now regulated; and in effect, whatever its motives, the whole complex of American oil legislation tends to operate as a price support programme. But this programme works inside one nation; though state governments are responsible for the output controls, the law that prevents widespread evasion of these controls is federal, as are the import restrictions that have had to be invoked to aid proration. Another reason why proration works in the United States is that one dominant producer, Texas, has often been prepared to act as the balance-wheel, taking the biggest cuts in its own output to stabilize total supplies, even though some states do not control production at all. These circumstances may be essential to any successful proration of oil supplies—or even to OPEC's 'production programming'.

In some comments (and complaints) that he voiced about OPEC's initial production programme early in 1966, Shaikh Ahmed Yamani, Saudi Arabia's oil minister, argued that the percentage increases allotted to member governments should be worked out according to some clear and logical formula.[4] The formula he suggested recalled that suggested at the second Arab Petroleum Congress in November 1960; that year the kind of formula that one might use was discussed by one of the Saudi Arabian delegation. Mr M. J. Sladie, an American consultant, had suggested that the factors to be taken into consideration might be

(1) the average annual net export achieved during any three-year period preceding proration. Nations would be entitled to declare an average rate at less than the maximum achieved in the past if they wished, in order to conserve their resources;

(2) the proportion of each nation's reserves to the total reserves of all net exporting nations; and

(3) estimates of net world demand.

The formula he proposed would be 'the maximum declaration plus the product of the ratio of the exporting nation's reserves to the total reserves of all nations ready to export above their maximum declaration, and the difference between net world demand and the total of all nation's declarations'. Mr. Sladic made allowance for the introduction into such a scheme of new exporting nations; and also, notionally at least, for problems that might arise for companies whose production in any given area was held down through proration to a level that would sharply reduce their return on investment. He recognized the difficulties that would be encountered in carrying through any such scheme—such as the need to standardize estimates of reserves, conservation practice, the forecasting of market demand, and any necessary estimates of return on investment.[5]

That formulae could be worked out to govern an international proration scheme, even one going beyond OPEC's tentative 'programming', is not in doubt; and the international 'infra-structure' necessary to administer one might be formed and might just possibly be able to work. But two main obstacles to such a scheme seemed very hard to overcome: namely, that consumer countries would regard it as an oil producers' cartel run by governments, and that it would effectively remove a large part of the managerial control that oil companies possess over their own businesses. These two objections are linked. For the international oil companies' right to supply any given market from whatever source they choose means flexibility in maintaining supplies; and this is the main guarantee that consumer countries rely on when increasing their dependence on petroleum imports.

For the host governments themselves, the intrinsic difficulties of successful proration or programming would arise partly in reconciling the different interests of the different member countries. First, the major exporters would have to allow a disproportionate share of the growth of demand, however small this might be to start with, for newcomers and potential entrants to the world oil market. Secondly, the interests of the Middle East would have to be reconciled with those of Venezuela, at a time when that exporting country's 'natural markets' in North America are being protected against its supplies. Third, even within the Middle East there are some jealousies regarding rates of growth in production; it would need very obvious success in stabilizing and then pushing up prices to still all of these. And it must be remembered that countries with taxation already linked to posted prices would gain no direct benefit from any rise that might be achieved in actual market prices.

An increase in actual market prices, admittedly, could have an indirect effect upon the revenues per barrel of countries with taxes linked to posted prices, through the alterations due for 1967 and later years in the 'OPEC discount' applied to posted prices. OPEC also argued, in its explanation of 'production programming', that if actual sales prices were allowed to slip further they must 'debilitate . . . an already unsatisfactory structure of posted prices'.[6] This seemed to imply more readiness to assume that posted prices might be cut than OPEC members had manifested in the previous five years. But it is true that as host governments become more directly concerned with the market—through national companies, or even through the initiative they may soon acquire regarding their concessionaires' incremental sales—they will want the best prices that they can get.

Here I am referring to the possibility Professor Adelman is fond of citing—that national governments, with their concessionaires driven down to a barely acceptable return on capital, may have to decide whether to gain a sale by shading their own revenue per barrel or to lose it by sticking to the letter of their tax law. That may never happen with private concessionnaires' sales: it remains to be seen. I think it quite liable to happen where their own national companies are concerned, whether or not these are operating in partnership with private oil companies. Most of the recent partnership concession agreements do provide for agreed discounts of one kind or another that might be granted to secure business not otherwise obtainable.

This is a normally competitive situation. Whether it will arise between host governments, if these become the last people left making really fat returns out of crude oil, remains to be seen. But if it does, the very fatness of the margin that many of these retain, and the variability of their costs, may make going out for business alone a more practicable and attractive proposition for them than sticking together in a production programming cartel and hoping that it works.

The common interest of the governments of oil-producing countries, perhaps, is strongest when the private companies that produce their oil have really fat profits that can readily be squeezed. As the process is repeated, and this net profit margin earned by the companies grows slimmer, the gains to be achieved by collective pressure upon them become harder to achieve. Beyond these companies' leaner margins, there are always the customers, whom it may be possible to make pay more. But these are a little harder to reach; and have the chance, if pressed too hard, to go away to find some other fuel. They do not fall within any jurisdiction of the oil countries' governments; indeed, they have governments of their own. Collective action may continue to interest the producing governments more, or seem more dignified, than seeking their individual advantage competitively, in the coming years. But if it does and becomes effective, it may be faced with collective action by consumer governments.

In both kinds of government there are politicians inclined to argue that more direct contact between producers and consumers at this level need not in any way mean a collision of interests: and that it might serve both of their interests better than they are served now.[7] During the next decade, these more direct contacts will almost certainly increase in scope. Does that imply the likelihood of some shrinkage in the role of the international oil business itself?

Part Three

Part Three

CHAPTER XXI

Pressure from Producers

One of the first acts of the Organization of Petroleum Exporting Countries after it set up headquarters in Geneva in 1961 was to commission three Western economic intelligence agencies to look into the economic behaviour of the Western oil companies. These agencies reported, in the first place, in time for the OPEC meeting of spring 1962: their remits included studies of the rate of return on oil investment in production and other operations, of the pricing of crude oil and products, and of the financial arrangements between companies and host governments. These subjects, as patient readers of this book may appreciate, offer plenty of meat for study—and argument. The arguments, from interested personalities in the host countries, had never been lacking. What was new in OPEC's better organized approach was the determination that from now on such arguments need never again lack any documentation and briefing that the best impartial consultancy available anywhere can make available. It served notice on the international oil industry that within a very short time they would have to expect countries negotiating with them that have access to OPEC to be as well briefed as they are themselves. Since that time, a number of argumentative papers emanating from OPEC, and its rapid rejoinders to pronouncements from within major oil companies, have continued to emphasize how much this briefing has improved.

Even before OPEC arrived, these companies needed no notice that the petroleum exporting countries were dissatisfied with their existing financial arrangements with the industry, and bent on changing them. Since the late fifties, many ideas had been in the air about the revision of the basic financial relationships between these governments and the oil companies. And though the initiative came largely from the governments, oilmen were not lacking, even within the most conservative of companies, to feel that the existing formulae promised, for the future, little but trouble. It was easier, admittedly, to find people who felt the international companies had 'painted ourselves into a corner', or who would agree that the time had come for 'a breakthrough', than people who had any solution that they were confident about themselves, or that they could persuade many of their colleagues was worth taking seriously. But much more widely than was perhaps evident from their public pronouncements, there existed an acceptance within the companies—resigned or even bitter rather than hopeful—of the likelihood of considerable change soon.

From the side of the governments, the elements coming into prominence in new concession agreements and in demands for revision of existing ones, during the sixties, have been 'participation' for host governments in the production (and, they would hope, in later stages of operations) of oil from beneath their land; the demand, whether as formal partners or not, for consultation with host governments over prices; the returning element of 'relinquishment'; and continuing desire, under one formula or another, for a steadily larger government share of the profits. At the beginning of the sixties, these were accompanied by demands for the 'relinquishment' of concession acreage that the concessionnaire companies had not developed. By 1965, in most of the major Middle East concessions, this had been conceded: acreage representing between 50 and 90 per cent of the original concessions had been handed back. In Libya and Venezuela, too, there was plenty of free acreage for governments to let out on new terms—provided they could choose a formula and find takers.

Several newcomers to the Middle East, during the middle and later fifties, had made deals offering participation to host governments; since the beginning of the current decade, in many countries, these have become the rule. From 1961 onwards, the Middle East governments began to take up participation in, for example, the operations of the Japanese and Italian companies that had first made agreements providing for this in the late fifties. Some of the major international companies, such as Shell, made no bones about accepting such partnership terms. Others, such as Jersey, had still never done so up to the beginning of 1966. None of these majors were willing to concede as a right in the revision of past agreements what they might have to offer in new ones. But they or their associates were at the same time accepting quite high percentages of government partnership in exploring new territories in, for example, South America and India, or in producing gas in Holland.

The settlement that was initialled in 1965 in Iraq, though not ratified, provided for most of the original concessionnaires to join with the Iraq National Oil Company in a joint venture to develop part of the acreage that they had been forced to give up by Qasim's 1961 legislation. Once it was finally accepted, the formula seemed likely to spread elsewhere. For both sides, there could be advantages in such partnerships on relinquished acreage between existing concessionnaires—with existing markets—and the new national companies.

Access to the rest of these countries for new developers, on new and stiffer terms, was becoming an uneasy matter for the established companies. It threatens a further potential surge of extra oil on to the world market, from areas that have so far been sterilized for 'orderly development'. It has introduced new twists in the concession formulae to which, over the years, they might have to consider accommodating their own concessions. Yet opening new taps to increase the world's surplus of oil could possibly tend to shift the initiative further towards marketing even than it is shifting already. To that degree, it might reduce the ultimate pressures that producers can apply to the whole integrated operations of the international industry.

Relinquishment, forced or voluntary, is already bringing in fresh capital to the Middle East. This is still an intensely attractive area, in physical prospects, for any oil company, new or established, that is still prepared to spend large amounts of money on exploration; and most companies, including the established majors, still are. The chances of finding oil in unexplored or untested areas in such countries must be taken as far better than in some of the countries where it has never yet been found. To the extent that host governments have capital to invest, oil in such areas should logically rank fairly high among potential activities in which to invest it—unless a comparable return, through high revenues per barrel from private concessionnaires, can be had painlessly without any investment at all. Most of the governments making such deals, so far, have preferred a compromise. They have required the private partner to put up all or most of the capital until oil can be produced commercially. Then they have had some oil income accruing from which they can put up their share of the capital.

But over and above the economic return, government participation in oil operations, with capital that the nation genuinely subscribes, has many obvious attractions in principle and in national sentiment. As one British civil servant commented to me some years ago, 'How should we like to have Arabs running our steel industry?' And the sooner the national companies begin operating on their own responsibility in this business, the better. It is simply bad luck that these companies should have commenced business in a period when the market for oil is so soft. But they have been able to make better than knockdown bargains with many avid newcomers, and with some of the privare companies operating in their countries.

Many difficulties can be foreseen in a relationship between a government partner, wanting responsibility and initiative, and a local operating company that would not normally possess much of either. Any self-respecting government entering such a partnership will expect some say in the key decisions of the business; yet in integrated companies these key decisions are in fact taken elsewhere, by the international companies of which the local operating joint companies or consortia are generally mere technical instruments. The setting of prices is one of those key decisions, in which governments are claiming a share already. Deciding the volume of offtake from the operating country is the next; at present this is a function mainly of the international integrated supplier, which has to decide from which among its various sources it shall supply any given demand. With the best will in the world, a government participating in the operations—and the profits—of an operating company in its own country must in its own national interest be at pains to secure the largest possible production from that one country. At present the offtake from each country is governed partly by agreements between the major shareholders in each jointly-owned company, but basically by the incentive of each such integrated major to maximize its own net integrated profit across a wide network of business around the globe. How would these governmentally-urged but at present subordinate operating companies 'compete' for greater custom from these integrated parent buyers—and others? And would any resultant changes in the balance of oil logistics make for more economical oil supply in the world, or less? ('Economical' here perhaps begs a question: but it is not used simply from the standpoint of a consumer interested in cheap oil. It is used to mean the supply of requirements around the world at the lowest practicable real cost, regardless of how any profits made are shared.)

Responsible government partnership in local producing companies in which the other partners are internationally integrated companies may put considerable strain on the links of integration inside companies producing oil in a large number of different places. It may put less strain or simpler strains upon any integrated companies that produce mainly in one area of international oil and ship the oil mainly to one market or group of markets. This is the case with some of the few partnership operations that have so far come into commercial production. Such a company may not be faced within the group with choices between so many producing areas, though it may have local governments as partners in more than one. That is one reason why the 'national preference company', particularly when the consumer government on which it depended for the preference is involved too, is frequently ready to offer the most tempting 'participation' formula.

But it can hardly be argued that a flow of trade depending upon special government dispensations at one end (or both) is likely to minimize real cost. And outside such special cases, it could be argued that responsible government participation in producing companies could only become effective if the internationally integrated companies were to 'divorce', in effect if not in form, their logistic function of matching demand from their central choice of supply, and in effect to put their requirements out to tender from their own (and other?) producing companies. There is a sense in which this happens already, in that the central choice is made according to the lowest possible costs at which the integrated group can supply its various demands from its own sources; but it does not necessarily go outside for supplies.

The governmental-cum-private producing partnerships would then, in principle, be free to offer their oil on the most advantageous terms to these major middlemen, with their considerable integrated command of markets, and to other independent buyers, to whom these countries indeed sell oil today. Some might find, if they made the terms right, that their offtake of oil rose. If so, that of others would be likely to fall (unless, indeed, all these government-influenced companies were ready to push prices down to a level that might stimulate an even greater increase in consumption, which somehow one imagines would not be their first intention). The integrated middlemen (ignoring for a moment all the problems of disentanglement) would retain the countervailing power of going elsewhere for their oil. The cost advantage of cheap oil from elsewhere against more expensive oil from which one stood to draw part of the profits would set a series of interesting problems for these integrated buyers, and the further ramifications of tax credits and final net integrated return on investment would add a further set of twists. But it would be too much to argue that these complications, presuming it were possible to get from the present situation to the one we have postulated, would make logical commercial behaviour impossible for the integrated marketers. Is their commercial logic so much simpler nowadays?

If one were to postulate that gradually this principle of partnership for host governments became extended to more and more of the oil produced internationally, this production—and sale—of crude more completely within national jurisdiction would seem likely to have one rapid result, whatever its other repercussions. It would make the governments' high royalties and taxes simply one section of their total financial interest in the crude sold—and influence them to consider all of this financial return more commercially. That might be a good thing for the world oil market—though there ought to be simpler ways to get there than divorcement. But would it be a good thing for the participating governments? More important, would they think it so?

That is obviously not the only conclusion to which government participation in operating companies might lead. It postulates an extreme solution, which could be reached only through a considerable upheaval of established property relationships. One imagines that many of the integrated companies concerned would contemplate the process with as much distaste as some of the host governments might find cause, in hindsight, to contemplate its eventual consequences. These governments have to consider whether they would do better, as at present, out of revenues tied to attificially high posted prices for crude oil than by taking greater commercial responsibility—and commercial risks. This does not mean that in the long run they may not be wise to assume fuller commercial responsibility. But it does mean that the exaggerated apparent return on assets invested in oil production in the Middle East might be reduced automatically by a structural change towards something rather more closely resembling an independently competitive free market, even if some of the competitors were governments.

Participation that amounts in fact only to getting an eventually larger percentage of the profit shown at posted prices, without any real share in the control of the business, is another thing. Some of the partnership deals made in recent years, with their obligations for the private partner to take all the national company's crude at some 'halfway price', sound more like this. But will these satisfy the reasonable ambitions of the able and aspiring nationalists even as long as the 50:50 formula satisfied them? It may seem on the one hand reactionary to doubt whether most of these host governments are yet quite aware of the rigours of commercial partnership in a soft world market for oil; and on the other hand perversely radical to doubt whether further halfway houses between here and full commercial responsibility could long satisfy the nationalist aspirations that they whet. Yet one must bear in mind the limited experience of many of these countries in meeting the problems of industry, let alone an internationally integrated one. Some of their nationals are most skilled traders in merchandise or even in international currency; but few of them have much industry other than oil within their borders. Ignorance of anything but oil, and disregard of the oil industry beyond one's borders, is in no way a reproach; it can be encountered, for example, in Texas. But it may make anything approaching genuine government partnership in sections of this complex private business hard to manage reasonably, in the short run. The current partnership deals are fashionable, and may be the least risky way to learn the business. But it is hard to escape the feeling that when the exporting countries feel prepared to take on full commercial responsibility and risks in the oil business—as logically in time they must—they would be best placed as participants in their own national companies. If host governments become any more directly involved in this business than they are today, but still imagine their own total revenue from oil must go up and can never go down, they may simply hamper the ability and resolution of their commercial partners in reacting logically to competition. Their stake in the industry's present arrangements, indeed, already does so.

For even now, logical commercial behaviour for the integrated companies could be politically explosive. As one person prominent in a major international company put it to me at the end of 1960, 'On paper at least, returns on investment in oil operations in the Eastern hemisphere appear to be exceptionally high. That appearance is deceptive; but the apparent returns on production, in particular, keep on attracting more new capital in. One solution that might eventually discourage new capital from entering this business, and perhaps eventually clear some of the recent entrants out, would be to make posted prices more realistic—demonstrating that investment in integrated oil operations in this hemisphere yields no more nowadays than a normal manufacturing return'. There is some commercial logic there. Sceptics would probably argue that posted prices deceive nobody today. Comfortable margins are being made even at discounted prices. There might be almost no bottom to the depths to which you would have to drive down the apparent return on production before you drove out of it newcomers who have invested their money and found oil already.

But any move towards realism in posted prices, as things stand, would be politically impossible. For any cuts in posted prices that brought these more into line with the actual prices paid in independent deals would correspondingly reduce the governments' revenue per barrel, and cut down the increase in total revenue upon which they continue to count. The tendency, in the mid-sixties, is indeed for the few remaining governments whose revenues are tied to actual realized prices to wish to move over to a posted, or tax reference, price basis.

In the first edition of this book, in 1962, I raised the possibility of shifting over from the then pattern, of a small royalty credited within a 50 per cent income tax, to a much larger element of fixed royalty, or some 'minimum guarantee', which would insulate the governments' revenue from prices altogether, posted or realized. The idea was not particularly original for an outsider looking into this industry. I gather that it was one of the possibilities mentioned about the same time, quite independently, in the study commissioned by OPEC from the American consultancy Arthur D. Little. But it was an uncommon one, at the time, among the governments and the oil companies, and certainly this kind of formula for stabilizing governments' unit revenue has never been adopted by OPEC in any of its propositions to the companies.

The great change in concession patterns that most people on both sides of Middle East oil then remembered best was the shift to 50:50 that was initiated at the end of 1950 and carried through to its full form by the mid-fifties. This was basically a shift from a fixed royalty of four shillings gold per ton of oil to an income tax charged as 50 per cent of profits shown at posted prices. That royalty had originally been tied to gold as a hedge against exchange instability, inflation or deflation, which during the thirties it provided. But when crude oil prices veered sharply upwards during the war years, the price of gold remained frozen; the original gold hedge in the royalty was nullified, and in effect the intent of the earlier agreements, to give the governments a revenue that was likely to rise in value at least as much as the price of oil, was no longer being carried out.

When the new tax plus royalty formula was introduced, it offered the governments considerable benefits. By the time that it was modified to exclude discounts to shareholder companies, in the middle fifties, it offered the governments such impressive increases over their revenues before that ever since many discussions of further improvements in revenue from oil have tended to be argued out in terms of desirable percentages of royalty and tax, both by governments that would like to push their percentage up and by companies who sigh for the time when 50:50 was inviolable. But it might still be worth remembering that the earlier 'gold' royalty itself had derived from a revision of the Anglo-Iranian concession in the thirties, and had then been brought in to give the government concerned a higher and more stable revenue. That was a shift from basing government revenues partly on a percentage of profits, which at the time were so low as to give it virtually no revenue at all, to the fixed royalty based on volume. It is by no means automatically true that what it was recently fashionable to call 'profit-sharing'—i.e. an income tax basis with royalties either 'credited' or 'expensed'—would always be the most advantageous financial arrangement for a host country, particularly in dealings with an industry where over the years prices are fairly often under downward competitive pressure. Over any long period of surplus, profit-sharing formulae, whatever the percentage ruling, seem liable to lead inexorably to the governments' seeking first to control prices, and second to their trying to organize some producer-controlled cartel to try to make those prices stick.

The only circumstances in which the companies could practicably have cut posted prices for crude as the prices actually paid have slipped downwards would have been by revising their formulae in the direction of insulating the governments' revenues from the effect of cuts in postings. This might mean, in some way or another, moving back towards a larger element of flat-rate revenue per barrel for the governments, and a smaller element varying with the swings of the market; either a return towards the royalty pattern, or supplementary payments for the governments at any time that it became commercially expedient to cut postings, to make up what would otherwise be their loss in revenue per barrel. This would have meant acknowledging openly that the governments' level of revenue per barrel are as virtually irreducible. Even in the fifties, in practice, their total annual revenues from oil were taken as irreducible, though this was never spelt out as a formal principle in any agreement. The steady and fairly high rate of growth in offtake of oil from these countries, at the time that cuts were made in posted prices in 1959 and 1960, made it possible to demonstrate that the host governments' total oil revenues for the next year, in spite of a somewhat lower revenue per barrel, would still come out higher.

In practice, as we have seen, the Middle East governments of OPEC, since the first edition of this book was written, have effectively achieved a minimum guarantee of their oil revenues. But they have not done so by the method of enlarging the fixed element in the pattern of these revenues. Their royalty remains the same in amount—12½ per cent of the posted price of their crude. It is now payable separately, before reckoning taxable income, and therefore not lost within the amount of the 50 per cent income tax liability. The posted price, formally, is still liable to revision by the oil companies, without any promise of consultation with governments. But the percentage discount allowed off this posted price for tax purposes, from 1967 onwards, can only be changed by the companies after considering what the governments concerned have to argue about the state of the market. And this discount, by agreement, will in no circumstances be increased—i.e. the difference between the tax reference price and the posted price will not be widened. There is a minimum guarantee, that is to say, applied to the discount below the posted price, though the posted price itself, theoretically, remains open to change. This is an anomalous pattern, in theory. In practice, posted prices in the Middle East have not been cut, in spite of the continued fall in arm's-length prices for crude and in final prices for products, since 1960. Any cut now would run the company that posted it into more trouble than the companies have been ready to provoke over the last five years; and would invite the kind of treatment that Libya was ready to apply to its concessionnaires at the beginning of 1966.

Formally, the effect of royalty expensing is to bring about a larger tax payment in the host country than before because royalty is not offset. In principle, this would create a larger tax credit for the internationally-integrated companies against their home tax liability on foreign income. But whether this has been of any use to an international company in moderating the net effect of the host countries' tax change will have depended on the extent to which the tax credits to which it was already entitled happen to be utilized already. Its tax credit available might already have exceeded its home tax liability on total foreign income. Allowing for depletion allowances and other charges against their home income, those of American internationally integrated companies often do; and following the shift in Britain in 1965–66 to a corporation tax at a lower rate than the income taxes of virtually any oil company, all international oil companies domiciled there are left with an unusable margin of 'excess foreign tax credit'. So the increase in foreign tax credit arising from the royalty expensing settlement seems unlikely to have been of much help in offsetting the cost of the higher tax in the producing country to the integrated companies. Circumstances might however arise that could increase American companies' home tax liability on foreign income—such as some senators' advertised desire to reduce foreign depletion allowances. If that were to happen— the companies hope it will not—then additional tax credit overseas might become extremely useful, and the net cost of allowing foreign governments a higher tax share, or a stable revenue per barrel when posted prices went down, might be considerably reduced.

To the outside observer, this tortuous approach to a minimum guarantee may look an unnecessarily complicated one. But two points may be made about it. The first, which was argued some years ago by Professor Adelman, is that the more elements there remain to argue about in oil concession arrangements, the less likelihood there may be of the governments feeling deceived if it proves impossible to maintain the revenues they believe to be guaranteed. The second, which I believe more important in the circumstances of oil nationalism, is that it would be contrary to the present temper of the host governments to apply any formula that ostensibly insulated them further from the market. What I, as an outside observer, failed to give sufficient importance was the deep desire of these countries to take a fuller share of responsibility for the development of their national oil resources. For the present, that remains stronger than any strictly economic calculation of the easiest way to get the highest revenue with the least effort.

So far, as we have seen, this national desire has been fulfilled with a considerable degree of economic prudence. In most cases, the national companies through which these governments seek to participate in oil operations do not have to risk any of their own national capital until the oil is found and production from it established to be commercially worthwhile. From then on, their responsibility for pre-production investment and later development can be offset against their entitle- ment to oil from the concession. And in most of the partnership deals there are provisions for the national company to require its commercial partner to take over all of its (the national company's) entitlement of oil on request at some pre-arranged price, if the national company cannot sell this itself. In a real sense, there is an element of minimum guarantee built into these deals too.

Yet it seems unwise to assume that the governments, having com- mitted themselves this far into the commercial operations of the oil business, would simply lean back on this minimum guarantee and depend on the private partner to get rid of all the oil. If prices in the world market improve generally, they would presumably be able to get a better price for their own share than would be available under the terms of the agreement. If prices continue to decline, and say the private partner is unable to dispose of its own or the national partner's oil for enough to cover that 'half-way price' including tax, then the governments will face an inevitable managerial decision, sooner or later. Do they go on developing the concession for sales at these prices, and oblige the private partner to take all the crude? In that case, the private partner will be unable before long to continue investing in development. Or will the governments, as the only partners in the business still obtaining really fat 'net profits', accept some reduction in their own take in order to secure the business? Finally, they could turn the business away—providing they can be sure that no other government and national company, with or without a private partner, will be prepared to accept the lower price to get it.

One healthy side-effect of this entry of governments, via national companies, into these partnership deals has been to restore real meaning to the word 'partnership' in oil. In public relations terminology during the fifties, the whole set of existing tax arrangements were too often clothed in phrases that suggested Arab governments, as recipients of royalties and tax-gatherers, had become 'partners' in this business. This was always disingenuous; and such terminology was of little use to either side of the oil bargain. In the United States and other developed economies income taxes often take some 50–55 per cent of the profits of business firms. But one does not often have companies in these countries describing their governments as 'profit-sharing partners' in their enterprise.

The attractiveness of 50:50, from the beginning, was that it sounded like a principle of fairness. But did it in fact embody any principle at all? Why should the share of profits in any given oil deal be 50:50, rather than 40:60, or 60:40? (and in passing it may be noted that examples of both these divisions, in recent years, have been labelled as 'according to the 50:50 principle'). One advantage of the emerging minimum guarantee for government revenues from oil may be that this at least can be seen to be clearly what in essence it is—the result of a commercial bargain, not some exercise in dubious principle about some 'right' or 'fair' percentage. In ordinary economic terms, the proceeds that these governments draw from the exploitation of oil or other mineral resources would mainly be classed as a rent or a mining royalty. One may note that Sir Maurice Bridgeman, chairman of British Petroleum, when he discussed government revenues from oil in his annual report to shareholders for 1961—stoutly defending the fairness of the existing 50:50 deal—spoke of 'the rent we pay our landlords'. It would be unreasonable to attribute any motive to Sir Maurice but the preference for clear English; but this certainly seemed a better description.

The oil rent in Venezuela, for example, has obviously in recent years been set rather too high—so long as the oil companies were in a position to shift the emphasis of their operations towards better bargains elsewhere. They did not cease taking huge exports of oil out of Venezuela: but they did cut down the increase. Doing without Middle East oil, on the other hand, has been attempted only once by the West and the oil companies, with relative success but in an expensive emergency operation. Doing without Middle East and Venezuelan oil at once never has. Doing without the oil companies, on the other hand, was attempted once, by Iran; it was a failure. Abadan and Suez are ugly object lessons that neither the petroleum exporting countries, the Western consuming nations, nor the oil companies might care to contemplate as benchmarks setting the limits of successful bargaining; they are on record, rather, as the danger signs showing where good sense foundered in the past. All parties to this bargaining, understandably, have since increased their insurance provisions. The petroleum-exporting countries did so by creating OPEC and agreeing not to benefit at the expense of other member countries involved in disputes with oil companies (a resolution regarded cynically in the West, but liable to become more durable as time passes). The oil companies, egged on by consumer governments, did so by some diversification of oil development into new productive areas. But neither of these two parties, as yet, seems to have achieved really 'comprehensive cover' through these measures of insurance.

It would be a rash man who would guess what the eventual bargaining pattern between the oil companies and their growing throng of host governments around the world will look like by the seventies. It may not remain uniform; at least, it may display diversity with less pretence of uniformity than concession arrangements used to. It will certainly come to include significant elements of government partnership with international companies—established ones as well as newcomers. The producing governments' own national oil companies will be playing a larger part, and the 'national preference' companies from consuming countries certainly will. Whatever form has then been reached is unlikely to be permanent: at best, the bargaining will still be going on. The biggest question mark, as ever, relates to the future state of the market. With prices, even at current discounts, well above the costs of bringing fresh reserves into production—since the governments' revenue per barrel is still a handsome one—it is hard to see any economic reason for any sustained hardening in prices, while competition prevails. The governments from now on, more than ever before, will have the choice between taking individual advantage of that competition, or sticking together to try to stabilize and then push up prices for every producer. Which they choose—and which might pay them better—will depend partly on the elasticity of oil demand to price, but mainly on the chances of making a producers' cartel, or maybe a commodity agreement bringing in consumers, really stick. Not all the consuming countries in the world, certainly, are very anxious to see oil prices come down further. But whether that will make them more amenable to price-fixing by producers alone is highly debatable.

CHAPTER XXII

Pressure from Consumers

F ew people in the oil business, when this book was written, were
prepared to take the pressures upon them from consumer governments as seriously as those from producer governments; and in the
short run they were obviously right. The dramatic demands, the
explicit or implicit threats to cut off their supplying operations, come
from the host governments in producing countries. Moreover, their
relations with those hosts are ultimately crystallized into contractual
arrangements: improvement or deterioration in such relations either
fortifies an agreement or brings arguments for its modification. In consuming countries where the oil industry operates simply as a processor
and marketer, its contractual arrangements until recently were only with
private individuals. Its relations with governments, and the favour or
disfavour it receives in their policies, are generally more detached. Some
of these consuming countries, again, are the homes of the great international companies: these companies make a significant contribution
to national wealth and may expect, though they do not invariably
receive it, some special consideration. And yet the world oil market is in
surplus; consumers throughout the importing countries are seeking to
take as much advantage of this as they can; and energy is so vital to
every consuming country nowadays that no government can ignore its
strategic, commercial and fiscal significance. Moreover, there is one
point of uncertainty regarding oil that consumer governments share
with producers. Petroleum is brought to their shores from various
sources, just as it is taken away from the producing countries towards
various destinations, chosen according to the convenience of international companies operating largely beyond their jurisdiction. They
cannot always assume that the companies' commercial convenience will
be more than incidentally identical with their own national interests.

The present circumstances in which this growing concern of consumer governments with oil may grow in importance are those of

surplus, which strengthens their leverage. To any other business it would seem a rather odd kind of surplus, since world demand for oil is continuing to grow at about 5 per cent per year, and outside the United States it is doubtful whether there is a real surplus of physical capacity. But at current prices enormous amounts of crude in proved reserves could readily be developed to afford a comfortable return. That is quite enough of a surplus to keep a downward pressure on prices. It is no part of this book's purpose, fortunately, to provide specific guesswork about the continuation of rates of growth in the world eceonomy. But most informed forecasts for the next 15–25 years—for example, those of Sir Maurice Bridgeman in 1963 and Mr J. H. Loudon in 1965[1]— imply that demand for oil will continue to grow fairly steadily without the pace accelerating much, though within the total the importance of newly-developing countries, already rising much faster than those already industrialized, will gradually increase.

Where short-term surpluses of physical capacity had been built up, they are disappearing. For some years tankers have not been ordered at the rate they were in the late fifties; a good deal of the oldest existing tonnage has been scrapped and in any case there is no real surplus of the really large tankers, which alone can offer the level of crude movement costs operators need to compete in today's market. Refining capacity in Europe, again, has of late been growing a little more slowly than it was, and perhaps more slowly than demand for petroleum products in certain areas; but given the rapid rate of growth in demand, there was never any general surplus in this area. In other parts of the world, certainly, where this is associated with the defence or penetration of particular markets, investment in refineries is still going on somewhat in advance of what the market potential might really require. But in terms of foreign exchange and national aspirations for the consuming country concerned, this may be less wasteful than it may look in terms of theoretically free world trade. And it does not amount to any very large margin of capacity. Investment in marketing is certainly still growing in most areas of the world. These are responses to a surplus; what about investment in exploration and production, which might be considered as what brings surpluses about? Right across the industry, investment in exploration has certainly fallen a little in recent years; but no major company can afford to cease to explore, and those that find oil in commercial quantities are often under legal obligations to develop it rapidly into production. As for the newcomers, whose oil has now been on the market for some years, there is little sign that even with growing government payments, these are yet beginning to find the present level of prices unremunerative.

Some experts feel that the prices of certain refined products, in parts of the world at least, are passing bottom. For example, late in 1965, Mr Haider of the Jersey group commented:

'We believe the worst is behind us and that prospects are brighter. . . . My own view is that this year represents the last phase of a period of transition and product price adjustments which has been caused, first, by the entry of many new competitors into the European market; second, by the abundant crude oil production capacity of both the established companies and the newcomers; and, third, by the strong competitive efforts of Europe's older marketers.'[2]

Mr Haider did not think product prices would regain the levels of five years before; but he thought they were stabilizing. In 1964 and 1965, indeed, the international majors, including Jersey, were able to buy up some independent refiner-marketers in the two markets in Europe where prices had sunk lowest, Germany and Switzerland. Libya's increase in government take put further pressure on the crude suppliers of cut-price products. And some hardening of fuel oil prices was achieved by the governments of oil-consuming countries themselves, for example Germany and Japan.

Consuming governments, with some cold-blooded exceptions, show considerable inhibitions about really behaving like oil consumers. From the United States outwards, developed countries with established domestic fuel industries have gone on valuing their investment in these industries fairly highly in the balance against the cheapness of imported energy. Moreover, little that has recently developed in the politics of Latin America, the Arab countries or Africa—which comprise virtually all the significant present and imminent exporters of petroleum—could reasonably have reduced these importers' concern with the strategic security of supply. Western Europe will no doubt remain more shame-faced than the United States about maintaining relatively high-cost indigenous fuel industries; its ways of doing so are probably less waste-ful; but it may not be very much more prepared to run those industries right down to the levels to which unrestricted imports of cheap oil might drive them.

Consumer governments, organizations of governments, and study groups appointed by governments will remain prepared to expatiate upon the benefits that taking full advantage of cheap energy would confer on the West—though their enthusiasm will no doubt continue to vary inversely with their degree of actual responsibility for acting upon such liberal views. Few responsible governments in such countries, however, are prepared wholly or even largely to supplant old or new indigenous fuel industries by imports of cheap energy—which they would probably accept as a factor, but by no means a determining one, in economic growth. To cite Professor E. S. Mason:[3]

> 'If low-cost energy was essential to economic development, we would expect to find some association between the price of energy and the state of economic development. Plotting national income per capita against energy prices in fact indicates no significant correlation. . . . There are some under-developed countries with low and some with high fuel costs. There are also some highly industrialized countries with low and some with high fuel costs. We also sometimes find within a country differences in fuel costs and energy prices almost as wide as average energy cost differences from country to country. Within the United States we have areas where fuel prices are ten times as high as those of the areas of lowest fuel prices.'

There is always a mixture of considerations: the short-run cost of energy, at home or on the trade balance, in some cases invisible income from ownership of international oil companies, the security of supply in the long run, and continuing uncertainty about the terms on which one may be able to continue to import one's fuel. If one were pushing the short-term logic of seeking cheap energy regardless, it could be argued that we might close down, or put on a 'care and maintenance basis', almost all the other fuel production in the world and rely on getting it all, over the next generation, as oil out of the Middle East and Russia. Nobody is prepared to suggest that, at least outside these two regions. Consciously or not, even the most liberal advocates of cheap energy imports put some bounds upon their enthusiasm.

Mixed motives remain evident also in the supra-national economic groupings that have appeared in Western Europe, the world's main importing region for energy. There is a desire to gain the benefits of cheap imports—up to a point; and a readiness to rationalize one's own older fuel industries—down to a point. This will probably grow as the share of oil continues to rise; the sense in holding general energy costs high to protect one's domestic energy industry looks increasingly questionable as its importance in the whole energy market declines. But these groups of governments, perhaps more than the single consumer governments, are moreover disturbed at the possibility of being held up by any cartel of producers. They are probably not entirely convinced that the existing commercial suppliers of the oil industry are always as competitive in pricing as they might be. But they are certainly even more apprehensive of any incipient cartel of oil-producing governments.

While the surplus lasts, one can certainly expect pressure from many consuming governments to get improved bargains in foreign exchange for their oil imports: and this is liable to occur at the point of import or processing by affiliates of the international groups. Many developing countries, for example, are anxious to take a financial interest in the import or refining of oil products in their countries. This was often derided by economists in the first postwar decade as matter simply of fashion, but it has begun to acquire considerably more logic as the world market moved into surplus. It is no longer simply a matter of laying out one's scarce capital, or attracting foreign capital from outside, to tie up in a prestigious but not over-remunerative item of industrial plant. It offers an opportunity of exacting a price, on behalf of the country's consumers and their governmental assets, for access to one's probably developing market. This is capital a nation might not otherwise come by, which oil suppliers are ready and anxious to put in to help them maintain or achieve their integrated return on a network of assets reaching back across the world. The newly independent African nations, in particular, have exacted this price of access to their markets, not only by seeking bids for government participation in refineries but by driving quite hard bargains about the pricing of the crude oil put into these refineries. This is a kind of government participation that major and minor oil companies in the world market have perforce become ready to accept.

Partnerships with consuming governments in refineries or marketing networks, during a period of world oil surplus, may be a fairly logical move for both participants in such joint enterprises. Over the history of the oil industry, the periods of incipient surplus have probably been longer than those of apparent or real shortage. Some of the toughest buyers of refined products or nowadays of crude oil include governmental import monopolies; these have often during surplus had the best bargain prices for their oil and not lost much during the periods of shortage. Government participation in a refinery or an importing concern can generally, liberal principles notwithstanding, guarantee the refinery's products preferential treatment in the internal market. 'Processing rights' may be guaranteed to existing marketers (but seldom to any new ones): but the partner in refining can generally hope for the lion's share of any expansion (until the time comes for an extension or another refinery). In such deals, the commercial partner must be assumed to know his own mind; so must the government. One may have ideological objections to state trading of any kind, or objections in simple fairness to governments which give their own trading bodies, or partnerships with commercial associates, privileged treatment in competition with purely private competitors. But that does not make their behaviour less likely or in their own interests less logical.

Privileged access to markets can be offered to producing countries, not merely to oil companies seeking outlets. What one of the major groups has christened 'the national preference companies' could grow in importance and increasingly affect private oil companies in the world market. The main example has been set by the French Saharan companies. These have survived Algeria's attainment of independence (and some of them have been venturing afield). Following the Franco-Algerian Accord of 1965, the form of further development of new Algerian oil has changed. But it remains linked with France. The main significance of this continued linkage has been the privileged access to the country's markets, an advantage shared also by the Japanese company in the Middle East. It has not been surprising that other consuming countries have been offering the same kind of deal. Preferential access to a sizeable or rapidly growing market, even when the business that can offer this has a large share of consumer government participation, may well be a tempting incentive to the governments of producing countries in a surplus. Where the consuming country too is not accustomed to fully competitive markets, as for example in the case of Spain's negotiations with Kuwait and France's new deal with Iran, the temptations are mutual.

The preference that such markets may offer oil from sources of which they particularly approve can come in various forms. Agreements recommending ideal rules of international trade, over the long run, ought in theory at least to whittle down the opportunity for governments to discriminate between imports by special tariffs or quotas. One current of argument about world trade in the sixties, symbolized perhaps by the 'Kennedy Round', favours further attempts to reduce such restrictions. It seems at present however rather more likely that developing regional trading areas—the European Economic Community has been followed by a wide variety of imitators—will reduce trade barriers and trade discrimination within their borders but retain some protection against the outside world. Certainly while France retains any hold on Saharan oil and gas it seems likely to seek preferential treatment for these fuels within its EEC partners' markets—and if necessary specific restrictions on crude as well as products from other sources. Apart from tariff preference, consumer governments are likely while their bargaining advantage lasts to enter into commercial competition in marketing: one has already seen recent examples of somewhat varying types in France, India and Ceylon.

The continuance of surplus might logically be expected, perhaps, to reduce consumer governments' interest in another form of intervention into oil which some have subsidized in recent years—exploration for oil within their own borders. But one rather doubts whether it will wholly deter any government. Has surplus, after all, deterred many international oil companies from going on exploring? A government, certainly, is not moved by one incentive that on occasion may encourage companies to keep up their exploration budgets, the possibility of tax advantage here or there. But the rewards of successful exploration can be so dramatic even for highly developed economies—as for example the gas finds in the Po Valley, Southern France and Holland have successively shown—that some national gamble for such prizes may seem sensible regardless of a surplus that might indeed be gone by the time that any petroleum found comes into production. (ENI developed the Po Valley gas; that of Lacq was located by French government explorers. Slochteren gas was found by Shell and Esso working together, but in the development of the Dutch gas too government participation has entered.) Moreover, any petroleum found at home becomes indigenous fuel: a benefit to local economic resources and to the balance of payments. It has, of course, a good chance of becoming economic, through sheer closeness to market. But whether economic or not, it may get produced anyway: local oil, in particular, is sometimes just another domestic industry queueing up for protection. Many of the private exploration ventures begun since the mid-fifties, moreover, have recognized the value consuming governments attach to this; there has been quite a shift in drilling activity to countries where, if the oil is found, it will command a ready market.

For many developing countries in the sixties, oil now weighs as heavy on the balance of payments as it did in Western Europe in the forties and early fifties. Investment in exploration in these countries, too, is likely to continue, by private companies, joint ventures, or state-hired contractors. But a period during which the actual landed prices of oil slip downward, even if postings should be held immovable for fear of reactions from exporting governments, ought to moderate that import cost. And unless the private Western companies are prepared to moderate the net foreign exchange cost of oil imported by such developing countries—either by spending more in these countries, or investing it there, or in helping them secure other foreign aid from Western countries to offset the cost—there is unfortunately little doubt that the Russians will get much of the business, by quoting low prices and accepting non-convertible currencies. Countries such as India, that is to say, remain well placed to put the screws on the Western oil marketer; and they are likely to find this for a time worth at least as much governmental expenditure of effort trying to find their own oil. Such countries, with limited markets and hence limited commercial bargaining power, feel they have been subject to price discrimination; hence their recourse to state trading. Pressure for government participation in oil-importing countries, therefore, seems likely to continue, and companies that complain of it in one country may find it convenient for themselves in another. Ambitions to engage in or share in exploration, however, might moderate somewhat in countries lacking oil, if the surplus lasts. And where such countries find it, they will ensure it preference for internal consumption. This, indeed, may not be quite the violation of received economic doctrine that it might appear at first sight to free traders —and importers. Local petroleum may not be the cheapest oil that a country could lay hands on. But can any country be sure that the operations of its present international suppliers at present ensure that it gets the cheapest? Can it be demonstrated that what gives the best net integrated return to an international supply complex is necessarily the best bargain that each particular country could get?

Most consumer governments, moreover, are not unmixedly anxious to have black oil prices pressed further down, though they might like gasoline prices down further. Indeed, the competition of low-cost fuel oil is one of the reasons why some of the consumer nations have been considering combined energy policies. Does this open any possibility of accommodation between the standpoints of consumer nationalism and producer nationalism?

In 1963, at the United Nations Conference on Trade and Development, some representatives of oil-producing countries did suggest petroleum as one of the commodities for which some kind of stabilization scheme might be devised. A year or two before, when the idea was mooted in the Organization of American States, there seems to have been some sympathy for the idea in parts at least of the American State Department. The idea has obvious parallels with OPEC's ideas about production programming, though the two concepts are not identical. Such a scheme, if it could ever be achieved, might offer exporting countries a very real participation in the international logistics of petroleum; but they would be face to face with the equally direct concern of consumer governments. Is there any real chance that the two groups could overcome mutual distrusts in a world commodity scheme, with both groups of governments in the game?

Certain world commodity schemes have had a limited degree of success before and since the war—mainly covering various pastoral commodities and metals. Moreover, several of the developed industrial nations have made friendly noises from time to time about such schemes in principle; and the idea may gain more general acceptance if the primary producing nations' income continues to fall. But few schemes have ever concerned commodities for which the increase in demand has been anything like as steady as it is for petroleum; or from which the countries and companies involved in production have continued to enjoy so comfortable a level of income. Most of them, too, have dealt with materials in the supply of which internationally integrated companies play only a limited part. Certain metals that have on occasion come under cartels or commodity schemes, such as aluminium, are produced by international, integrated companies; but few of them carry operations as far through from the mineral resource to the final consumer, as many oil companies do. Some form of world commodity agreement for petroleum, in principle, might not be inherently impossible. But it would require the reconciliation of many differing, and some violently opposed interests.

Some penetrating analysts of this industry, such as Dr. Paul Frankel, would argue that such external control, of one kind or another, is a natural response to the peculiar economic behaviour to which this industry tends uncontrolled. He has suggested that when one such form of control, such as was exercised in the international oil market by the major companies after the war, breaks down, some other will have to be instituted to replace it. It is for this reason that he has suggested that the 'informal prorationing' that was once possible among the major companies may have to be replaced by something that brings in other interests as well.[4] Even the casual observer may feel convinced that the pressure by the governments at both ends of this business for greater influence over the oil market—control necessitated partly by what Dr. Frankel calls 'lack of self-balancing factors in the market'—will recur and strengthen if no more conventional stabilization comes about. But there are more forms than one in which control might be re-established in this international market, at least temporarily. (Dr Frankel is fond of Lenin's question, 'Who whom?' It seems to me a relevant one in discussion of international agreements to control the oil market.) And it is perhaps likely that for some years we shall see continued evolution of the existing patterns of the industry rather than any openly radical shift in its organization.

For no such scheme could ever come into existence, in a free world, without the co-operation of the oil companies, whose financial stake in this is the largest of all. And whether any scheme controlled largely by governments with different interests could ever fit in with the major companies' widely and differently dispersed patterns of commercial interest is very doubtful. (Where governments and companies have co-operated in emergency schemes, as for example during the Suez crisis, these have been essentially governments of one kind, representing consumers.) This industry has, admittedly, adapted itself to many distortions and emergencies imposed from outside upon its pattern of commercial operations. But no emergency that it has met successfully ever postulated any continuing supervision over its main job of management, in a business that it is conducting successfully on the basis of unquestionable legal rights of private enterprise.

Politically, too, the parent countries of the existing international oil companies are among the most powerful of the Western world; these would tend to line up against any control that abrogated the property rights of the oil industry. Indeed, the whole current of thinking in the industrialized countries of the West, while not averse to some extension of national or even supra-national control, does for the present seem more favourable towards private enterprise than it may have done, say, at the end of the last war. Planning is coming back into vogue; but planning without socialism and certainly without expropriation.

The most important consuming countries, so far, are all based mainly upon private enterprise. Property is guaranteed rights within a stable and comprehensive legal system; when companies come to argue with such governments, they are arguing about the same things within the same frame of reference. This makes their relationships with such governments easier than with the governments of most producing nations, though no less complicated in detail (as the companies perforce concerned with European energy policies have certainly found out). But it does not necessarily guarantee the continuance of the present structure of the industry, within and between nations.

CHAPTER XXIII

The Business in Between

N one of the interests concerned with the international oil trade—consuming nations, exporting nations, or the companies in between—wants the oil to stop flowing; but all would like to see it flowing on slightly different terms. There are, however, inherent limitations to the extent to which most consumer governments, at any rate, would push what might seem to be their short-run self interest; and whether or not this is true of the exporting nations, there are some obvious commercial limitations upon the extent to which any of these could push up their rewards from oil. Each group of governments may think of the companies, from time to time, as ganging up with the other against it; the oil business may sometimes consider the possibility of these two ultimate bargainers combining to squeeze the middleman, but has never yet had to face such a reality. Ideologically, not many governments outside the Communist sphere appear to cherish much desire to take oil operations inside their borders entirely under government ownership; this industry is beset primarily by pragmatic nationalism, rather than theoretical socialism. Equally, few substantial companies in the oil business generally behave as if they believe in *laisser faire*, though some on occasion feel constrained to talk as if they did. They may be driven into extremes of short-run competitive behaviour from time to time; but most prefer a steadier form of competition looking towards their interests in at any rate the medium run. And whatever their philosophical attitudes towards government intervention in business, oilmen in practice have had years of experience in living with it.

Nowadays, bargaining between governments and companies about many aspects of the oil business goes on virtually without pause; and that it should not stop is perhaps more important to the world than the precise nature of the formulae discussed. But the central subject of the bargaining is being looked at a little differently. It is no longer simply a question of what a government, say, should get out of oil as a reward for geographical ownership: it is shifting round to what the company should get out of it as a reward for business enterprise. This question of the proper rate of return for the risk-taking international entrepreneur in this business is what, in essence, the bargaining always has been about; but today it is being openly discussed as such. And indeed, if producing and consuming governments were ever to get together over the industry's head, they would be faced with the same questions. What are the essential—and irreducible—functions of this prodigious middleman, the international oil industry? And how much return does one need to offer capital to enter or stay in it?

One easy and partly adequate answer to the second question may seem to excuse governments from considering the first. The going price that capital needs in each part of the business, the governments may answer, is simply the lowest rate of return that any fresh entrepreneurs coming into the business are prepared to accept. Let each producing government get the best terms it can on any fresh concessions that it grants; and then squeeze the holders of its existing concessions to come into line. On this reasoning relinquishment deals would have an additional attraction for the governments; they might enable a continuing series of fresh bargains to be struck, with the extra benefits of each being translated back, in due course, to all existing deals. The Libyan government, so recent an entrant into the business, has clearly learned this game: it had begun revising its oil law even before a barrel of commercial oil had been shipped, back in 1961, and as we have seen quite recently, is still managing to stay ahead of the game. And at the other end of the oil business, consumer governments have learned this game too. Using their bargaining power in a buyer's market for products, they are exacting special arrangements from some of the major companies that are less advantageously placed in marketing, or from newcomers seeking to enter their markets; then making similar demands on those already established.

Such pressures, tactical considerations in bargaining at both ends of this business, do not remove the question of the essential functions of risk capital in this business and of the return that needs to be paid on integrated operations to make them worth while. Specialized deals of one kind and another, particularly those linking production in given countries to consumption in given countries, will probably multiply. But is or is not the role of the internationally integrated company, operating across the world market, essential to this industry? And if so, what is it worth?

Fractions of the answer to these questions are given daily by the major oil companies themselves. In deciding what they need not do themselves and can hire other people to do, they at once demonstrate what can be decentralized and put a price on the physical performance of it. A host government can hire an exploration contractor: the quotation it gets, set largely by what company customers will pay, should enable it to decide whether it would rather invest in the equipment—and the men—itself, and will also give it an idea of the rate of return that capital invested in the physical operations concerned, without the element of risk, can competitively command. It can finance its own tankers—or bargain with independent operators. It can perhaps conclude refining contracts for its own production or 'royalty crude' with independent refiners. Consuming governments can fairly easily ascertain the amount of capital required and the minimum return that some marketers find acceptable for entry into a market: the capital cost of entry, today, will usually be fairly high, but the rate of return acceptable will depend partly on whether the marketer is integrated, and how much oil he can get rid of elsewhere. These are all functions of which the internationally integrated company, on occasion, is ready to divest itself, paying the going rate on other people's capital to do the job, though generally retaining most of the choices, and hence the risks itself. It may, similarly, have some of its technical research done outside, though it cannot delegate the technical management function of identifying, at any time, what its key technical problems really are.

What then, are the central functions that it cannot leave to anyone outside? And what rate of return is necessary to get these functions, apart from the many physical operations that it can hire, performed efficiently in the short, the medium and possibly the long run? Asked these questions, various oilmen offer a variety of overlapping answers. But to an outsider the essential operational function of an internationally integrated oil company may seem to be logistic—the disposition of supplies from many sources to meet many different demands, and the setting of relative prices. Its main technical and social function may be one of selecting and training good managers of all nationalities and imbuing them with wider than national experience in management. Its main financial function is perhaps that of acting as a specialized investment bank with exceptional experience in a particularly risky and complex technology, with a long enough view to ensure the steady development of an internationally essential resource. And all these functions, as exercised today, need an international viewpoint detached from the special interest of any one nation—which makes such a company, perforce, a political as well as an economic middleman between nations.

The logistic function of each internationally integrated oil company is carried out, within the limits of its own operations, as a kind of 'invisible hand'. It produces, moves, and markets oil around the world not quite simply according to the 'principle of comparative costs' of free trade economics, but in accordance with the maximizing of net profit after tax across each company's own integrated chain of oil operations in many countries. Physically, within each company's sphere of operations, the resulting movement of oil from source to market will be designed to minimize its costs. No company has quite 'the average' pattern. There are some constraints through joint offtake rules, or peculiarities in each company's geographical or cost pattern, though the widespread practice of exchanging crudes and products between companies tends to reduce the extra costs that might arise from these. It is true that neither producing nor consuming governments, considering the structure of this industry and the assorted interests of the many integrated companies involved, are likely to trust that these companies' decisions best serve all interests quite as much as classical economists would have producers and consumers trust the free play of market forces. Tax considerations, moreover, enter into each company's logistic exercise; and an integrated company may have other not simply economic incentives to consider A as against B, arising largely from the different governmental pressures under which it does business in different places. One may regret these complications of taxation and these political pressures, or accept them as inevitable. What one can hardly do is to argue that any new set of operators, set up by governments likely to follow their own individual economic interests rather than the broader medium-run interest of world oil development in general, would be less susceptible to political pressures—or that they could readily expect to perform this operation at lower total cost than that with which oil is nowadays moved from well to market.

It has to be borne in mind that the regulation of permitted exports that some governments wish to impose on the companies would on balance cut across their tax advantages here and there, raise the cost of the operation and the tax liability involved, and reduce the net return on the capital employed in it. That has already happened at the other

end, where consumer governments dictate preferential imports of particular crudes. This reduction, certainly, arises largely from the particular dispersion of interests of particular companies. Moreover, taxes are
things a government can alter to suit its own convenience, as oil companies have plenty of reason to know. But whether any concert of
governments at either end of the oil business or both could 'maximize
the return' or reduce the net expenditure of resources on this central
exercise of oil management to the degree that uncommitted third parties
—such as the present wide variety of integrated and other oil companies—may in practice, would seem most doubtful.

Developing and properly employing oilmen of all kinds—including
those managers who have to identify the right areas for technical research—is not less important. Any one intelligent oilman represents a
substantial asset to this industry, in which time and money will have
been invested: developing a succession of them is a searching and continuous exercise, and cannot be done on the cheap. Over the years an oil
company generates experience embodied in people just as financially it
generates capital. Some businessmen would argue that men of the
calibre that international oil has now in quite large numbers could not
be trained or would not stay in organizations ultimately controlled by
governments: I do not find that ideological argument convincing. The
quality of French technicians in the Sahara, of ENI's gas marketing
men—or so far as one can judge from outside by results, of Mr Gurov's
Soviet oilmen—does not seem to me obviously inferior to that of their
counterparts in the privately-owned groups. Venezuelans and Arabs,
to the extent that they are given the chance, are already proving their
abilities in the private companies' oil management; and the judgment
displayed by managers of some of the producing countries' national
companies is already impressive. On the other hand, there are dangers
that political decisions affecting a government-dominated company
might frustrate intelligent action for reasons wholly foreign to its
business interest more often than in the privately-owned group (though
neither frustration nor bureaucracy is absent there either).

Anyone who has seen anything of the fairly ruthless process of
cost-cutting set in train by the biggest international oil groups over
the last few years may retain doubts, too, whether any government-
owned organization could set about slimming itself so drastically. The
strength of political considerations and influence, at any rate, might
slow such a process. Without belittling the efforts in recent years to
recruit and train nationals of the oil-producing states inside the major

companies, it is objectively a pity that the process has not been even faster, and that responsible top management in the great international companies is still almost exclusively confined to white Westerners. But the internationally integrated oil company can, at its best, offer a possibility of employment all round the world, in different national situations but not of them, that may bring a refinement of managerial judgment for international operations difficult to achieve either if governments played a more dominant role in the oil trade or if the demand for the exclusive employment of nationals develops much further everywhere.

The final central function of the integrated oil company, which impinges directly upon the question of the return that capital in this business requires, seems to me to be its activity as a generator and investor of capital, a specialized investment bank. It happens that this industry since the war has generated and retained internally most of the capital that it goes on investing in such great amounts: but the deployment rather than the provenance of these capital resources seems to me the essential function. The exceptional risks involved in exploration and the huge rewards that accrued for the lucky risk-taker, no doubt, set the pattern of self-financing. Oilmen who struck it rich acquired the money as well as the taste for more gambling in oil, while few capitalists outside felt competent to risk sums of such magnitude in so chancy a business (until this acquired special tax advantages in some countries). From time to time, the business began to look less chancy, and attracted large amounts of outside capital in: much of it has stayed, but some of the newcomers, from time to time in the history of this industry, have burned their fingers and withdrawn. The latest influx of new capital occurred when it began to become clear how fabulous a money-spinner the Middle East, in a favourable market, could be. We are not over the results of that yet. Moreover, it was the exceptional profits earned there that made possible the virtually complete self-financing of the major companies in the fifties. This has been eroded, and may be eroded further.

Making decisions about the deployment of further capital investment in this industry—which venture to back where next, out of the many constantly on offer—is the ultimate job that no internationally-integrated company would consider delegating to outsiders in its normal business operations. It might be hard for individual governments, or some 'supranational' committee of producer and consumer governments, to get these decisions right as often as the industry, on balance, manages to do. No sensible oilman would suggest that investment policy is always right now, or always decided now purely in economic terms without the least attention to political considerations. Like other heavily-capitalized industries since the war, the world petroleum industry has been subject to 'fashions' in investment, waves of imitative capital expenditure that predictably and fairly quickly have led to short-term surplus capacity in particular stages of the business. These should be distinguished from the tax incentives thrown in by some governments to encourage investment in particular stages of it—which still seem to be encouraging so much investment as to develop more lasting situations of surplus in some relatively high-cost oil areas.

Ought the industry to be investing as much in looking for oil as it still is? Is heavy investment in refining and marketing justified to hold or extend the share that every company has of every market? Is petrochemicals quite the escape route to higher returns than can be obtained on oil that it seemed to these central oil managers a few years ago? How far should the industry be looking for gas on its own (and whenever it finds gas, how ought it to price the stuff in relation to oil products)? These are not questions about which anyone can be confident of getting the right answer all the time. But long experience in having to consider them is a pretty valuable commodity. So is a degree of insulation from sectional political interest in selecting answers. And the degree that even now these investment managers still enjoy may on balance be of considerable service to the whole international economy.

Each international oil group's spread of interests, true, will be biased or lopsided in one way or another, giving it a different background for decision from other groups in the industry (or from some ideally-weighted cross-section of the 'whole' world oil industry. But who would do the weighting?). Not every decision or initiative from even the most broadly-based groups is popular with other oil companies or always, considered in hindsight, advantageous for the industry as a whole. But these decisions are usually less one-sided than the decision a single national government engaged in oil might take, and less simply null than the lowest common denominator of decision acceptable to several such governments around a table might be. They are also, nowadays at least, more open to competitive test in the market—though if the governments seek to take over the decisions, they will not be able to avoid competition either.

Governments seeking to discover the proper rate of return on capital in the oil business, I have suggested, might find that many of the physical operations, provided they assumed all the risk themselves, could perhaps be financed for the bare cost of borrowing the money. The oil companies are indeed doing this today with fairly low-coupon bonds (though their credit may still be rather better than that of some governments). Moreover, the need to keep producer government revenues stable and hence posted prices of crude up has of late involved the integrated companies in showing only nominal rates of return or even losses on their later stages of operations, even though the total integrated return is actually earned on the whole operation. That exaggerates the return on production to an embarrassingly high level; and with an irony that the companies may consider somewhat cruel, they are now being questioned, by the very governments who benefit most from it, about the justification of such a high return. It is possible to mount some rationalizations to support the belief of many oilmen that the profit not only is, but should be, 'in the crude'. But in the Middle East, the prices that put it there were a result of decision, not of any automatic working of market forces. Many of the governments dealing with them still credit the few large international companies, at any rate, with unaltered powers of decision over the world oil market. But in the meantime, across huge areas of their operations, these companies have become far more susceptible to the competition of other companies and the countervailing power of consumers. It would be hardly too much to say that the rate of return on production, in the Middle East, which arose from deliberate decisions by these companies (and the governments of the United States and Britain), has remained high because they have become almost helpless to change it.

In contrast to this continuing high rate of apparent return on production, during the early sixties, some of the major companies in the oil industry were showing an integrated return in the Eastern hemisphere (on production and everything else) that was lower than the return capital could get less riskily in normal manufacturing in developed countries. The increases in their revenue per barrel recently gained by Middle East governments, like the increase in tax that Venezuela brought in a few years ago, tend in effect to depress the return even further on the industry's 'downstream' (and in value much larger) investment. This illustrates some of the difficulties that would arise in practice from the idea often toyed with in government departments all around the world—of imposing upon the oil industry some kind of 'international public utility' rate of return. Assume that governments could agree on what rate of return they would consider proper for internationally integrated companies in this business (which enjoy neither the guaranteed monopoly nor the relative freedom from risk that are ordinarily associated with public utilities). Can one see different governments agreeing about how much of that controlled rate of return ought to be shown at each stage of the business—in all the different countries concerned?

Part of the seemingly excessive return on Middle East crude, it is clear, arises simply from accounting that was once convenient for the companies and is now the reverse. The Eastern hemisphere comparison is admittedly not the ideal one. Economically, there seems no reason why the profits on Middle East oil—made all the way down the stream, wherever they may be shown—should need automatically to cover investment in less remunerative oil operations elsewhere. This they were able to do to some considerable extent during the earlier postwar years. In circumstances of oligopoly, the companies adjusted the prices down more slowly than they might have come down in an utterly competitive market; kept in being some higher-cost producing areas that utter competition from low-cost Middle East oil might have put out of business; and themselves financed from the profits much of the further investment that utterly competitive entrepreneurs might have had to seek from the world's capital market. The producer governments shared these profits of oligopoly made during that period, and have been protected from the later decline in those profits as the degree of oligopoly crumbled. The consumer governments benefited from the diversity of supply sources that a large part of the profits left with the companies were invested to bring about. Both, inevitably, feel that the others, along with the companies, did too well out of it.

One key question that producer governments, here, put to the companies goes to the heart of the international situation of these companies, and is one that producers would have to argue out with consumer governments, throughout any joint public utility operation that they might combine to set up. How much investment in exploration does the international oil industry need to go on doing—and where? This is a direct confrontation of producer versus consumer interests, as well as of the short-term interest of any producing area against the long-term interest of international companies, or any conceivable successors to them as continuing suppliers of oil.

It is hardly going to be possible to persuade a Saudi Arabian or

Kuwaiti, sitting on what may be a century's oil at the rate it is now being taken out, that the entrepreneurial net return on developing his oil need be such as to allow exploration elsewhere for the purpose of finding a developing capacity that might eventually replace, but will immediately compete with, production in Arabia. 'Explore, yes,' one can imagine him saying. 'Explore here! Find the next Abquiq or the next Burgan, or drill up the reserves here—and a sight more easily, in all probability, than by wasting years and millions in Papua or Australia.'

Any established producing government's enthusiasm about the need for financing exploration is likely to be temperate and somewhat localized. One might indeed suspect the same of certain major companies that are particularly well-placed in single regions, if it were not for the growing interest, always potentially unwelcome, of host governments there. This governmental interest has limited the extent to which any oil company dare 'accentuate the positive' of one rich region. So its business incentive to keep up with the rest, maintaining or improving its share of low-cost or cheaply-situated oil, is supplemented by a concern with the security of maintainable supplies that makes diversification in the search for oil an end in itself.

This is one of the kinds of questions of management, quite apart from direct bargaining over price and offtake, that would come up again and again for answer in any world commodity scheme for oil, any proration scheme, or any other machinery by which diverse governments may seek to take over or regulate this business that works in between them. It is possible from the outside to have many doubts about the total rate of exploration of the international oil industry in given periods and particular areas, and to feel that some tax incentives that help to engender it, representing the frozen decision of certain governments long ago to encourage local oil development, now encourage it everywhere to a degree that exacerbates and prolongs surplus. But that makes it no easier to see how other governments would answer the same set of questions—particularly governments with opposite kinds of interests in oil.

For this diversification, this high rate of exploration in unlikely places as well as likely, is something in which the consumer government's interest is strong and almost unmixed. Such a government may not be anxious to have oil prices forced down to levels that would put its own domestic fuel industries out of business. But it certainly prefers, at any time, to have just a little more oil on tap than it really requires, and from as many different sources as possible. It is likely, nowadays, to promote exploration for oil and gas within its own home borders and indeed elsewhere; and if it finds any, to protect, or give oil 'its own companies' have found some import preference. Equally, the governments of prospective areas for exploration, which have as yet found no oil but not much of anything else either, have certainly an interest in attracting the oil entrepreneur to take his gamble in their land, where he may win so much for them along with himself.

One cogent if partial answer from the middlemen to this question of how much further exploration, and where, the profits made on oil from established producing areas should be partly utilized to finance would no doubt be that if you want consumers to switch to oil they will have to feel safe in doing so. The great consuming countries, in spite of some protection of their home fuel industries, have in fact been switching to oil as a general fuel at a pretty rapid pace. Among the additional producing countries that have been brought into being since the Suez incident, perhaps only Libya has yet made any great difference to the West's ability to get all the oil it needs at low cost. But the implicit assurance that diverse sources of oil are constantly being explored, as part of the normal behaviour of the international oil industry, does play a part in the policies of consumer governments.

The companies operating internationally, of course, have other motives for going on exploring as well as keeping consumers confident. They want to find it, if they can, really near to developing markets. However much low-cost oil they command elsewhere it can always be somewhat devalued if somebody else finds, say, huge natural gas reserves in North-West Europe. They want to balance their supplies and marketing capacity in the short run and to pre-empt possible discoveries in new areas and maintain their competitive position in the long run. They are quite often concerned, in bidding for new concessions, less with finding new oil quickly than in making sure it is 'in strong hands'—which can mean that it may not soon become so bitterly competitive with established producing areas as established host governments fear. The established groups are no more anxious for 'competition amongst the many' than any established producing government. But there is no reason why the corporate and national rivals of both should accept this joint 'oil establishment' as uniquely entitled to conduct this business.

In this many-sided bargaining, indeed, some of the key issues lie really between governments—the landlord from whose territory the oil comes, his neighbours who would like a bonanza too, and the ultimate consumer who finally pays the price and confers a value on it. The entrepreneurs who put their capital into developing the resource and finding it a market for the producing nation, or into securing a cheap and convenient fuel for the consumer, are already being squeezed at both ends of the business they have built up. In theory, they might become quite resigned to sit back and let landlords and customers wrangle over some of the refinements of this ultimate bargain. Some people in the companies, at times, are prepared to debate upon the possibilities of 'retreating to the marketing function' and using their buying power fully against the producing companies that they presently own; or even of shifting large parts of their aggregated capital out of the oil business. So far, however, the industry as a whole has certainly not resigned itself to letting producer and consumer governments argue over its head. The entrepreneurs distrust further government encroachment on their business. They fear that even if confrontation were to demonstrate to governments of both kinds that the shared problems of oil are less simple than they look from one side alone, whatever was finally worked out would still tend to be at the companies' expense. These fears are naturally self-interested. Can one argue that they are not realistic?

One quite useful service of this industry to the world economy, to the outsider, may seem to be simply that it does not leave consuming countries to argue direct with producers, and that in this trade the governments whose interests are opposed remain relatively insulated from one another. Like other international institutions in a world where nationalism is not visibly declining, it cannot expect to be popular. It is certainly not an ideal international economic institution. Its control is heavily biased towards the Western industrialized countries, though most of its production comes from underdeveloped countries. In economic performance, it is at best workably rather than fully competitive; and its frequent attempts to reduce instability do not guarantee any rapid re-adjustment back into equilibrium. The very large companies that play so large a part within it display some considerable built-in resistances to change, in spite of operational flexibility. They are also quite dominating aggregations of economic power in some of the countries where they operate, and indeed large and rather remote, suspect ones to most of the countries where they do business. Their formal duty is to shareholders, not to the national aspirations of the countries where they work; and in practice, shareholders do not appear to exercise their theoretical control either. Regard for shareholders may sometimes hamper the companies' ability to adjust their dealings with governments—particularly when they fear that the end of successive adjustments must eventually be at their shareholders' expense, which is certainly a considerable possibility. The big company's interest in survival is always likely to counsel moderation in short-term gains. But if its managers have a feeling of '*après moi la deluge*'—and clearheaded men at the top of the integrated companies must have some excuse for such a feeling—are they justified in forgoing short-term gains for the sake of amicable future relations with governments that they do not honestly believe can stay amicable?

From most but not all the governments they have to deal with, private enterprise can probably claim some theoretical approval. But in theory this approval attaches to atomistically competitive private enterprise: in practice, also, to private enterprise operating wholly within a government's own economic sphere. The oil business is not quite either of these. There is no general and automatic acceptance of its private, international 'legitimacy'. It can act as a cushion, if not an arbiter, between the claims of different countries, without the political friction that continuous confrontation of national interests would cause. Yet at both ends of its business, the governments may doubt whether in the last resort it is responsible to anyone. They may feel confronted with some kind of 'Shell Company of Atlantis'. Every international oil company, in a sense, must seem to those who deal with it to live on an imaginary island.

What may seem to constitute the companies' virtues, from a world view, are not much more likely to be popular with governments than their defects. Whatever bounds different governments put upon their legitimate interest in this business, the international oil industry from now on seems fairly certain to have to get accustomed to operating with governments breathing down its neck. That may be uncomfortable, but not impossible.

The internally integrated companies are still, even now, glad enough to go on ploughing capital into this business: it would be stupid to suggest that they have been driven to a point where it is really losing its fascination or its rewards for them. But there could obviously come a limit to the readiness of international capital to invest in this international business, if these growing encroachments should begin even more seriously to whittle down the independent efficiency of international operations, the security of tenure, and in a market like the present the total integrated return. There are other forms of investment into which capital and management of the quantity and quality that the international oil industry deploys could go—and which could, at some point, become equally attractive. And there still seems to me no prospect of any alternative structure formed out of overlapping nationalism that offers a hope of handling this international job of logistics and of deploying investment with anything like the same, reasonably impartial degree of efficiency.

There is still plenty of room for legitimate bargaining about sharing the wealth that the international development of oil is bringing into being. But the bargaining needs to be conducted in the recognition that the capitalist is worthy of his hire; and that his labour—which is ultimately one of reaching a fair balance between different commercial and national interests at many points, as a continuing operation—cannot be avoided. The international oil industry, and within it the major oil companies, have not yet fully fitted themselves for and into their role as an international economic institution; there remain, oddly enough, considerable vestiges of nationalist arrogance in their own makeup and behaviour. But if this international institution did not exist it would be necessary to invent one.

Table I

WORLD ENERGY CONSUMPTION, COMMERCIAL FUELS:
Orders of Magnitude

	1929	1937	1950	1965	1971 (forecast)
Million metric tons Coal Equivalent					
Solid Fuels	1,367	1,361	1,569	2,260	2,698
Hydro-Electricity	14	22	41	114	166
Natural Gas	76	115	273	892	1,309
Oil	255	328	636	2,118	2,951
Nuclear Electricity	—	—	—	3	23
Total	1,712	1,826	2,519	5,387	7,147

Percentages					
Solid Fuels	80	75	62	42	38
Hydro-Electricity	1	1	2	2	3
Natural Gas	4	6	11	17	18
Oil	15	18	25	39	41
Nuclear Electricity	—	—	—	—	—
	100	100	100	100	100

Source: Figures to 1950, 'World Energy Supplies' United Nations, 1965 and forecast 1971, oil company estimates.

Table II

ENERGY CONSUMPTION, 1965 ESTIMATES, BY AREAS

In million metric tons 'coal equivalent' and percentages (in brackets)	Solid Fuels	Hydro Electric Power	Natural Gas	Oil	Nuclear Electricity	Total	%
North America	473	38	652	848	1	2,012	(37)
	(24)	(2)	(32)	(42)	—	(100)	
Latin America	10	5	17	116	—	148	(3)
	(7)	(3)	(11)	(79)		(100)	
Western Europe	525	36	27	540	2	1,130	(21)
	(46)	(3)	(2)	(48)	—	(100)	
Africa, Middle and Far East	182	15	13	293	—	503	(9)
	(36)	(3)	(3)	(58)		(100)	
Oceania	29	2	—	31	—	62	(1)
	(47)	(3)		(50)		(100)	
Free World	1,219	96	709	1,828	3	3,855	(71)
	(32)	(3)	(18)	(47)	—	(100)	
Soviet bloc	1,041	18	183	290	—	1,532	(29)
	(68)	(1)	(12)	(19)		(100)	
Total World	2,260	114	892	2,118	3	5,387	(100)

Note: Percentages do not necessarily add to 100 owing to rounding.

Table III

OIL: RESERVES, PRODUCTION, AND CONSUMPTION,

By Areas, 1965

(*In metric tons and barrels*)	*Reserves at end 1965*	*Production 1965*	*Consumption 1965*
North America	6,100 m. tons	492·3 m. tons	618
	47,100 m. bbl	10,325 'ooo b/d	12,810
Caribbean	2,700 m. tons	198·2 m. tons	37
	19,300 m. bbl	3,810 'ooo b/d	720
South America	800 m. tons	23·8 m. tons	46
	5,900 m. bbl	475 'ooo b/d	920
Western Hemisphere	9,600 m. tons	714·3 m. tons	701
	72,300 m. bbl	14,610 'ooo b/d	14,450
Western Europe	400 m. tons	21·9 m. tons	376
	2,600 m. bbl	440 'ooo b/d	7,730
Africa	3,000 m. tons	105·6 m. tons	34
	23,000 m. bbl	2,210 'ooo b/d	680
Middle East	28,900 m. tons	408·9 m. tons	33
	214,900 m. bbl	8,340 'ooo b/d	660
East Indies	1,300 m. tons	30·3 m. tons	6
	10,000 m. bbl	605 'oco b/d	128
Japan	6 m. tons	0·7 m. tons	89
	45 m. bbl	12·8 'ooo b/d	1,770
U.S.S.R.	4,300 m. tons	239·2 m. tons ⎫	
	32,000 m. bbl	4,840 'ooo b/d ⎬ 220	
E. Europe and	200 m. tons	24·8 m. tons ⎭ 4,500	
China	1,500 m. bbl	505 'ooo b/d	
Australasia and other	130 m. tons	4·5 m. tons	55
E. Hem.	1,000 m. bbl	91 'ooo b/d	1,132
Eastern Hemisphere	38,300 m. tons	834·7 m. tons	813
	285,000 m. bbl	17,090 'ooo b/d	16,600
World	47,900 m. tons	1,549·0 m. tons	1,514
	357,300 m. bbl	31,700 'ooo b/d	31,050

Source: British Petroleum Company.

Table IV

CRUDE OIL RESERVES AND PRODUCTION, MAJOR INTERNATIONAL COMPANIES

| | CRUDE OIL RESERVES, END 1963[1] | | | | | | Total | | CRUDE PRODUCTION[2] 1963 | | | RESERVE-PRODUCTION RATIO | |
	U.S.A. and Canada	Venezuela	Western Hemisphere	Middle East	Africa	Eastern Hemisphere	incl. U.S.A. and Canada	excl. U.S.A. and Canada	U.S.A. and Canada	Western Hemisphere	Eastern Hemisphere	U.S.A. and Canada	World outside N. America
	(in Million tons)								(in Million tons)			(in Years' Output)	
Gulf Oil	300	100	400	4,650	50	4,750	5,100	4,850	20·5	29·3	57·9	14·6	71·2
Mobil	200	50	250	1,650	100	1,800	2,050	1,850	14·8	22·2	24·6	13·5	57·8
Standard Oil of California	300	50	350	2,800	—	3,150	3,500	3,200	21·3	23·9	34·9	14·1	85·3
Standard Oil of New Jersey	600	1,250	1,900	3,250	300	3,650	5,500	4,900	40·1	114·1	56·0	15·0	38·0
Texaco	400	50	500	2,800	—	3,150	3,650	3,250	30·6	49·4	35·5	13·1	73·4
British Petroleum	—	—	50	7,850	200	8,050	8,100	8,100	0·3	2·2	103·8	—	78·1
Royal Dutch/Shell	200	550	800	1,650	200	2,150	2,950	2,750	24·6	72·9	37·9	8·1	24·8
Compagnie Francaise	—	—	—	1,550	200	1,750	1,750	1,750	—	—	30·4	—	57·6
Eight Major Companies (Total all Companies)	2,000 (5,750)	2,000 (2,400)	4,200 (9,150)	26,150 (27,850)	1,050 (2,150)	28,400 (31,950)[2]	32,650 (41,000)[2]	30,650 (35,250)[2]	142·2 (449·7)	315·0 (676·8)	381·0 (438·5)[2]	14·1 (12·8)	55·3 (72·8)

[1] Reserve estimates rounded to nearest 50 million tons.
[2] Excludes U.S.S.R., Eastern Europe, China.

Source of reserve estimates: Petroleum Economics Ltd.

Table V

SHAREHOLDINGS OF MAIN MIDDLE EAST OIL CONCESSIONS

Countries and Concessions	British Petroleum	Compagnie Française des Pétroles	Gulf Oil	Standard Oil of New Jersey	Socony Mobil	Royal Dutch/Shell	Standard Oil of California	Texas Company
ABU DHABI								
Onshore concession[1]	(23·75%)	(23·75%)	—	(11·875%)[3]	(11·875%)[3]	(23·75%)	—	—
Offshore concession	66·6%	33·3%						
BAHREIN							50%	50%
IRAN								
Consortium	40%	6%	7%	7%	7%	14%	7%	7%
Offshore[2]						50%		
IRAQ								
IPC, BPC, MPC concessions[1]	23·75%	23·75%	—	11·875%[3]	11·875%[3]	23·75%	—	—
KUWAIT								
Onshore concession	50%	—	50%					
OMAN								
Onshore concession						85%		
QATAR Onshore[1]	(23·75%)	(23·75%)	—	(11·875%)[3]	(11·875%)[3]	(23·75%)		
Offshore						100%		
SAUDI ARABIA	—	—	—	30%	10%	—	30%	30%

[1] IPC owns Qatar and Abu Dhabi (onshore) operating companies. [2] Other 50% held by National Iranian Oil Company, which is also in partnership with other companies offshore (but no other international majors). [3] Exercised through half ownership of Near East Development Corporation, which owns 23·75 per cent of IPC stock.

Short Bibliography

Adelman, Professor Morris A. *The Supply and Price of Natural Gas.* Oxford, 1962.
Oil Prices in the Long Run, 1963–75. Journal of Business. University of Chicago, 1964.
The World Oil Outlook. In 1963 Forum on The Role of Natural Resources in International Development.
Oil Production Costs in Four Areas. Paper to the American Mining Metallurgical & Petroleum Engineers' annual meeting, March 1966.
Ayres, Eugene, and Scarlott, Charles. *Energy Sources: the Wealth of the World.* McGraw Hill. New York, 1952.
Cassady, Ralph jr. *Price Making and Price Behaviour in the Petroleum Industry.* Yale University Press. New Haven, 1954.
Chase Manhattan Bank. Monographs:
Future Growth and Financial Requirements of the World Petroleum Industry. New York, 1956.
Investment Patterns in the World Petroleum Industry. New York, 1956.
Future Growth of the World Petroleum Industry. New York, 1961.
Capital Investments by the World Petroleum Industry. New York, 1961, 1962 and 1964.
de Chazeau, Melvin E., and Kahn, Alfred E. *Integration and Competition in the Petroleum Industry.* Yale University Press, New Haven, 1959.
European Coal/Steel Authority, Luxembourg:
Étude sur les Perspectives Energetiques à long terme de la Communauté. Luxembourg, 1964.
Nouvelles Reflexions sur les Perspectives. Luxembourg, 1966.
Inter-Executive Memorandum on Energy Policy. Luxembourg, July 1962.
Economic Commission for Europe, Geneva:
The Price of Oil in Western Europe. Geneva. United Nations, 1955.
Relationship Between Coal and Black Oils in Western Europe. Geneva. United Nations, 1954.

395

European Economic Commission, Brussels:
Première note de la Commission au Conseil sur la Politique de la Communauté en Matiere de petrole et de gaz natural. Brussels, February 1966.

First National City Bank. Monographs:
Petroleum in the Eastern Hemisphere. New York, 1959.
Oil Prospects and Profits in the Eastern Hemisphere. New York, 1961.
Oil Advances in the Eastern Hemisphere, 1962.
Eastern Hemisphere Oil, 1963.
Future Price and Availability Trends for Hydrocarbon Raw Materials outside the United States. New York, 1961.

Frank, Helmut J. The Price of Oil in the Middle East: A Study in Oligopolistic Price Behaviour. Frederick A. Praeger Inc., New York, 1966.

Frankel, Paul H. Essentials of Petroleum: A Key to Oil Economics. Chapman & Hall, London, 1946.
'Integration in the Oil Industry'. Journal of Industrial Economics. Oxford, July 1953.
'The Significance of Marginal Capacity in the Oil Industry'. Journal of Industrial Economics. March 1962.
Oil: The Facts of Life. Weidenfeld and Nicolson, 1962.
Mattei: Oil and Power Politics. Faber & Faber, London, 1966.

Issawi, Charles, and Yeganeh, Mohammed. The Economics of Middle East Oil. Frederick A. Praeger Inc., New York, 1962.

Kabbani, I. K. Elasticity of Demand for Crude Oil: Its Implications for Exporting Countries. OPEC, Geneva, 1964.

Leeman, Wayne A. The Price of Middle East Oil. Cornell University Press, Ithica, 1962.

Lenczowski, George. Oil and State in the Middle East. Cornell University Press, Ithica, New York, 1960.

Levy, Walter J. The Past, Present and Likely Future Price Structure for the International Oil Trade. Proceedings of the Third World Petroleum Congress. The Hague, 1951.
'World Oil in Transition'. The Eeonomist, August 1961.
The World Oil Industry in the Sixties. Before the Ottawa Branch of the Canadian Industry of Mining and Metallurgy. March 1960.

Longrigg, Stephen H. Oil in the Middle East: Its Discovery and Development. Oxford University Press. Revised edition, 1961.

Lovejoy, W. F., and Homan, Paul T. A Study of Methods of Estimating

Reserves of Crude Oil, Natural Gas and Natural Gas Liquids. Southern Methodist University, 1964.

Economic Aspects of Petroleum Conservation Regulation. Southern Methodist University, 1964.

MacEvoy, Paul W. *Price Formation in Natural Gas Fields.* Yale University Press, 1962.

Maclean, John H., and Haigh, Robert W. *The Growth of Integrated Oil Companies.* Graduate School of Business Administration, Harvard University, Boston, 1954.

Mikdashi, Zuhayr. *A Financial Analysis of Middle Eastern Oil Concessions 1901–1965.* Frederick A. Praeger, New York, 1966.

Mughraby, Muhammad A. *Permanent Sovereignty over Oil Resources,* Middle East Publishing Centre, 1966.

Organization of European Economic Co-operation. Two independent reports:

Europe's Growing Needs of Energy. How Can They Be Met? (By a Commission headed by Sir Harold Hartley) Paris, 1956.

Towards a New Energy Pattern in Europe. (By a Commission headed by Professor E. A. G. Robinson) Paris, 1960.

Organization of the Petroleum Exporting Countries. (OPEC)

From Concessions to Contracts. Cairo, March 1965.

OPEC and the Principle of Negotiation. Cairo, March 1965.

The Price of Crude Oil, A Rational Approach. Beirut, November 1963.

Pricing Problems: Further Considerations. Geneva, September 1963.

Taxation Economics in Crude Production. Cairo, March 1965.

Ovens, David. *Crude Oil Prices: The Next Five Years* in *Competitive Aspects of Oil Operations.* Institute of Petroleum, London, 1958.

Parra, F. R. *Demand Patterns and Crude Gravities.* OPEC, Geneva, 1963.

The Development of Petroleum Resources Under the Concession System in Non-Industrialized Countries. OPEC, Geneva, 1964.

The Oil Industry's Organization in the Middle East and some of its Fiscal Consequences. OPEC, Geneva, November 1963.

OPEC and the Oil Industry in the Middle East. Geneva, October 1962.

Penrose, E. T. 'Profit Sharing Between Producing Countries and Oil Companies in the Middle East'. *The Economic Journal.* London, June 1959.

'Middle East Oil: The International Distribution of Profits and Income Taxes'. *Economica.* London, August 1960.

Monopoly and Competition in the International Petroleum Industry. Stevens & Sons, London, 1964.

'Vertical Integration with Joint Control of Raw-Material Production'. *Journal of Development Studies,* April 1965.

Political and Economic Planning. *A Fuel Policy for Britain* (group report drafted by J. E. Hartshorn). PEP, London, 1966.

Schurr, Sam H. and Netschert, Bruce C. *Energy in the American Economy, 1850–1975. Its History and Prospects.* Resources for the Future Inc. The Johns Hopkins Press, Baltimore, 1960.

Shwadran, Benjamin. *The Middle East, Oil, and Great Powers.* Council for Middle Eastern Affairs Press. New York, 1959.

Tugendhat, Georg. 'A World Market in Upheaval'. *Fortune,* October 1960.

The Political Economy of Energy. Three Lectures to The London School of Economics, 1959.

United States Federal Trade Commission. *The International Petroleum Cartel.* Washington, 1952.

Zimmermann, Erich W. *Conservation in the Production of Petroleum.* Yale University Press, New Haven, 1957.

Notes

Chapter I. By Way of Introduction

1. Continental Oil is now one of the eight American 'big independent' companies that together own 5 per cent of the Iranian Consortium. These companies exercise their rights through the Iricon Agency Ltd; Iricon was party to the Supplemental Agreement made by the Consortium with the Iranian government in 1965 to implement agreement on the royalty expensing settlement of the OPEC negotiations. Continental, as the owner of a 0·417 per cent shareholding in the Consortium, was thus formally committed to the settlement with Iran (where taxes were already reckoned on the basis of posted prices).

2. Seven independent companies holding out against acceptance of the revised Libyan law, in November 1965, issued a detailed justification of their position; and the Libyan government, in reply, issued an even more detailed rebuttal and account of its own position in December 1965. See *Petroleum Intelligence Weekly*, November 1965–January 1966; and *Arab Oil*, Tripoli, over the same period.

Chapter II. Oil as a General Fuel

1. United Nations, *World Energy Statistics*, 1959 to 1963; and oil company estimates.

2. The United Nations uses an energy conversion coefficient for electricity (0·125 metric tons per 1,000 kilowatt-hours) that tends to put a low value on hydro-electricity when compared with the fossil fuels burned in thermal power plants. This gives a relatively low value for hydro-electricity as an element in total primary energy, by comparison with conversion methods that value electricity at the average thermal equivalent of the primary fossil fuels used in generation.

3. Some recent forecasts include: an expert symposium at the British Association, September 1965, published in *The Advancement of Science*, Vol. 22, No. 99, September 1965; *World-Wide Production—Its Prospects and Problems*, by Sir Maurice Bridgeman, to the American Petroleum Institute, November 1963; *Is There Enough Oil?*, J. McAfee and W. B. Davis, American Institute of Mining Engineers, February 1964; *World Energy Requirements and the Economics of Nuclear Power*, H. J. Bhabha and M. Dayal, Third United Nations International Conference on the Peaceful Uses of Atomic Energy, Geneva, 1964; *Energy Policy: Problems and Objectives*, OCED Energy Committee, Paris, August 1966, and *Nouvelles Réfléctions sur Les Perspectives*, European Coal-Steel Authority, Luxembourg.

Notes

Chapter III. Geography: Sources and Markets

1. D. C. Ion, *Oil Resources in the Next Half Century*, in *Factors in the Development of the Oil Industry*, Institute of Petroleum, 1956.
2. W. F. Lovejoy and P. T. Homan, *A Study of Methods of Estimating Reserves of Crude Oil, Natural Gas and Natural Gas Liquids*, Southern Methodist University, 1964.
3. M. A. Adelman, *The Supply and Price of Natural Gas*, Oxford, Basil Blackwell, 1962.
4. S. H. Schurr and B. C. Netschert, *Energy in the American Economy, 1850–1975*. Resources for the Future, 1960.

Chapter IV. Operating Economics: I. Crude Oil

1. *Oil and Gas Journal* annual surveys.
2. Adelman, *op. cit.* (SPNG), 1962.
3. W. L. Newton, *The Long Term Development of the Tanker Freight Market*. Institute of Petroleum, April 1964.

Chapter VI. Operating Economics: III. Natural Gas

1. P. W. MacAvoy, *Price Formation in Natural Gas Fields*, Yale, 1962.
2. Adelman, *op. cit.* (SPNG), 1962.

Chapter VII. Investment and Returns.

1. *Oil Today*. Oil Sub-committee of OECD, 1964.
2. *Capital Investments by the World Petroleum Industry, 1964*. Chase Manhattan Bank, 1965.
3. A. S. Ashton, paper to the Institute of Petroleum, February 1965.
4. M. A. Adelman, *Crude Oil Supply and Costs*. Lectures given in Japan, 1966. (Privately circulated.)
5. *Petroleum in the Eastern Hemisphere*, 1959. *Oil Prospects and Profits in the Eastern Hemisphere*, 1961. E. D. Symonds, First National City Bank.
6. *Oil Advances in the Eastern Hemisphere*, 1962. *Eastern Hemisphere Petroleum*, 1963. But see also: Francisco R. Parra, *The Eastern Hemisphere—Oil Profits in Focus*, OPEC, Geneva, 1963.
7. A. D. Little, *Economic Aspects of the International Petroleum Industry*. A report to OPEC, 1962. (Unpublished.) Cited in, for example, in
8. As apparently calculated by Professor G. Fua in a report to OPEC early in 1962. This report has never been officially published, but a summary of its conclusions was published by *Petroleum Intelligence Weekly*, May 7th, 1962.

Chapter VIII. Bigness in the Oil Business

1. E.g. in *Report of the National Fuels and Energy Study Group*. U.S. Government Printing Office, 1962.
2. J. H. MacLean and R. H. Haigh, *The Growth of Integrated Oil Companies*, Harvard University, 1954.
3. Interstate Oil Compact Commission, *A Study of Oil and Gas Conservation in the United States*, 1964.
4. *Financial Analysis of (32) Petroleum Companies*, Chase Manhattan Bank, annual publication.

Notes

Chapter IX. Pricing: Appearance and Reality

1. W. J. Levy, *The Past, Present and Likely Future Price Structure for the International Oil Trade*, 1952; P. H. Frankel, *Oil: The Facts of Life*, 1962; D. J. Ovens, *Crude Oil Prices—The Next Five Years*, 1958; M. A. Adelman, *Oil Prices in the Long Run*, 1964; *The World Oil Outlook*, 1964; R. J. Cassady, *Price Making and Price Behaviour in the Petroleum Industry*, 1952; M. G. de Chazeau and A. E. Kahn, *Integration and Competition in the Petroleum Industry*, 1959; W. A. Leeman, *The Price of Middle East Oil*, 1962.

2. Abd' Allah Tariki, *The Pricing of Middle East Crude Oil and Refined Products*, 1960; Ashraf T. Lutfi, *Royalty Oil Economics*, 1965; Ramadan Ahmed Kamel, *Arab Oil Prices: Justice Versus Fact*, 1965. (First paper to the Second Arab Petroleum Congress, 1960; second and third to the Fifth Arab Petroleum Congress, 1965.)

3. *The Price of Crude Oil*, 1963; *The Development of Petroleum Resources under the Concession System*, 1965; *Elasticity of Demand for Crude Oil* (Isam T. Kabbani), 1964. OPEC, Geneva.

4. *Current International Oil Pricing Problems*, 1963; *International Oil Prices*, F. J. Gripaios, 1964.

5. Adelman, *op. cit.* (*The World Oil Outlook*), 1964.

6. Gripaios, *op. cit.*

7. Examples in the last five years include tax departments in Germany, Switzerland, and the United Kingdom in Europe; also Australia and New Zealand.

8. *The Economist*, 'What Price Libyan Oil?' August 5, 1961.

9. *Petroleum Intelligence Weekly*, 18th January 1965.

10. W. J. Levy, *op. cit.*

11. D. J. Ovens, *op. cit.*

12. Abd' Allah Tariki, *op. cit.*

13. R. A. R. Pattman, Institute of Petroleum Review, 1956.

14. Adelman, *op. cit.* (*Oil Prices in the Long Run, 1965–1975*) (1964).

Chapter X. Orderly Competition: As Was

1. Notably: *The International Petroleum Cartel*. Staff report to the Federal Trade Commission, 1952.

2. The prohibition of inter-company agreements to fix prices, allocate territories, markets or customers, limit sales and output and exclude competition, in the 'World Oil Consent Decree' was made subject to exception if foreign governments or supra-national authorities required the major oil companies concerned to do so by law, official request, or official pronouncement of policy. (United States *v.* Standard Oil of New Jersey, U.S. District Court, Civil Action No. 86–27. November 14th, 1960.)

3. Monopolies Commission, *A Report on the Supply of Petrol to Retailers in the UK*, 1965.

4. See P. H. Frankel, *Essentials of Petroleum*, 1946.

5. Dr Edith Penrose, *Vertical Integration with Joint Control of Raw Material Production*. Journal of Development Studies, April 1965.

Chapter XI. Oil Companies as Taxpayers

1. No adequate summary of the tax regulations applying to oil companies operating internationally has ever been published, though certain independent studies were commissioned by the European Economic Commission in Brussels in 1965–66, in the course of considering fiscal incentives that

might be offered to European companies to develop a greater degree of international integration. Up to the time that this book was completed, those studies had not been published.
2. Erich W. Zimmerman, *Conservation in the Production of Petroleum*, Yale University Press, 1957.
3. See, e.g., H. J. Barnett and C. Morse, *Scarcity and Growth*. Resources for the Future, 1963.

Chapter XII. Self-sufficiency in Oil: I. The United States

1. Interdepartmental Petroleum Study Committee, U.S. Government, Conclusions and Recommendations, 1963.
2. Interstate Oil Compact Commission, *A Study of Conservation of Oil and Gas*, 1964.
3. W. F. Lovejoy and P. T. Homan, *Economic Aspects of Petroleum Conservation Regulation*, Southern Methodist University, 1964.
4. E. W. Zimmerman, *op. cit.*
5. Schurr and Netschert, *op. cit.*
6. Petroleum Study Committee, *op. cit.*
7. M. A. Adelman, *Efficiency of Resource Use in Crude Petroleum*, American Economic Journal, October 1964.
8. S. H. Schurr, *Foreign Trade Policies Affecting Mineral Fuels in the United States and Western Europe*, 1960. But see also M. Iskander, *World Oil Supplies in relation to United States Imports, Depletion and Proration Policies*, 1965.

Chapter XIII. Self-sufficiency in Oil: II. The Soviet Bloc

1. R. E. Ebel, *The Petroleum Industry of the Soviet Union*. American Petroleum Institute, 1961.
2. Ebel, *op. cit.*
3. National Petroleum Council. *Impact of Oil Exports from the Soviet Bloc*, 1962. *Supplement*, 1964.

Chapter XIV. Seeking Their Own Petroleum

1. Following upon the report of the Royal Commission on Canada's Economic Prospects, 1961.
2. Antonio J. Bermudez, *The Mexican Petroleum Industry; a Case Study in Nationalisation*. Stanford, 1963.

Chapter XV. Customers Commanding Oil

1. Political and Economic Planning. *A Fuel Policy for Britain*, 1966.
2. *Fuel Policy*, Cmnd. 2798. HMSO, 1965.
3. F. Huizinga, Papers, e.g. *The Potential Contribution of Gas with Special Reference to Natural Gas*, to British Association, 1965.
4. Denis Touret, *Le Régime Français d'Importation du Petrole et La Communaute Economique Européene*. Université de Paris, 1966.
5. *Accord Petrolier Franco-Algerien*. Journaux Officiels, Paris, 1965.

Chapter XVI. Consumers in the Market-Place

1. *Untersuchung über die Entwicklung der gegenwartigen und zukünftigen Struktur von Augebot und Nachfrage in der Energuwirtschaft der Bundesrepublik*, Berlin, 1961.

2. *The Petroleum Industry in Japan*, 1963, 1964, 1965. Japanese National Committee of the World Petroleum Congress.
3. R. W. Stocking, *The Arabian Oil Company: Progress and Prospects*. Middle East Economic Survey, September 1964.
4. M. A. Adelman, *op. cit. (World Oil Outlook)*, 1964.

Chapter XVII. Consumers: Interests in Common

1. Economic Commission for Europe, *Tne Price of Oil in Western Europe*, 1955.
2. Organization for European Economic Co-Operation (later OECD). *Europe's Need for Oil; Implications and Lessons of the Suez Crisis*, 1958. *Oil: The Outlook for Europe*, 1956. *Oil Today*, 1964.
3. OEEC. *Europe's Growing Needs of Energy: How Can They Be Met?* (Hartley Report), OEEC, 1956.
4. OEEC. *Towards a New Energy Pattern in Europe*. (Robinson Report), OEEC, 1960.
5. J. E. Hartshorn, *An Energy Policy for EEC?* Political and Economic Planning, 1963.
6. European Coal-Steel Authority, *Premier Rapport sur la portée et des effets des mesures prises dans la domaine de la politique énergetique*, Luxembourg, 1959.
7. European Coal-Steel Authority, *Inter-Executive Memorandum on Energy Policy*, 1962.
8. European Coal Steel Authority, *Etude sur les Perspectives Energetiques a long terme de la Communauté*, 1964.
9. European Coal-Steel Authority, *Protocole d'accord en matiere d'Energie*, April 1964.
10. European Economic Commission, *Note au Conseil sur la Politique de la Communauté en matiere de Petrole et du Gaz Naturel*, February 1966.

Chapter XVIII. Producers for Export: The Western Hemisphere

1. A. Parra and G. Escobar, *Financial Obligations of the Venezuelan Petroleum Industry*. Paper to the Third Arab Petroleum Congress, 1962.
2. *The International Position of Venezuelan Oil*. John Trimmer. Paper to a seminar at the London School of Economics, 1963 (unpublished).
3. *The Economist*, 'Venezuela Faces the Market', October 23, 1965, and 'Venezuela Seeks a New Formula', October 30, 1965.

Chapter XIX. Producers for Export: The Eastern Hemisphere

1. F. Hendryx, Papers to the First and Second Arab Petroleum Congresses, 1959 and 1960.
2. Muhammad A. Mughraby, *Permanent Sovereignty over Oil Resources*. Middle East Publishing Center, 1966.
3. B. A. Schwadran, , *The Middle East, Oil and the Great Powers*, 1960.
4. Zuhayr Miqdashi, *A Financial Analysis of Middle Eastern Oil Concessions: 1901–65*, 1966.
5. *Middle East Economic Survey*, 7th October 1966.
6. Summarized in *Middle East Economic Survey*, 24th December 1965.

Chapter XX. Producers: Interests in Common

1. P. H. Frankel, *op. cit. Essentials of Petroleum*, 1946.
2. Omar Haliq. Paper circulated privately. 1960. See *The Economist*, April 18, 1959.

Notes

3. OPEC, *OPEC and the Principle of Negotiation.* Paper to the Fifth Arab Petroleum Congress, 1965.
4. *Middle East Economic Survey,* 11th February 1966.
5. M. T. Sladic, *An Approach to International Prorationing.* Paper to Second Arab Petroleum Congress, 1960.
6. OPEC Explanatory Memorandum. Ninth Congress, July 1965.
7. Fuad al-Kabazi, quoted in *Middle East Economic Survey,* 12th August 1966.

Chapter XXII. Pressure from Consumers

1. Sir Maurice Bridgeman, *World-Wide Production. Its Prospects and Problems.* A paper to the American Petroleum Institute, 1963. J. H. Loudon, *A Look into the Future.* 7th annual Cadman Lecture. Institute of Petroleum, 1965.
2. M. L. Haider, to the New York Society of Investment Analysts, 1965.
3. E. S. Mason, *Energy Requirements and Economic Growth.* National Planning Association, 1955. See also *L'Influence de la Prix de l'Energie sur la Developpement Economique,* European Economic Commission, 1966.
4. P. H. Frankel, *op. cit. Oil—The Facts of Life,* 1962.

Index